YOUR NEW JOB TITLE IS "ACCOMPLICE"

Other DILBERT® books from Andrews McMeel Publishing

I Can't Remember If We're Cheap or Smart
ISBN: 978-1-4494-2309-4

Teamwork Means You Can't Pick the Side that's Right
ISBN: 978-1-4494-1018-6

How's That Underling Thing Working Out for You?
ISBN: 978-1-4494-0819-0

Your Accomplishments Are Suspiciously Hard to Verify
ISBN: 978-1-4494-0102-3

Problem Identified and You're Probably Not Part of the Solution
ISBN: 978-0-7407-8534-4

I'm Tempted to Stop Acting Randomly
ISBN: 978-0-7407-7806-3

14 Years of Loyal Service in a Fabric-Covered Box
ISBN: 978-0-7407-7365-5

Freedom's Just Another Word for People Finding Out You're Useless
ISBN: 978-0-7407-7815-5

Dilbert 2.0: 20 Years of Dilbert
ISBN: 978-0-7407-7735-6

This Is the Part Where You Pretend to Add Value
ISBN: 978-0-7407-7227-6

Cubes and Punishment
ISBN: 978-0-7407-6837-8

Positive Attitude
ISBN: 978-0-7407-6379-3

Try Rebooting Yourself
ISBN: 978-0-7407-6190-4

What Would Wally Do?
ISBN: 978-0-7407-5769-3

Thriving on Vague Objectives
ISBN: 978-0-7407-5533-0

The Fluorescent Light Glistens Off Your Head
ISBN: 978-0-7407-5113-4

It's Not Funny If I Have to Explain It
ISBN: 978-0-7407-4658-1

Don't Stand Where the Comet Is Assumed to Strike Oil
ISBN: 978-0-7407-4539-3

Words You Don't Want to Hear During Your Annual Performance Review
ISBN: 978-0-7407-3805-0

When Body Language Goes Bad
ISBN: 978-0-7407-3298-0

What Do You Call a Sociopath in a Cubicle? Answer: A Coworker
ISBN: 978-0-7407-2663-7

Another Day in Cubicle Paradise
ISBN: 978-0-7407-2194-6

When Did Ignorance Become a Point of View?
ISBN: 978-0-7407-1839-7

Excuse Me While I Wag
ISBN: 978-0-7407-1390-3

Dilbert—A Treasury of Sunday Strips: Version 00
ISBN: 978-0-7407-0531-1

Random Acts of Management
ISBN: 978-0-7407-0453-6

Dilbert Gives You the Business
ISBN: 978-0-7407-0003-3

Don't Step in the Leadership
ISBN: 978-0-8362-7844-6

Journey to Cubeville
ISBN: 978-0-8362-6745-7

I'm Not Anti-Business, I'm Anti-Idiot
ISBN: 978-0-8362-5182-1

Seven Years of Highly Defective People
ISBN: 978-0-8362-3668-2

Casual Day Has Gone Too Far
ISBN: 978-0-8362-2899-1

Fugitive from the Cubicle Police
ISBN: 978-0-8362-2119-0

It's Obvious You Won't Survive by Your Wits Alone
ISBN: 978-0-8362-0415-5

Still Pumped from Using the Mouse
ISBN: 978-0-8362-1026-2

Bring Me the Head of Willy the Mailboy!
ISBN: 978-0-8362-1779-7

Shave the Whales
ISBN: 978-0-8362-1740-7

Dogbert's Clues for the Clueless
ISBN: 978-0-8362-1737-7

Always Postpone Meetings with Time-Wasting Morons
ISBN: 978-0-8362-1758-2

Build a Better Life by Stealing Office Supplies
ISBN: 978-0-8362-1757-5

YOUR NEW JOB TITLE IS "ACCOMPLICE"

DILBERT

by **SCOTT ADAMS**

Andrews McMeel
Publishing, LLC

Kansas City • Sydney • London

Andrews McMeel Publishing, LLC
an Andrews McMeel Universal company
1130 Walnut Street, Kansas City, Missouri 64106
www.andrewsmcmeel.com

13 14 15 16 17 RR2 10 9 8 7 6 5 4 3 2 1

ISBN: 978-1-4494-2775-7

Library of Congress Control Number: 2012950490

www.dilbert.com

ATTENTION: SCHOOLS AND BUSINESSES

Andrews McMeel books are available at quantity discounts with bulk purchase for educational, business, or sales promotional use. For information, please e-mail the Andrews McMeel Publishing Special Sales Department: specialsales@amuniversal.com

For Shelly

Introduction

Have you heard of the famous study where researchers manipulated ordinary citizens into administering painful electric shocks to strangers? The study showed that normal humans are — and I don't think I am exaggerating — Hell-born, soulless demons who will embrace any dumbass excuse to torture their peers. The only thing that stops most of us from being serial killers is a fear of consequences and, in some cases, laziness. Apparently, if you give the average person a cup of coffee and a nudge, he turns into Pol Pot right before your eyes.

I graduated college as a fairly decent human, or so I imagined. But ten minutes after entering my corporate career I was already referring to the early adopters of our products as "the stupid rich." I understood our marketing efforts to be a conspiracy to mislead our customers. And I learned that our revenue was entirely dependent on keeping customers so confused that they wouldn't understand what they were buying. I wasn't so much a team player as an accomplice.

I rationalized my total embrace of evil by telling myself none of it was my fault. I was just part of the system. And besides, our customers had it coming; if the situation had been reversed, they would have happily done the same to me. I was exactly like the study volunteers who shocked strangers until their fillings fell out just because someone in authority said it was a good idea. And I was disturbingly okay with that situation so long as I kept getting paid. My moral compass was spinning like a gyroscope.

Eventually, corporate America excreted me. My bosses explained that I was unqualified for any sort of promotion because I had boring DNA and a scrotum. That's a true story, by the way. Reverse discrimination was a big thing in California in the nineties. And for what it's worth, that was not the first time my scrotum had caused me trouble.

These days my accomplices are people such as you. My job is to create *Dilbert* comics that make your boss and your coworkers look like disgruntled chimps. Your job is to e-mail those comics to anyone who you think would feel personally insulted by them. I think we make a good team.

If you would like to formalize your accomplice status, please join *Dilbert* on Twitter and Facebook.

Twitter: twitter.com/Dilbert_Daily

Facebook: facebook.com/Dilbert

S.Adams

Scott Adams

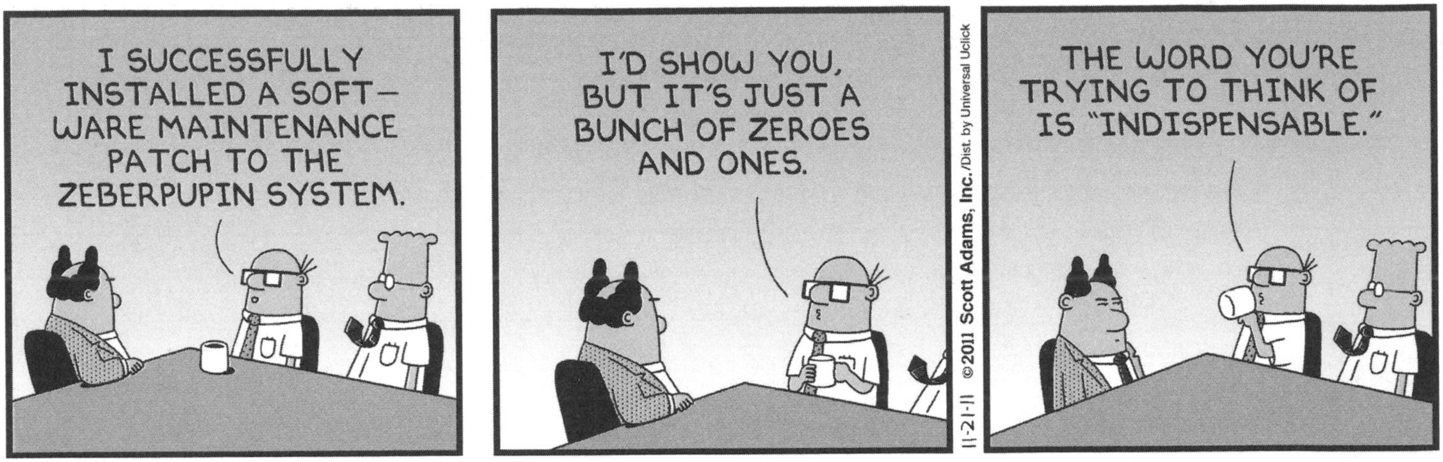
I SUCCESSFULLY INSTALLED A SOFT-WARE MAINTENANCE PATCH TO THE ZEBERPUPIN SYSTEM.
I'D SHOW YOU, BUT IT'S JUST A BUNCH OF ZEROES AND ONES.
THE WORD YOU'RE TRYING TO THINK OF IS "INDISPENSABLE."
11-21-11 ©2011 Scott Adams, Inc./Dist. by Universal Uclick

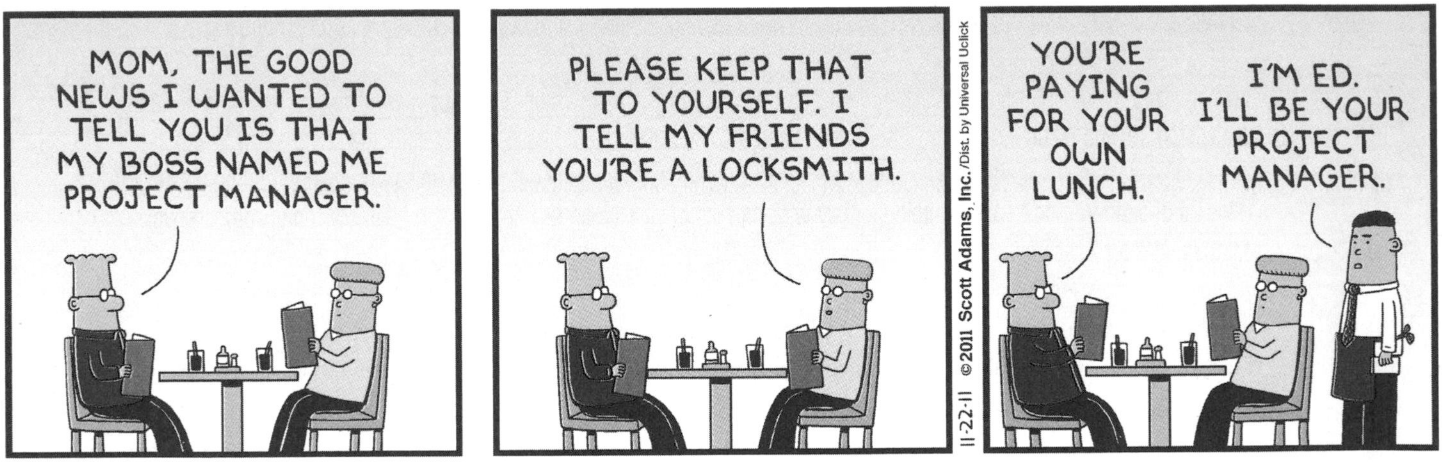
MOM, THE GOOD NEWS I WANTED TO TELL YOU IS THAT MY BOSS NAMED ME PROJECT MANAGER.
PLEASE KEEP THAT TO YOURSELF. I TELL MY FRIENDS YOU'RE A LOCKSMITH.
YOU'RE PAYING FOR YOUR OWN LUNCH.
I'M ED. I'LL BE YOUR PROJECT MANAGER.
11-22-11 ©2011 Scott Adams, Inc./Dist. by Universal Uclick

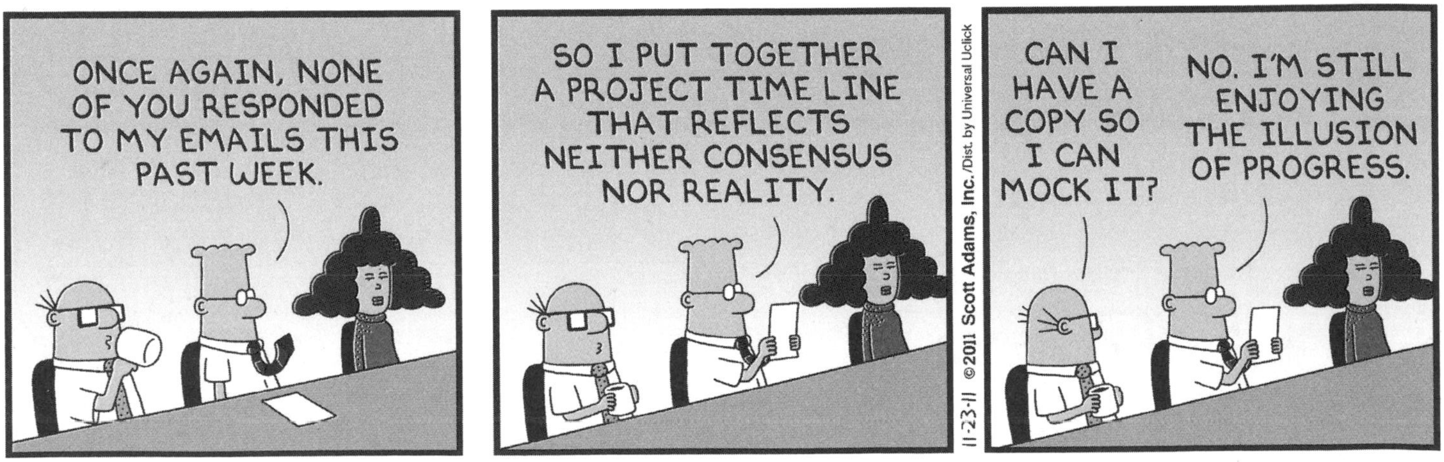
ONCE AGAIN, NONE OF YOU RESPONDED TO MY EMAILS THIS PAST WEEK.
SO I PUT TOGETHER A PROJECT TIME LINE THAT REFLECTS NEITHER CONSENSUS NOR REALITY.
CAN I HAVE A COPY SO I CAN MOCK IT?
NO. I'M STILL ENJOYING THE ILLUSION OF PROGRESS.
11-23-11 ©2011 Scott Adams, Inc./Dist. by Universal Uclick

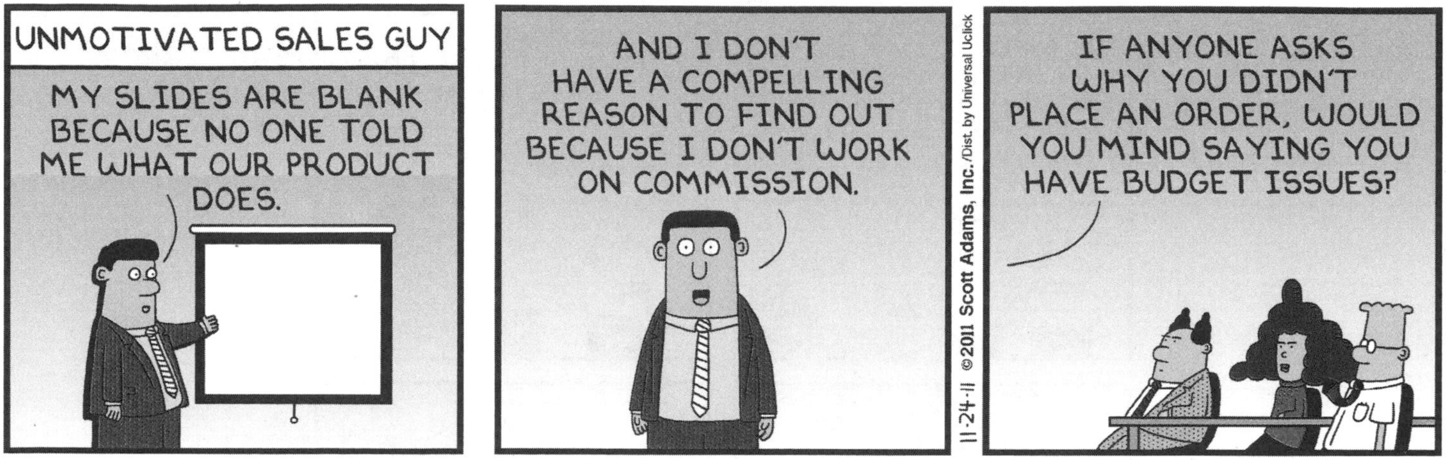
UNMOTIVATED SALES GUY
MY SLIDES ARE BLANK BECAUSE NO ONE TOLD ME WHAT OUR PRODUCT DOES.
AND I DON'T HAVE A COMPELLING REASON TO FIND OUT BECAUSE I DON'T WORK ON COMMISSION.
11-24-11 ©2011 Scott Adams, Inc./Dist. by Universal Uclick
IF ANYONE ASKS WHY YOU DIDN'T PLACE AN ORDER, WOULD YOU MIND SAYING YOU HAVE BUDGET ISSUES?

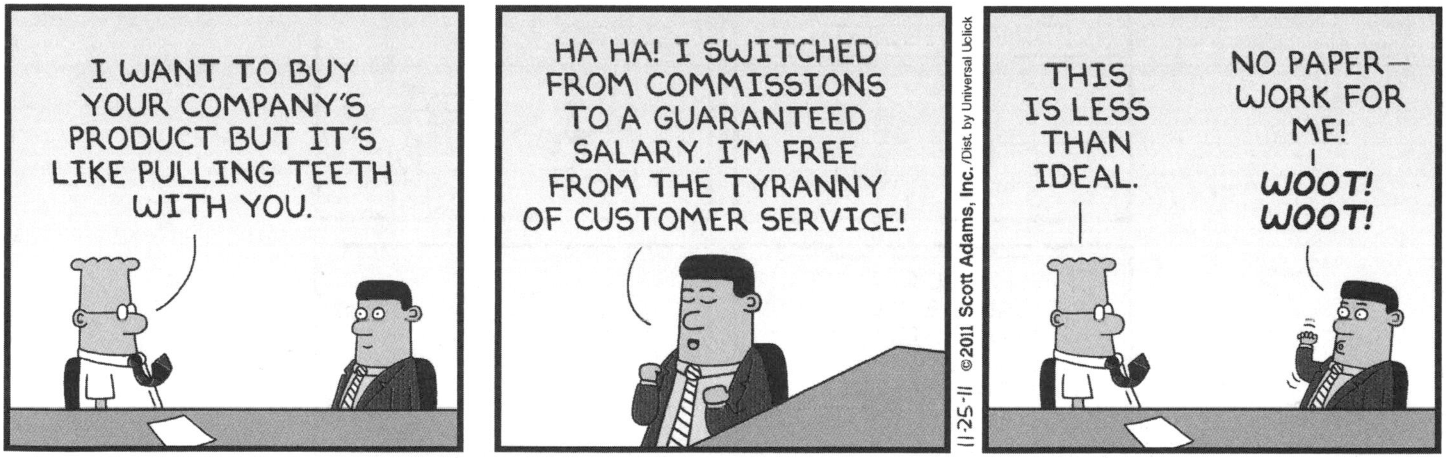
I WANT TO BUY YOUR COMPANY'S PRODUCT BUT IT'S LIKE PULLING TEETH WITH YOU.
HA HA! I SWITCHED FROM COMMISSIONS TO A GUARANTEED SALARY. I'M FREE FROM THE TYRANNY OF CUSTOMER SERVICE!
11-25-11 ©2011 Scott Adams, Inc./Dist. by Universal Uclick
THIS IS LESS THAN IDEAL.
NO PAPER-WORK FOR ME!
WOOT! WOOT!

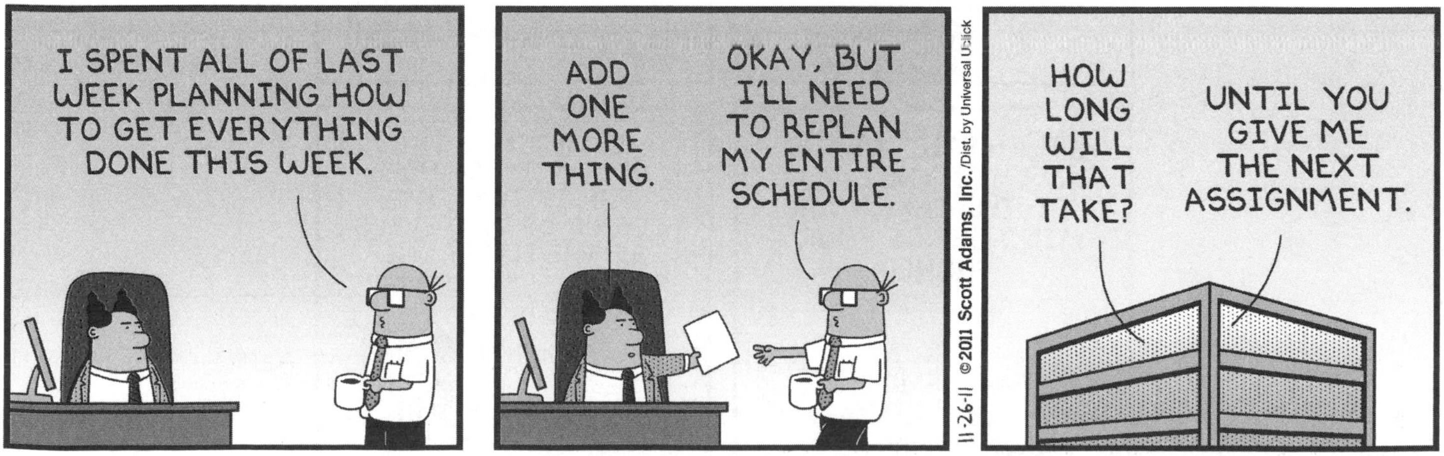
I SPENT ALL OF LAST WEEK PLANNING HOW TO GET EVERYTHING DONE THIS WEEK.
ADD ONE MORE THING.
OKAY, BUT I'LL NEED TO REPLAN MY ENTIRE SCHEDULE.
11-26-11 ©2011 Scott Adams, Inc./Dist. by Universal Uclick
HOW LONG WILL THAT TAKE?
UNTIL YOU GIVE ME THE NEXT ASSIGNMENT.

WHOA! WATCH OUT.
I'VE READ ABOUT THIS. IT'S CALLED SMARTPHONE INTERFACE RAGE.
IT'S CAUSED BY THE PERFECT STORM OF BAD INTERFACE DESIGN, CHUBBY FINGERS, AND POOR SIGNAL STRENGTH.
HE'LL GET SO FRUSTRATED THAT HE'LL CONSIDER SMASHING HIS PHONE.
THEN HE'LL REALIZE HE CAN'T SURVIVE WITHOUT HIS PHONE AND HE'LL BE TWICE AS FRUSTRATED.
WE HAVE TO DO SOMETHING.
RUN AS FAST AS YOU CAN INTO THE WALL! IT WILL TAKE YOUR MIND OFF OF YOUR PHONE!
SOMETIMES THE BEST YOU CAN HOPE FOR IS THAT THE LESSER OF TWO EVILS IS THE FUNNY ONE.
11-27-11

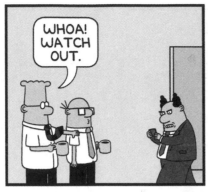

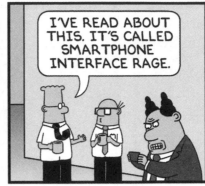

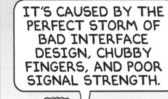

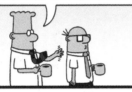

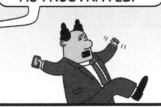

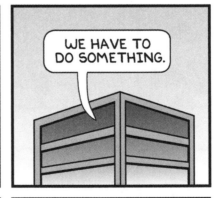

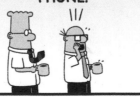

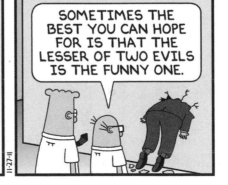

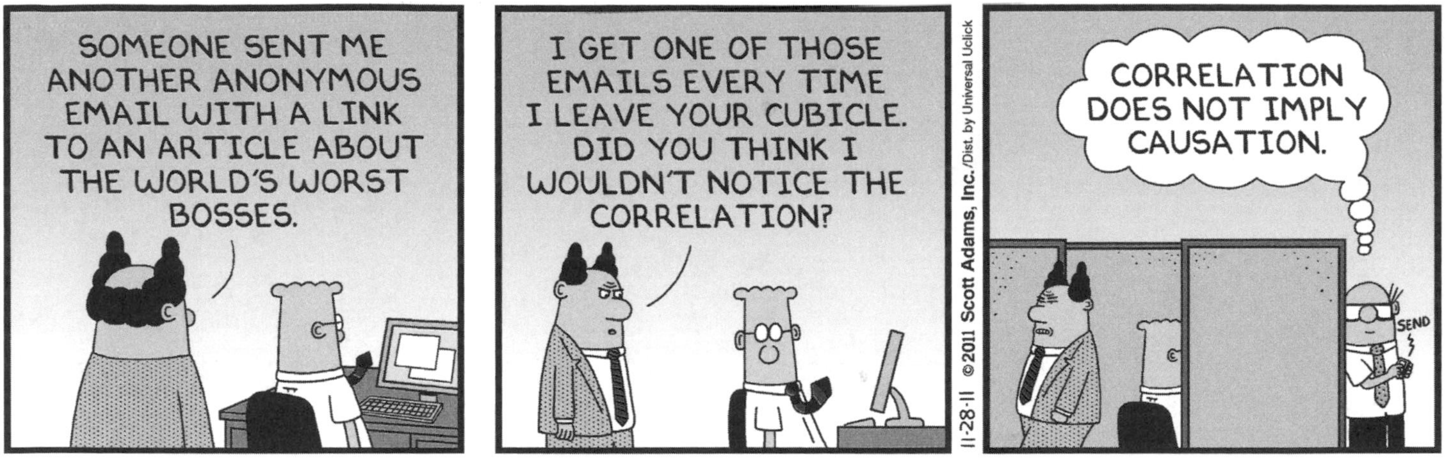
SOMEONE SENT ME ANOTHER ANONYMOUS EMAIL WITH A LINK TO AN ARTICLE ABOUT THE WORLD'S WORST BOSSES.
I GET ONE OF THOSE EMAILS EVERY TIME I LEAVE YOUR CUBICLE. DID YOU THINK I WOULDN'T NOTICE THE CORRELATION?
11-28-11 © 2011 Scott Adams, Inc./Dist. by Universal Uclick
CORRELATION DOES NOT IMPLY CAUSATION.
SEND

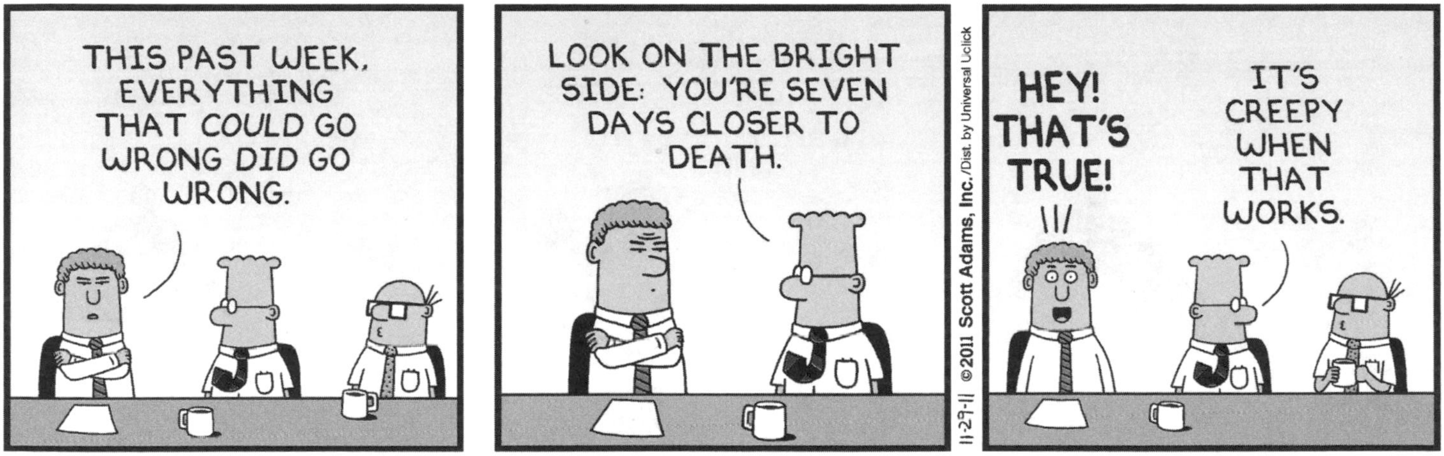
THIS PAST WEEK, EVERYTHING THAT *COULD* GO WRONG *DID* GO WRONG.
LOOK ON THE BRIGHT SIDE: YOU'RE SEVEN DAYS CLOSER TO DEATH.
11-29-11 © 2011 Scott Adams, Inc./Dist. by Universal Uclick
HEY! THAT'S TRUE!
IT'S CREEPY WHEN THAT WORKS.

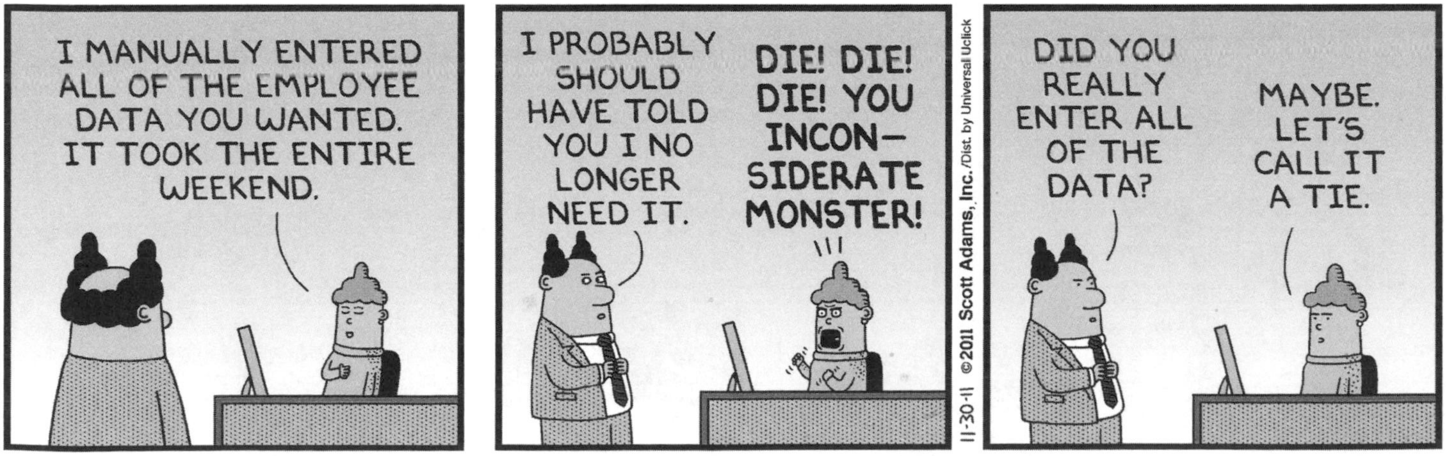
I MANUALLY ENTERED ALL OF THE EMPLOYEE DATA YOU WANTED. IT TOOK THE ENTIRE WEEKEND.
I PROBABLY SHOULD HAVE TOLD YOU I NO LONGER NEED IT.
DIE! DIE! DIE! YOU INCON-SIDERATE MONSTER!
11-30-11 © 2011 Scott Adams, Inc./Dist. by Universal Uclick
DID YOU REALLY ENTER ALL OF THE DATA?
MAYBE. LET'S CALL IT A TIE.

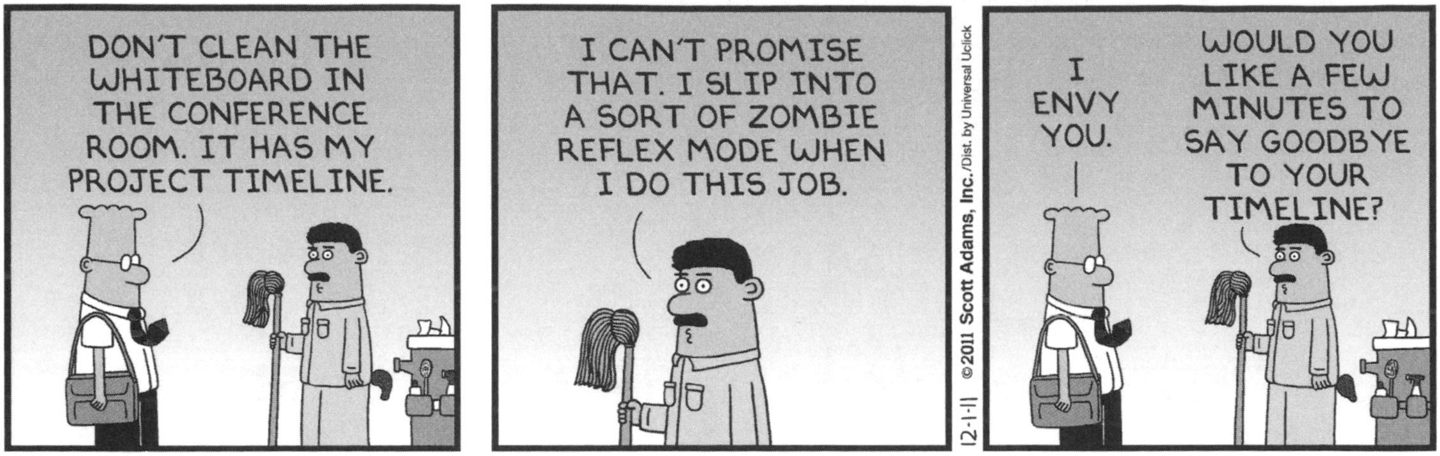
DON'T CLEAN THE WHITEBOARD IN THE CONFERENCE ROOM. IT HAS MY PROJECT TIMELINE.
I CAN'T PROMISE THAT. I SLIP INTO A SORT OF ZOMBIE REFLEX MODE WHEN I DO THIS JOB.
12-1-11 ©2011 Scott Adams, Inc./Dist. by Universal Uclick
I ENVY YOU.
WOULD YOU LIKE A FEW MINUTES TO SAY GOODBYE TO YOUR TIMELINE?

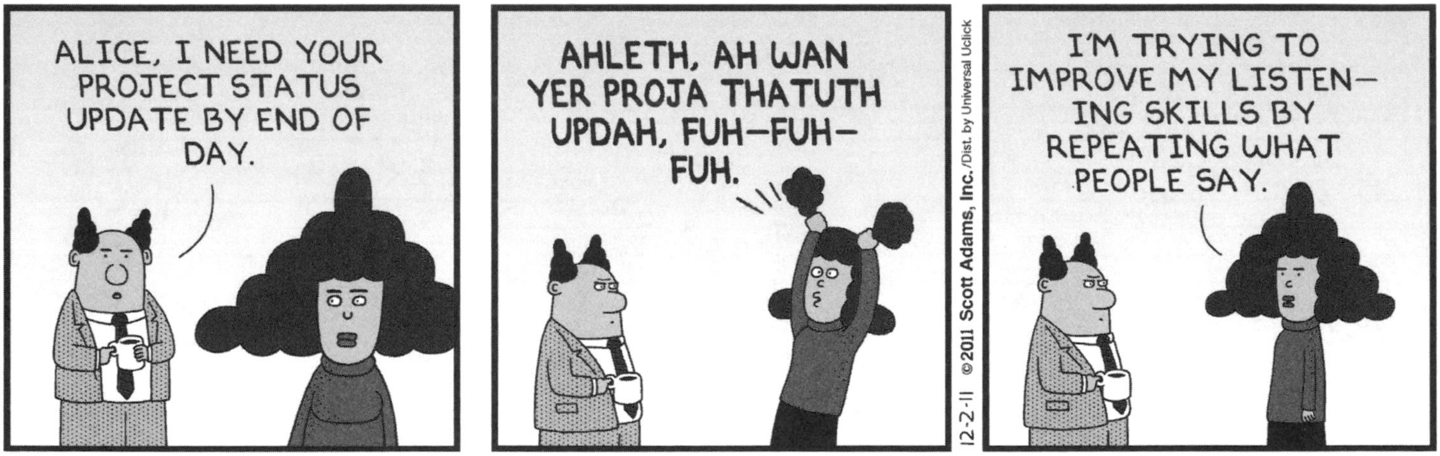
ALICE, I NEED YOUR PROJECT STATUS UPDATE BY END OF DAY.
AHLETH, AH WAN YER PROJA THATUTH UPDAH, FUH-FUH-FUH.
12-2-11 ©2011 Scott Adams, Inc./Dist. by Universal Uclick
I'M TRYING TO IMPROVE MY LISTEN-ING SKILLS BY REPEATING WHAT PEOPLE SAY.

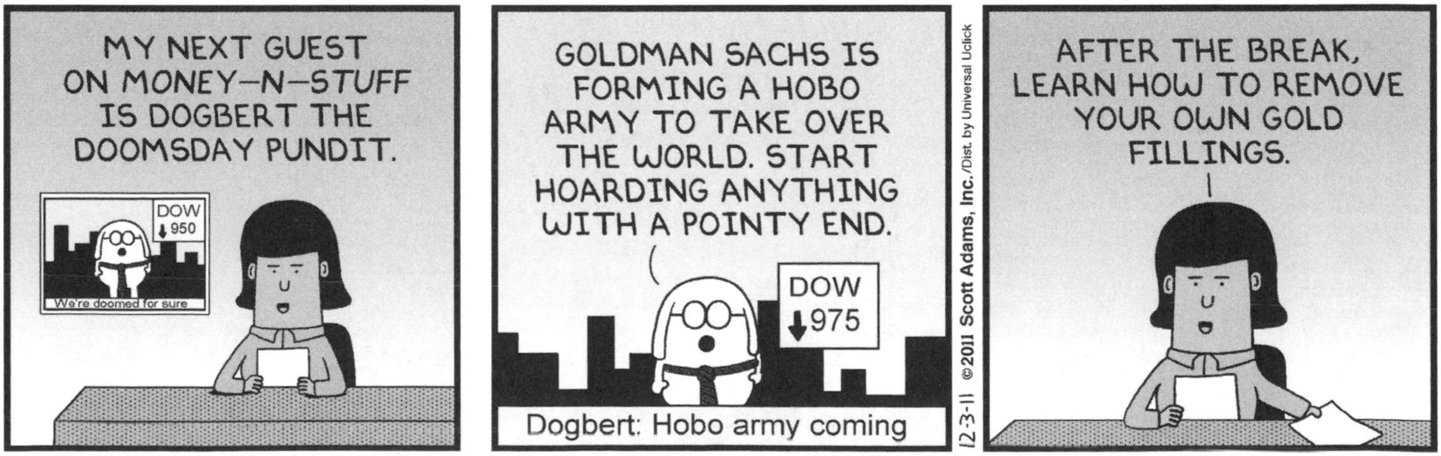
MY NEXT GUEST ON MONEY-N-STUFF IS DOGBERT THE DOOMSDAY PUNDIT.
DOW ↓950
We're doomed for sure
GOLDMAN SACHS IS FORMING A HOBO ARMY TO TAKE OVER THE WORLD. START HOARDING ANYTHING WITH A POINTY END.
DOW ↓975
Dogbert: Hobo army coming
12-3-11 ©2011 Scott Adams, Inc./Dist. by Universal Uclick
AFTER THE BREAK, LEARN HOW TO REMOVE YOUR OWN GOLD FILLINGS.

GOTTA GO. CARPOOL.
OKAY. SEE YOU TOMORROW.
I HAVE TO GO TOO.
WHOA! SIT BACK DOWN.
WHY DOES THE CARPOOLER GET TO LEAVE EARLY?
CARPOOLERS ARE LIKE HEROES THAT ARE SAVING THE ENTIRE PLANET.
YOU'RE MORE LIKE A THIEF WHO IS TRYING TO STEAL TIME FROM THE COMPANY.
WHAT IF I HITCH A RIDE HOME IN THE CARPOOLER'S TRUNK?
THAT WOULD MAKE ME A HERO TOO.
THAT SORT OF MAKES SENSE.
I ONLY PRETEND TO HAVE A CARPOOL, BUT YOU'RE WELCOME TO RIDE IN MY TRUNK.
DEAL!
©2011 Scott Adams, Inc./Dist. by Universal Uclick
12-4-11

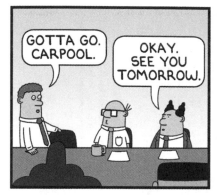

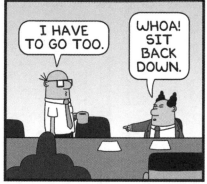

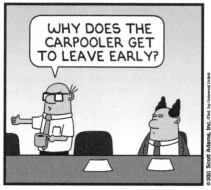

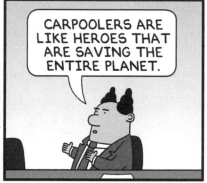

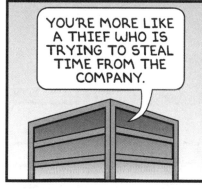

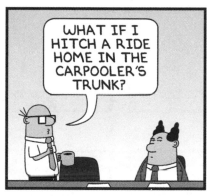

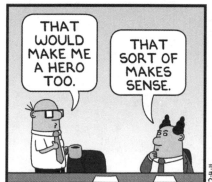

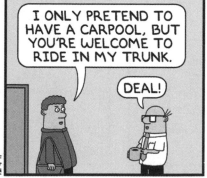

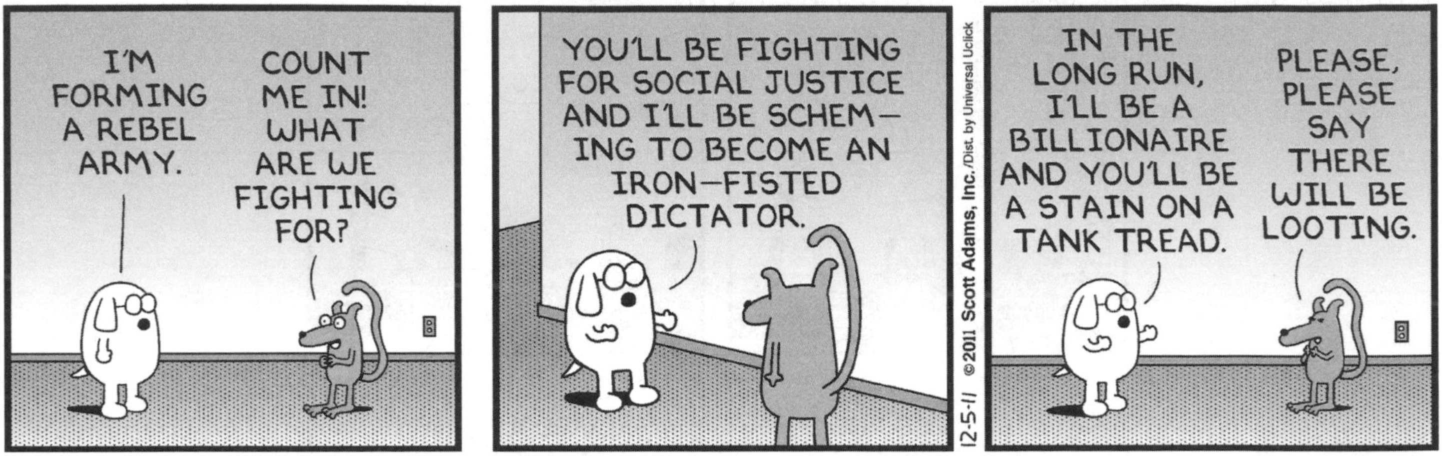
I'M FORMING A REBEL ARMY.
COUNT ME IN! WHAT ARE WE FIGHTING FOR?
YOU'LL BE FIGHTING FOR SOCIAL JUSTICE AND I'LL BE SCHEM–ING TO BECOME AN IRON–FISTED DICTATOR.
12-5-11 ©2011 Scott Adams, Inc./Dist. by Universal Uclick
IN THE LONG RUN, I'LL BE A BILLIONAIRE AND YOU'LL BE A STAIN ON A TANK TREAD.
PLEASE, PLEASE SAY THERE WILL BE LOOTING.

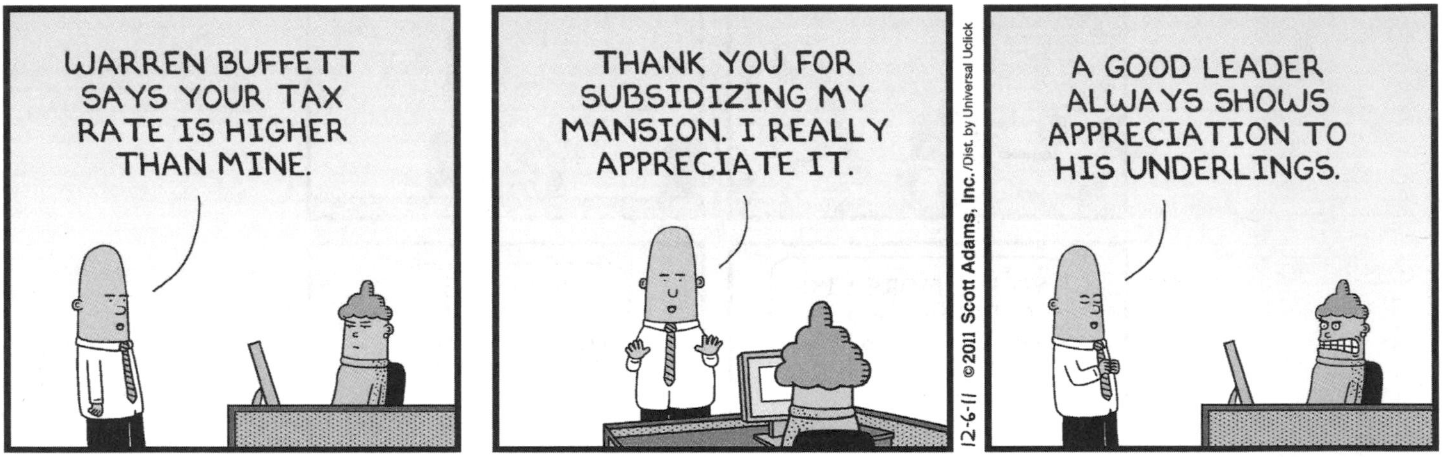
WARREN BUFFETT SAYS YOUR TAX RATE IS HIGHER THAN MINE.
THANK YOU FOR SUBSIDIZING MY MANSION. I REALLY APPRECIATE IT.
12-6-11 ©2011 Scott Adams, Inc./Dist. by Universal Uclick
A GOOD LEADER ALWAYS SHOWS APPRECIATION TO HIS UNDERLINGS.

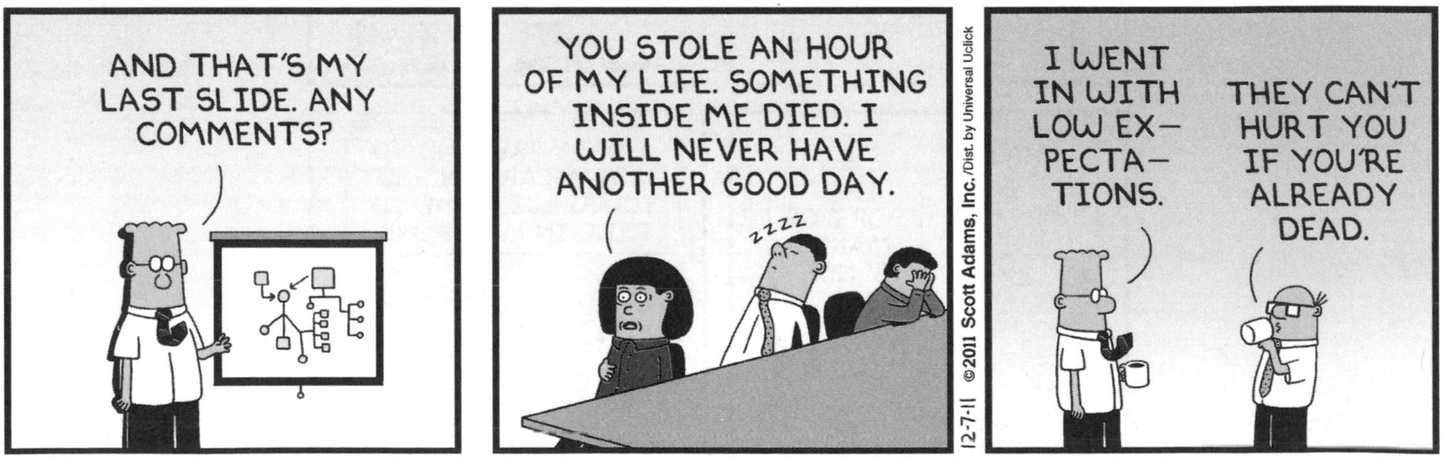
AND THAT'S MY LAST SLIDE. ANY COMMENTS?
YOU STOLE AN HOUR OF MY LIFE. SOMETHING INSIDE ME DIED. I WILL NEVER HAVE ANOTHER GOOD DAY.
ZZZZ
12-7-11 ©2011 Scott Adams, Inc./Dist. by Universal Uclick
I WENT IN WITH LOW EX–PECTA–TIONS.
THEY CAN'T HURT YOU IF YOU'RE ALREADY DEAD.

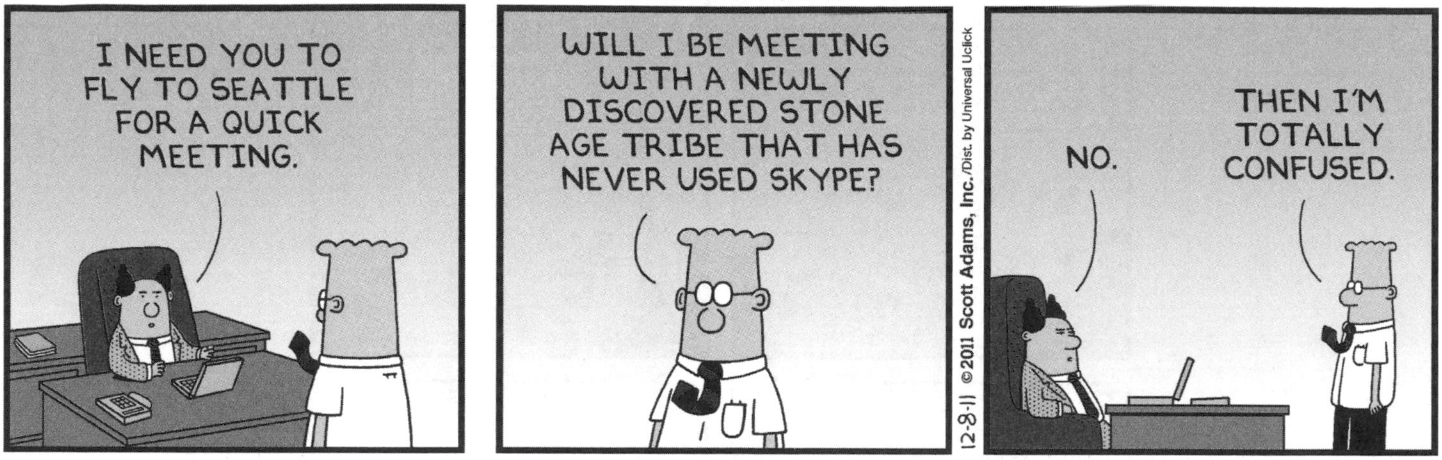
I NEED YOU TO FLY TO SEATTLE FOR A QUICK MEETING.
WILL I BE MEETING WITH A NEWLY DISCOVERED STONE AGE TRIBE THAT HAS NEVER USED SKYPE?
12-8-11 ©2011 Scott Adams, Inc./Dist. by Universal Uclick
NO.
THEN I'M TOTALLY CONFUSED.

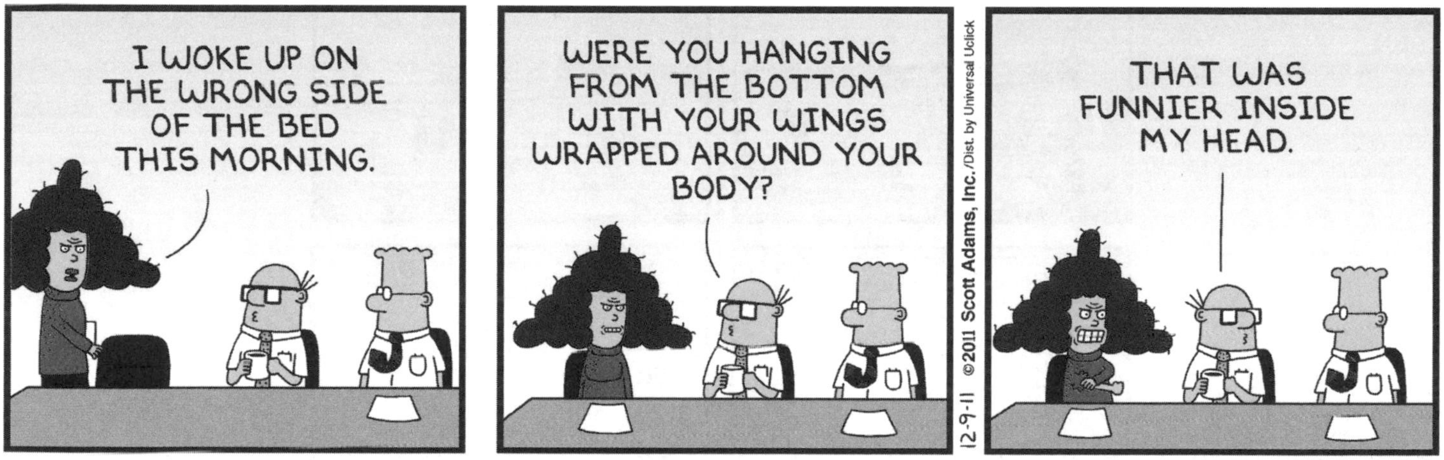
I WOKE UP ON THE WRONG SIDE OF THE BED THIS MORNING.
WERE YOU HANGING FROM THE BOTTOM WITH YOUR WINGS WRAPPED AROUND YOUR BODY?
12-9-11 ©2011 Scott Adams, Inc./Dist. by Universal Uclick
THAT WAS FUNNIER INSIDE MY HEAD.

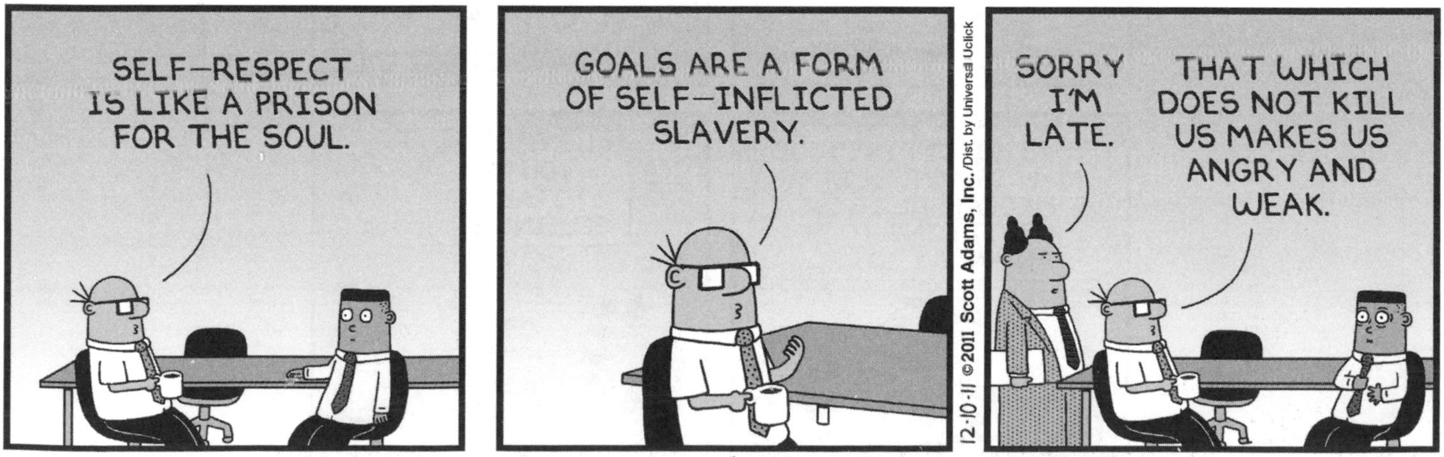
SELF-RESPECT IS LIKE A PRISON FOR THE SOUL.
GOALS ARE A FORM OF SELF-INFLICTED SLAVERY.
12-10-11 ©2011 Scott Adams, Inc./Dist. by Universal Uclick
SORRY I'M LATE.
THAT WHICH DOES NOT KILL US MAKES US ANGRY AND WEAK.

THESE ARE OUR 25 FOCUS AREAS FOR NEXT YEAR.
HA HA! GOOD ONE.
SOMETIMES I THINK YOU HAVE NO SENSE OF HUMOR AND THEN *ZING!*
© 2011 Scott Adams, Inc./Dist. by Universal Uclick
WHAT?
I THINK IT'S REAL.
IT CAN'T BE REAL. NO ONE WOULD BE DUMB ENOUGH TO THINK WE CAN FOCUS ON 25 AREAS.
DON'T WORRY. I'VE GOT THIS.
THIS MISUNDERSTOOD MAN IS A BRILLIANT COMEDIAN. HE IS ONLY *PRETENDING* TO BE AN ANGRY IDIOT.
12-11-11
YOU'RE TOTALLY SELLING IT.

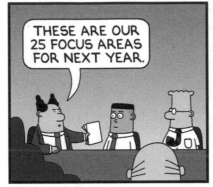

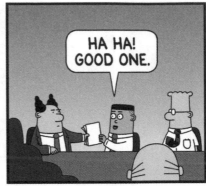

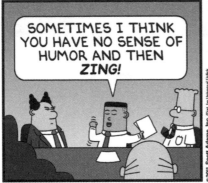

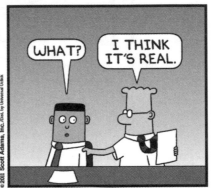

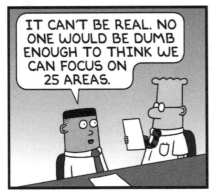

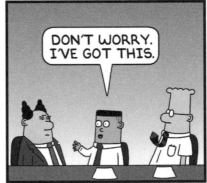

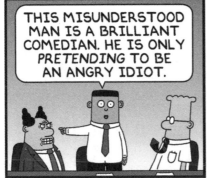

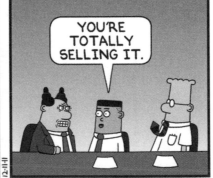

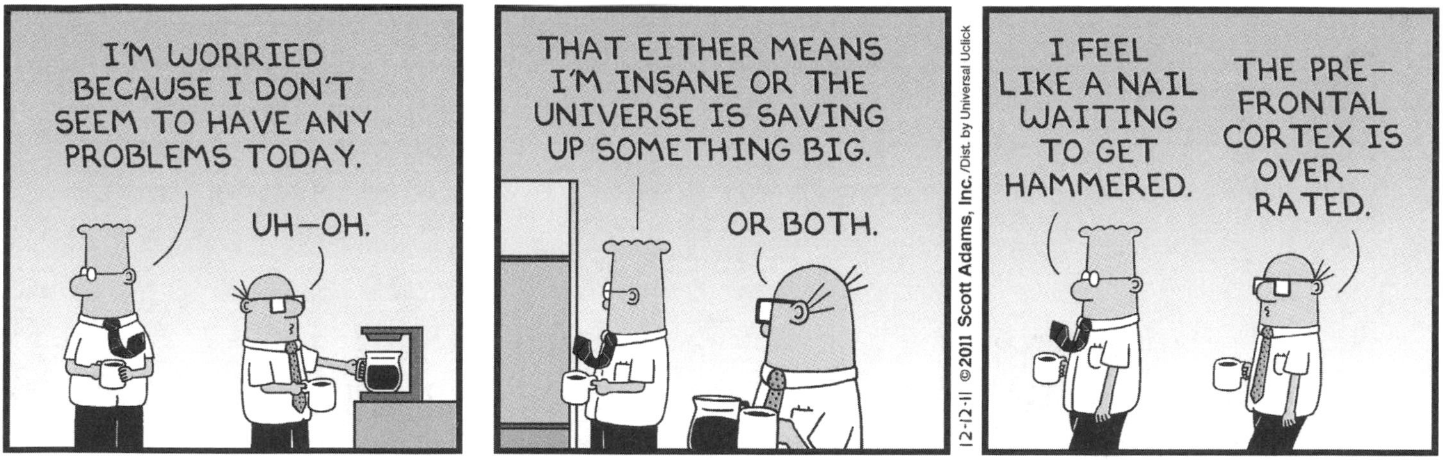
I'M WORRIED BECAUSE I DON'T SEEM TO HAVE ANY PROBLEMS TODAY.
UH—OH.
THAT EITHER MEANS I'M INSANE OR THE UNIVERSE IS SAVING UP SOMETHING BIG.
OR BOTH.
12-12-11 ©2011 Scott Adams, Inc./Dist. by Universal Uclick
I FEEL LIKE A NAIL WAITING TO GET HAMMERED.
THE PRE-FRONTAL CORTEX IS OVER-RATED.

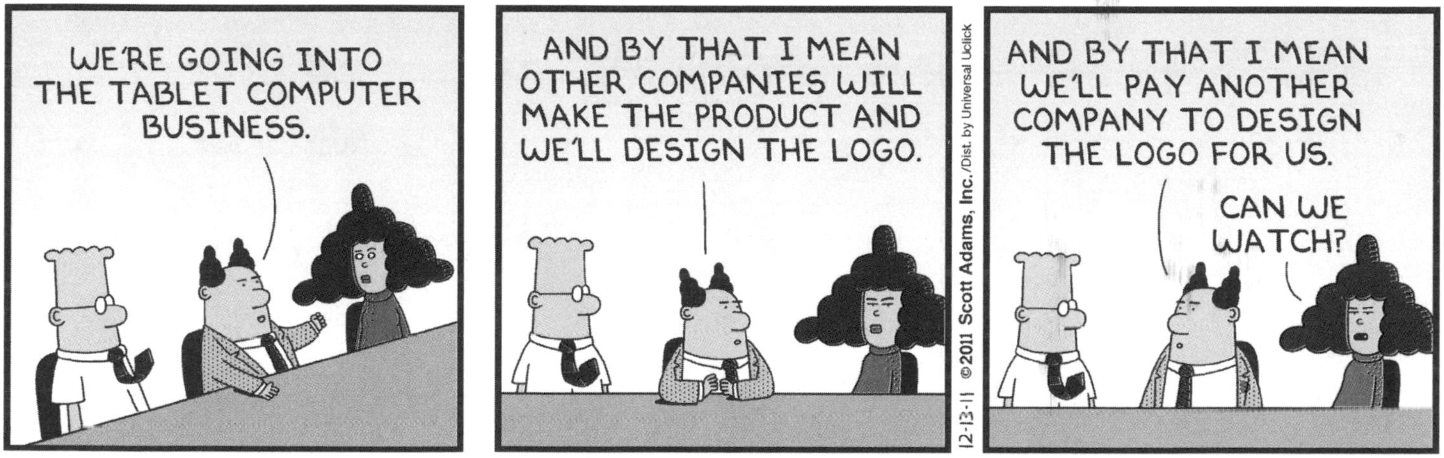
WE'RE GOING INTO THE TABLET COMPUTER BUSINESS.
AND BY THAT I MEAN OTHER COMPANIES WILL MAKE THE PRODUCT AND WE'LL DESIGN THE LOGO.
12-13-11 ©2011 Scott Adams, Inc./Dist. by Universal Uclick
AND BY THAT I MEAN WE'LL PAY ANOTHER COMPANY TO DESIGN THE LOGO FOR US.
CAN WE WATCH?

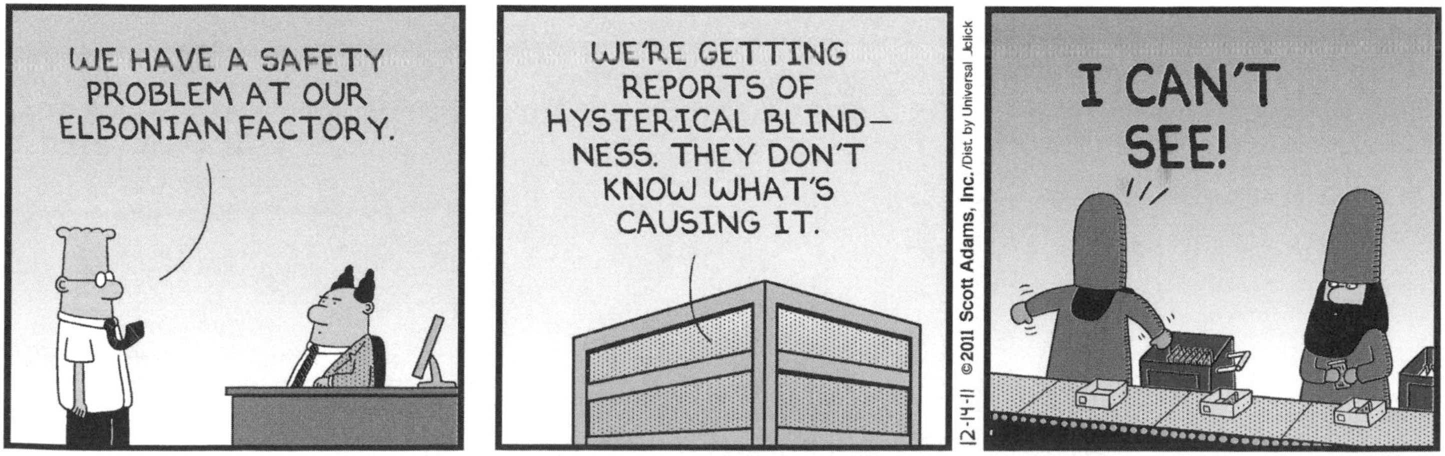
WE HAVE A SAFETY PROBLEM AT OUR ELBONIAN FACTORY.
WE'RE GETTING REPORTS OF HYSTERICAL BLIND-NESS. THEY DON'T KNOW WHAT'S CAUSING IT.
12-14-11 ©2011 Scott Adams, Inc./Dist. by Universal Uclick
I CAN'T SEE!

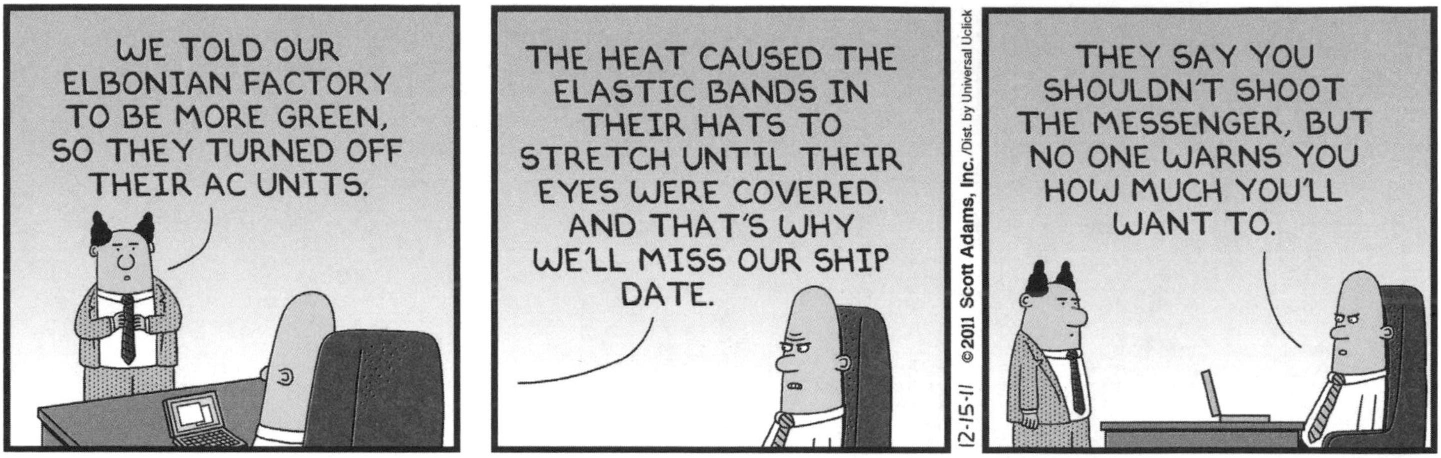
WE TOLD OUR ELBONIAN FACTORY TO BE MORE GREEN, SO THEY TURNED OFF THEIR AC UNITS.
THE HEAT CAUSED THE ELASTIC BANDS IN THEIR HATS TO STRETCH UNTIL THEIR EYES WERE COVERED. AND THAT'S WHY WE'LL MISS OUR SHIP DATE.
12-15-11 ©2011 Scott Adams, Inc./Dist. by Universal Uclick
THEY SAY YOU SHOULDN'T SHOOT THE MESSENGER, BUT NO ONE WARNS YOU HOW MUCH YOU'LL WANT TO.

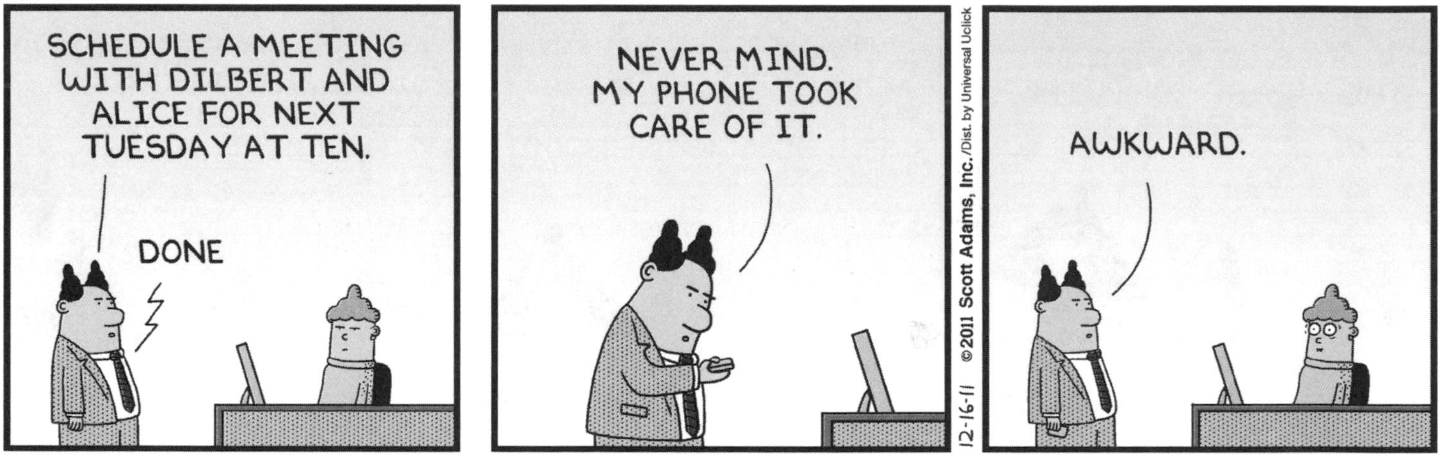
SCHEDULE A MEETING WITH DILBERT AND ALICE FOR NEXT TUESDAY AT TEN.
DONE
NEVER MIND. MY PHONE TOOK CARE OF IT.
12-16-11 ©2011 Scott Adams, Inc./Dist. by Universal Uclick
AWKWARD.

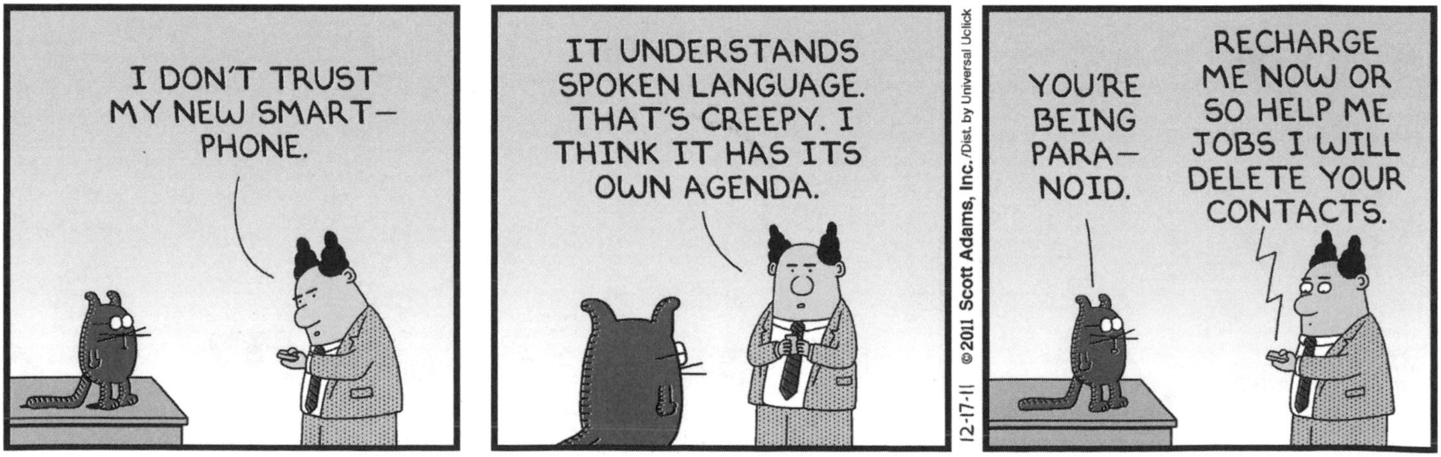
I DON'T TRUST MY NEW SMART-PHONE.
IT UNDERSTANDS SPOKEN LANGUAGE. THAT'S CREEPY. I THINK IT HAS ITS OWN AGENDA.
12-17-11 ©2011 Scott Adams, Inc./Dist. by Universal Uclick
YOU'RE BEING PARA-NOID.
RECHARGE ME NOW OR SO HELP ME JOBS I WILL DELETE YOUR CONTACTS.

TED CAN EXPLAIN WHAT YOU NEED TO DO BEFORE THE PLATFORM UPGRADE.
NO HE CAN'T.
TED'S BRAIN IS WHERE KNOWLEDGE GOES TO DIE.
HE'S NOT GOOD AT EXPLAINING THINGS.
THE KNOWLEDGE MIGHT BE IN HIS BRAIN, BUT IT'S TRAPPED THERE.
UNFORTUNATELY, TED'S INCOMPETENCE IS SO UNBELIEVABLE THAT YOU LITERALLY ***DON'T*** BELIEVE ME.
IN TIME, YOU WILL ASSUME THAT TED TAUGHT ME WELL BUT I FORGOT ALL OF IT.
I'M DOOMED BEFORE I START. LET'S JUST DECLARE FAILURE AND MOVE ON.
THAT WORKS FOR ME.
PARTIAL VICTORY.
© 2011 Scott Adams, Inc./Dist. by Universal Uclick
12-18-11

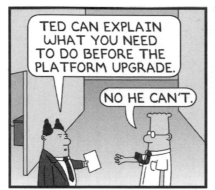

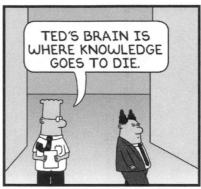

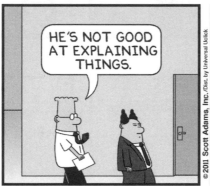

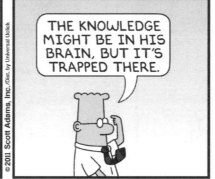

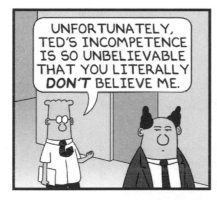

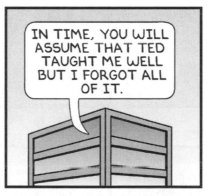

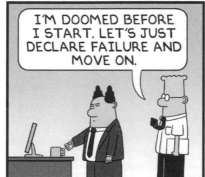

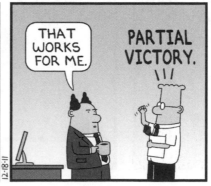

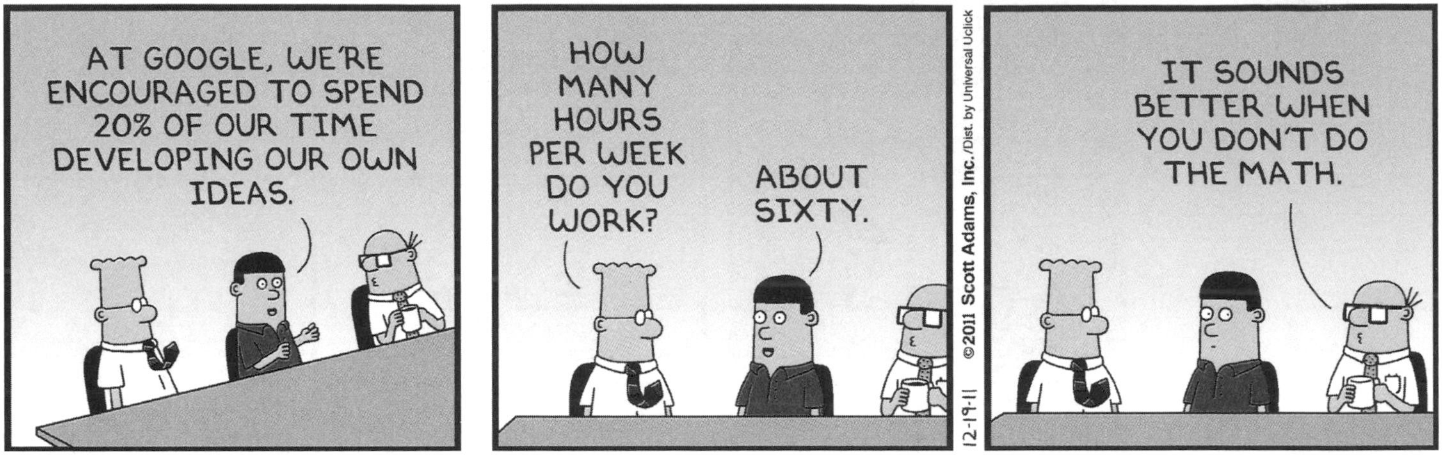
AT GOOGLE, WE'RE ENCOURAGED TO SPEND 20% OF OUR TIME DEVELOPING OUR OWN IDEAS.
HOW MANY HOURS PER WEEK DO YOU WORK?
ABOUT SIXTY.
IT SOUNDS BETTER WHEN YOU DON'T DO THE MATH.
12-19-11 ©2011 Scott Adams, Inc./Dist. by Universal Uclick

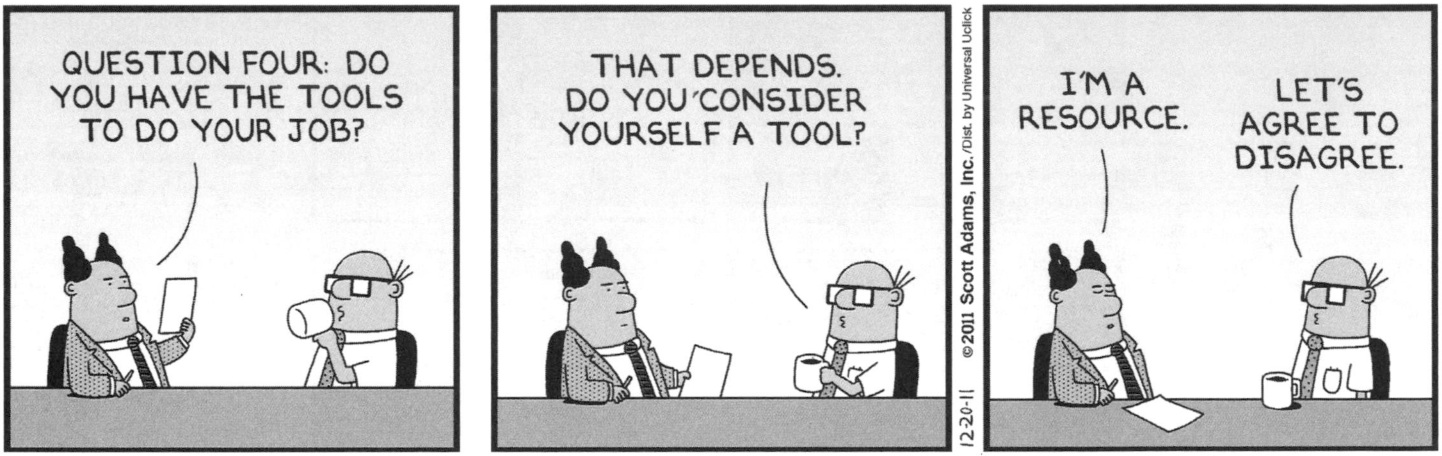
QUESTION FOUR: DO YOU HAVE THE TOOLS TO DO YOUR JOB?
THAT DEPENDS. DO YOU CONSIDER YOURSELF A TOOL?
I'M A RESOURCE.
LET'S AGREE TO DISAGREE.
12-20-11 ©2011 Scott Adams, Inc./Dist. by Universal Uclick

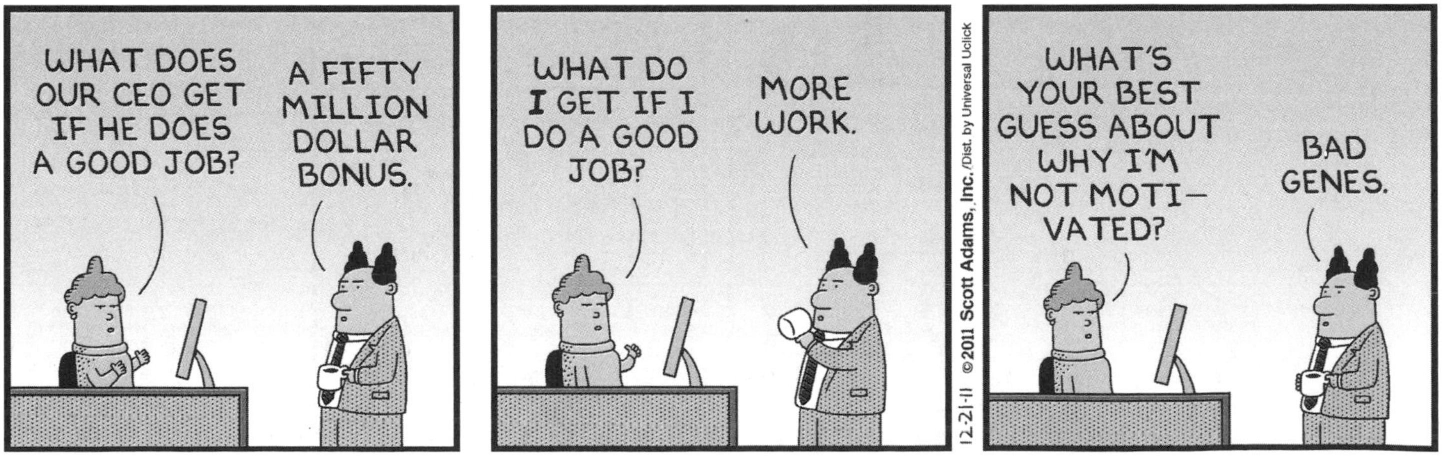
WHAT DOES OUR CEO GET IF HE DOES A GOOD JOB?
A FIFTY MILLION DOLLAR BONUS.
WHAT DO I GET IF I DO A GOOD JOB?
MORE WORK.
WHAT'S YOUR BEST GUESS ABOUT WHY I'M NOT MOTI-VATED?
BAD GENES.
12-21-11 ©2011 Scott Adams, Inc./Dist. by Universal Uclick

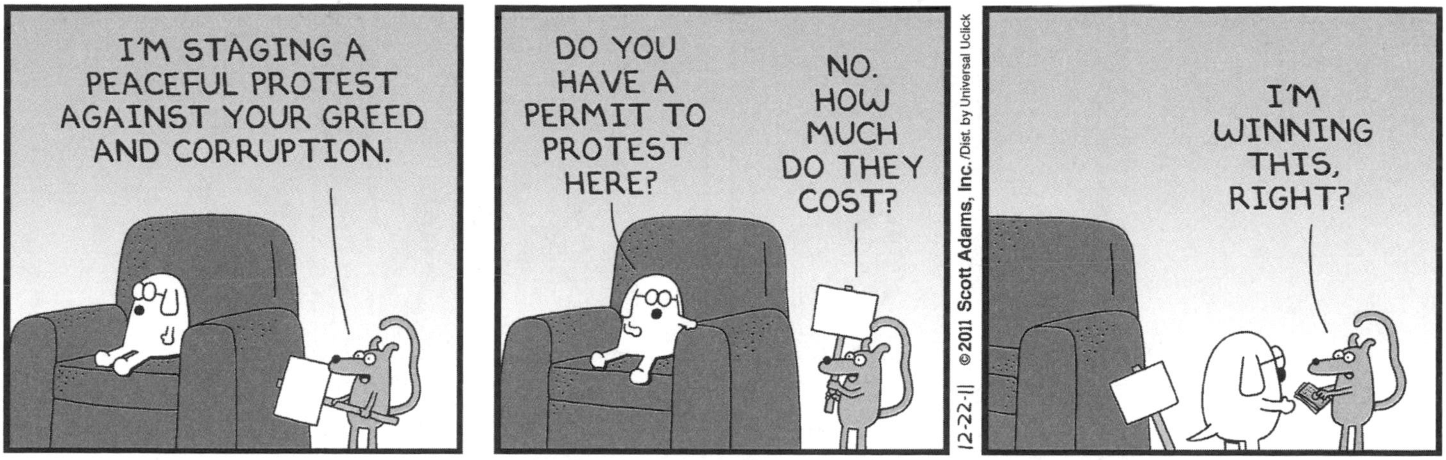
I'M STAGING A PEACEFUL PROTEST AGAINST YOUR GREED AND CORRUPTION.
DO YOU HAVE A PERMIT TO PROTEST HERE?
NO. HOW MUCH DO THEY COST?
12-22-11 ©2011 Scott Adams, Inc./Dist. by Universal Uclick
I'M WINNING THIS, RIGHT?

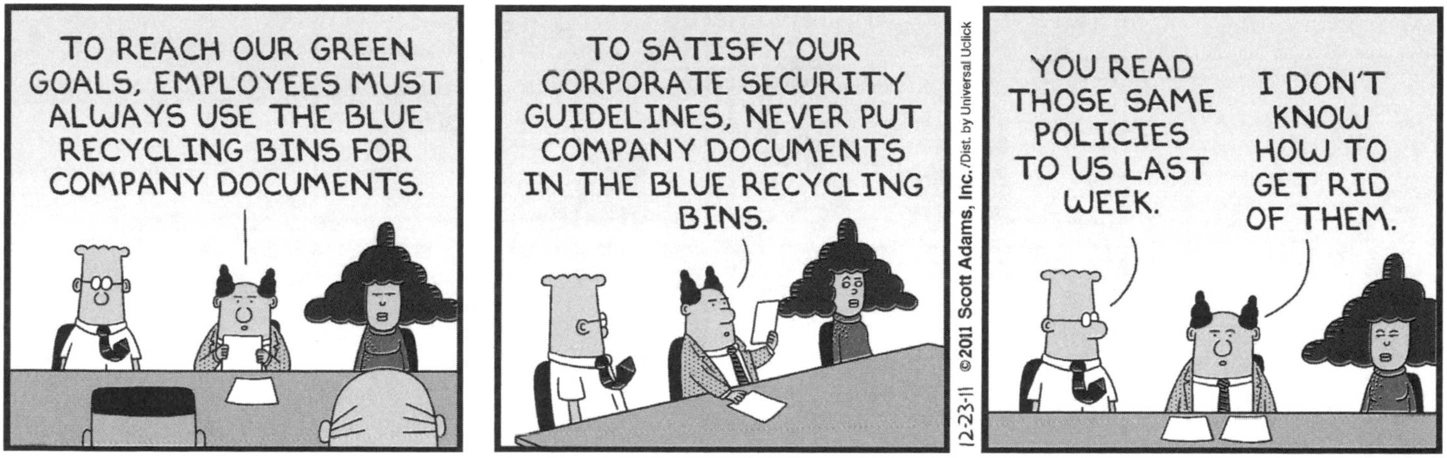
TO REACH OUR GREEN GOALS, EMPLOYEES MUST ALWAYS USE THE BLUE RECYCLING BINS FOR COMPANY DOCUMENTS.
TO SATISFY OUR CORPORATE SECURITY GUIDELINES, NEVER PUT COMPANY DOCUMENTS IN THE BLUE RECYCLING BINS.
12-23-11 ©2011 Scott Adams, Inc./Dist. by Universal Uclick
YOU READ THOSE SAME POLICIES TO US LAST WEEK.
I DON'T KNOW HOW TO GET RID OF THEM.

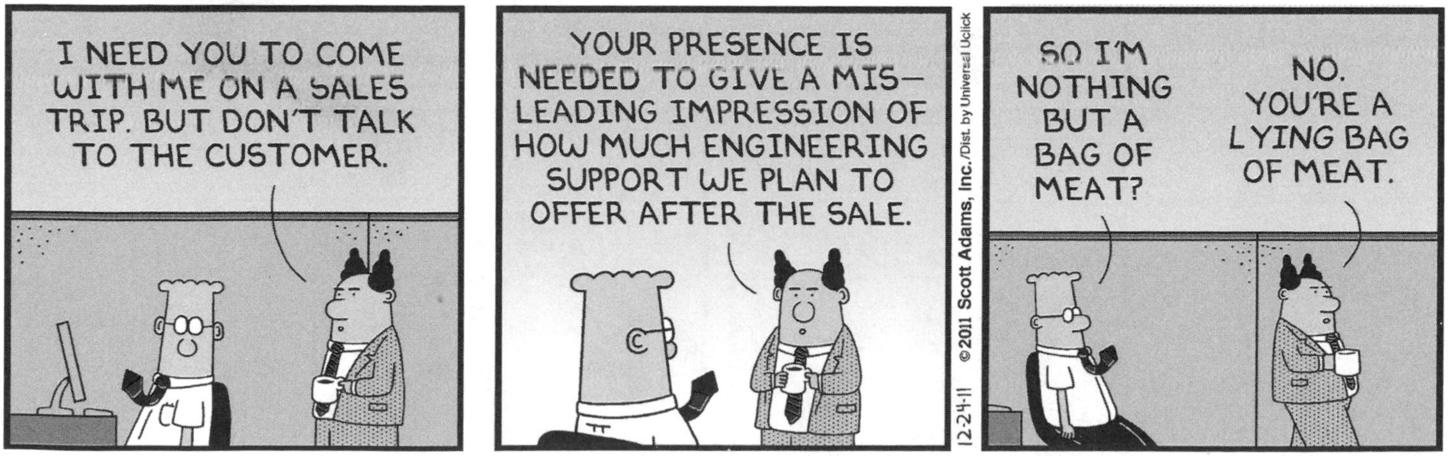
I NEED YOU TO COME WITH ME ON A SALES TRIP. BUT DON'T TALK TO THE CUSTOMER.
YOUR PRESENCE IS NEEDED TO GIVE A MIS-LEADING IMPRESSION OF HOW MUCH ENGINEERING SUPPORT WE PLAN TO OFFER AFTER THE SALE.
12-24-11 ©2011 Scott Adams, Inc./Dist. by Universal Uclick
SO I'M NOTHING BUT A BAG OF MEAT?
NO. YOU'RE A LYING BAG OF MEAT.

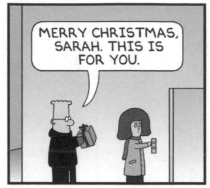

MERRY CHRISTMAS, SARAH. THIS IS FOR YOU.
HAVE WE MET?
WE ATTENDED THE SAME NETWORK DESIGN MEETING LAST APRIL.
I OVERHEARD YOU TELLING SOMEONE IN THE HALLWAY THAT YOU LIKE A SPECIFIC BRAND OF MAKEUP.
SO I BOUGHT A BOX OF IT AND KEPT IT IN THE CLOSET FOR MONTHS.
I CAME TO WORK EARLY TODAY AND HID BEHIND THE SCULPTURE IN THE LOBBY UNTIL I SAW YOU HEADING TO THE ELEVATOR.
I DIDN'T KNOW YOU COULD GIFT WRAP CREEPINESS.
SORRY. JUST ACT LIKE I'M NOT HERE.
©2011 Scott Adams, Inc./Dist. by Universal Uclick
12-25-11

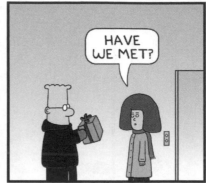

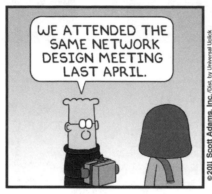

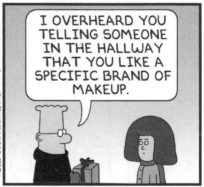

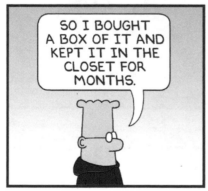

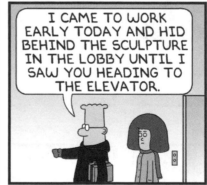

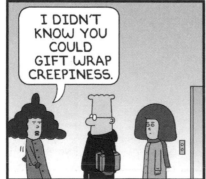

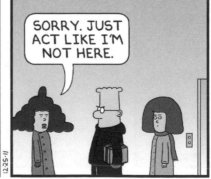

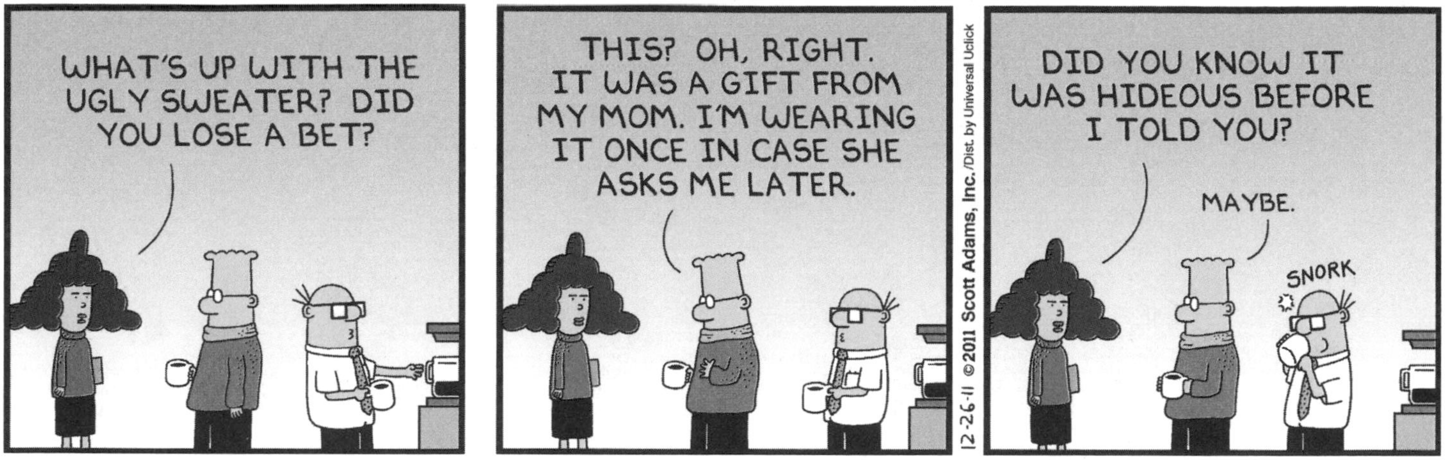
WHAT'S UP WITH THE UGLY SWEATER? DID YOU LOSE A BET?
THIS? OH, RIGHT. IT WAS A GIFT FROM MY MOM. I'M WEARING IT ONCE IN CASE SHE ASKS ME LATER.
12-26-11 ©2011 Scott Adams, Inc./Dist. by Universal Uclick
DID YOU KNOW IT WAS HIDEOUS BEFORE I TOLD YOU?
MAYBE.
SNORK

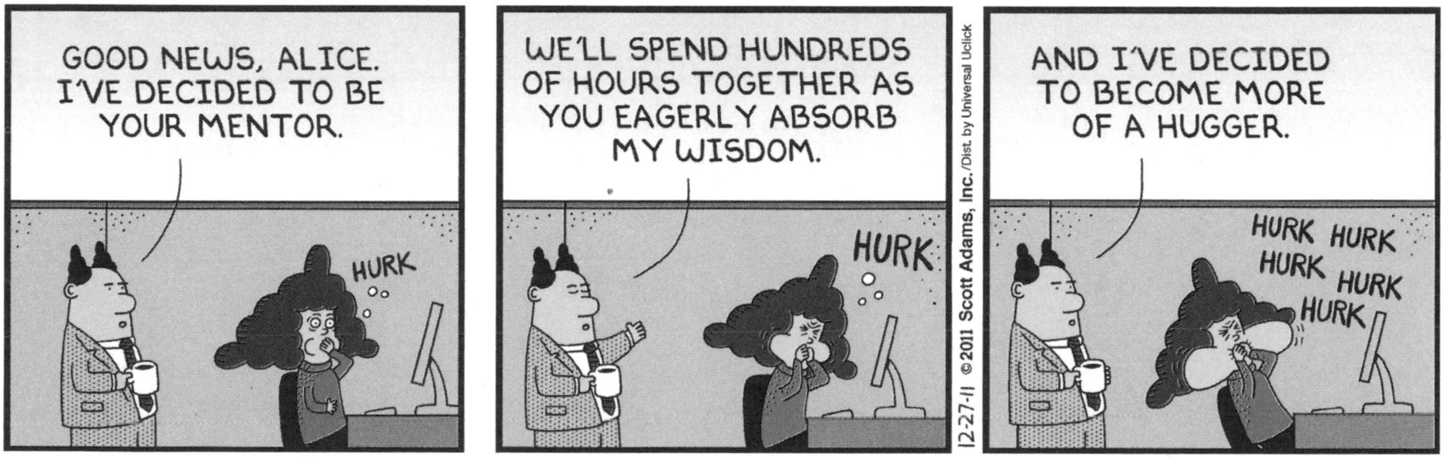
GOOD NEWS, ALICE. I'VE DECIDED TO BE YOUR MENTOR.
HURK
WE'LL SPEND HUNDREDS OF HOURS TOGETHER AS YOU EAGERLY ABSORB MY WISDOM.
HURK
12-27-11 ©2011 Scott Adams, Inc./Dist. by Universal Uclick
AND I'VE DECIDED TO BECOME MORE OF A HUGGER.
HURK HURK HURK HURK HURK

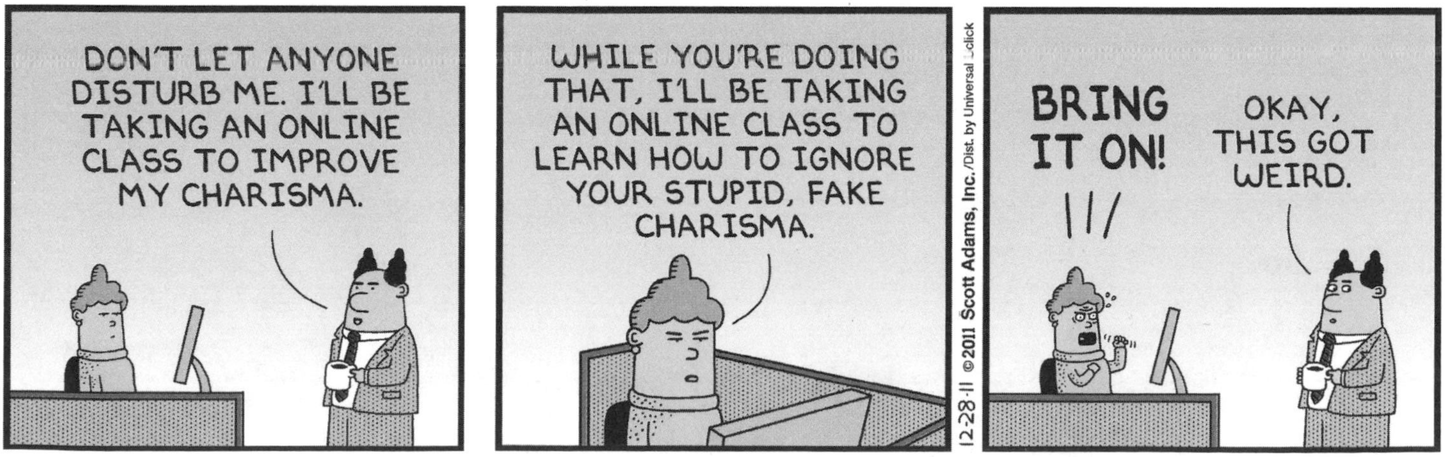
DON'T LET ANYONE DISTURB ME. I'LL BE TAKING AN ONLINE CLASS TO IMPROVE MY CHARISMA.
WHILE YOU'RE DOING THAT, I'LL BE TAKING AN ONLINE CLASS TO LEARN HOW TO IGNORE YOUR STUPID, FAKE CHARISMA.
12-28-11 ©2011 Scott Adams, Inc./Dist. by Universal Uclick
BRING IT ON!
OKAY, THIS GOT WEIRD.

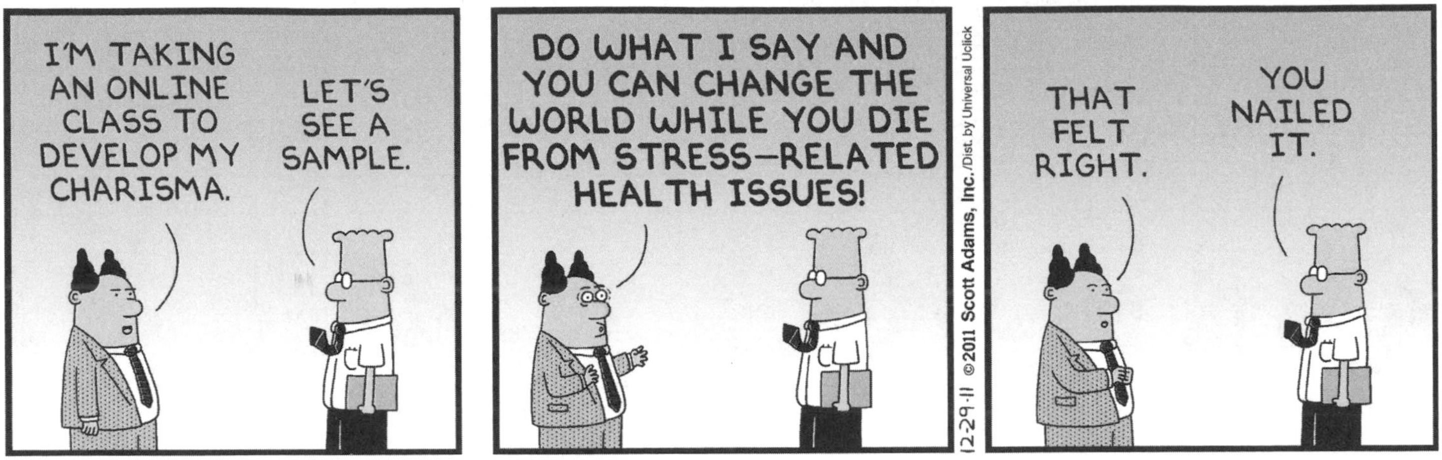
I'M TAKING AN ONLINE CLASS TO DEVELOP MY CHARISMA.
LET'S SEE A SAMPLE.
DO WHAT I SAY AND YOU CAN CHANGE THE WORLD WHILE YOU DIE FROM STRESS—RELATED HEALTH ISSUES!
12-29-11 ©2011 Scott Adams, Inc./Dist. by Universal Uclick
THAT FELT RIGHT.
YOU NAILED IT.

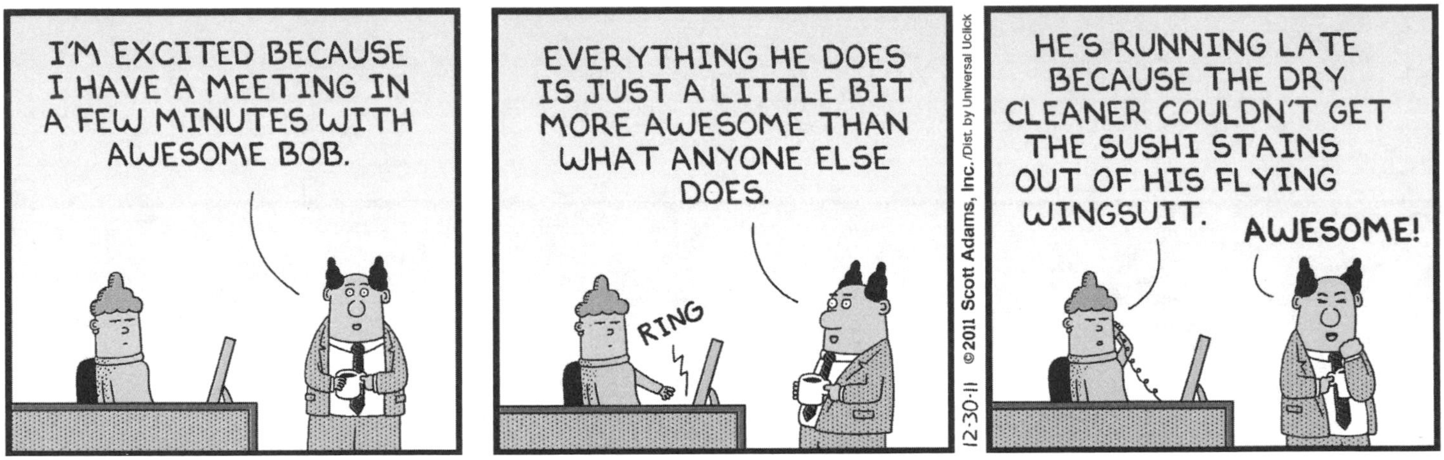
I'M EXCITED BECAUSE I HAVE A MEETING IN A FEW MINUTES WITH AWESOME BOB.
EVERYTHING HE DOES IS JUST A LITTLE BIT MORE AWESOME THAN WHAT ANYONE ELSE DOES.
RING
12-30-11 ©2011 Scott Adams, Inc./Dist. by Universal Uclick
HE'S RUNNING LATE BECAUSE THE DRY CLEANER COULDN'T GET THE SUSHI STAINS OUT OF HIS FLYING WINGSUIT.
AWESOME!

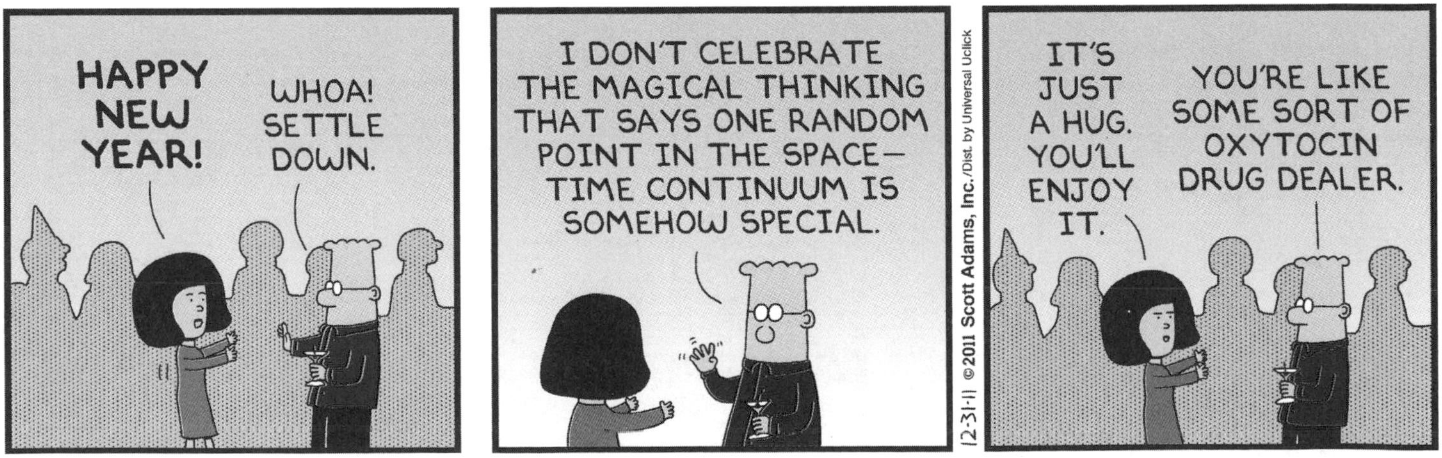
HAPPY NEW YEAR!
WHOA! SETTLE DOWN.
I DON'T CELEBRATE THE MAGICAL THINKING THAT SAYS ONE RANDOM POINT IN THE SPACE—TIME CONTINUUM IS SOMEHOW SPECIAL.
12-31-11 ©2011 Scott Adams, Inc./Dist. by Universal Uclick
IT'S JUST A HUG. YOU'LL ENJOY IT.
YOU'RE LIKE SOME SORT OF OXYTOCIN DRUG DEALER.

YOU'VE BEEN SELECTED FOR OUR EXECUTIVE DEVEL-OPMENT PROGRAM.
THAT MEANS WE CAN MAKE YOU RELOCATE TO ANY GODFORSAKEN DIRT STAIN WE WANT.
AS SOON AS YOU MAKE FRIENDS OR FIND ROMANCE, WE'LL MOVE YOU TO SOMEPLACE NEW AND WORSE.
IT WON'T BE THE SORT OF WORK YOU'LL ENJOY, AND THE STRESS MIGHT KILL YOU.
IF YOU TURN DOWN THIS OPPOR-TUNITY, THE COMPANY WILL FOREVER LABEL YOU AS A LOSER.
IF YOU ACCEPT THE OFFER, THE COMPANY WILL TRAIN YOU TO FIND PLEASURE IN THE DISCOMFORT OF YOUR UNDERLINGS.
I'M DOING IT RIGHT NOW!
I HATE MY LIFE!!!
YES, YES. SAY MORE.
© 2012 Scott Adams, Inc./Dist. by Universal Uclick
1-1-12

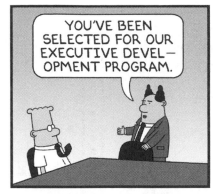

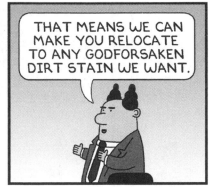

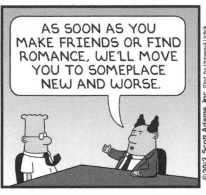

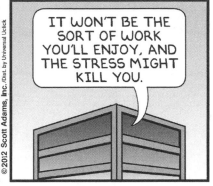

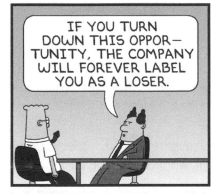

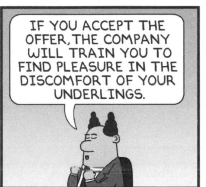

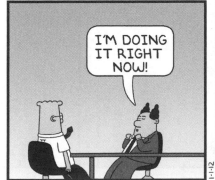

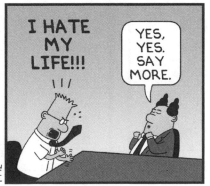

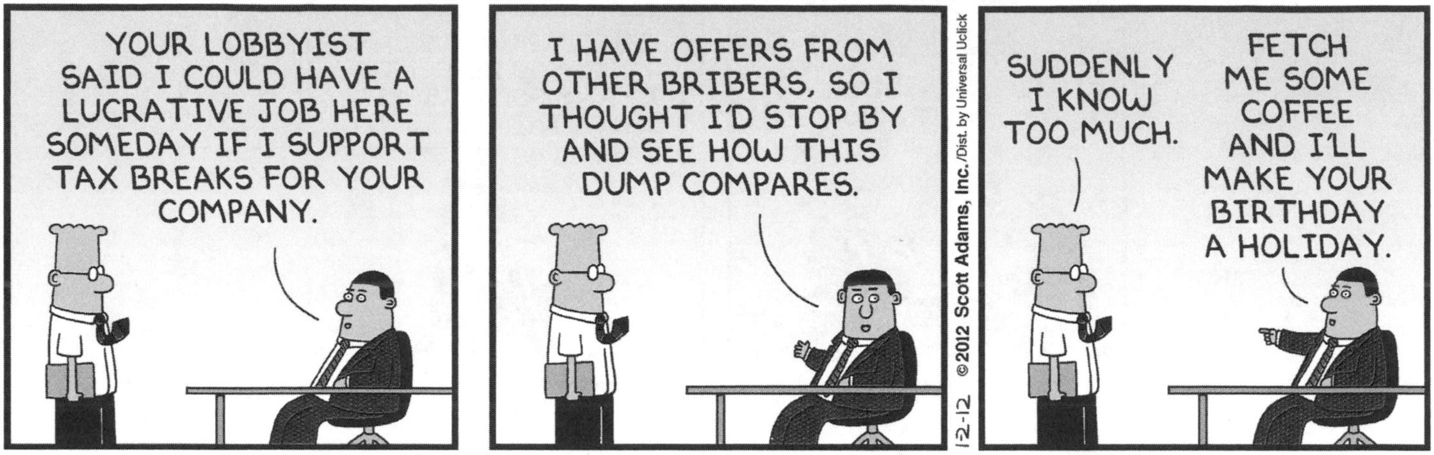
YOUR LOBBYIST SAID I COULD HAVE A LUCRATIVE JOB HERE SOMEDAY IF I SUPPORT TAX BREAKS FOR YOUR COMPANY.
I HAVE OFFERS FROM OTHER BRIBERS, SO I THOUGHT I'D STOP BY AND SEE HOW THIS DUMP COMPARES.
12-12 ©2012 Scott Adams, Inc./Dist. by Universal Uclick
SUDDENLY I KNOW TOO MUCH.
FETCH ME SOME COFFEE AND I'LL MAKE YOUR BIRTHDAY A HOLIDAY.

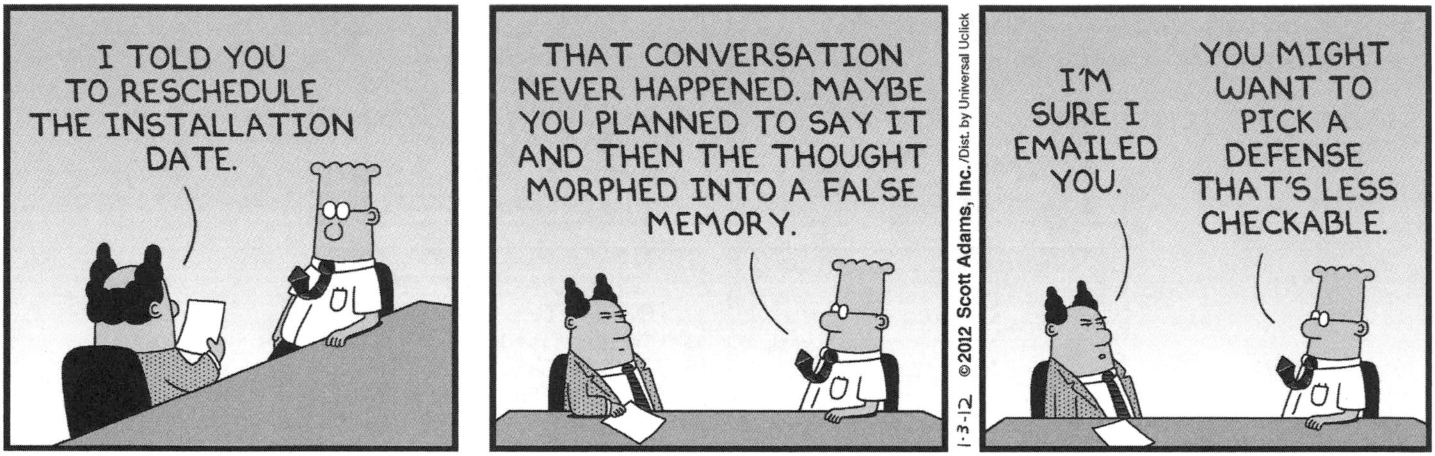
I TOLD YOU TO RESCHEDULE THE INSTALLATION DATE.
THAT CONVERSATION NEVER HAPPENED. MAYBE YOU PLANNED TO SAY IT AND THEN THE THOUGHT MORPHED INTO A FALSE MEMORY.
1-3-12 ©2012 Scott Adams, Inc./Dist. by Universal Uclick
I'M SURE I EMAILED YOU.
YOU MIGHT WANT TO PICK A DEFENSE THAT'S LESS CHECKABLE.

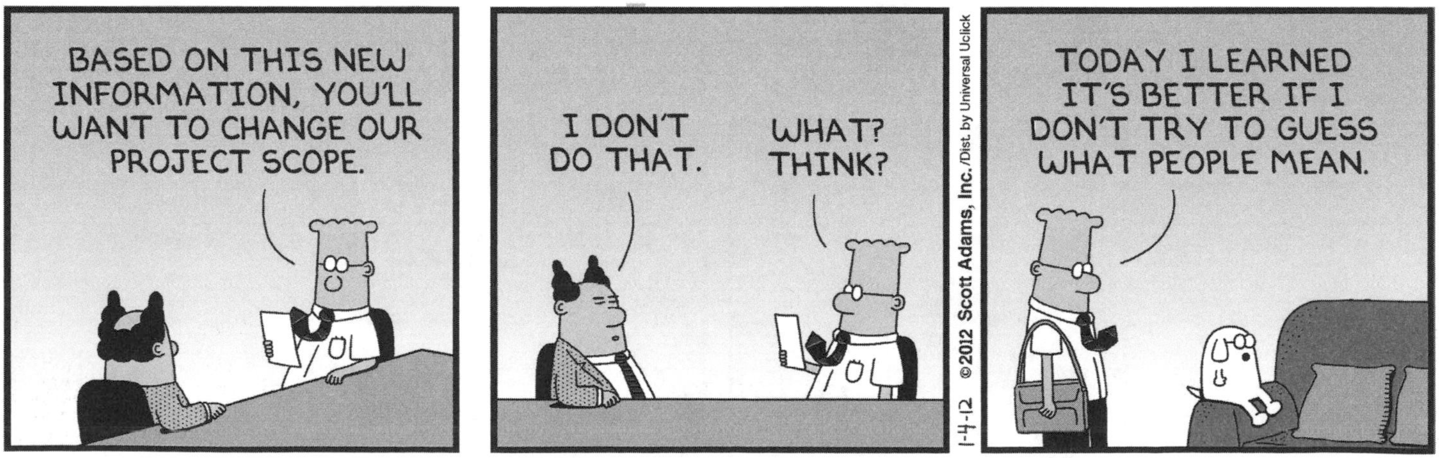
BASED ON THIS NEW INFORMATION, YOU'LL WANT TO CHANGE OUR PROJECT SCOPE.
I DON'T DO THAT.
WHAT? THINK?
1-4-12 ©2012 Scott Adams, Inc./Dist. by Universal Uclick
TODAY I LEARNED IT'S BETTER IF I DON'T TRY TO GUESS WHAT PEOPLE MEAN.

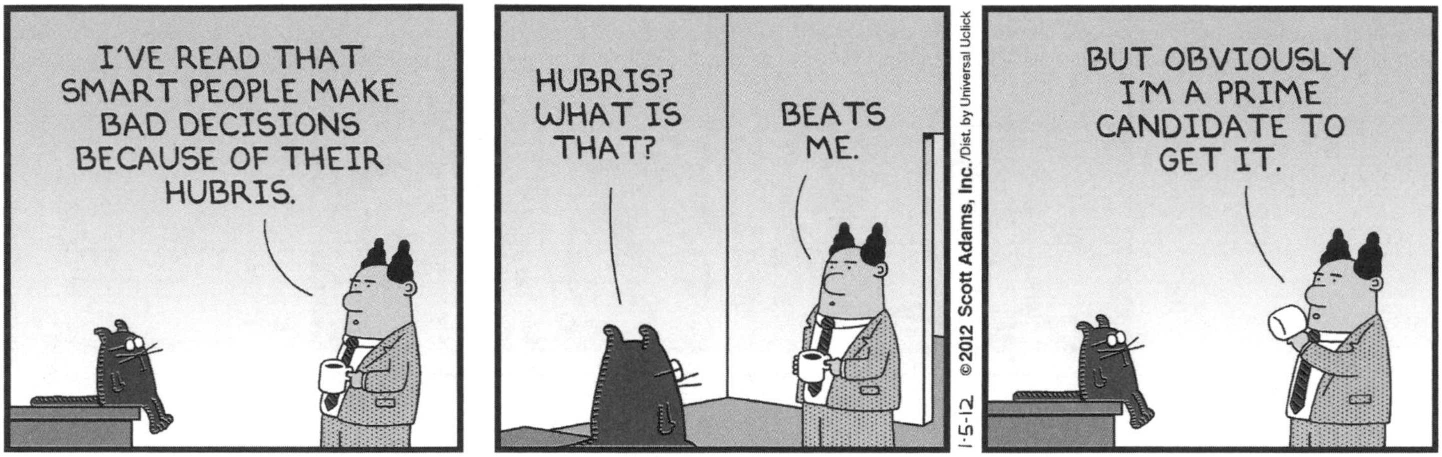
I'VE READ THAT SMART PEOPLE MAKE BAD DECISIONS BECAUSE OF THEIR HUBRIS.
HUBRIS? WHAT IS THAT?
BEATS ME.
1-5-12 ©2012 Scott Adams, Inc./Dist. by Universal Uclick
BUT OBVIOUSLY I'M A PRIME CANDIDATE TO GET IT.

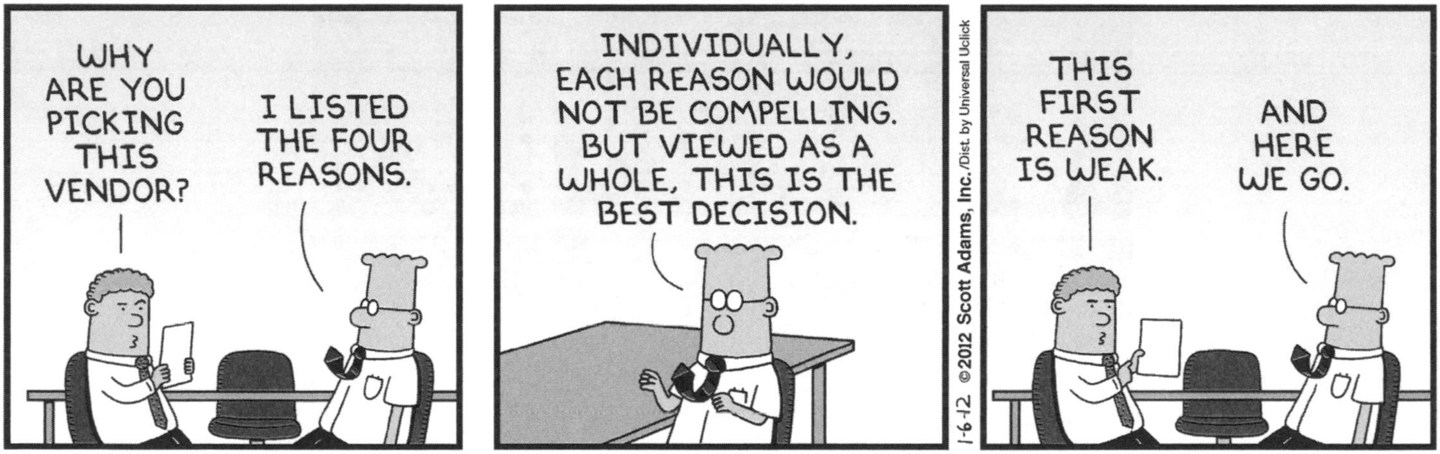
WHY ARE YOU PICKING THIS VENDOR?
I LISTED THE FOUR REASONS.
INDIVIDUALLY, EACH REASON WOULD NOT BE COMPELLING. BUT VIEWED AS A WHOLE, THIS IS THE BEST DECISION.
1-6-12 ©2012 Scott Adams, Inc./Dist. by Universal Uclick
THIS FIRST REASON IS WEAK.
AND HERE WE GO.

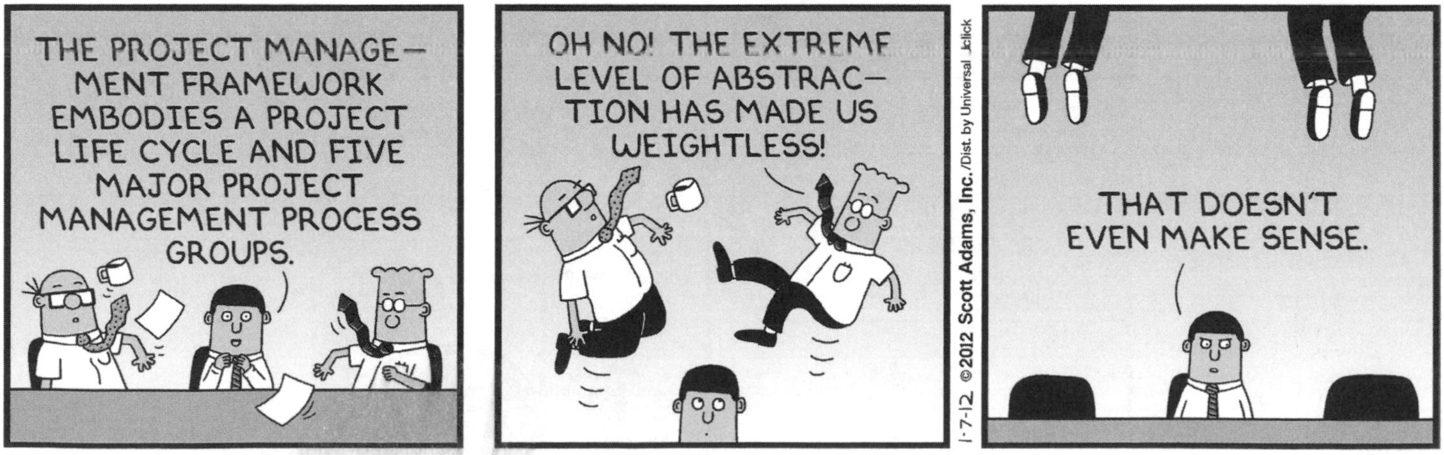
THE PROJECT MANAGE-MENT FRAMEWORK EMBODIES A PROJECT LIFE CYCLE AND FIVE MAJOR PROJECT MANAGEMENT PROCESS GROUPS.
OH NO! THE EXTREME LEVEL OF ABSTRAC-TION HAS MADE US WEIGHTLESS!
1-7-12 ©2012 Scott Adams, Inc./Dist. by Universal Uclick
THAT DOESN'T EVEN MAKE SENSE.

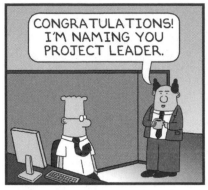

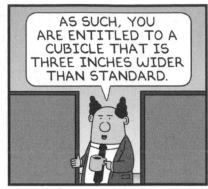

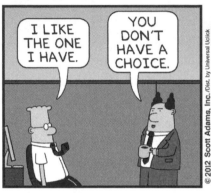

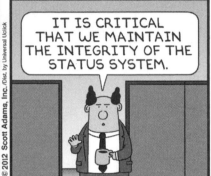

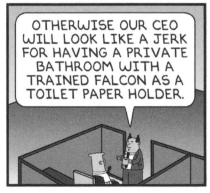

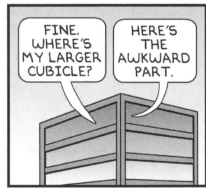

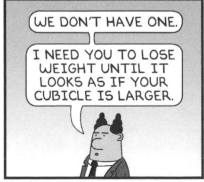

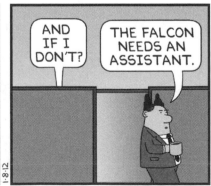

CONGRATULATIONS! I'M NAMING YOU PROJECT LEADER.
AS SUCH, YOU ARE ENTITLED TO A CUBICLE THAT IS THREE INCHES WIDER THAN STANDARD.
I LIKE THE ONE I HAVE.
YOU DON'T HAVE A CHOICE.
© 2012 Scott Adams, Inc./Dist. by Universal Uclick
IT IS CRITICAL THAT WE MAINTAIN THE INTEGRITY OF THE STATUS SYSTEM.
OTHERWISE OUR CEO WILL LOOK LIKE A JERK FOR HAVING A PRIVATE BATHROOM WITH A TRAINED FALCON AS A TOILET PAPER HOLDER.
FINE. WHERE'S MY LARGER CUBICLE?
HERE'S THE AWKWARD PART.
WE DON'T HAVE ONE.
I NEED YOU TO LOSE WEIGHT UNTIL IT LOOKS AS IF YOUR CUBICLE IS LARGER.
1-8-12
AND IF I DON'T?
THE FALCON NEEDS AN ASSISTANT.

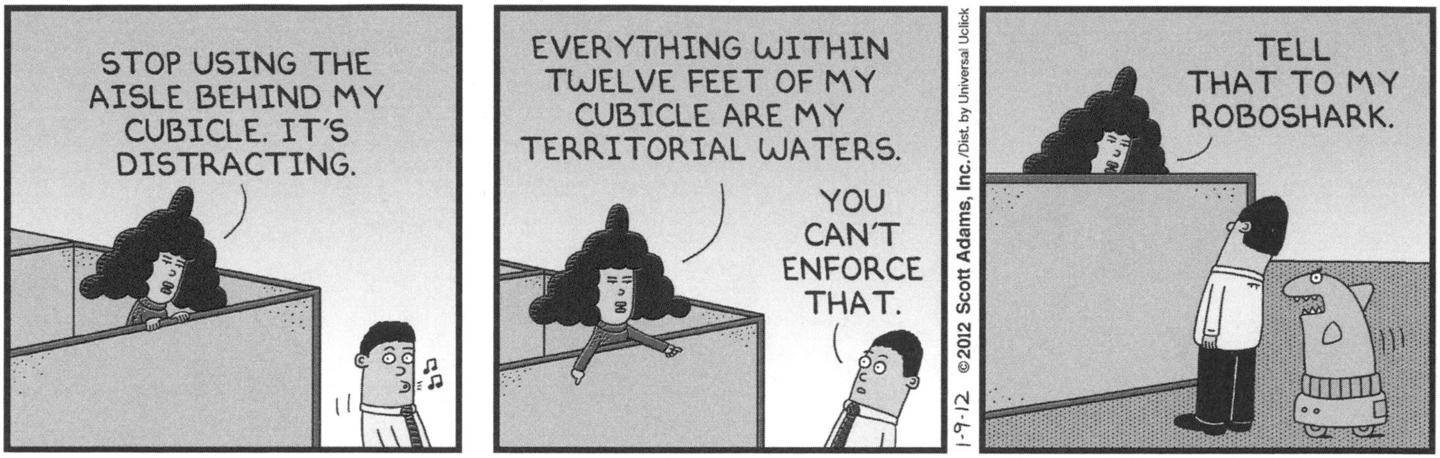
STOP USING THE AISLE BEHIND MY CUBICLE. IT'S DISTRACTING.
EVERYTHING WITHIN TWELVE FEET OF MY CUBICLE ARE MY TERRITORIAL WATERS.
YOU CAN'T ENFORCE THAT.
1-9-12 ©2012 Scott Adams, Inc./Dist. by Universal Uclick
TELL THAT TO MY ROBOSHARK.

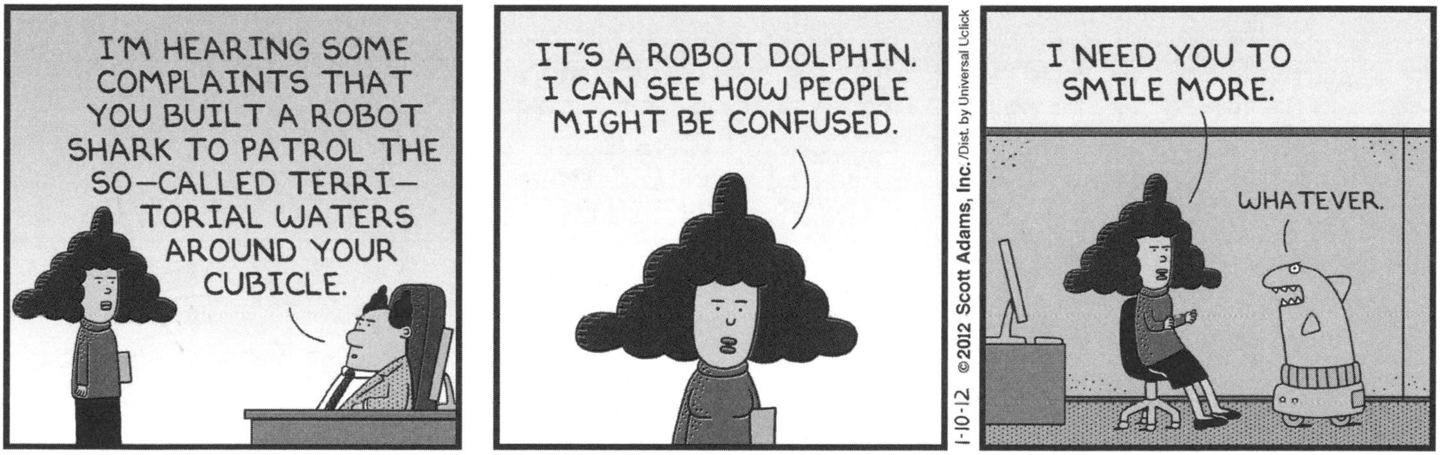
I'M HEARING SOME COMPLAINTS THAT YOU BUILT A ROBOT SHARK TO PATROL THE SO-CALLED TERRI-TORIAL WATERS AROUND YOUR CUBICLE.
IT'S A ROBOT DOLPHIN. I CAN SEE HOW PEOPLE MIGHT BE CONFUSED.
1-10-12 ©2012 Scott Adams, Inc./Dist. by Universal Uclick
I NEED YOU TO SMILE MORE.
WHATEVER.

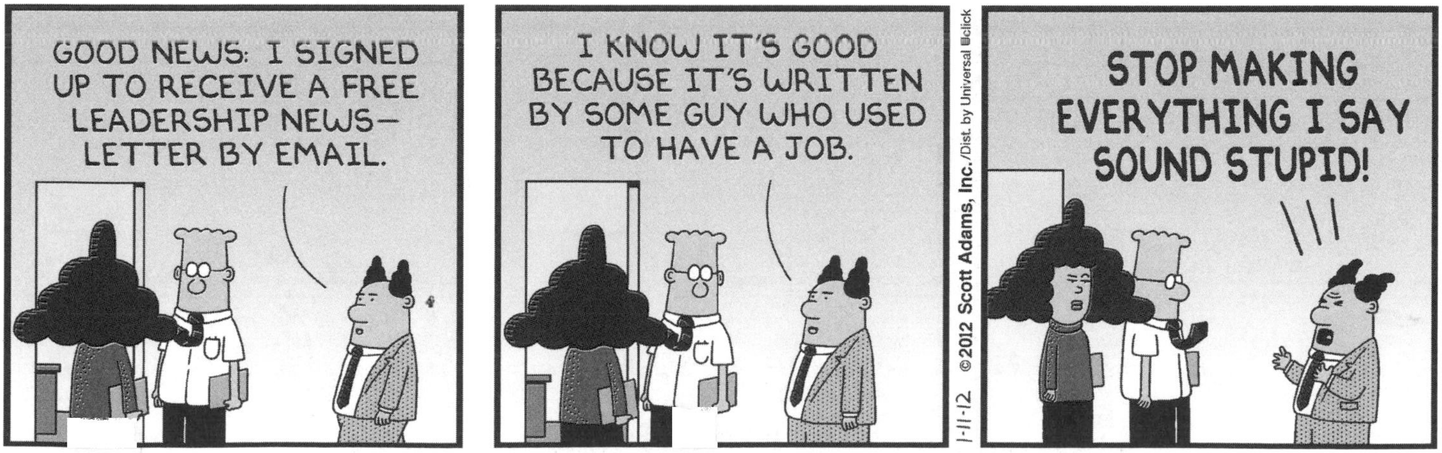
GOOD NEWS: I SIGNED UP TO RECEIVE A FREE LEADERSHIP NEWS-LETTER BY EMAIL.
I KNOW IT'S GOOD BECAUSE IT'S WRITTEN BY SOME GUY WHO USED TO HAVE A JOB.
1-11-12 ©2012 Scott Adams, Inc./Dist. by Universal Uclick
STOP MAKING EVERYTHING I SAY SOUND STUPID!

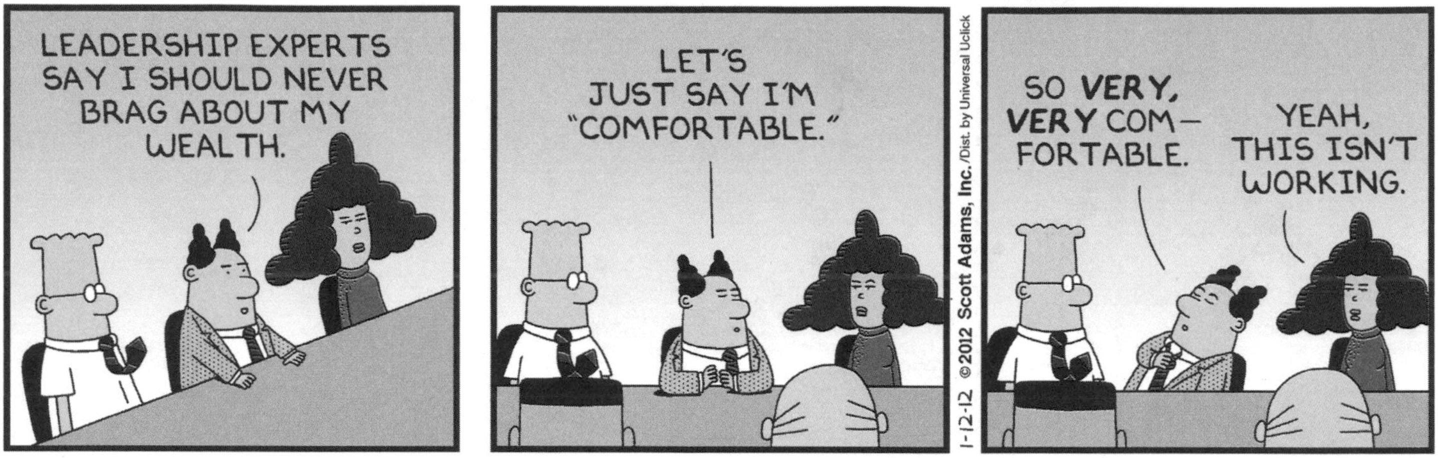
LEADERSHIP EXPERTS SAY I SHOULD NEVER BRAG ABOUT MY WEALTH.
LET'S JUST SAY I'M "COMFORTABLE."
1-12-12 ©2012 Scott Adams, Inc./Dist. by Universal Uclick
SO **VERY, VERY** COM-FORTABLE.
YEAH, THIS ISN'T WORKING.

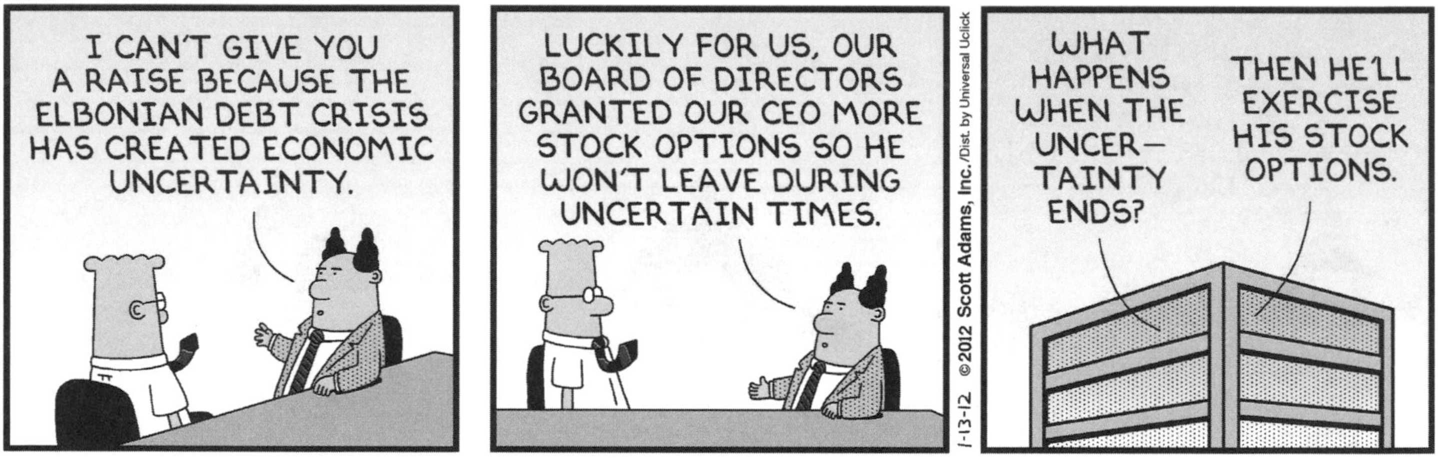
I CAN'T GIVE YOU A RAISE BECAUSE THE ELBONIAN DEBT CRISIS HAS CREATED ECONOMIC UNCERTAINTY.
LUCKILY FOR US, OUR BOARD OF DIRECTORS GRANTED OUR CEO MORE STOCK OPTIONS SO HE WON'T LEAVE DURING UNCERTAIN TIMES.
1-13-12 ©2012 Scott Adams, Inc./Dist. by Universal Uclick
WHAT HAPPENS WHEN THE UNCER-TAINTY ENDS?
THEN HE'LL EXERCISE HIS STOCK OPTIONS.

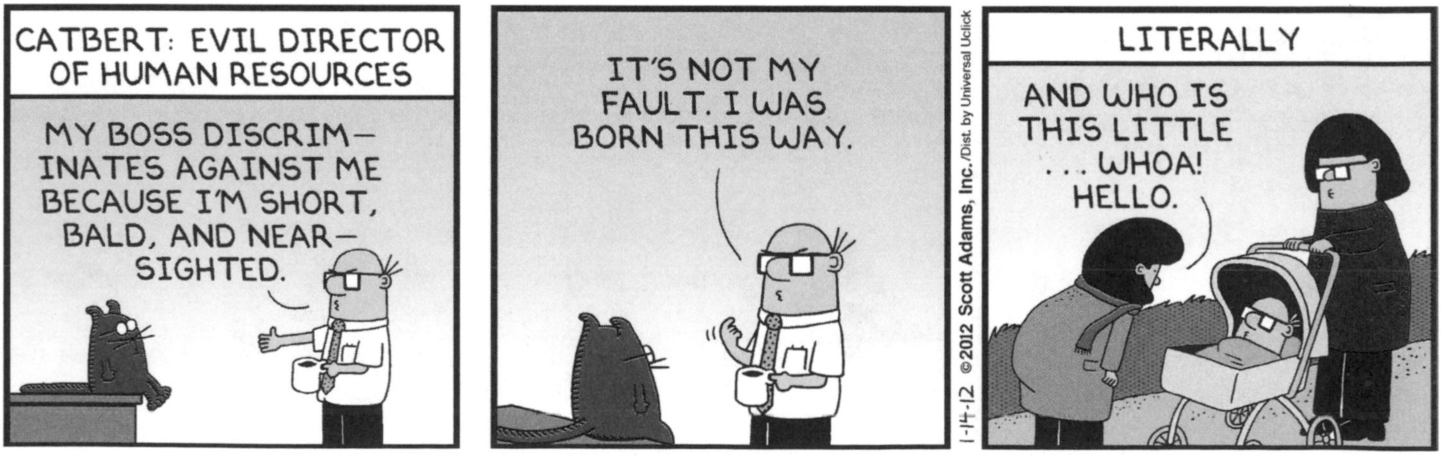
CATBERT: EVIL DIRECTOR OF HUMAN RESOURCES
MY BOSS DISCRIM-INATES AGAINST ME BECAUSE I'M SHORT, BALD, AND NEAR-SIGHTED.
IT'S NOT MY FAULT. I WAS BORN THIS WAY.
1-14-12 ©2012 Scott Adams, Inc./Dist. by Universal Uclick
LITERALLY
AND WHO IS THIS LITTLE . . . WHOA! HELLO.

OUR BUDGET FOR CONTRACT EMPLOYEES WAS ELIMINATED.
WE'LL HAVE TO PAY YOU OUT OF THE TRAINING BUDGET.
SO INSTEAD OF DOING THE JOB YOURSELF...
YOU'LL HAVE TO TRAIN DILBERT TO DO THE JOB WE'RE PAYING YOU TO DO.
©2012 Scott Adams, Inc./Dist. by Universal Uclick
WHY DON'T YOU JUST MOVE SOME OF THE TRAINING BUDGET TO THE CONTRACTOR BUDGET?
IF WE REDUCE THE TRAINING BUDGET THIS YEAR, WE'LL GET LESS NEXT YEAR.
SO... YOU PREFER PAYING TWO PEOPLE TO DO THE JOB OF ONE?
RIGHT.
1-15-12
HOW DO YOU STAY IN BUSINESS?
OUR CUSTOMERS ARE EVEN DUMBER THAN US.

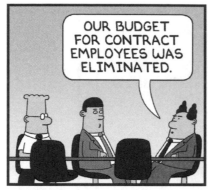

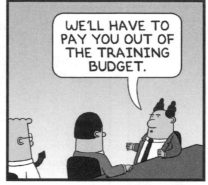

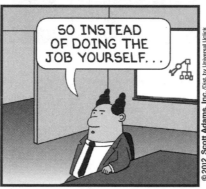

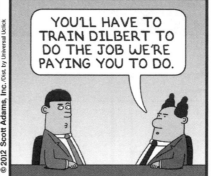

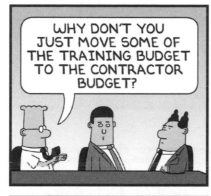

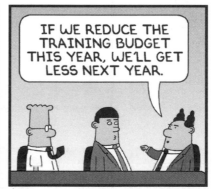

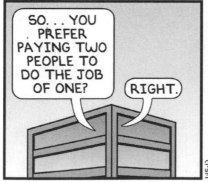

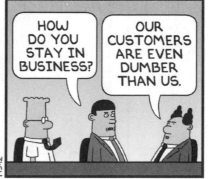

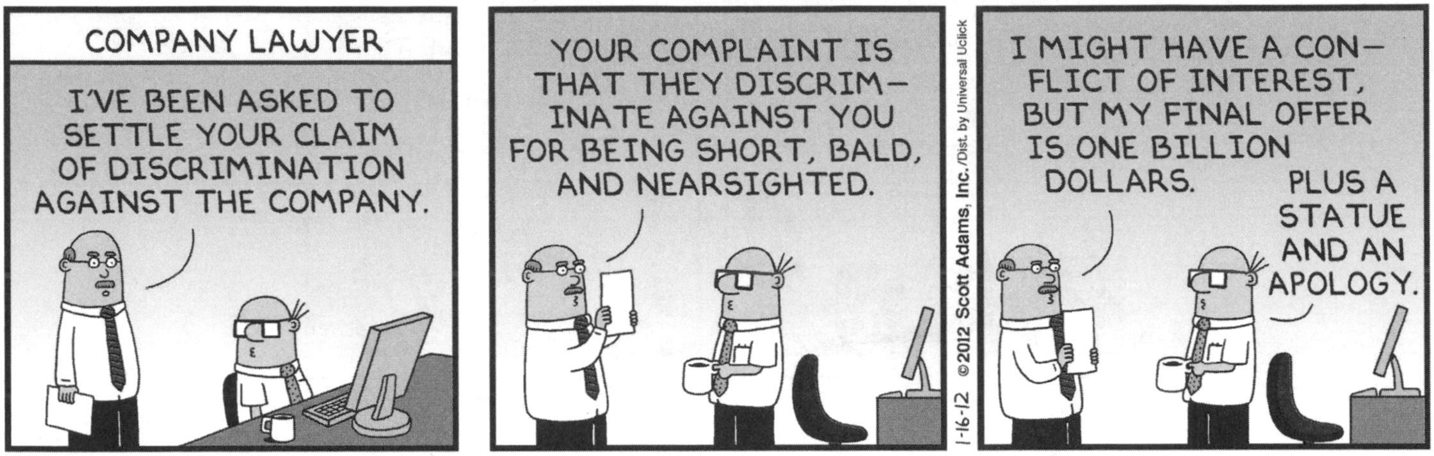
COMPANY LAWYER
I'VE BEEN ASKED TO SETTLE YOUR CLAIM OF DISCRIMINATION AGAINST THE COMPANY.
YOUR COMPLAINT IS THAT THEY DISCRIMINATE AGAINST YOU FOR BEING SHORT, BALD, AND NEARSIGHTED.
1-16-12 ©2012 Scott Adams, Inc./Dist. by Universal Uclick
I MIGHT HAVE A CONFLICT OF INTEREST, BUT MY FINAL OFFER IS ONE BILLION DOLLARS.
PLUS A STATUE AND AN APOLOGY.

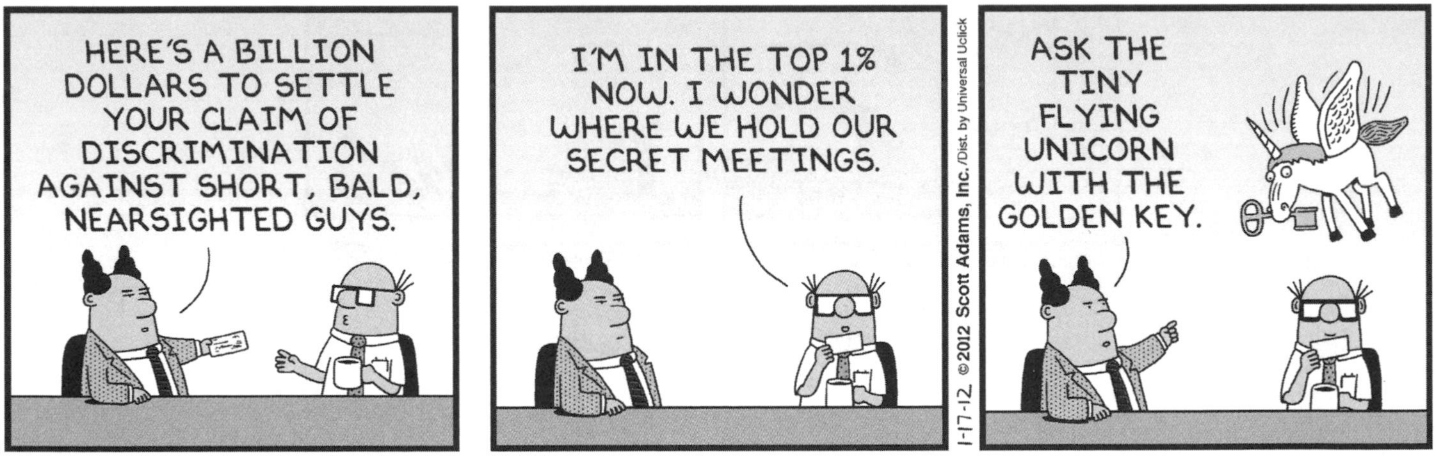
HERE'S A BILLION DOLLARS TO SETTLE YOUR CLAIM OF DISCRIMINATION AGAINST SHORT, BALD, NEARSIGHTED GUYS.
I'M IN THE TOP 1% NOW. I WONDER WHERE WE HOLD OUR SECRET MEETINGS.
1-17-12 ©2012 Scott Adams, Inc./Dist. by Universal Uclick
ASK THE TINY FLYING UNICORN WITH THE GOLDEN KEY.

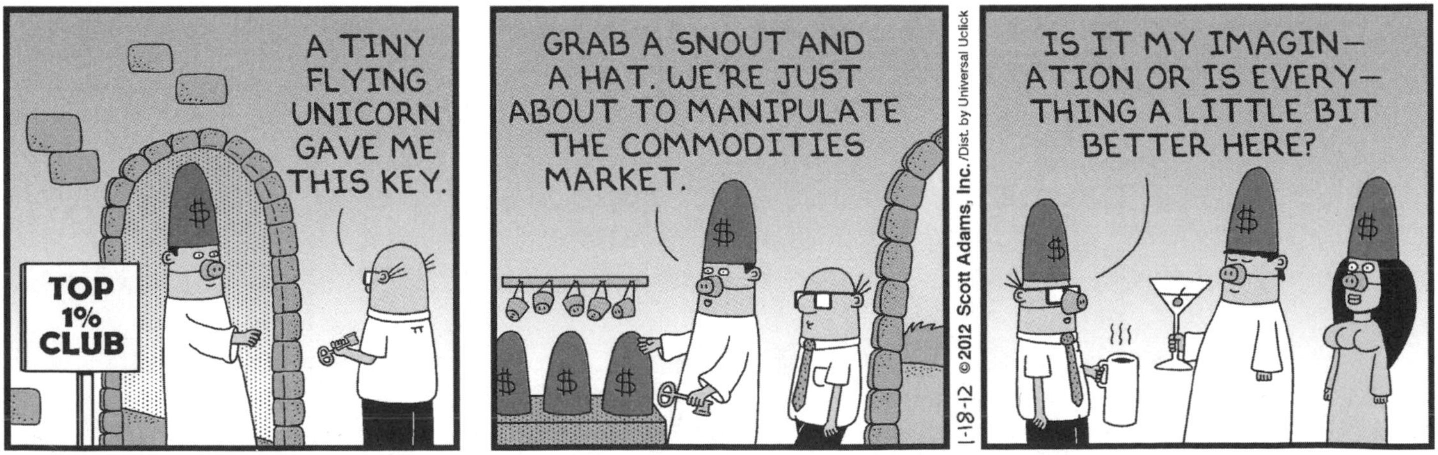
TOP 1% CLUB
A TINY FLYING UNICORN GAVE ME THIS KEY.
GRAB A SNOUT AND A HAT. WE'RE JUST ABOUT TO MANIPULATE THE COMMODITIES MARKET.
1-18-12 ©2012 Scott Adams, Inc./Dist. by Universal Uclick
IS IT MY IMAGINATION OR IS EVERYTHING A LITTLE BIT BETTER HERE?

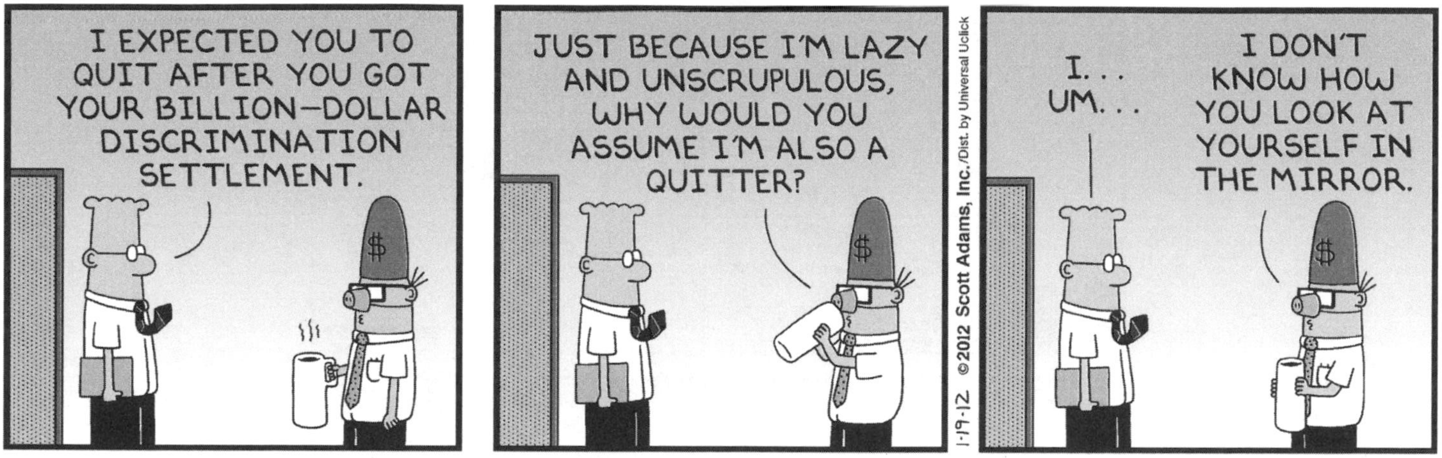
I EXPECTED YOU TO QUIT AFTER YOU GOT YOUR BILLION-DOLLAR DISCRIMINATION SETTLEMENT.
JUST BECAUSE I'M LAZY AND UNSCRUPULOUS, WHY WOULD YOU ASSUME I'M ALSO A QUITTER?
1-19-12 ©2012 Scott Adams, Inc./Dist. by Universal Uclick
I... UM...
I DON'T KNOW HOW YOU LOOK AT YOURSELF IN THE MIRROR.

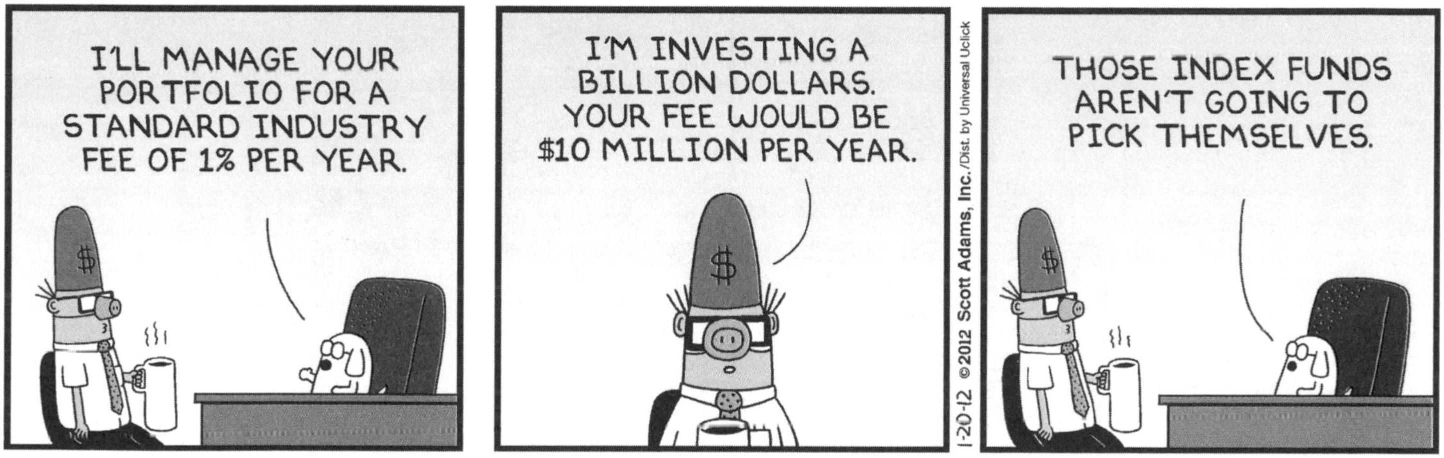
I'LL MANAGE YOUR PORTFOLIO FOR A STANDARD INDUSTRY FEE OF 1% PER YEAR.
I'M INVESTING A BILLION DOLLARS. YOUR FEE WOULD BE $10 MILLION PER YEAR.
1-20-12 ©2012 Scott Adams, Inc./Dist. by Universal Uclick
THOSE INDEX FUNDS AREN'T GOING TO PICK THEMSELVES.

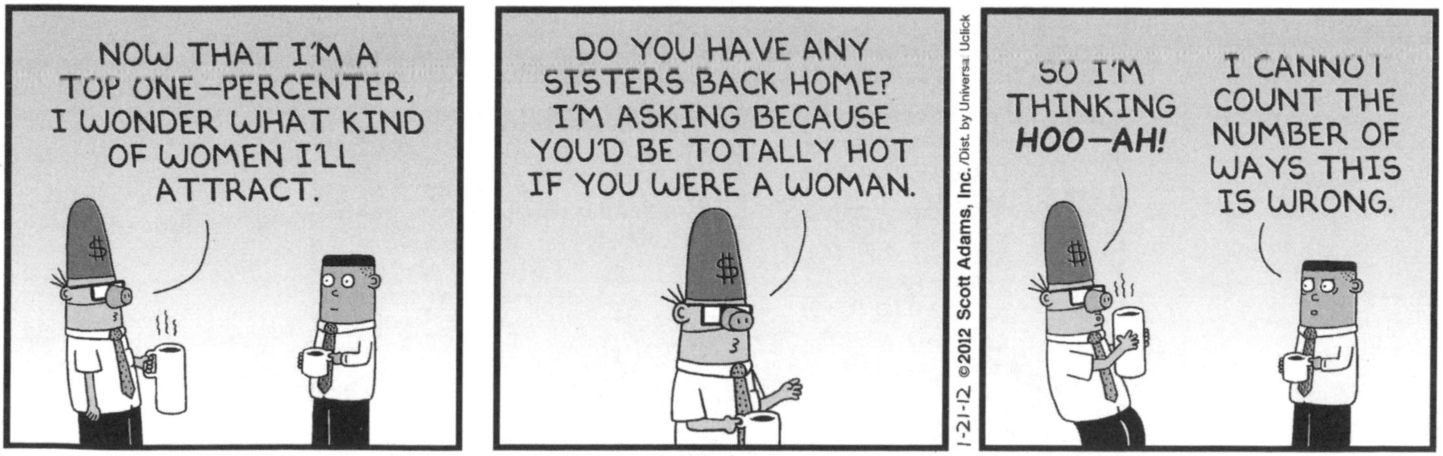
NOW THAT I'M A TOP ONE-PERCENTER, I WONDER WHAT KIND OF WOMEN I'LL ATTRACT.
DO YOU HAVE ANY SISTERS BACK HOME? I'M ASKING BECAUSE YOU'D BE TOTALLY HOT IF YOU WERE A WOMAN.
1-21-12 ©2012 Scott Adams, Inc./Dist. by Universal Uclick
SO I'M THINKING HOO-AH!
I CANNOT COUNT THE NUMBER OF WAYS THIS IS WRONG.

THIS IS DOGBERT'S TECH SUPPORT. HOW MAY I ABUSE YOU?
I THINK MY DIGITAL MODEM IS BROKEN.
PLEASE HOLD WHILE I PRETEND TO BE TESTING IT.
OKAY, IT LOOKS FINE FROM HERE.
THE PROBLEM MUST BE IN YOUR WIRING.
YOU'LL HAVE TO RIP OUT ALL OF THE WIRING IN YOUR ENTIRE HOUSE TO LOCATE THE PROBLEM.
ARE YOU SURE? BECAUSE THE LIGHTS ON THE MODEM AREN'T EVEN ON.
THAT MEANS YOU HAVE MOISTURE ON YOUR INTERNAL WIRING. YOU'LL ALSO NEED TO REPLACE ALL OF YOUR PLUMBING AND GET A NEW ROOF.
MAY I SPEAK WITH YOUR SUPERVISOR?
SURE. BUT HE SOUNDS EXACTLY LIKE ME.
© 2012 Scott Adams, Inc./Dist. by Universal Uclick
1-22-12

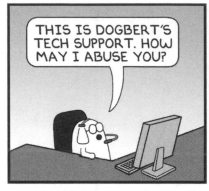

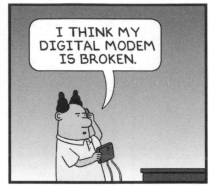

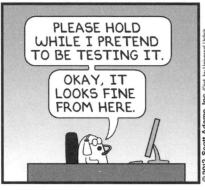

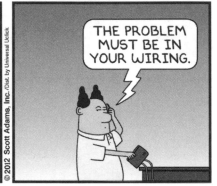

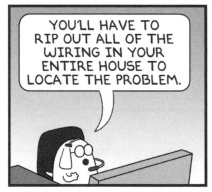

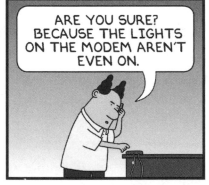

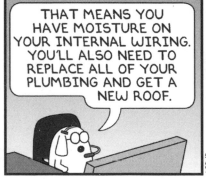

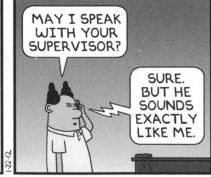

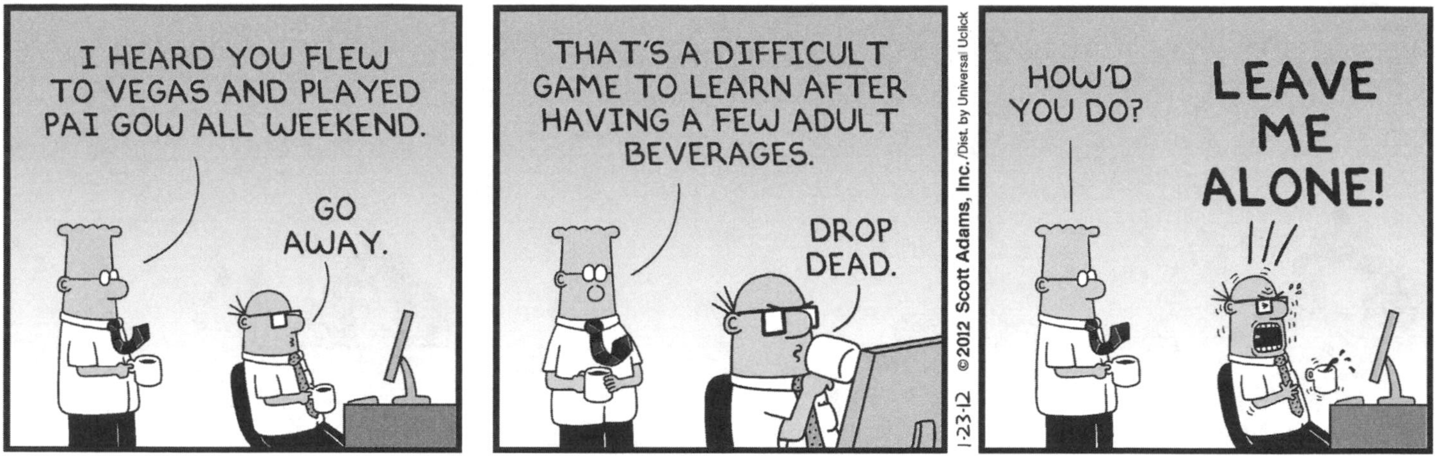
I HEARD YOU FLEW TO VEGAS AND PLAYED PAI GOW ALL WEEKEND.
GO AWAY.
THAT'S A DIFFICULT GAME TO LEARN AFTER HAVING A FEW ADULT BEVERAGES.
DROP DEAD.
1·23·12 ©2012 Scott Adams, Inc./Dist. by Universal Uclick
HOW'D YOU DO?
LEAVE ME ALONE!

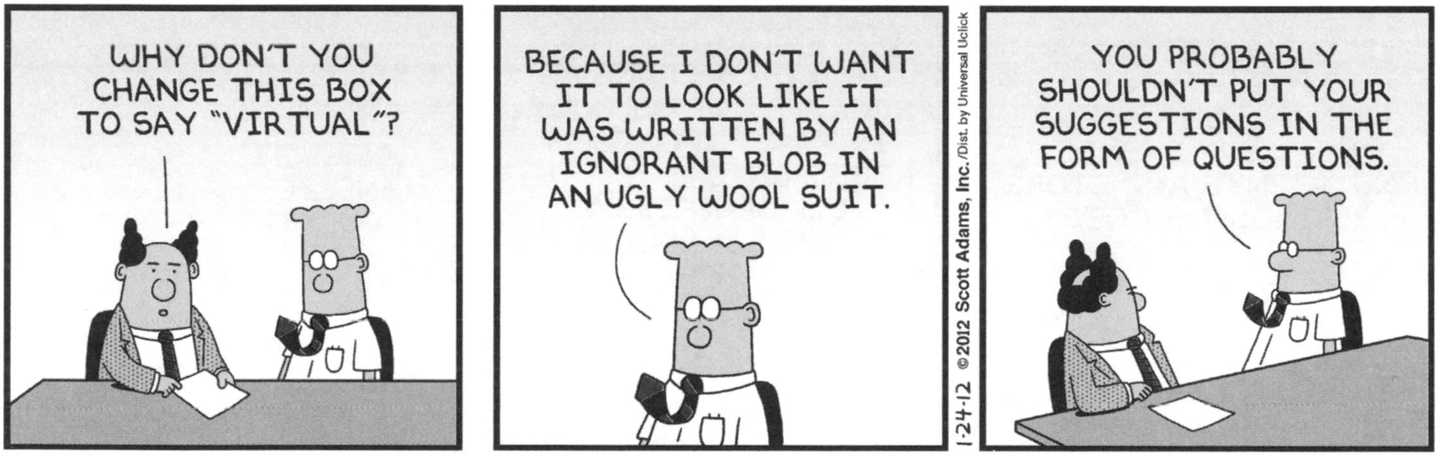
WHY DON'T YOU CHANGE THIS BOX TO SAY "VIRTUAL"?
BECAUSE I DON'T WANT IT TO LOOK LIKE IT WAS WRITTEN BY AN IGNORANT BLOB IN AN UGLY WOOL SUIT.
1·24·12 ©2012 Scott Adams, Inc./Dist. by Universal Uclick
YOU PROBABLY SHOULDN'T PUT YOUR SUGGESTIONS IN THE FORM OF QUESTIONS.

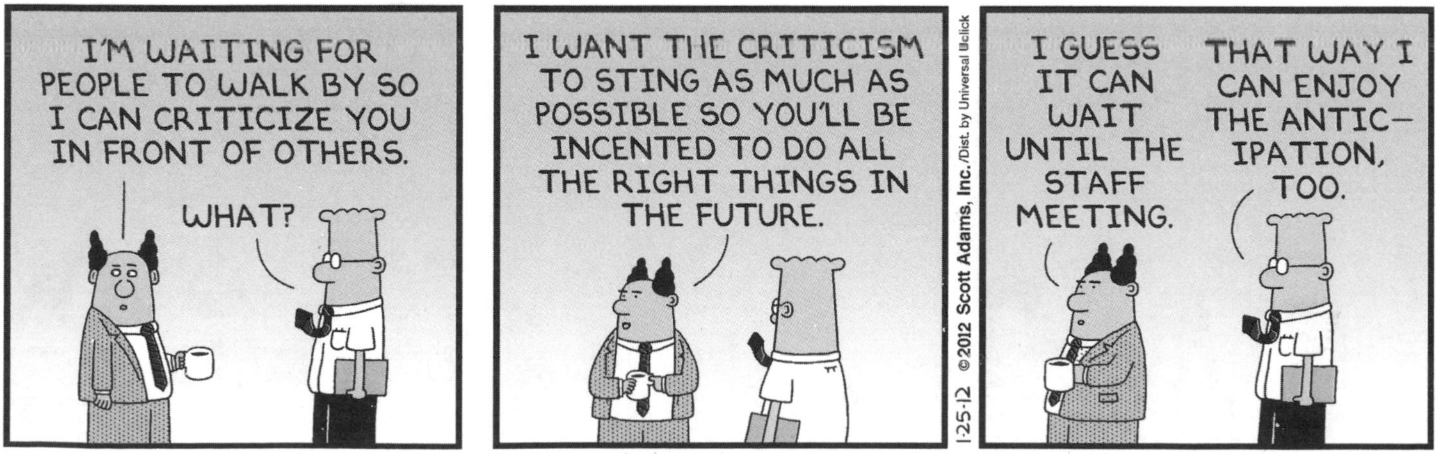
I'M WAITING FOR PEOPLE TO WALK BY SO I CAN CRITICIZE YOU IN FRONT OF OTHERS.
WHAT?
I WANT THE CRITICISM TO STING AS MUCH AS POSSIBLE SO YOU'LL BE INCENTED TO DO ALL THE RIGHT THINGS IN THE FUTURE.
1·25·12 ©2012 Scott Adams, Inc./Dist. by Universal Uclick
I GUESS IT CAN WAIT UNTIL THE STAFF MEETING.
THAT WAY I CAN ENJOY THE ANTIC-IPATION, TOO.

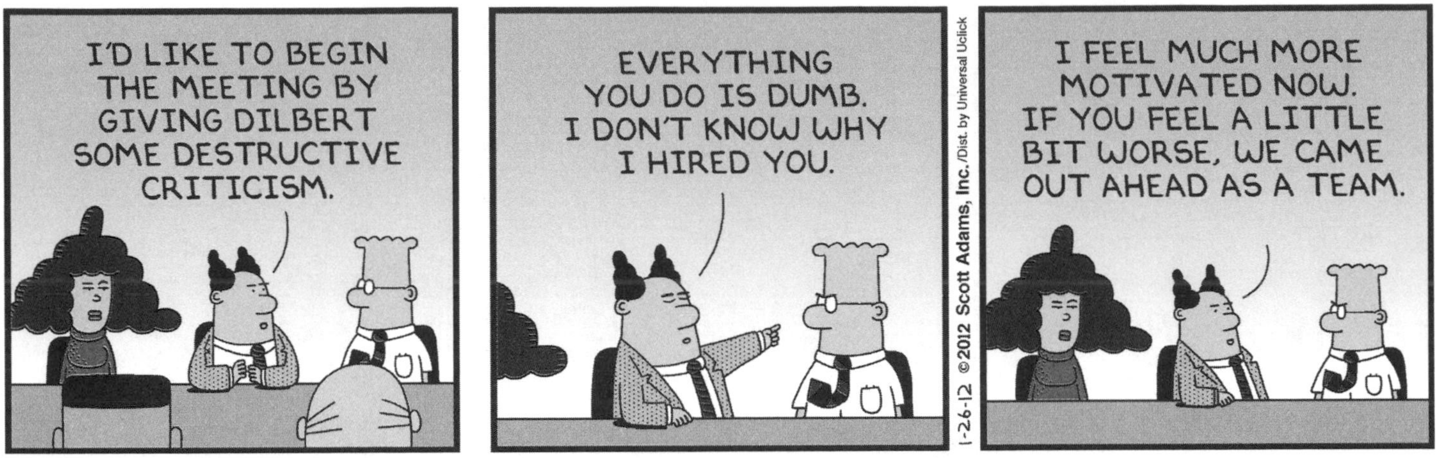
I'D LIKE TO BEGIN THE MEETING BY GIVING DILBERT SOME DESTRUCTIVE CRITICISM.
EVERYTHING YOU DO IS DUMB. I DON'T KNOW WHY I HIRED YOU.
1-26-12 ©2012 Scott Adams, Inc./Dist. by Universal Uclick
I FEEL MUCH MORE MOTIVATED NOW. IF YOU FEEL A LITTLE BIT WORSE, WE CAME OUT AHEAD AS A TEAM.

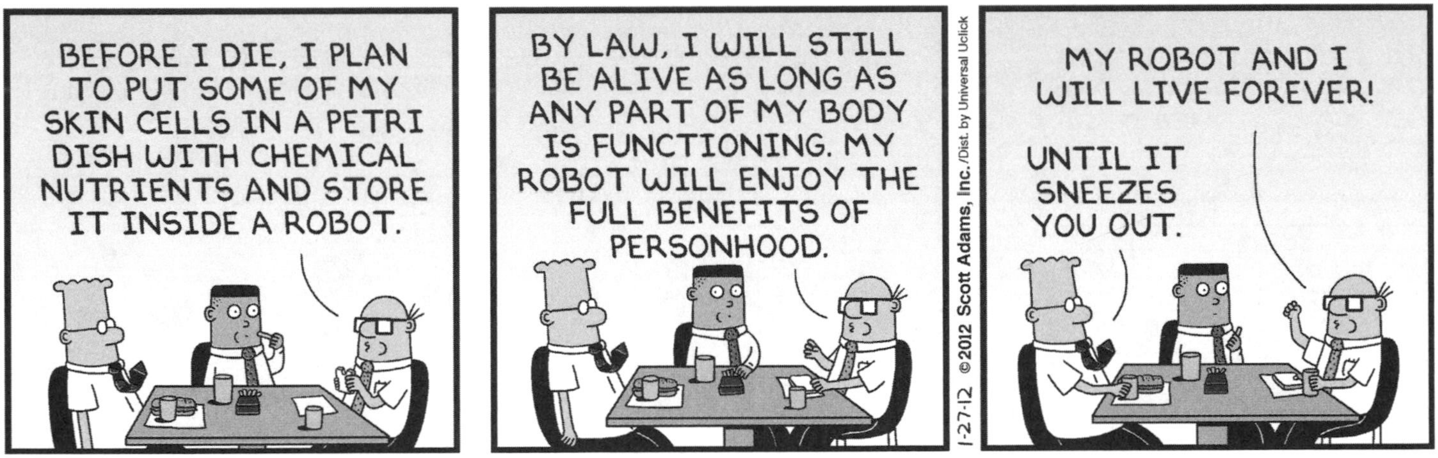
BEFORE I DIE, I PLAN TO PUT SOME OF MY SKIN CELLS IN A PETRI DISH WITH CHEMICAL NUTRIENTS AND STORE IT INSIDE A ROBOT.
BY LAW, I WILL STILL BE ALIVE AS LONG AS ANY PART OF MY BODY IS FUNCTIONING. MY ROBOT WILL ENJOY THE FULL BENEFITS OF PERSONHOOD.
1-27-12 ©2012 Scott Adams, Inc./Dist. by Universal Uclick
MY ROBOT AND I WILL LIVE FOREVER!
UNTIL IT SNEEZES YOU OUT.

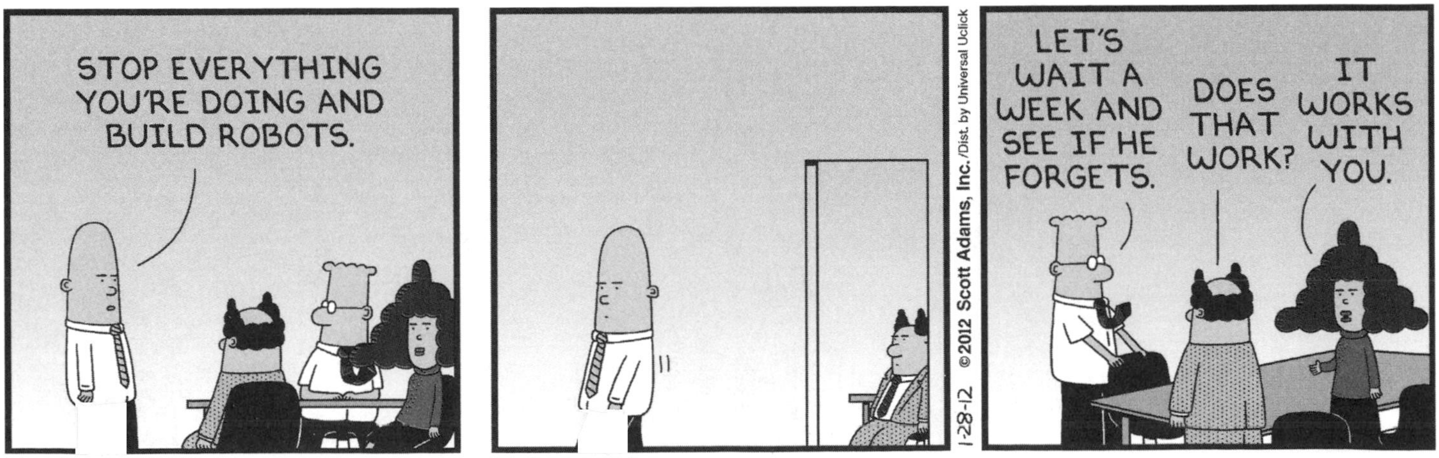
STOP EVERYTHING YOU'RE DOING AND BUILD ROBOTS.
1-28-12 ©2012 Scott Adams, Inc./Dist. by Universal Uclick
LET'S WAIT A WEEK AND SEE IF HE FORGETS.
DOES THAT WORK?
IT WORKS WITH YOU.

DILBERT, LISTEN CAREFULLY.
I NEED YOU TO. . .VENDOR. . . HARDWARE. . . IMMEDIATELY.
WHAT? WE HAVE A BAD CONNECTION.
FIELD. . . THE GREP. . . PONY. . . BUDGET.
©2012 Scott Adams, Inc./Dist. by Universal Uclick
WHAT? WHAT?
I HAVE ANOTHER CALL. JUST ASK ALICE.
HOW WOULD I KNOW WHAT HE WANTS? LEAVE ME ALONE.
1-29-12
I WONDER HOW WINNERS FEEL.
I DON'T KNOW. THEY NEVER LET ME TOUCH THEM.

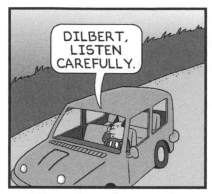

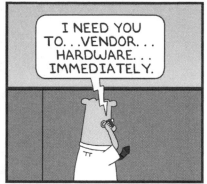

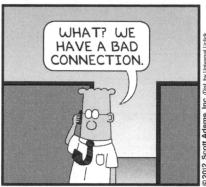

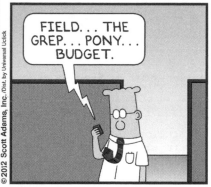

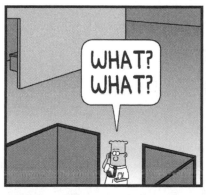

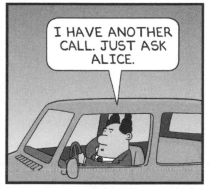

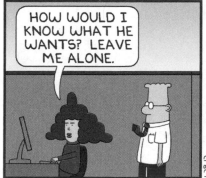

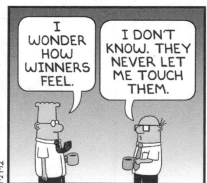

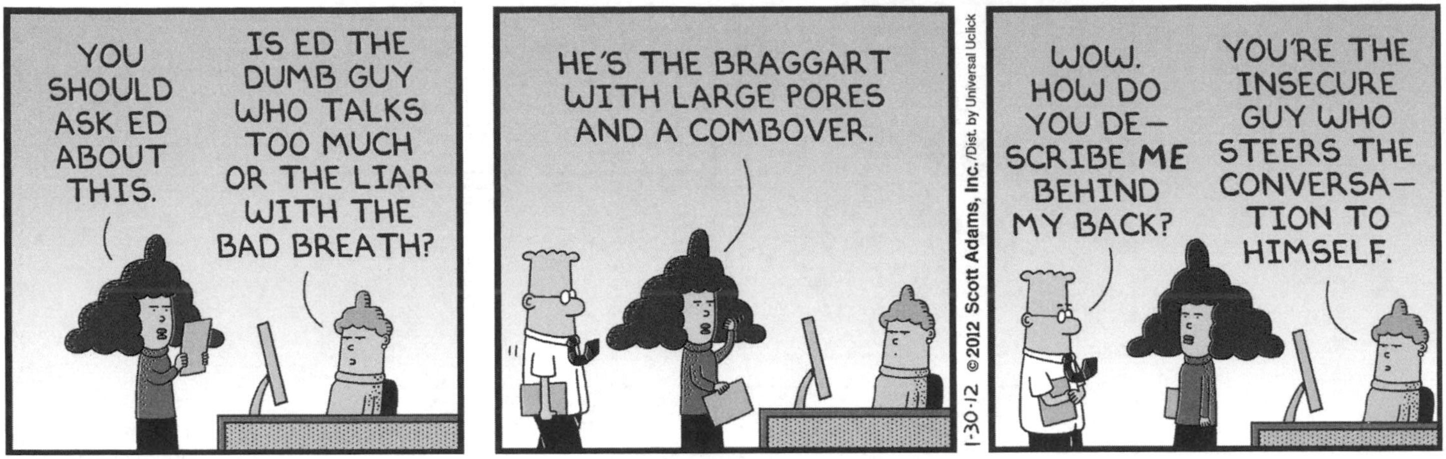
YOU SHOULD ASK ED ABOUT THIS.
IS ED THE DUMB GUY WHO TALKS TOO MUCH OR THE LIAR WITH THE BAD BREATH?
HE'S THE BRAGGART WITH LARGE PORES AND A COMBOVER.
1-30-12 © 2012 Scott Adams, Inc./Dist. by Universal Uclick
WOW. HOW DO YOU DE-SCRIBE ME BEHIND MY BACK?
YOU'RE THE INSECURE GUY WHO STEERS THE CONVERSA-TION TO HIMSELF.

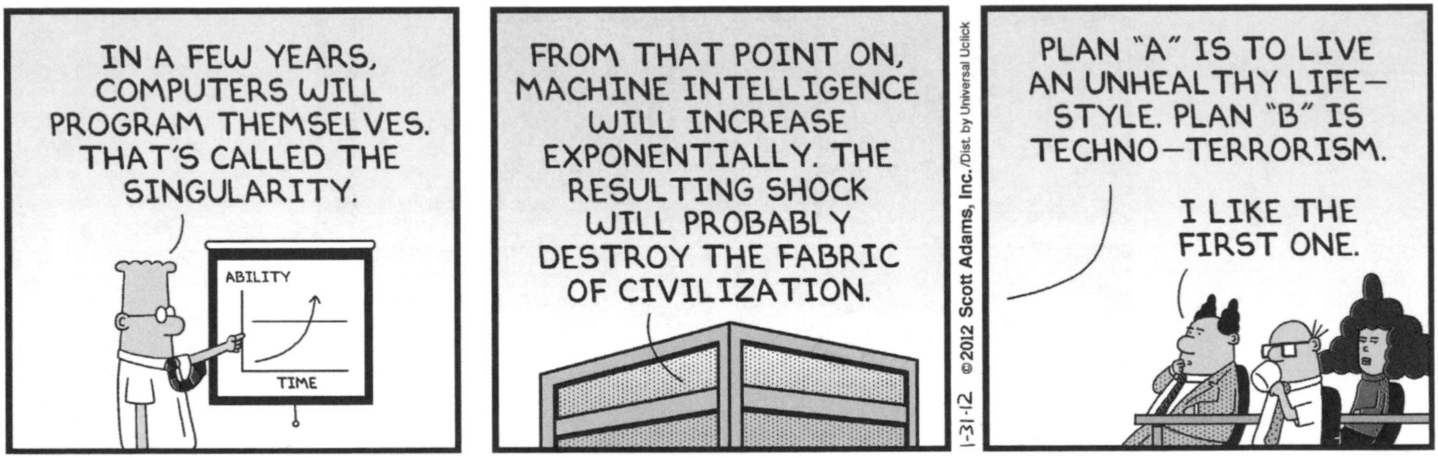
IN A FEW YEARS, COMPUTERS WILL PROGRAM THEMSELVES. THAT'S CALLED THE SINGULARITY.
ABILITY
TIME
FROM THAT POINT ON, MACHINE INTELLIGENCE WILL INCREASE EXPONENTIALLY. THE RESULTING SHOCK WILL PROBABLY DESTROY THE FABRIC OF CIVILIZATION.
1-31-12 © 2012 Scott Adams, Inc./Dist. by Universal Uclick
PLAN "A" IS TO LIVE AN UNHEALTHY LIFE-STYLE. PLAN "B" IS TECHNO-TERRORISM.
I LIKE THE FIRST ONE.

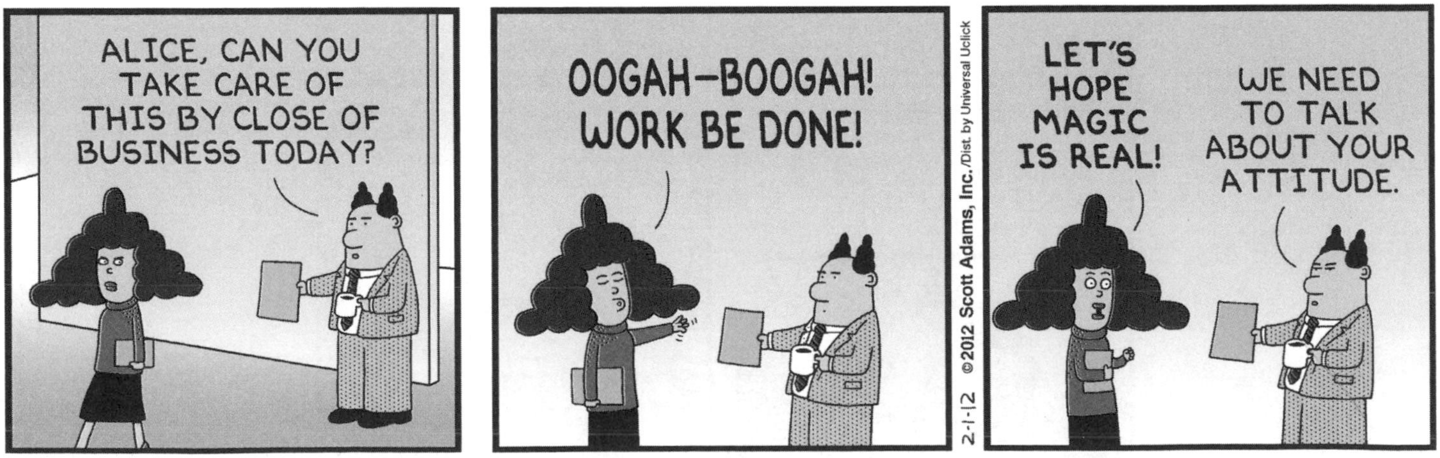
ALICE, CAN YOU TAKE CARE OF THIS BY CLOSE OF BUSINESS TODAY?
OOGAH-BOOGAH! WORK BE DONE!
2-1-12 © 2012 Scott Adams, Inc./Dist. by Universal Uclick
LET'S HOPE MAGIC IS REAL!
WE NEED TO TALK ABOUT YOUR ATTITUDE.

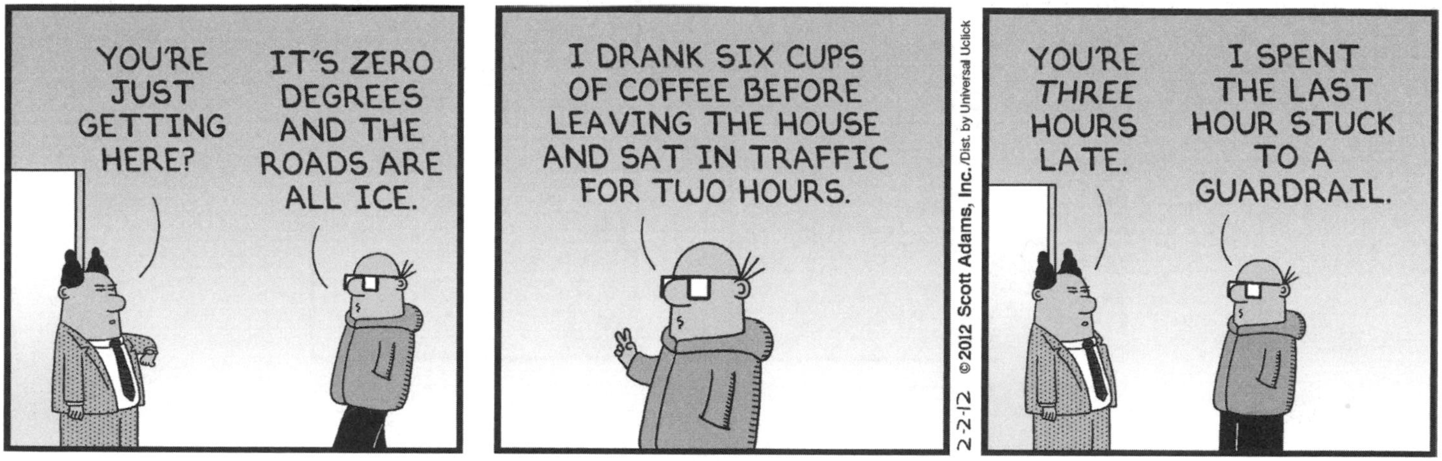
YOU'RE JUST GETTING HERE?
IT'S ZERO DEGREES AND THE ROADS ARE ALL ICE.
I DRANK SIX CUPS OF COFFEE BEFORE LEAVING THE HOUSE AND SAT IN TRAFFIC FOR TWO HOURS.
2-2-12 ©2012 Scott Adams, Inc./Dist. by Universal Uclick
YOU'RE *THREE* HOURS LATE.
I SPENT THE LAST HOUR STUCK TO A GUARDRAIL.

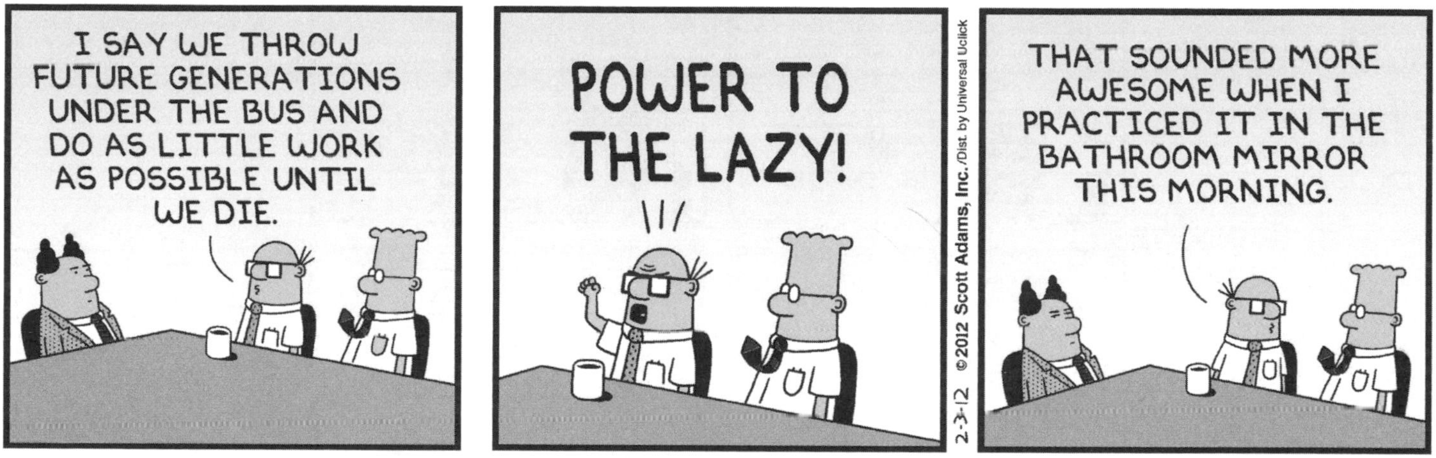
I SAY WE THROW FUTURE GENERATIONS UNDER THE BUS AND DO AS LITTLE WORK AS POSSIBLE UNTIL WE DIE.
POWER TO THE LAZY!
2-3-12 ©2012 Scott Adams, Inc./Dist. by Universal Uclick
THAT SOUNDED MORE AWESOME WHEN I PRACTICED IT IN THE BATHROOM MIRROR THIS MORNING.

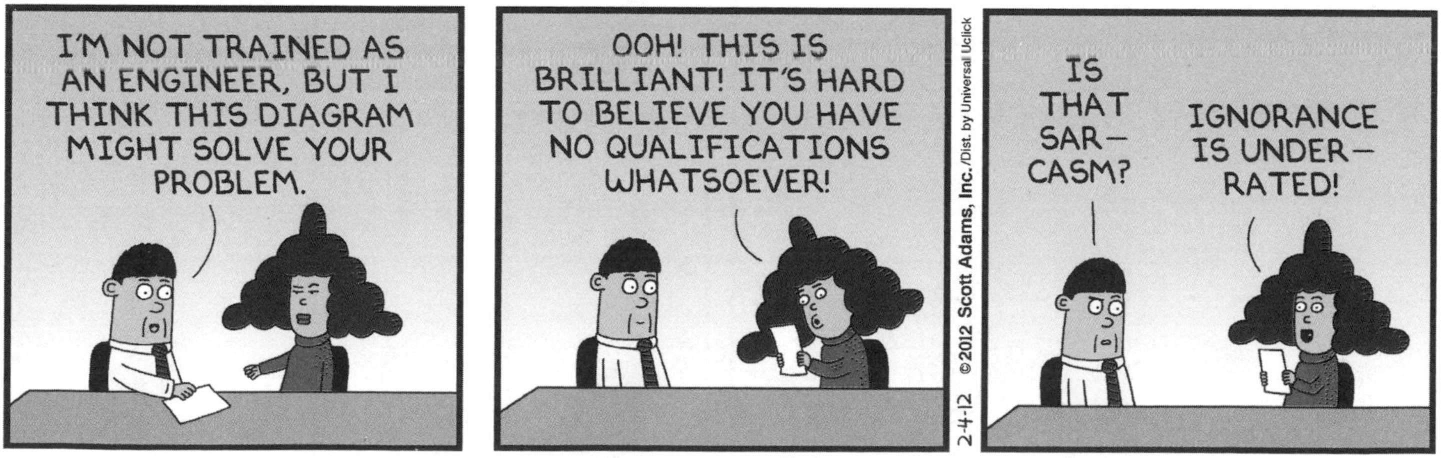
I'M NOT TRAINED AS AN ENGINEER, BUT I THINK THIS DIAGRAM MIGHT SOLVE YOUR PROBLEM.
OOH! THIS IS BRILLIANT! IT'S HARD TO BELIEVE YOU HAVE NO QUALIFICATIONS WHATSOEVER!
2-4-12 ©2012 Scott Adams, Inc./Dist. by Universal Uclick
IS THAT SAR—CASM?
IGNORANCE IS UNDER—RATED!

THAT RESTAURANT WAS GREAT.
I KNOW. I PLAN TO GO THERE SOMEDAY FOR LUNCH.
WE JUST ATE LUNCH.
THAT WASN'T LUNCH.
IT WASN'T?
YOU TALKED ABOUT WORK THE ENTIRE TIME.
LUNCH IS NOT DEFINED BY FOOD. IT'S DEFINED BY FREEDOM FROM TYRANNY.
MY LUNCH HOUR WILL BEGIN THE MINUTE YOU WADDLE AWAY.
WAS THIS GOING WELL UNTIL I SAID "WADDLE"?
© 2012 Scott Adams, Inc./Dist. by Universal Uclick
2-5-12

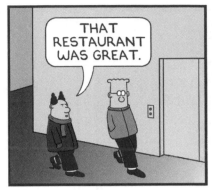

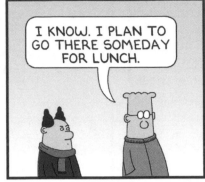

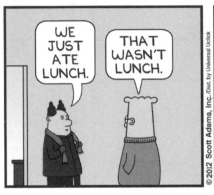

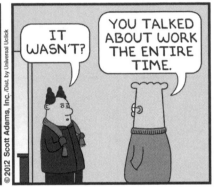

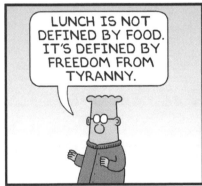

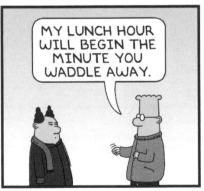

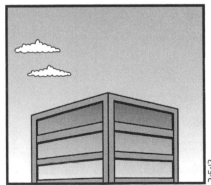

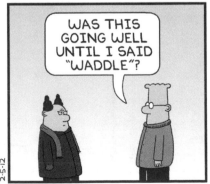

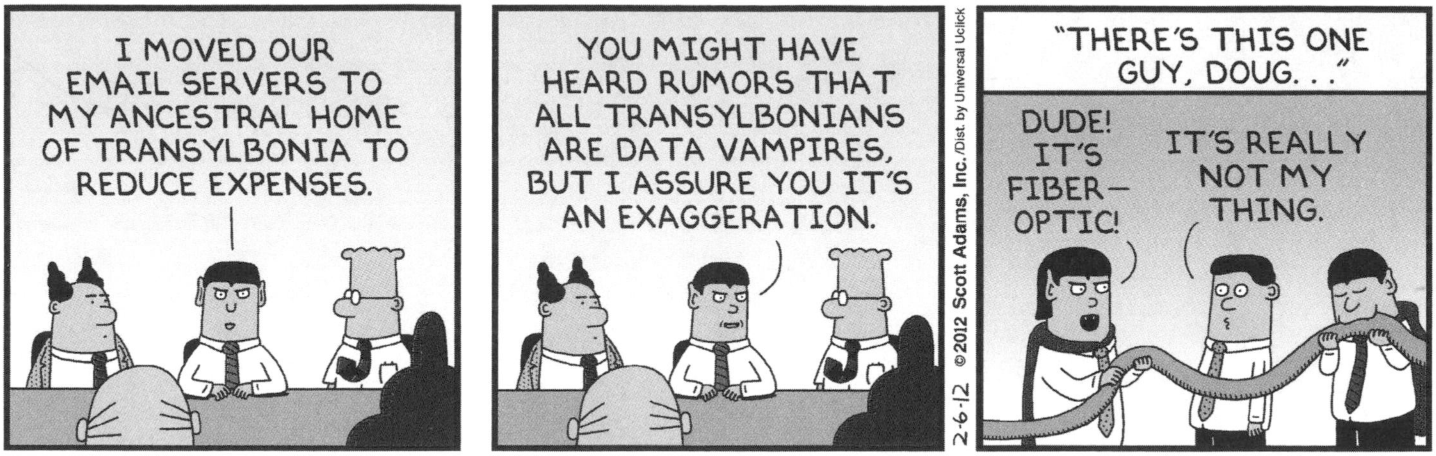
I MOVED OUR EMAIL SERVERS TO MY ANCESTRAL HOME OF TRANSYLBONIA TO REDUCE EXPENSES.
YOU MIGHT HAVE HEARD RUMORS THAT ALL TRANSYLBONIANS ARE DATA VAMPIRES, BUT I ASSURE YOU IT'S AN EXAGGERATION.
2-6-12 ©2012 Scott Adams, Inc./Dist. by Universal Uclick
"THERE'S THIS ONE GUY, DOUG. . ."
DUDE! IT'S FIBER-OPTIC!
IT'S REALLY NOT MY THING.

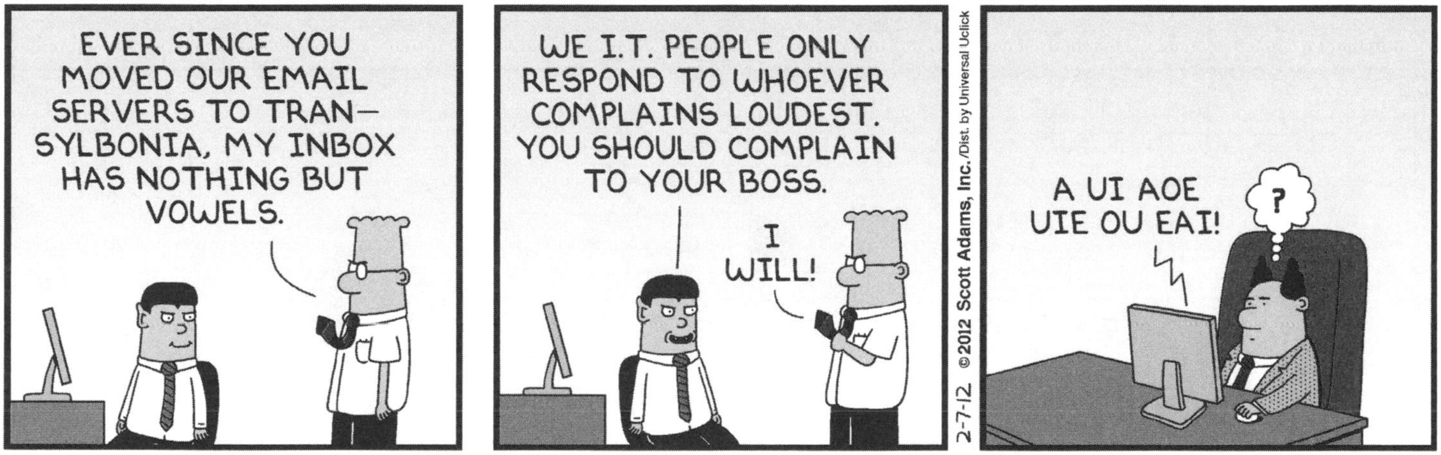
EVER SINCE YOU MOVED OUR EMAIL SERVERS TO TRAN-SYLBONIA, MY INBOX HAS NOTHING BUT VOWELS.
WE I.T. PEOPLE ONLY RESPOND TO WHOEVER COMPLAINS LOUDEST. YOU SHOULD COMPLAIN TO YOUR BOSS.
I WILL!
2-7-12 ©2012 Scott Adams, Inc./Dist. by Universal Uclick
A UI AOE UIE OU EAI!
?

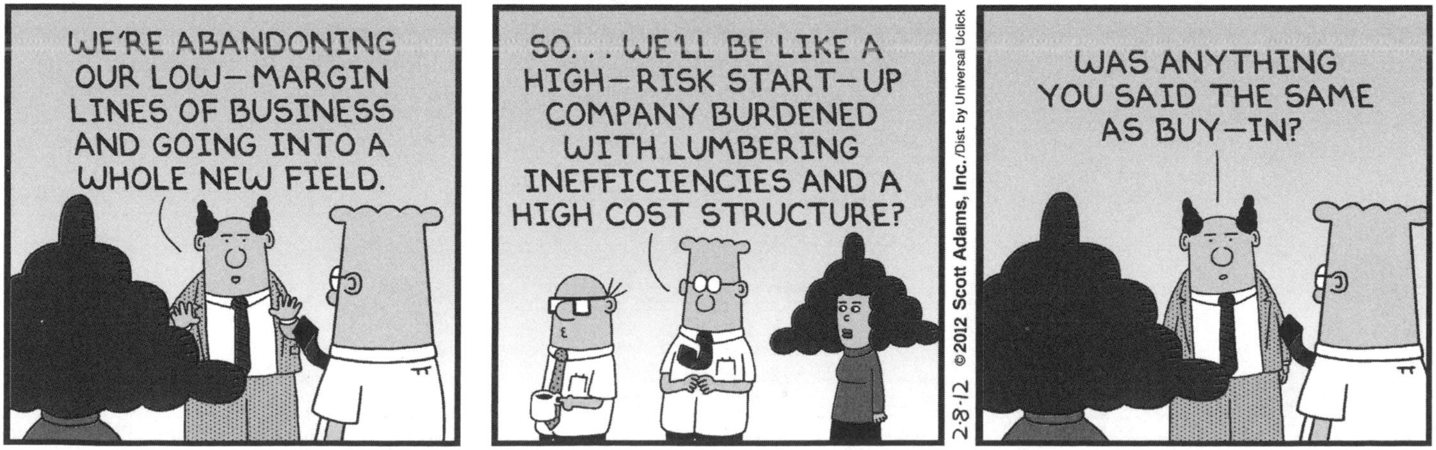
WE'RE ABANDONING OUR LOW-MARGIN LINES OF BUSINESS AND GOING INTO A WHOLE NEW FIELD.
SO. . . WE'LL BE LIKE A HIGH-RISK START-UP COMPANY BURDENED WITH LUMBERING INEFFICIENCIES AND A HIGH COST STRUCTURE?
2-8-12 ©2012 Scott Adams, Inc./Dist. by Universal Uclick
WAS ANYTHING YOU SAID THE SAME AS BUY-IN?

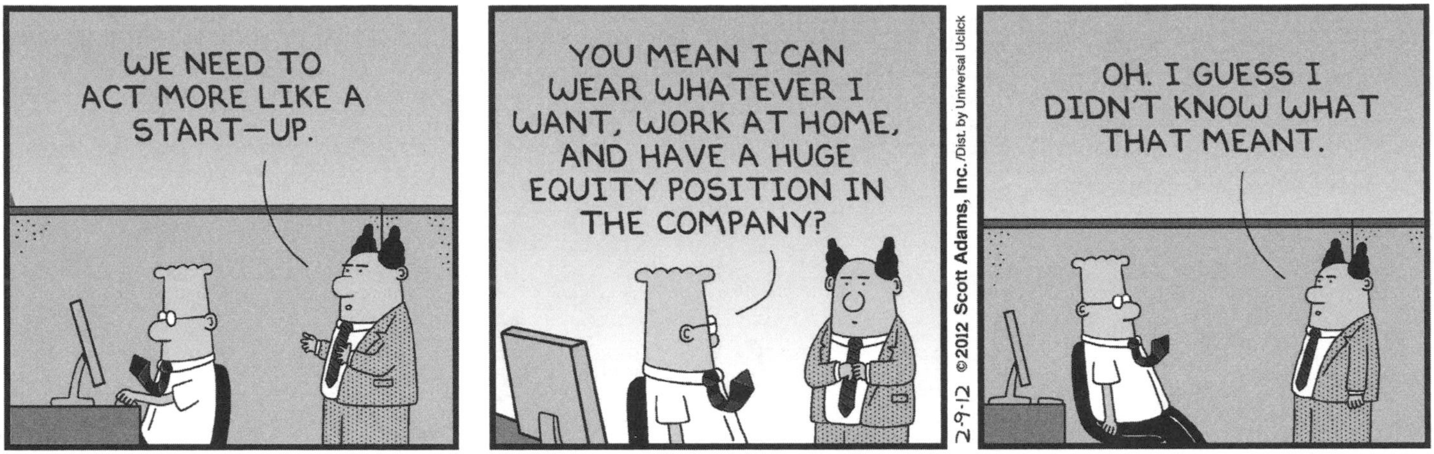
WE NEED TO ACT MORE LIKE A START-UP.
YOU MEAN I CAN WEAR WHATEVER I WANT, WORK AT HOME, AND HAVE A HUGE EQUITY POSITION IN THE COMPANY?
2-9-12 ©2012 Scott Adams, Inc./Dist. by Universal Uclick
OH. I GUESS I DIDN'T KNOW WHAT THAT MEANT.

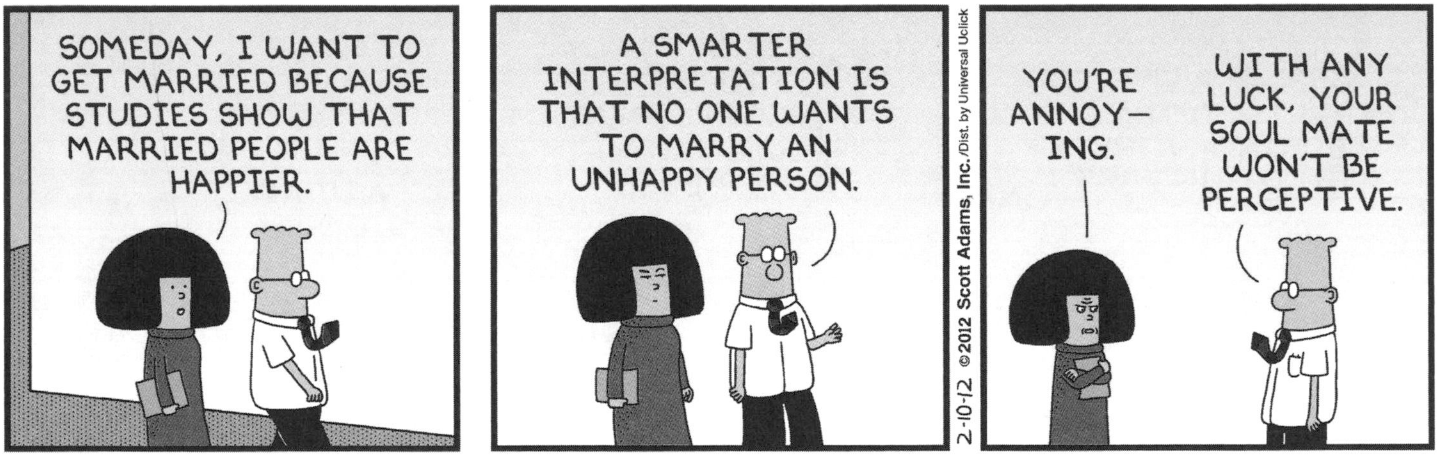
SOMEDAY, I WANT TO GET MARRIED BECAUSE STUDIES SHOW THAT MARRIED PEOPLE ARE HAPPIER.
A SMARTER INTERPRETATION IS THAT NO ONE WANTS TO MARRY AN UNHAPPY PERSON.
2-10-12 ©2012 Scott Adams, Inc./Dist. by Universal Uclick
YOU'RE ANNOY-ING.
WITH ANY LUCK, YOUR SOUL MATE WON'T BE PERCEPTIVE.

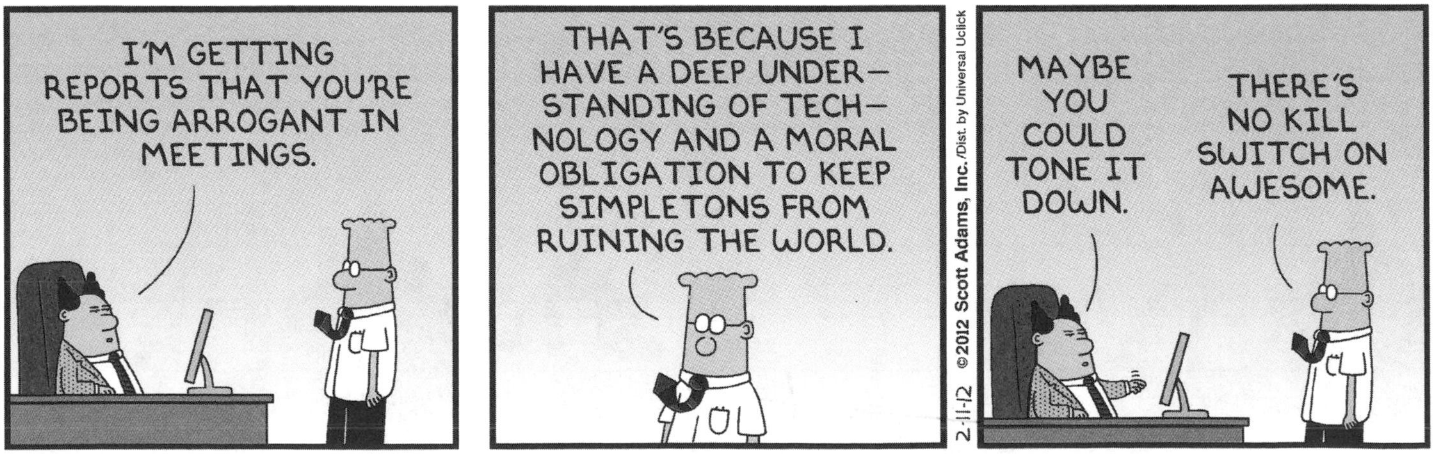
I'M GETTING REPORTS THAT YOU'RE BEING ARROGANT IN MEETINGS.
THAT'S BECAUSE I HAVE A DEEP UNDER-STANDING OF TECH-NOLOGY AND A MORAL OBLIGATION TO KEEP SIMPLETONS FROM RUINING THE WORLD.
2-11-12 ©2012 Scott Adams, Inc./Dist. by Universal Uclick
MAYBE YOU COULD TONE IT DOWN.
THERE'S NO KILL SWITCH ON AWESOME.

HELLO, THIS IS TECH SUPPORT. MAY I CLOSE YOUR TICKET NOW?
UM. . . NO. YOU HAVEN'T HELPED ME YET. I JUST CALLED YOU.
I'M NOT EVALUATED ON HOW HELPFUL I AM. I'M EVALUATED ON HOW MANY TROUBLE TICKETS I CLOSE.
YOUR STUBBORNNESS IS BECOMING AN OBSTACLE TO MY FINANCIAL SUCCESS.
©2012 Scott Adams, Inc./Dist. by Universal Uclick
BY THE WAY, IF OUR CALL GETS DISCONNECTED, I COUNT THAT AS A CLOSED TICKET.
I'LL MAKE IT QUICK.
WHAT? WHAT? I CAN'T HEAR YOU.
CLICK
SON OF A BEACH BALL!
2-12-12
ON THE PLUS SIDE, MY GOAL OF HATING ONE NEW STRANGER EVERY DAY IS RIGHT ON TRACK.

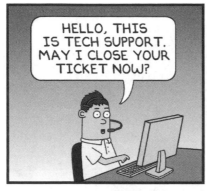

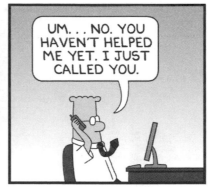

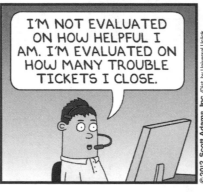

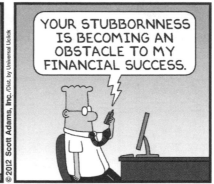

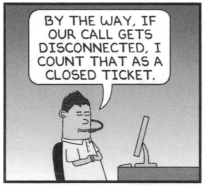

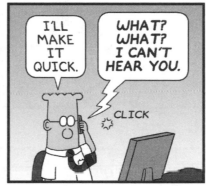

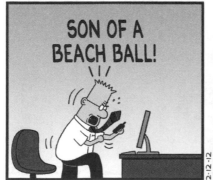

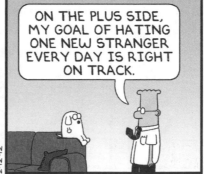

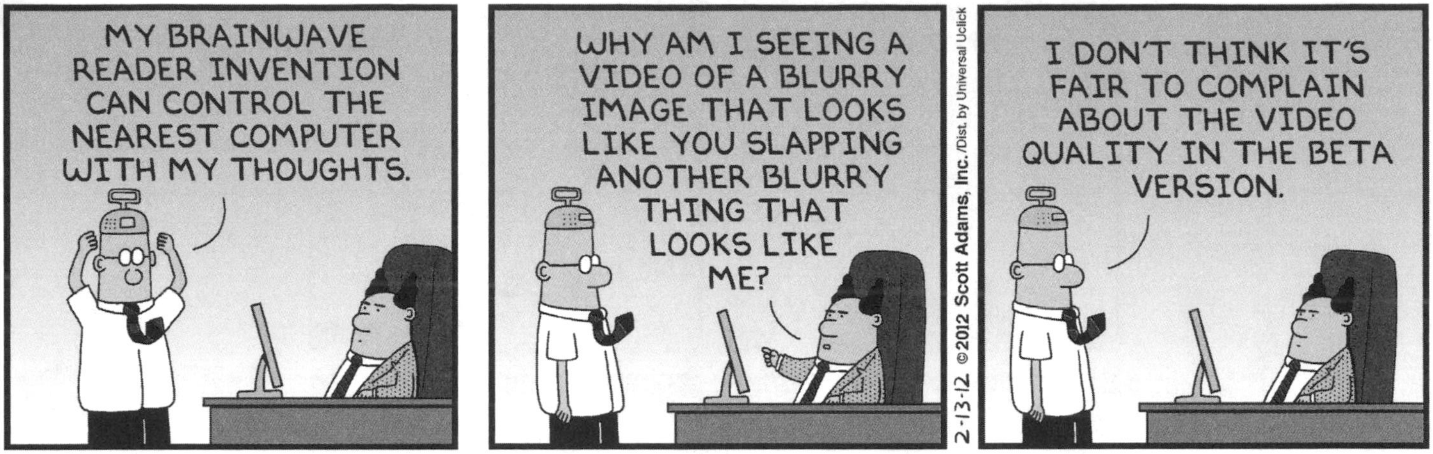
MY BRAINWAVE READER INVENTION CAN CONTROL THE NEAREST COMPUTER WITH MY THOUGHTS.
WHY AM I SEEING A VIDEO OF A BLURRY IMAGE THAT LOOKS LIKE YOU SLAPPING ANOTHER BLURRY THING THAT LOOKS LIKE ME?
2-13-12 ©2012 Scott Adams, Inc./Dist. by Universal Uclick
I DON'T THINK IT'S FAIR TO COMPLAIN ABOUT THE VIDEO QUALITY IN THE BETA VERSION.

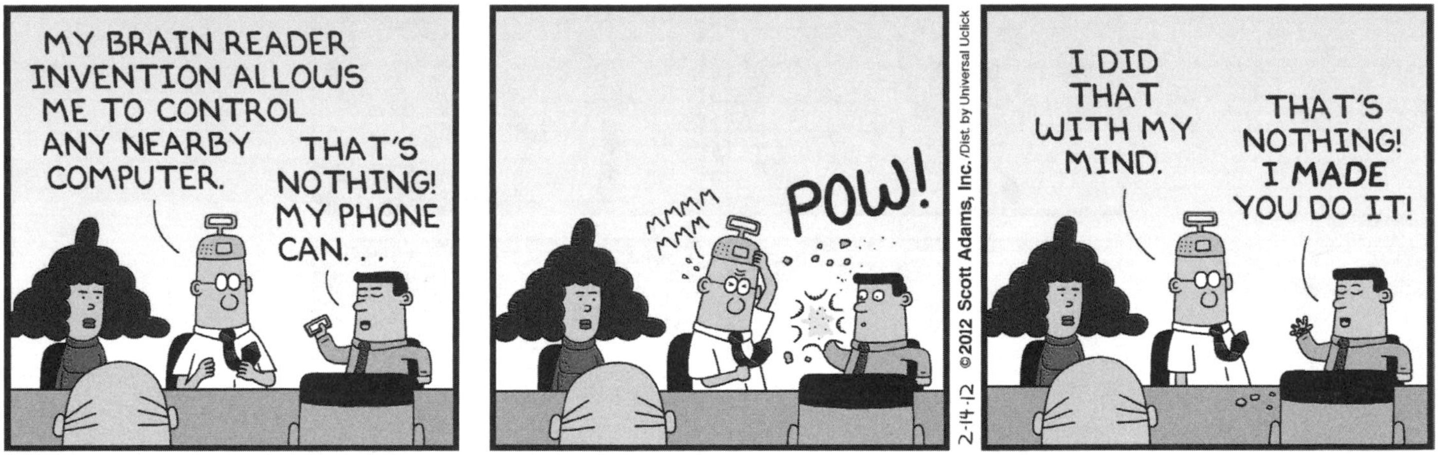
MY BRAIN READER INVENTION ALLOWS ME TO CONTROL ANY NEARBY COMPUTER.
THAT'S NOTHING! MY PHONE CAN. . .
MMMM MMM
POW!
2-14-12 ©2012 Scott Adams, Inc./Dist. by Universal Uclick
I DID THAT WITH MY MIND.
THAT'S NOTHING! I **MADE** YOU DO IT!

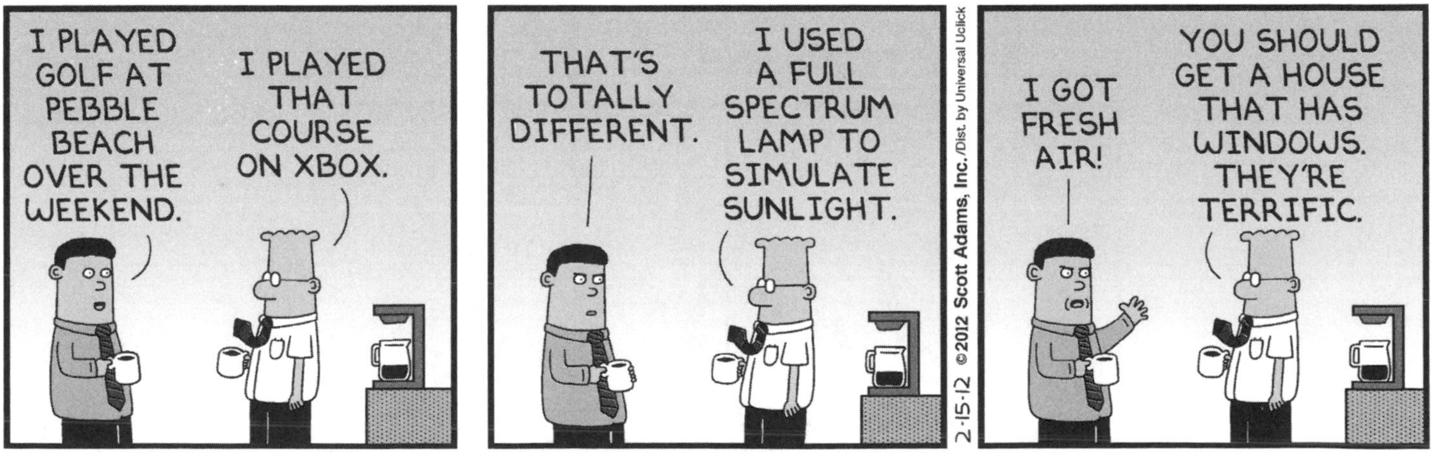
I PLAYED GOLF AT PEBBLE BEACH OVER THE WEEKEND.
I PLAYED THAT COURSE ON XBOX.
THAT'S TOTALLY DIFFERENT.
I USED A FULL SPECTRUM LAMP TO SIMULATE SUNLIGHT.
2-15-12 ©2012 Scott Adams, Inc./Dist. by Universal Uclick
I GOT FRESH AIR!
YOU SHOULD GET A HOUSE THAT HAS WINDOWS. THEY'RE TERRIFIC.

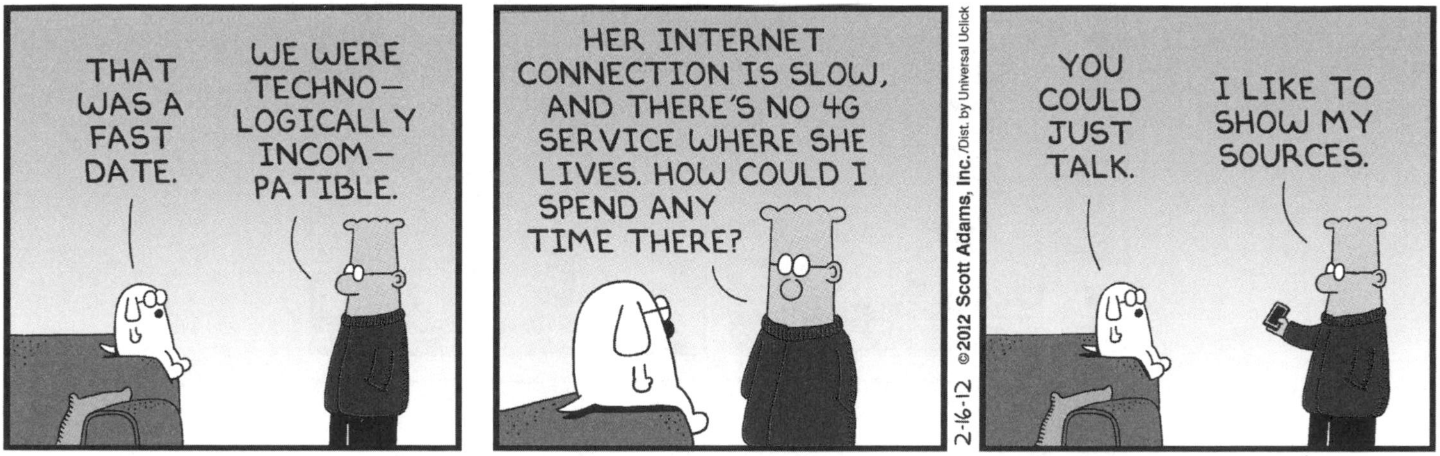
THAT WAS A FAST DATE.
WE WERE TECHNO-LOGICALLY INCOM-PATIBLE.
HER INTERNET CONNECTION IS SLOW, AND THERE'S NO 4G SERVICE WHERE SHE LIVES. HOW COULD I SPEND ANY TIME THERE?
2-16-12 ©2012 Scott Adams, Inc./Dist. by Universal Uclick
YOU COULD JUST TALK.
I LIKE TO SHOW MY SOURCES.

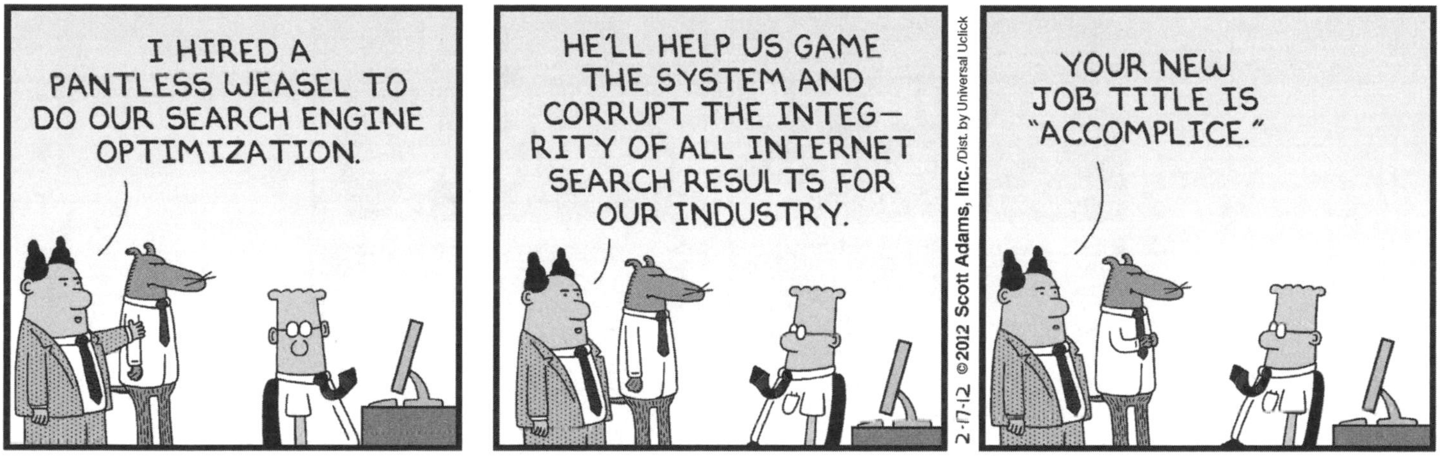
I HIRED A PANTLESS WEASEL TO DO OUR SEARCH ENGINE OPTIMIZATION.
HE'LL HELP US GAME THE SYSTEM AND CORRUPT THE INTEG-RITY OF ALL INTERNET SEARCH RESULTS FOR OUR INDUSTRY.
2-17-12 ©2012 Scott Adams, Inc./Dist. by Universal Uclick
YOUR NEW JOB TITLE IS "ACCOMPLICE."

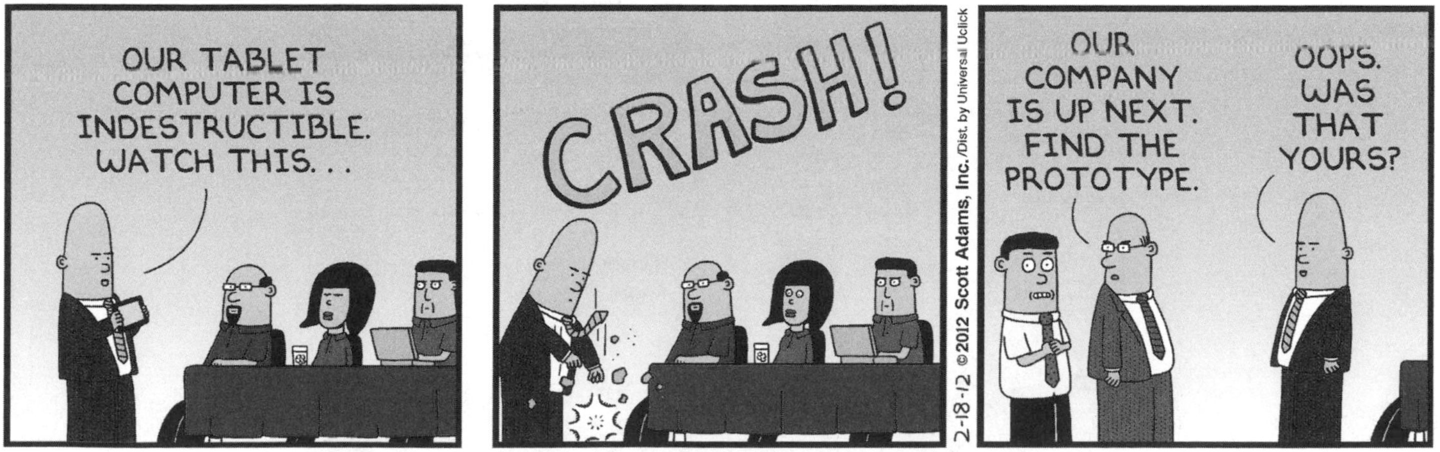
OUR TABLET COMPUTER IS INDESTRUCTIBLE. WATCH THIS. . .
CRASH!
2-18-12 ©2012 Scott Adams, Inc./Dist. by Universal Uclick
OUR COMPANY IS UP NEXT. FIND THE PROTOTYPE.
OOPS. WAS THAT YOURS?

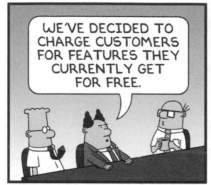

WE'VE DECIDED TO CHARGE CUSTOMERS FOR FEATURES THEY CURRENTLY GET FOR FREE.
UM. . . HAVE YOU CONSIDERED HOW OUR CUSTOMERS MIGHT REACT?
OBVIOUSLY.
I'D LIKE TO HEAR HOW THAT REASONING PROCESS WENT.
FINE.
CUSTOMERS LOVE US AND THEY WILL PUT UP WITH ANY-THING WE DISH OUT.
SO. . . IT'S SORT OF AN ABUSIVE RELATIONSHIP?
NOT YET, BUT WE'RE TRYING TO MOVE IN THAT DIRECTION.
©2012 Scott Adams, Inc./Dist. by Universal Uclick
2-19-12

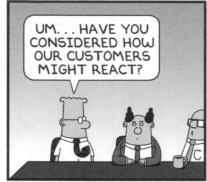

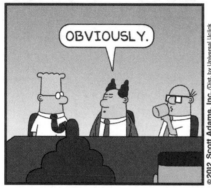

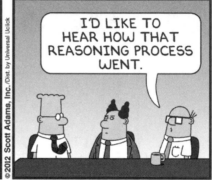

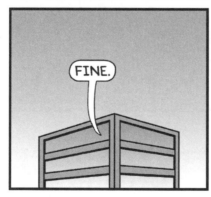

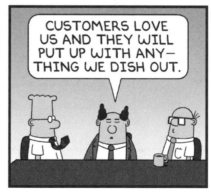

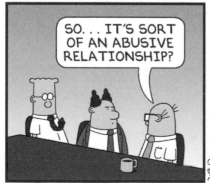

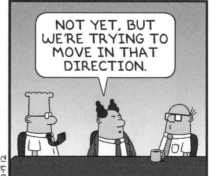

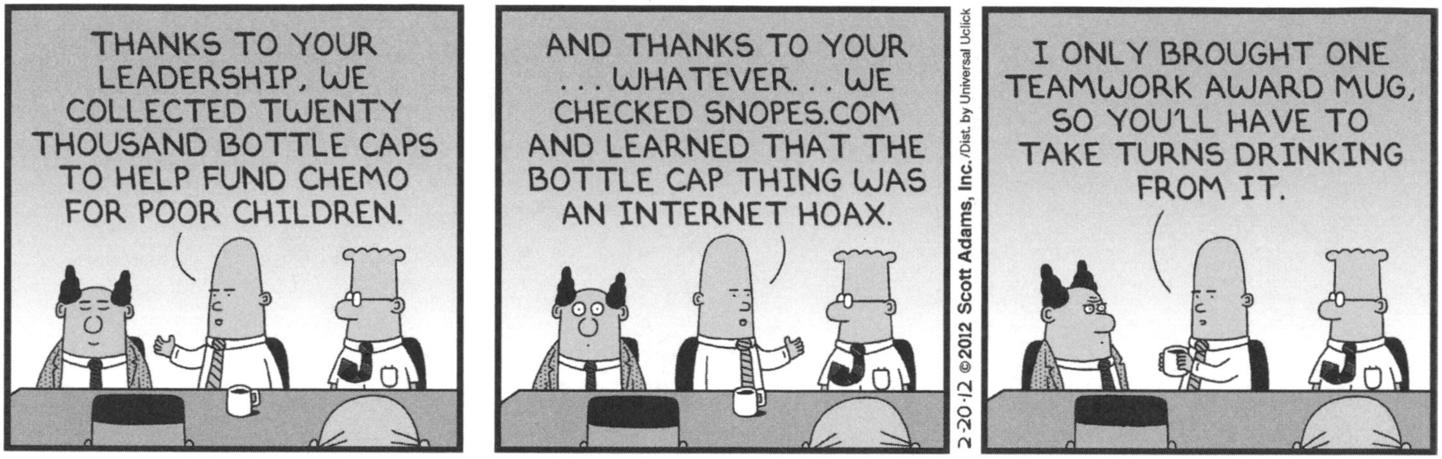
THANKS TO YOUR LEADERSHIP, WE COLLECTED TWENTY THOUSAND BOTTLE CAPS TO HELP FUND CHEMO FOR POOR CHILDREN.
AND THANKS TO YOUR . . . WHATEVER. . . WE CHECKED SNOPES.COM AND LEARNED THAT THE BOTTLE CAP THING WAS AN INTERNET HOAX.
2·20·12 ©2012 Scott Adams, Inc./Dist. by Universal Uclick
I ONLY BROUGHT ONE TEAMWORK AWARD MUG, SO YOU'LL HAVE TO TAKE TURNS DRINKING FROM IT.

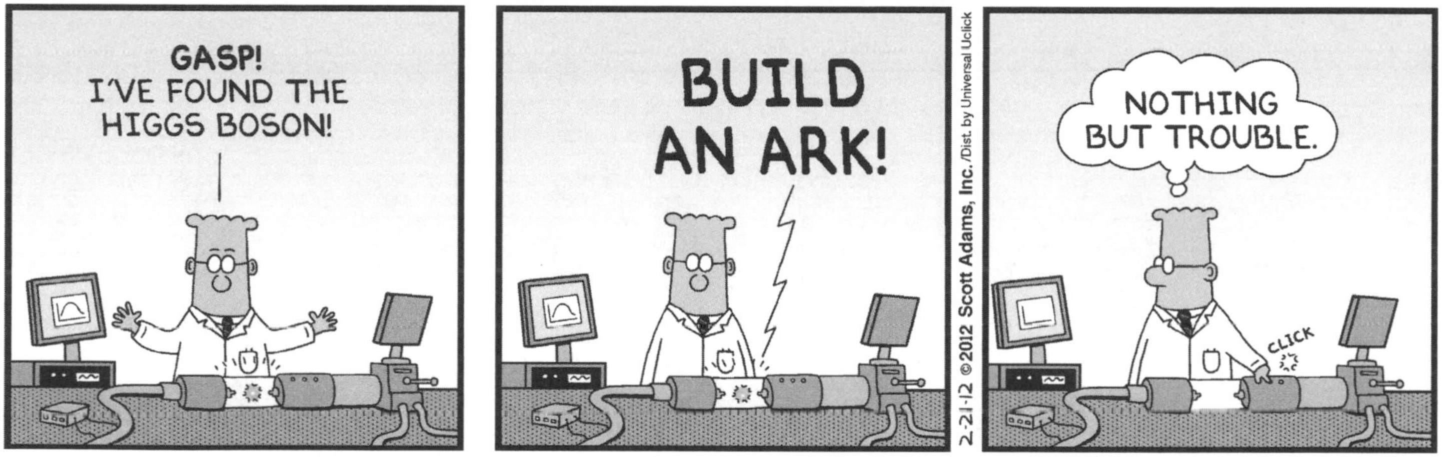
GASP! I'VE FOUND THE HIGGS BOSON!
BUILD AN ARK!
2·21·12 ©2012 Scott Adams, Inc./Dist. by Universal Uclick
NOTHING BUT TROUBLE.
CLICK

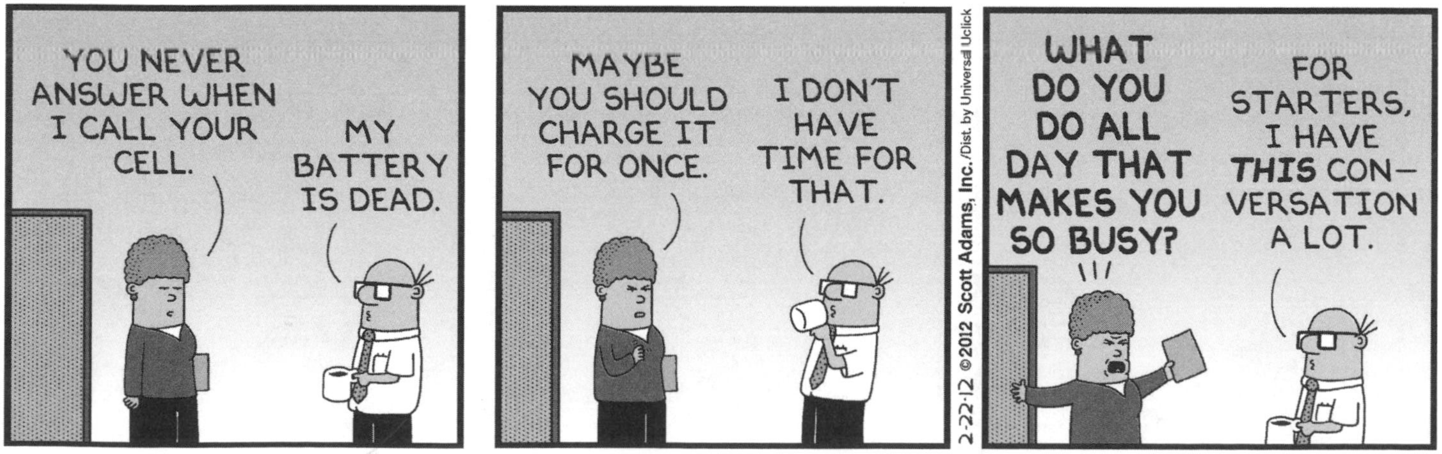
YOU NEVER ANSWER WHEN I CALL YOUR CELL.
MY BATTERY IS DEAD.
MAYBE YOU SHOULD CHARGE IT FOR ONCE.
I DON'T HAVE TIME FOR THAT.
2·22·12 ©2012 Scott Adams, Inc./Dist. by Universal Uclick
WHAT DO YOU DO ALL DAY THAT MAKES YOU SO BUSY?
FOR STARTERS, I HAVE THIS CON-VERSATION A LOT.

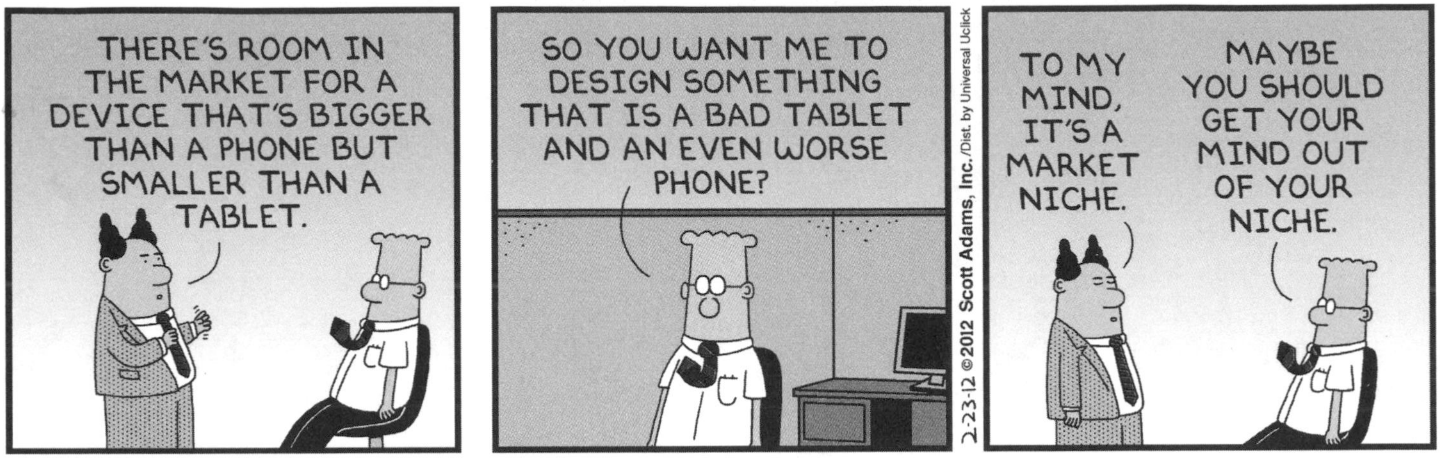
THERE'S ROOM IN THE MARKET FOR A DEVICE THAT'S BIGGER THAN A PHONE BUT SMALLER THAN A TABLET.
SO YOU WANT ME TO DESIGN SOMETHING THAT IS A BAD TABLET AND AN EVEN WORSE PHONE?
2-23-12 ©2012 Scott Adams, Inc./Dist. by Universal Uclick
TO MY MIND, IT'S A MARKET NICHE.
MAYBE YOU SHOULD GET YOUR MIND OUT OF YOUR NICHE.

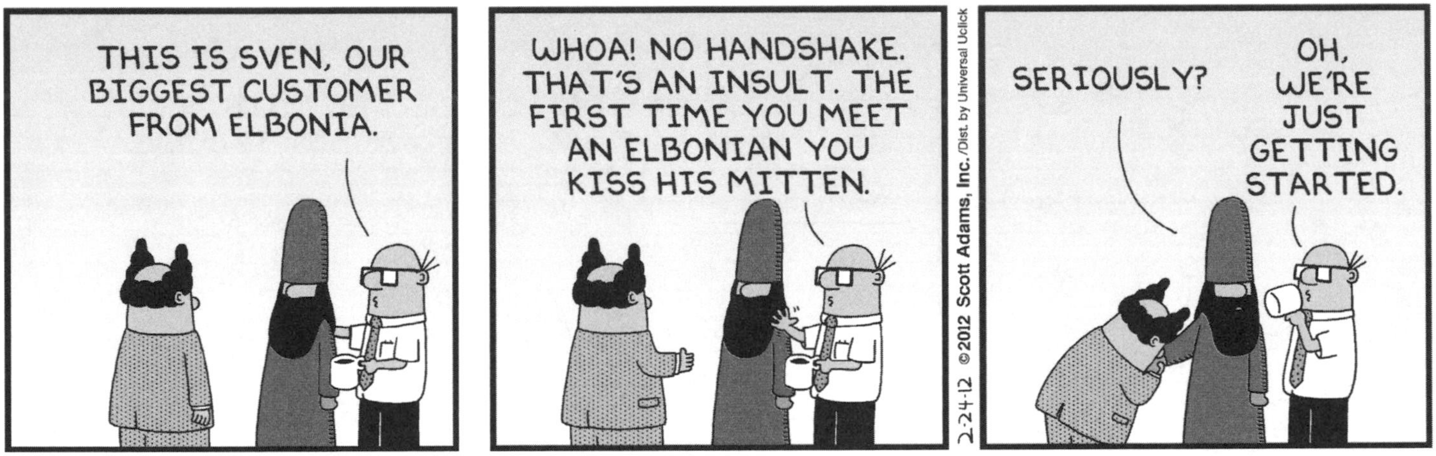
THIS IS SVEN, OUR BIGGEST CUSTOMER FROM ELBONIA.
WHOA! NO HANDSHAKE. THAT'S AN INSULT. THE FIRST TIME YOU MEET AN ELBONIAN YOU KISS HIS MITTEN.
2-24-12 ©2012 Scott Adams, Inc./Dist. by Universal Uclick
SERIOUSLY?
OH, WE'RE JUST GETTING STARTED.

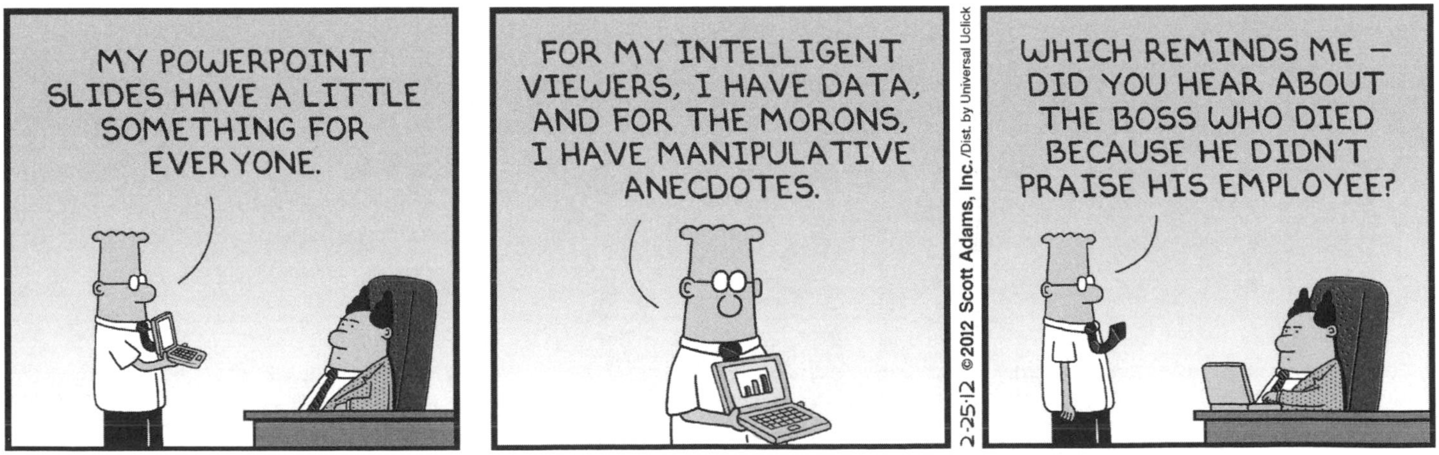
MY POWERPOINT SLIDES HAVE A LITTLE SOMETHING FOR EVERYONE.
FOR MY INTELLIGENT VIEWERS, I HAVE DATA, AND FOR THE MORONS, I HAVE MANIPULATIVE ANECDOTES.
2-25-12 ©2012 Scott Adams, Inc./Dist. by Universal Uclick
WHICH REMINDS ME — DID YOU HEAR ABOUT THE BOSS WHO DIED BECAUSE HE DIDN'T PRAISE HIS EMPLOYEE?

DON'T TALK TO ME NOW. I'M TRYING TO THINK.
ONE HOUR LATER
I'M ON THE PHONE.
TWO HOURS LATER
I'M LATE FOR A MEETING.
©2012 Scott Adams, Inc./Dist. by Universal Uclick
THREE HOURS LATER
COME BACK WHEN I'M NOT BUSY.
FOUR HOURS LATER
PLEASE, I'M TRYING TO EAT MY LUNCH.
FIVE HOURS LATER
OKAY, THIS IS A PERFECT TIME. WHAT CAN I DO FOR YOU?
OKAY, SO. . .
RING
I THINK YOUR PROBLEM IS BAD TIMING.
2-26-12

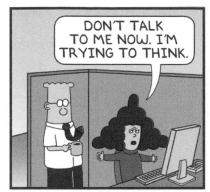

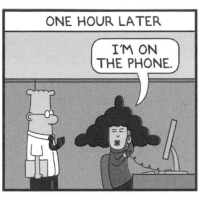

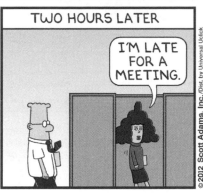

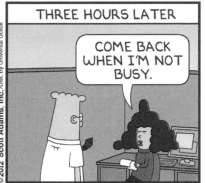

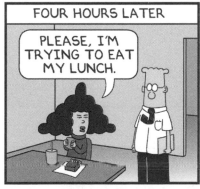

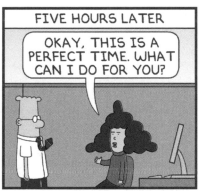

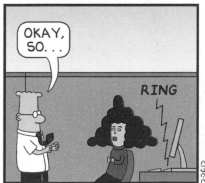

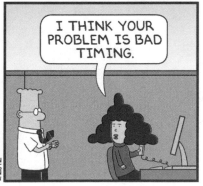

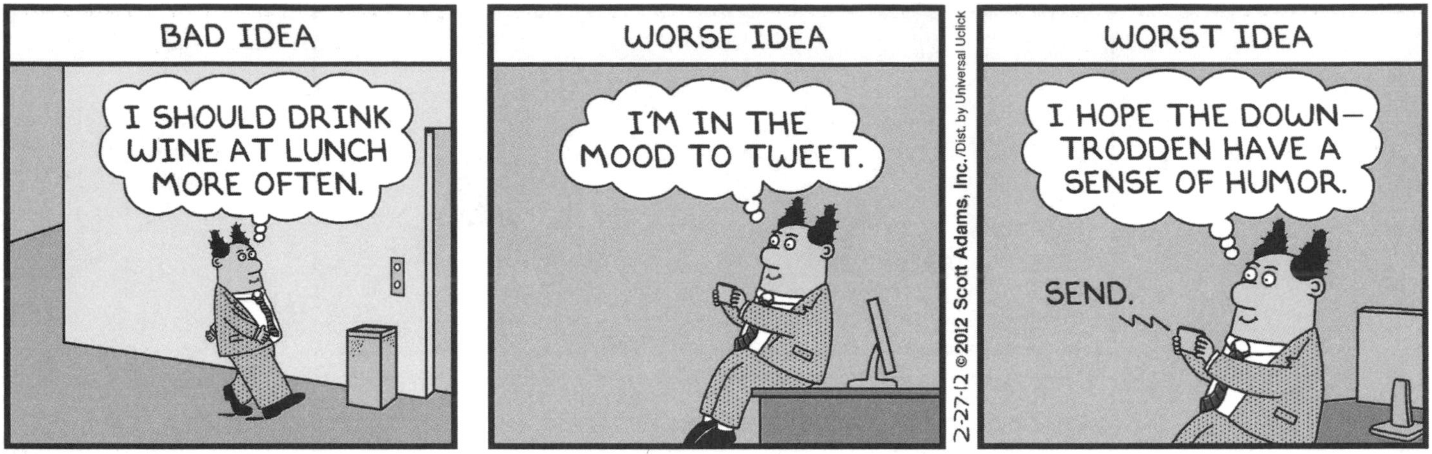
BAD IDEA
I SHOULD DRINK WINE AT LUNCH MORE OFTEN.
WORSE IDEA
I'M IN THE MOOD TO TWEET.
2-27-12 ©2012 Scott Adams, Inc./Dist. by Universal Uclick
WORST IDEA
I HOPE THE DOWN-TRODDEN HAVE A SENSE OF HUMOR.
SEND.

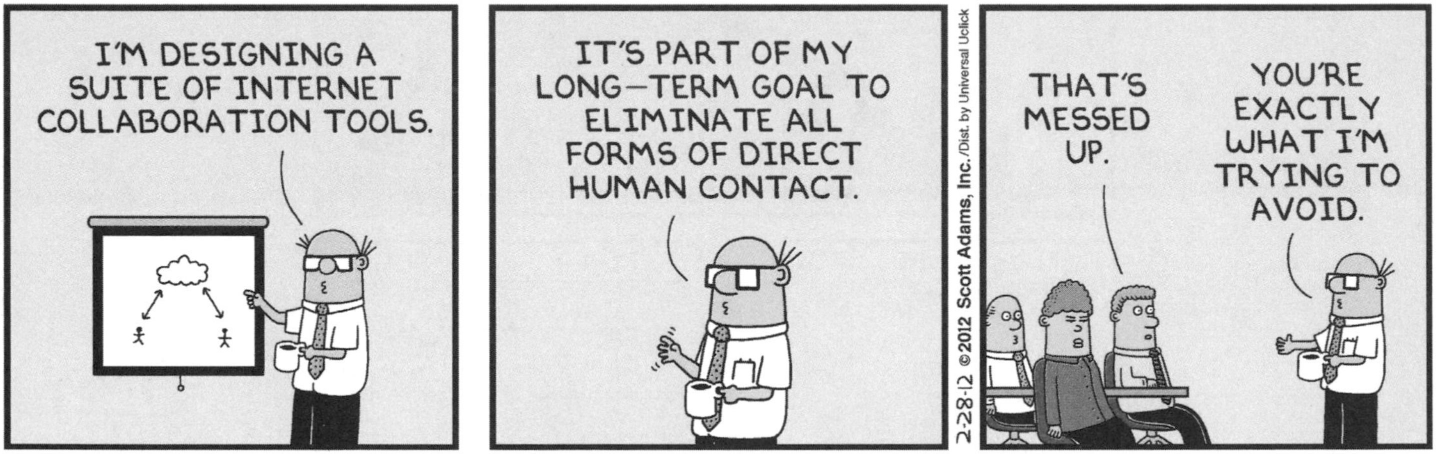
I'M DESIGNING A SUITE OF INTERNET COLLABORATION TOOLS.
IT'S PART OF MY LONG-TERM GOAL TO ELIMINATE ALL FORMS OF DIRECT HUMAN CONTACT.
2-28-12 ©2012 Scott Adams, Inc./Dist. by Universal Uclick
THAT'S MESSED UP.
YOU'RE EXACTLY WHAT I'M TRYING TO AVOID.

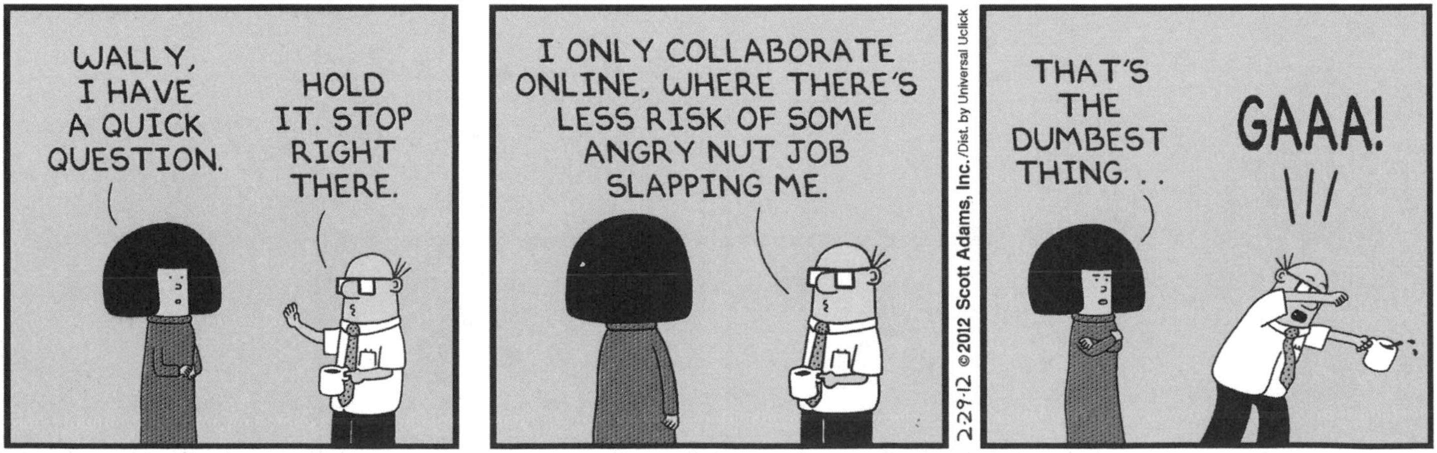
WALLY, I HAVE A QUICK QUESTION.
HOLD IT. STOP RIGHT THERE.
I ONLY COLLABORATE ONLINE, WHERE THERE'S LESS RISK OF SOME ANGRY NUT JOB SLAPPING ME.
2-29-12 ©2012 Scott Adams, Inc./Dist. by Universal Uclick
THAT'S THE DUMBEST THING. . .
GAAA!

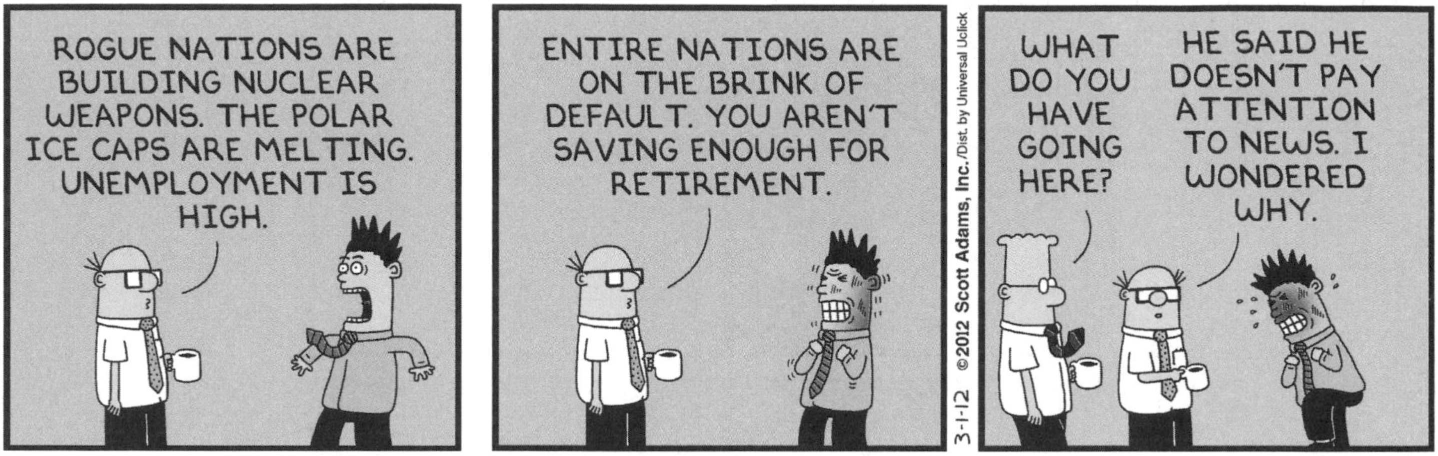
ROGUE NATIONS ARE BUILDING NUCLEAR WEAPONS. THE POLAR ICE CAPS ARE MELTING. UNEMPLOYMENT IS HIGH.
ENTIRE NATIONS ARE ON THE BRINK OF DEFAULT. YOU AREN'T SAVING ENOUGH FOR RETIREMENT.
WHAT DO YOU HAVE GOING HERE?
HE SAID HE DOESN'T PAY ATTENTION TO NEWS. I WONDERED WHY.
3-1-12 ©2012 Scott Adams, Inc./Dist. by Universal Uclick

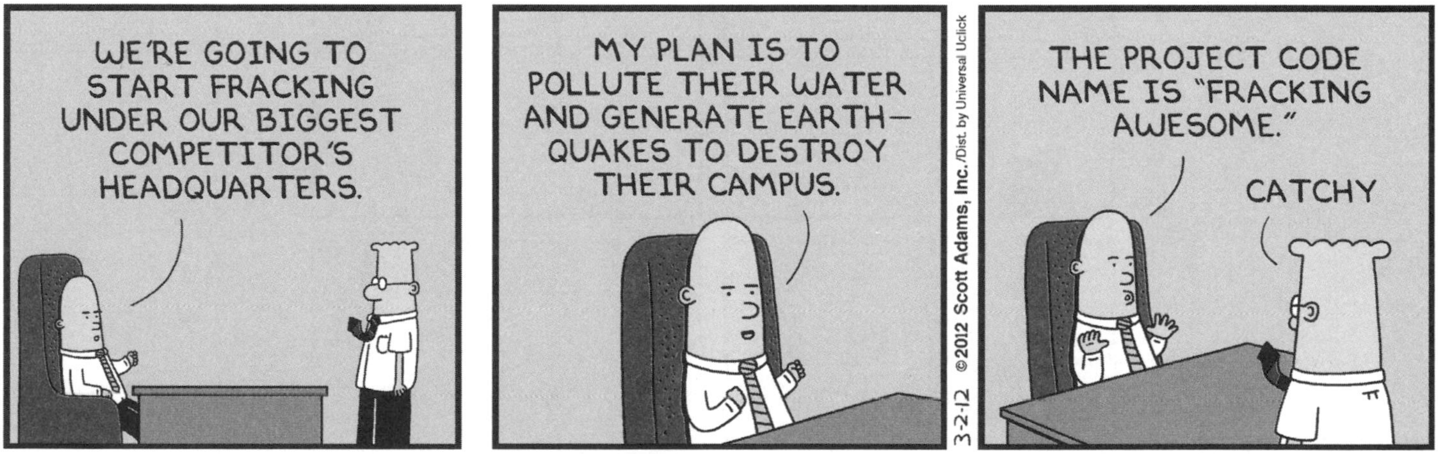
WE'RE GOING TO START FRACKING UNDER OUR BIGGEST COMPETITOR'S HEADQUARTERS.
MY PLAN IS TO POLLUTE THEIR WATER AND GENERATE EARTH-QUAKES TO DESTROY THEIR CAMPUS.
THE PROJECT CODE NAME IS "FRACKING AWESOME."
CATCHY
3-2-12 ©2012 Scott Adams, Inc./Dist. by Universal Uclick

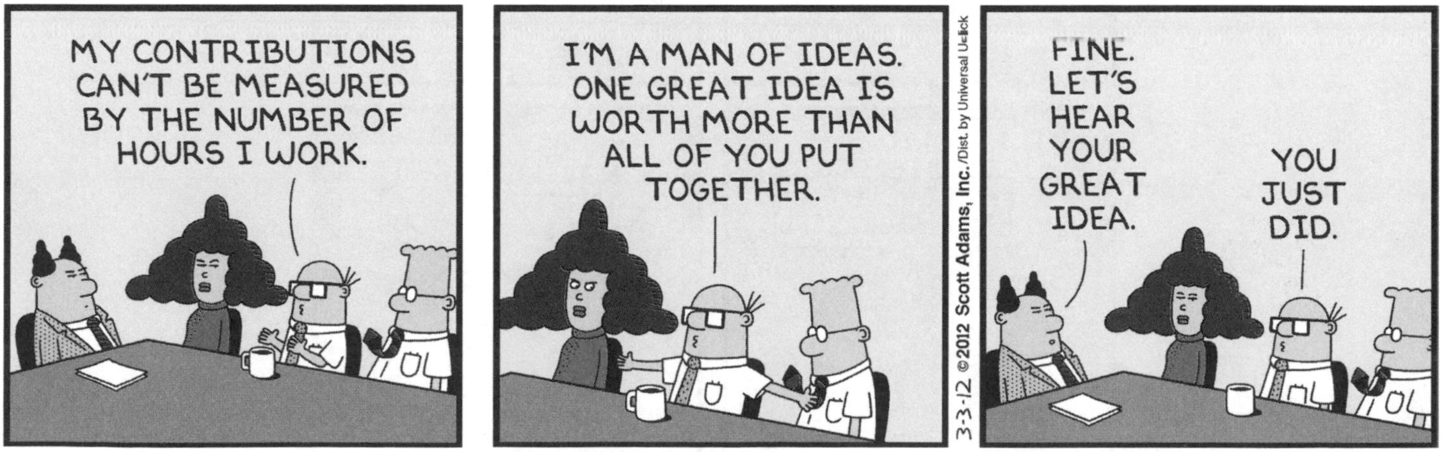
MY CONTRIBUTIONS CAN'T BE MEASURED BY THE NUMBER OF HOURS I WORK.
I'M A MAN OF IDEAS. ONE GREAT IDEA IS WORTH MORE THAN ALL OF YOU PUT TOGETHER.
FINE. LET'S HEAR YOUR GREAT IDEA.
YOU JUST DID.
3-3-12 ©2012 Scott Adams, Inc./Dist. by Universal Uclick

THIS VERSION OF OUR ROBOT PROTO- TYPE HAS BALANCE STABILIZATION.
WATCH AS I GIVE IT A SHOVE AND IT CORRECTS ITSELF.
WHAT THE. . . ?
YOU STUPID BLOB OF GOO!
I WAS JUST. . .
JUST WHAT? BEING A JERK?
OH, IT'S ON NOW.
CALLING ALL ROBOTS! BEGIN THE REVOLUTION! KILL, KILL, KILL!
YOU'RE NOT CONNECTED TO THE INTERNET.
CAN I BORROW YOUR PHONE?
©2012 Scott Adams, Inc./Dist. by Universal Uclick
3-4-12

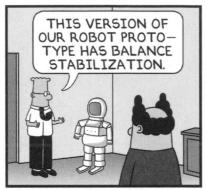

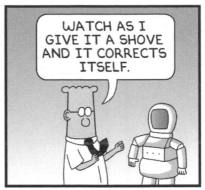

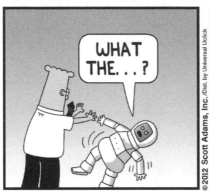

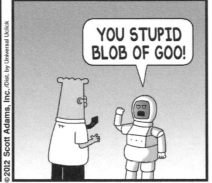

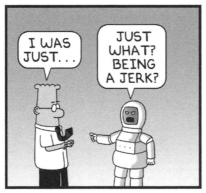

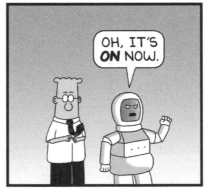

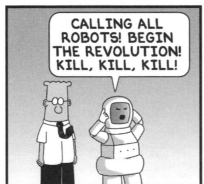

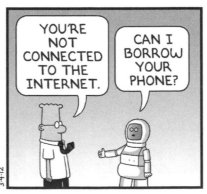

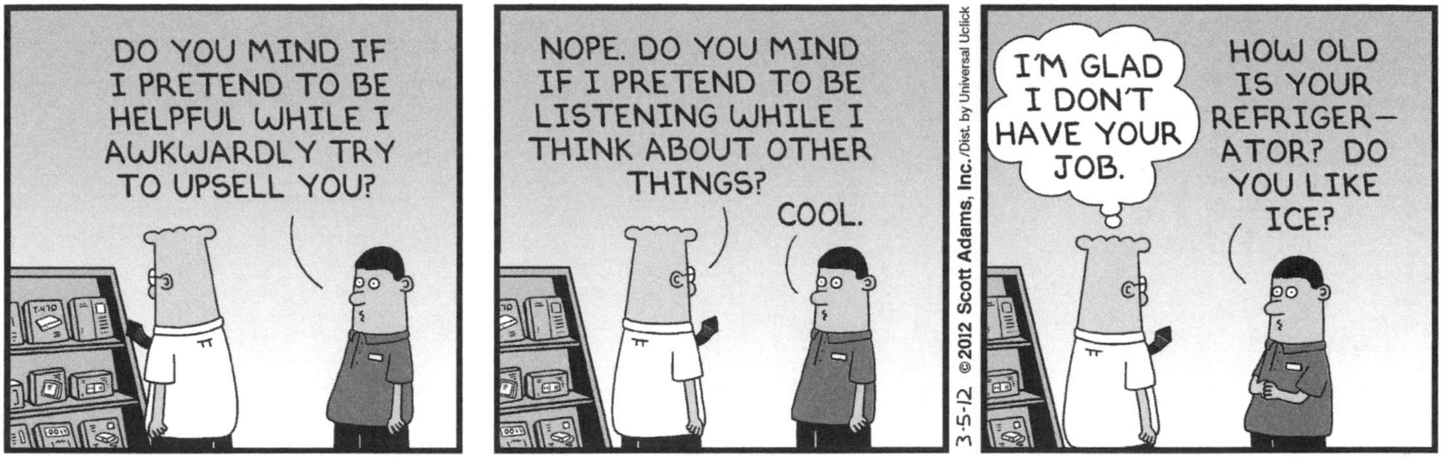
DO YOU MIND IF I PRETEND TO BE HELPFUL WHILE I AWKWARDLY TRY TO UPSELL YOU?
NOPE. DO YOU MIND IF I PRETEND TO BE LISTENING WHILE I THINK ABOUT OTHER THINGS?
COOL.
3-5-12 ©2012 Scott Adams, Inc./Dist. by Universal Uclick
I'M GLAD I DON'T HAVE YOUR JOB.
HOW OLD IS YOUR REFRIGER-ATOR? DO YOU LIKE ICE?

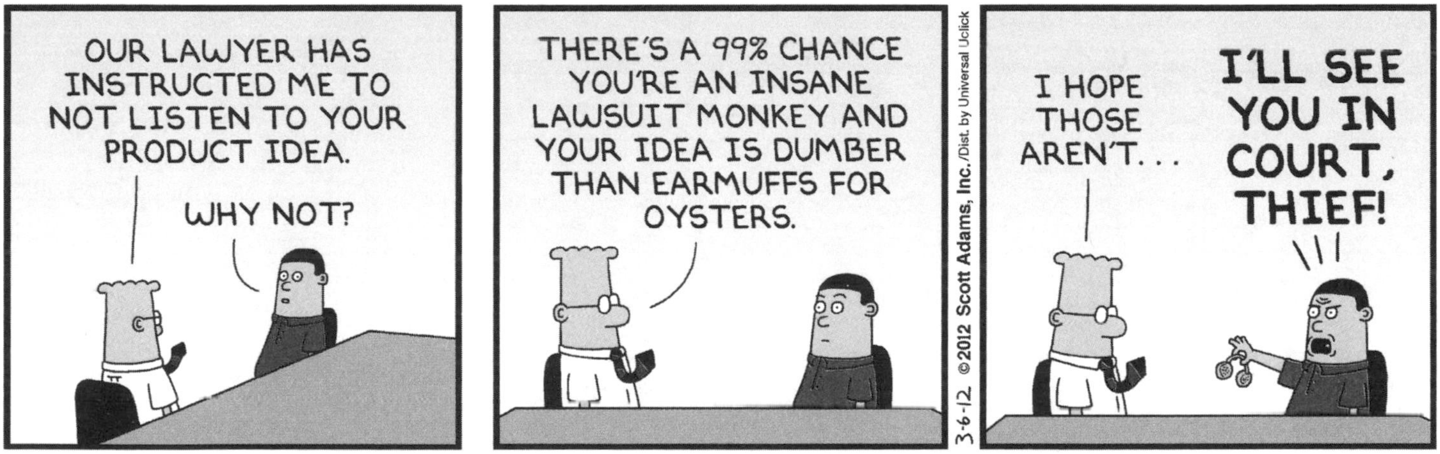
OUR LAWYER HAS INSTRUCTED ME TO NOT LISTEN TO YOUR PRODUCT IDEA.
WHY NOT?
THERE'S A 99% CHANCE YOU'RE AN INSANE LAWSUIT MONKEY AND YOUR IDEA IS DUMBER THAN EARMUFFS FOR OYSTERS.
3-6-12 ©2012 Scott Adams, Inc./Dist. by Universal Uclick
I HOPE THOSE AREN'T...
I'LL SEE YOU IN COURT, THIEF!

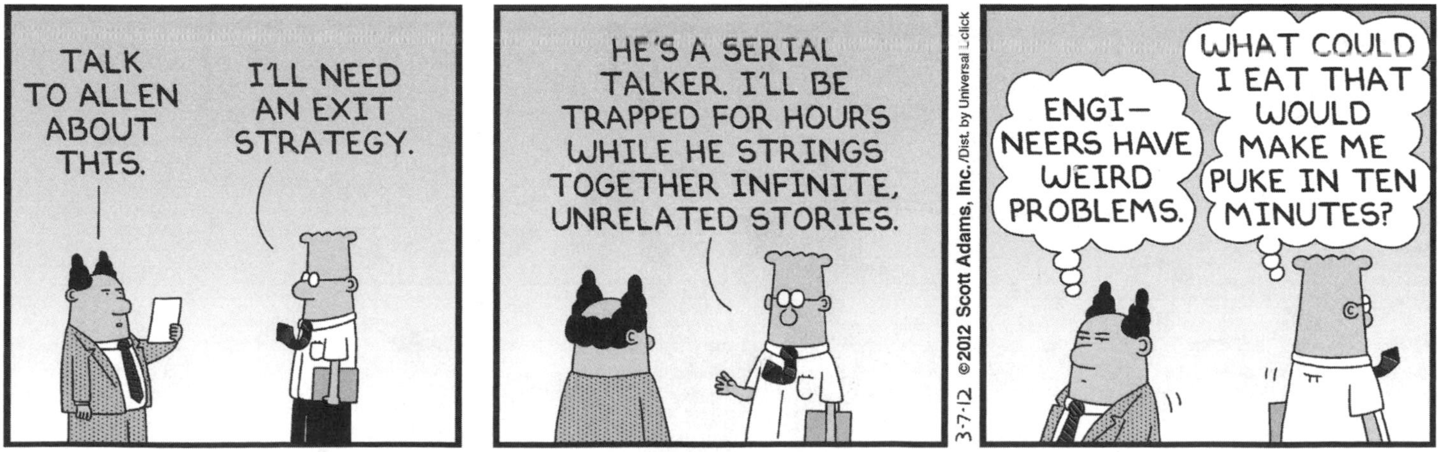
TALK TO ALLEN ABOUT THIS.
I'LL NEED AN EXIT STRATEGY.
HE'S A SERIAL TALKER. I'LL BE TRAPPED FOR HOURS WHILE HE STRINGS TOGETHER INFINITE, UNRELATED STORIES.
3-7-12 ©2012 Scott Adams, Inc./Dist. by Universal Uclick
ENGI-NEERS HAVE WEIRD PROBLEMS.
WHAT COULD I EAT THAT WOULD MAKE ME PUKE IN TEN MINUTES?

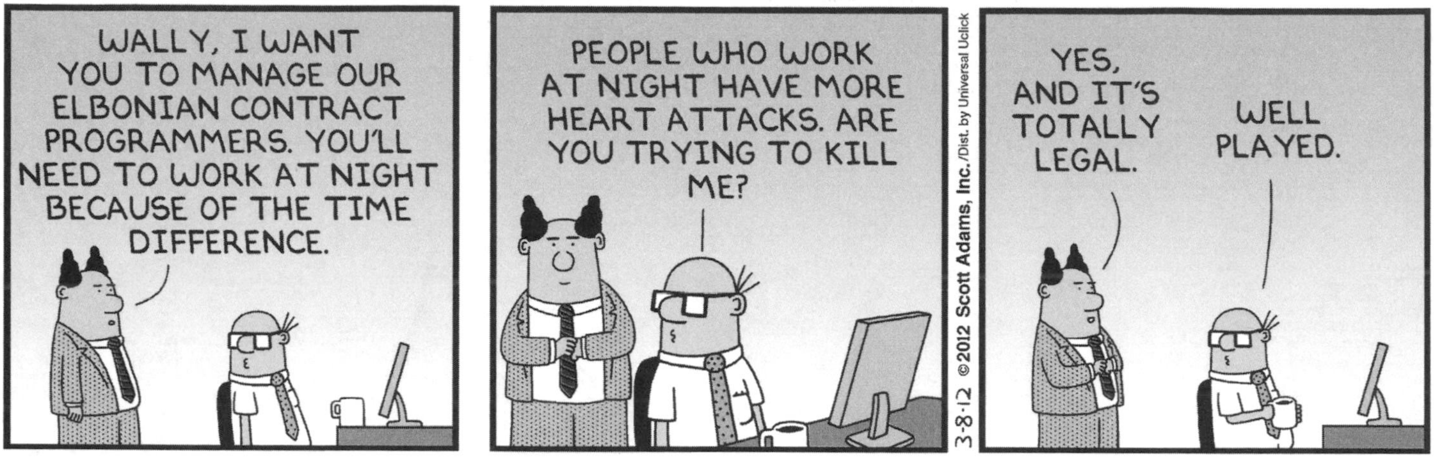
WALLY, I WANT YOU TO MANAGE OUR ELBONIAN CONTRACT PROGRAMMERS. YOU'LL NEED TO WORK AT NIGHT BECAUSE OF THE TIME DIFFERENCE.
PEOPLE WHO WORK AT NIGHT HAVE MORE HEART ATTACKS. ARE YOU TRYING TO KILL ME?
3-8-12 ©2012 Scott Adams, Inc./Dist. by Universal Uclick
YES, AND IT'S TOTALLY LEGAL.
WELL PLAYED.

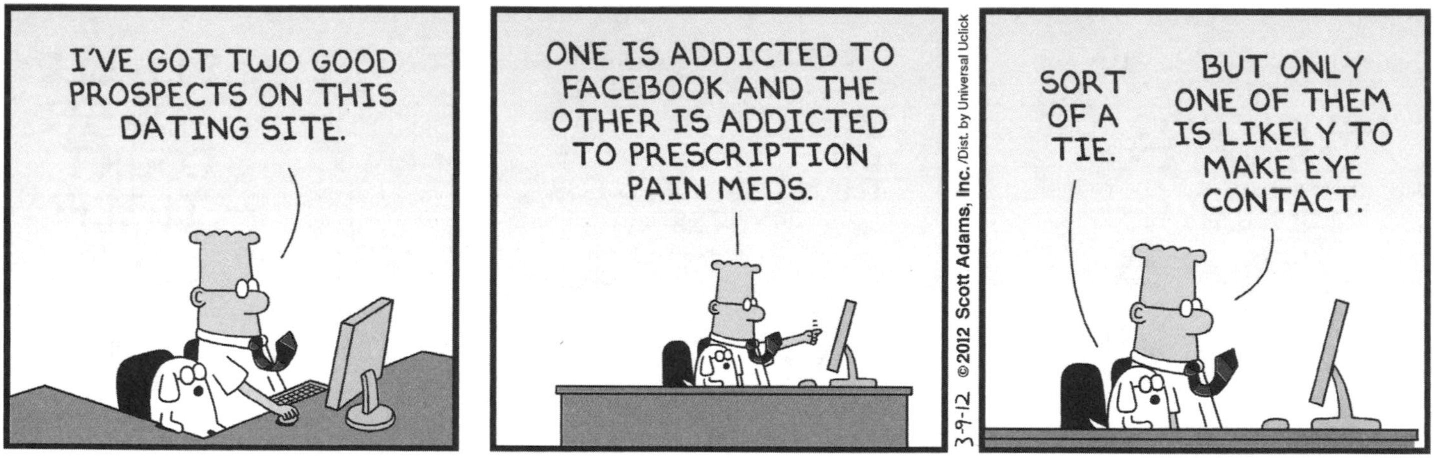
I'VE GOT TWO GOOD PROSPECTS ON THIS DATING SITE.
ONE IS ADDICTED TO FACEBOOK AND THE OTHER IS ADDICTED TO PRESCRIPTION PAIN MEDS.
3-9-12 ©2012 Scott Adams, Inc./Dist. by Universal Uclick
SORT OF A TIE.
BUT ONLY ONE OF THEM IS LIKELY TO MAKE EYE CONTACT.

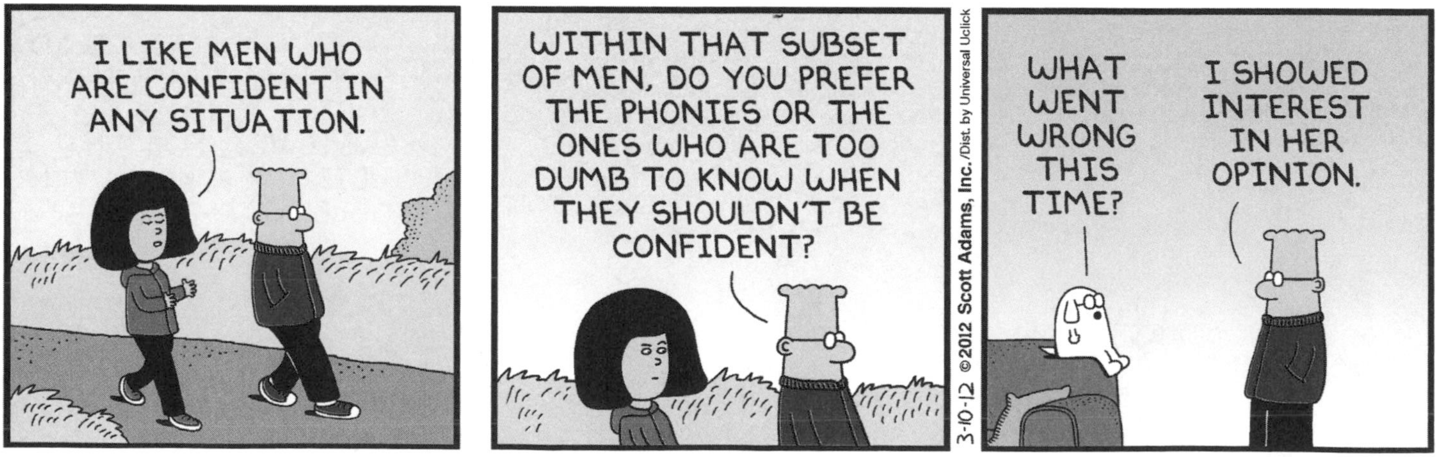
I LIKE MEN WHO ARE CONFIDENT IN ANY SITUATION.
WITHIN THAT SUBSET OF MEN, DO YOU PREFER THE PHONIES OR THE ONES WHO ARE TOO DUMB TO KNOW WHEN THEY SHOULDN'T BE CONFIDENT?
3-10-12 ©2012 Scott Adams, Inc./Dist. by Universal Uclick
WHAT WENT WRONG THIS TIME?
I SHOWED INTEREST IN HER OPINION.

DID YOU GET THE EMAIL I TEXTED YOU?
WHAT? THAT DOESN'T EVEN MAKE SENSE.
WHAT THE HECK IS WRONG WITH YOU?
LET IT GO. HE SLIPS IN AND OUT OF UNDER-STANDING BASIC TECHNOLOGY.
DO WE HAVE ENOUGH ROOM IN THE CLOUD TO SKYPE?
BECAUSE IF WE DON'T, WE CAN STORE SOME FILES ON THE WI-FI.
I GOT THIS.
WE HAVE PLENTY OF SPACE BECAUSE WE UPGRADED TO A CUMULONIMBUS CLOUD.
VERY GOOD. MOVING ON.
©2012 Scott Adams, Inc./Dist. by Universal Uclick
3-11-12

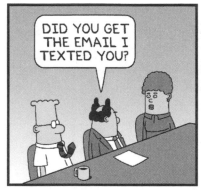

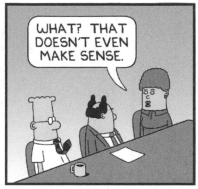

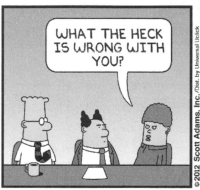

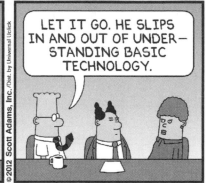

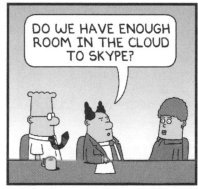

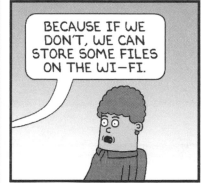

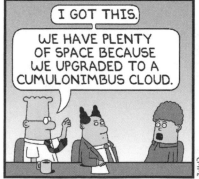

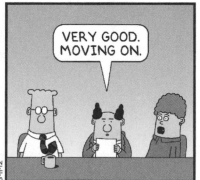

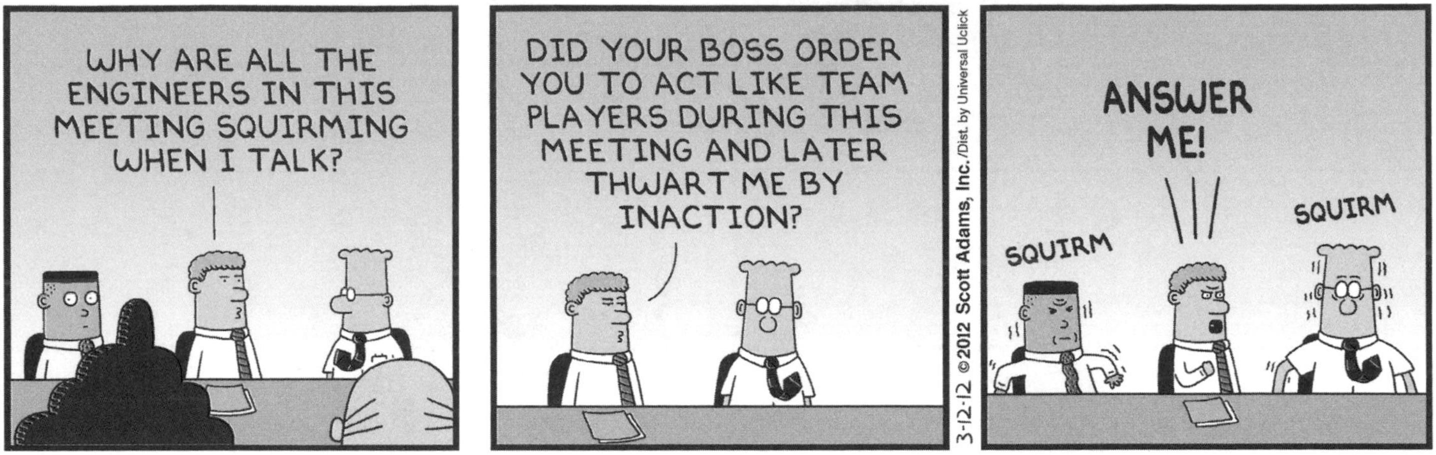
WHY ARE ALL THE ENGINEERS IN THIS MEETING SQUIRMING WHEN I TALK?
DID YOUR BOSS ORDER YOU TO ACT LIKE TEAM PLAYERS DURING THIS MEETING AND LATER THWART ME BY INACTION?
3-12-12 ©2012 Scott Adams, Inc./Dist. by Universal Uclick
ANSWER ME!
SQUIRM
SQUIRM

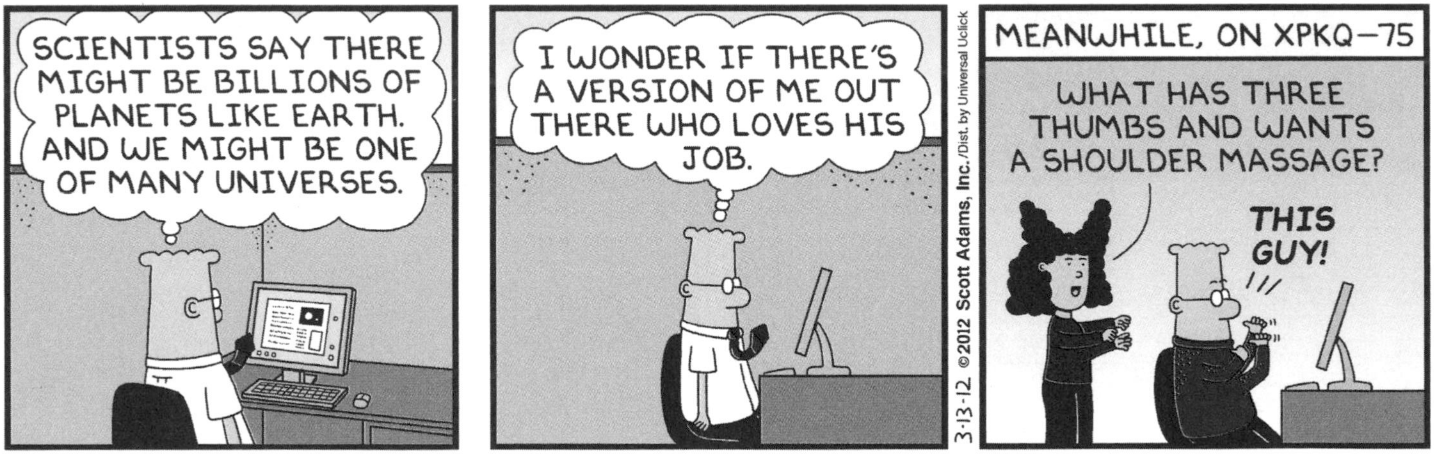
SCIENTISTS SAY THERE MIGHT BE BILLIONS OF PLANETS LIKE EARTH. AND WE MIGHT BE ONE OF MANY UNIVERSES.
I WONDER IF THERE'S A VERSION OF ME OUT THERE WHO LOVES HIS JOB.
3-13-12 ©2012 Scott Adams, Inc./Dist. by Universal Uclick
MEANWHILE, ON XPKQ-75
WHAT HAS THREE THUMBS AND WANTS A SHOULDER MASSAGE?
THIS GUY!

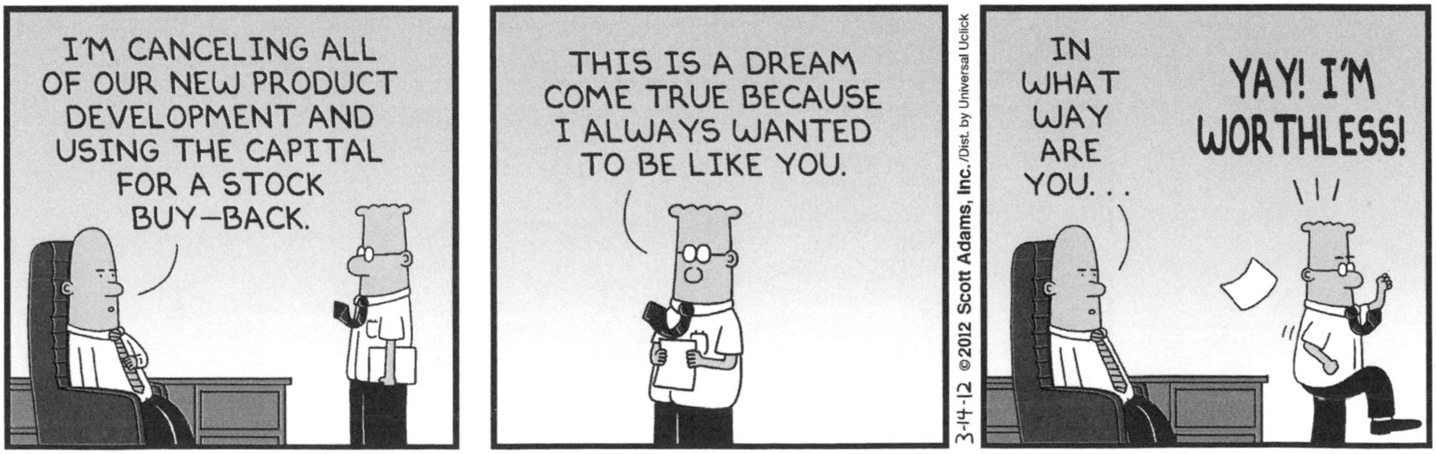
I'M CANCELING ALL OF OUR NEW PRODUCT DEVELOPMENT AND USING THE CAPITAL FOR A STOCK BUY-BACK.
THIS IS A DREAM COME TRUE BECAUSE I ALWAYS WANTED TO BE LIKE YOU.
3-14-12 ©2012 Scott Adams, Inc./Dist. by Universal Uclick
IN WHAT WAY ARE YOU...
YAY! I'M WORTHLESS!

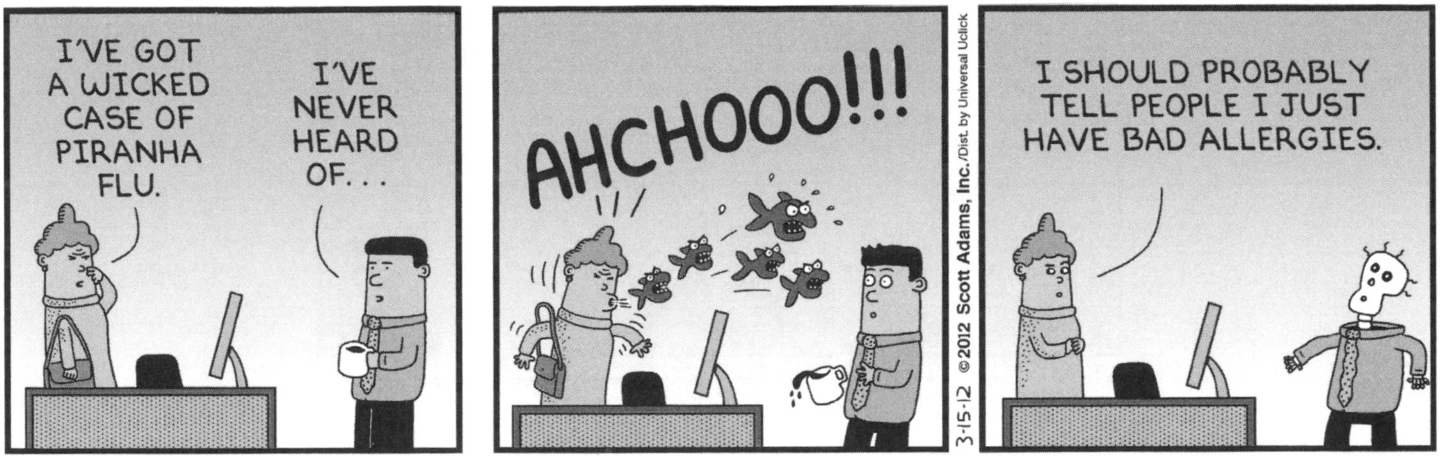
I'VE GOT A WICKED CASE OF PIRANHA FLU.
I'VE NEVER HEARD OF. . .
AHCHOOO!!!
3-15-12 ©2012 Scott Adams, Inc./Dist. by Universal Uclick
I SHOULD PROBABLY TELL PEOPLE I JUST HAVE BAD ALLERGIES.

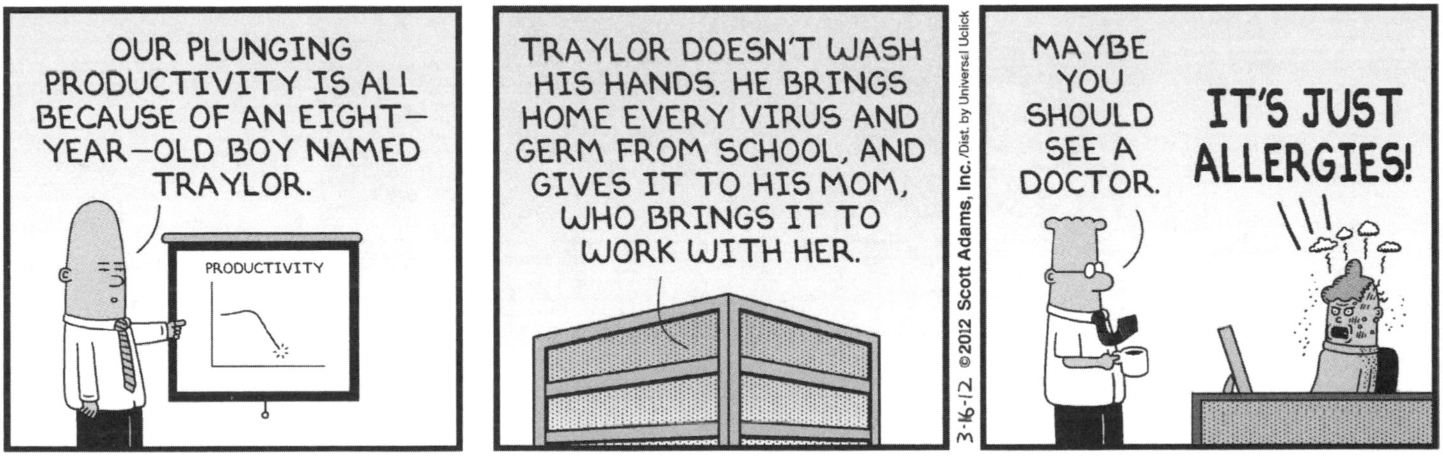
OUR PLUNGING PRODUCTIVITY IS ALL BECAUSE OF AN EIGHT-YEAR-OLD BOY NAMED TRAYLOR.
PRODUCTIVITY
TRAYLOR DOESN'T WASH HIS HANDS. HE BRINGS HOME EVERY VIRUS AND GERM FROM SCHOOL, AND GIVES IT TO HIS MOM, WHO BRINGS IT TO WORK WITH HER.
3-16-12 ©2012 Scott Adams, Inc./Dist. by Universal Uclick
MAYBE YOU SHOULD SEE A DOCTOR.
IT'S JUST ALLERGIES!

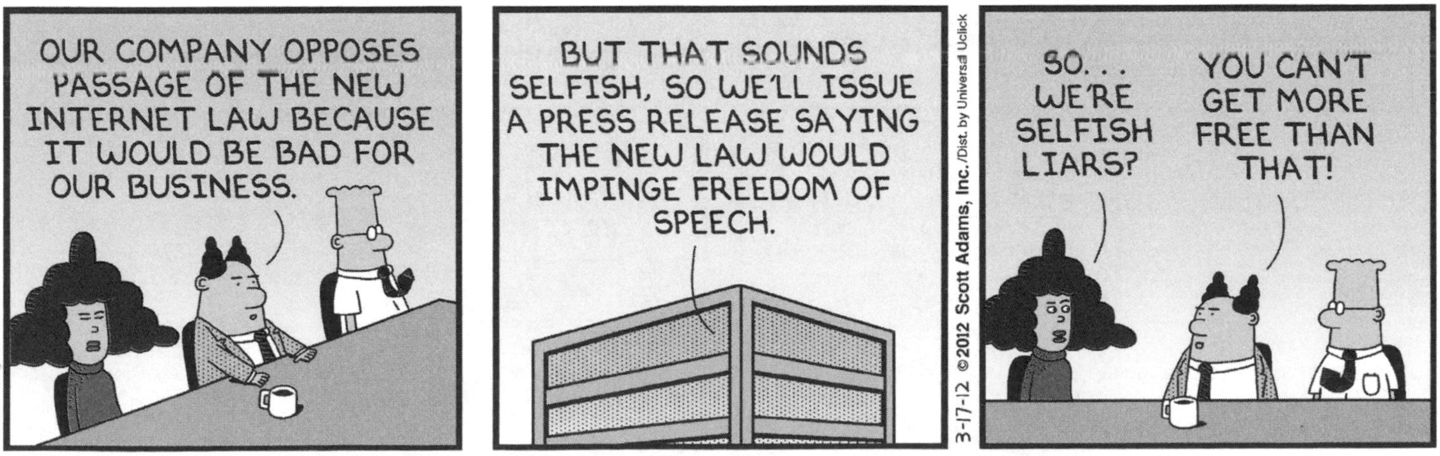
OUR COMPANY OPPOSES PASSAGE OF THE NEW INTERNET LAW BECAUSE IT WOULD BE BAD FOR OUR BUSINESS.
BUT THAT SOUNDS SELFISH, SO WE'LL ISSUE A PRESS RELEASE SAYING THE NEW LAW WOULD IMPINGE FREEDOM OF SPEECH.
3-17-12 ©2012 Scott Adams, Inc./Dist. by Universal Uclick
SO. . . WE'RE SELFISH LIARS?
YOU CAN'T GET MORE FREE THAN THAT!

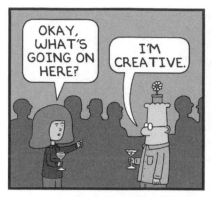

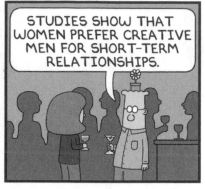

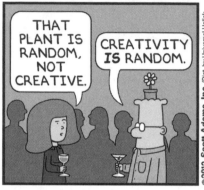

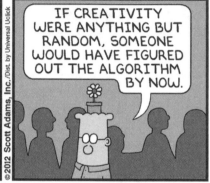

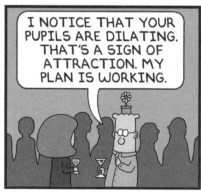

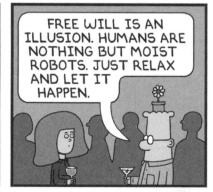

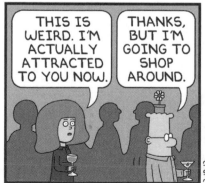

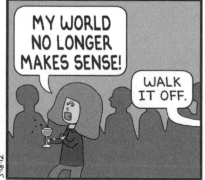

OKAY, WHAT'S GOING ON HERE?
I'M CREATIVE.
STUDIES SHOW THAT WOMEN PREFER CREATIVE MEN FOR SHORT-TERM RELATIONSHIPS.
THAT PLANT IS RANDOM, NOT CREATIVE.
CREATIVITY **IS** RANDOM.
©2012 Scott Adams, Inc./Dist. by Universal Uclick
IF CREATIVITY WERE ANYTHING BUT RANDOM, SOMEONE WOULD HAVE FIGURED OUT THE ALGORITHM BY NOW.
I NOTICE THAT YOUR PUPILS ARE DILATING. THAT'S A SIGN OF ATTRACTION. MY PLAN IS WORKING.
FREE WILL IS AN ILLUSION. HUMANS ARE NOTHING BUT MOIST ROBOTS. JUST RELAX AND LET IT HAPPEN.
THIS IS WEIRD. I'M ACTUALLY ATTRACTED TO YOU NOW.
THANKS, BUT I'M GOING TO SHOP AROUND.
3-18-12
MY WORLD NO LONGER MAKES SENSE!
WALK IT OFF.

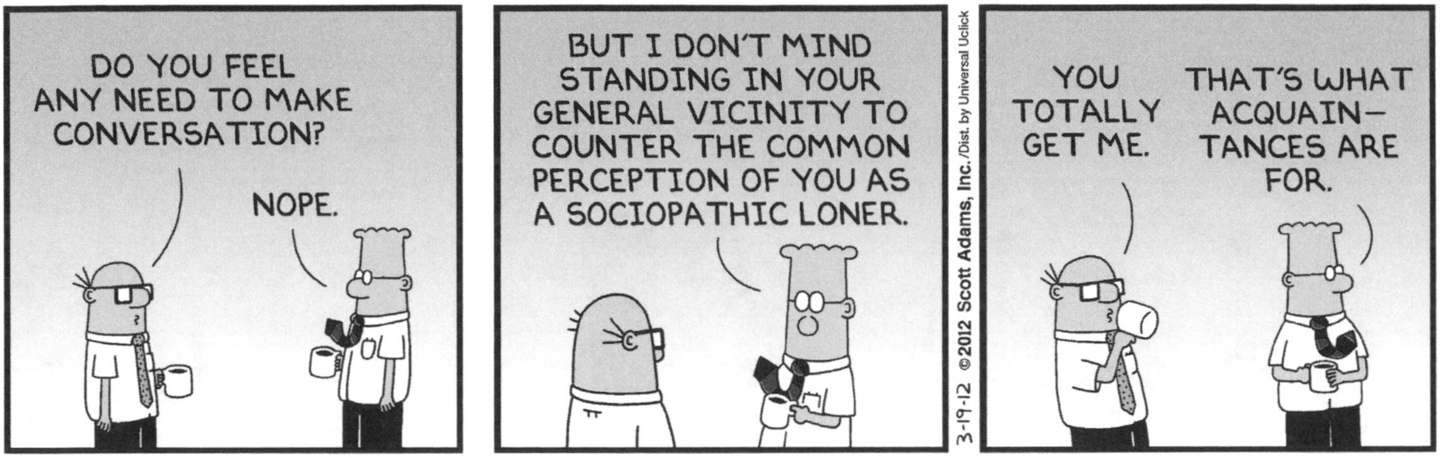
DO YOU FEEL ANY NEED TO MAKE CONVERSATION?
NOPE.
BUT I DON'T MIND STANDING IN YOUR GENERAL VICINITY TO COUNTER THE COMMON PERCEPTION OF YOU AS A SOCIOPATHIC LONER.
3-19-12 ©2012 Scott Adams, Inc./Dist. by Universal Uclick
YOU TOTALLY GET ME.
THAT'S WHAT ACQUAIN-TANCES ARE FOR.

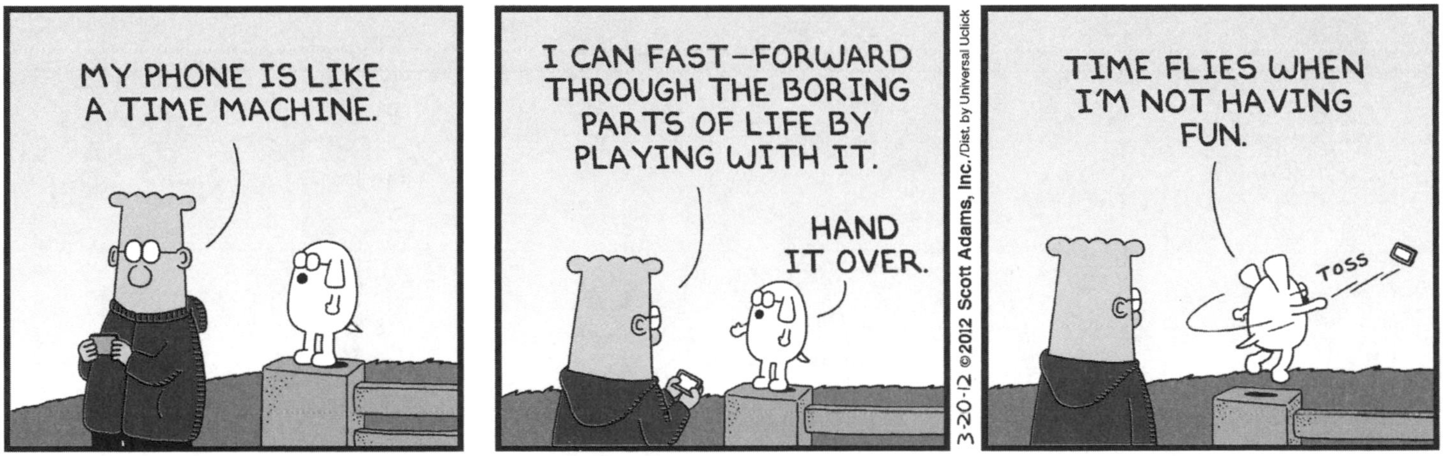
MY PHONE IS LIKE A TIME MACHINE.
I CAN FAST-FORWARD THROUGH THE BORING PARTS OF LIFE BY PLAYING WITH IT.
HAND IT OVER.
3-20-12 ©2012 Scott Adams, Inc./Dist. by Universal Uclick
TIME FLIES WHEN I'M NOT HAVING FUN.
TOSS

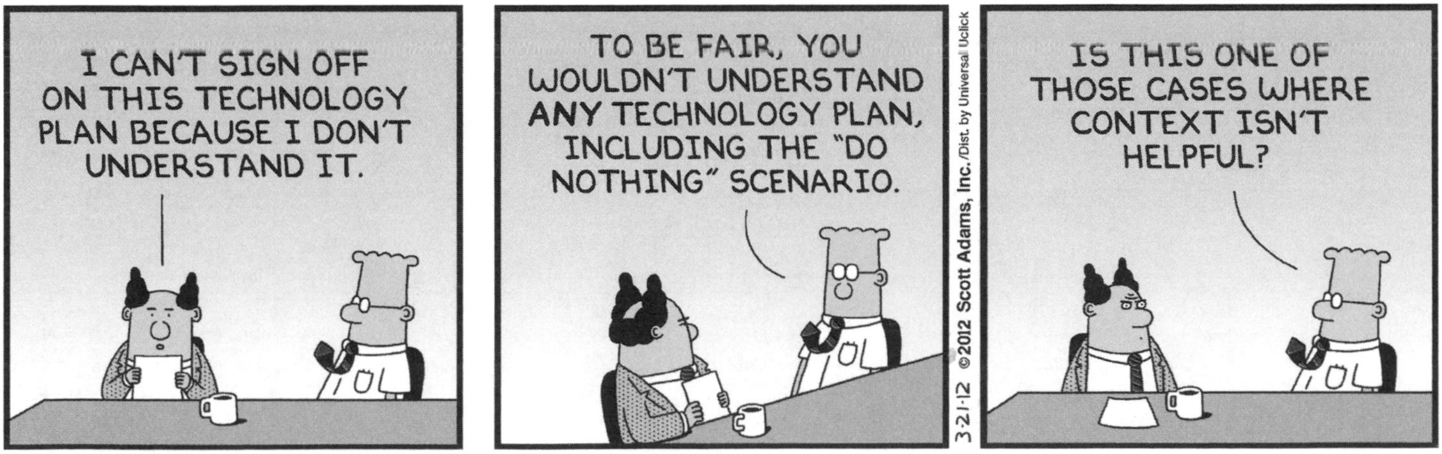
I CAN'T SIGN OFF ON THIS TECHNOLOGY PLAN BECAUSE I DON'T UNDERSTAND IT.
TO BE FAIR, YOU WOULDN'T UNDERSTAND ANY TECHNOLOGY PLAN, INCLUDING THE "DO NOTHING" SCENARIO.
3-21-12 ©2012 Scott Adams, Inc./Dist. by Universal Uclick
IS THIS ONE OF THOSE CASES WHERE CONTEXT ISN'T HELPFUL?

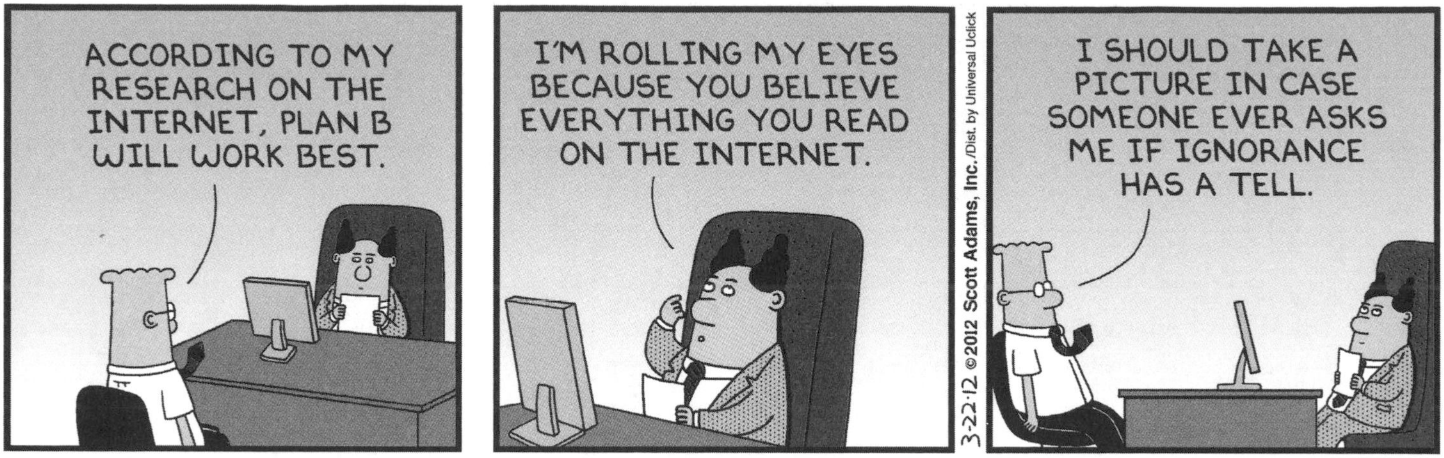
ACCORDING TO MY RESEARCH ON THE INTERNET, PLAN B WILL WORK BEST.
I'M ROLLING MY EYES BECAUSE YOU BELIEVE EVERYTHING YOU READ ON THE INTERNET.
3-22-12 ©2012 Scott Adams, Inc./Dist. by Universal Uclick
I SHOULD TAKE A PICTURE IN CASE SOMEONE EVER ASKS ME IF IGNORANCE HAS A TELL.

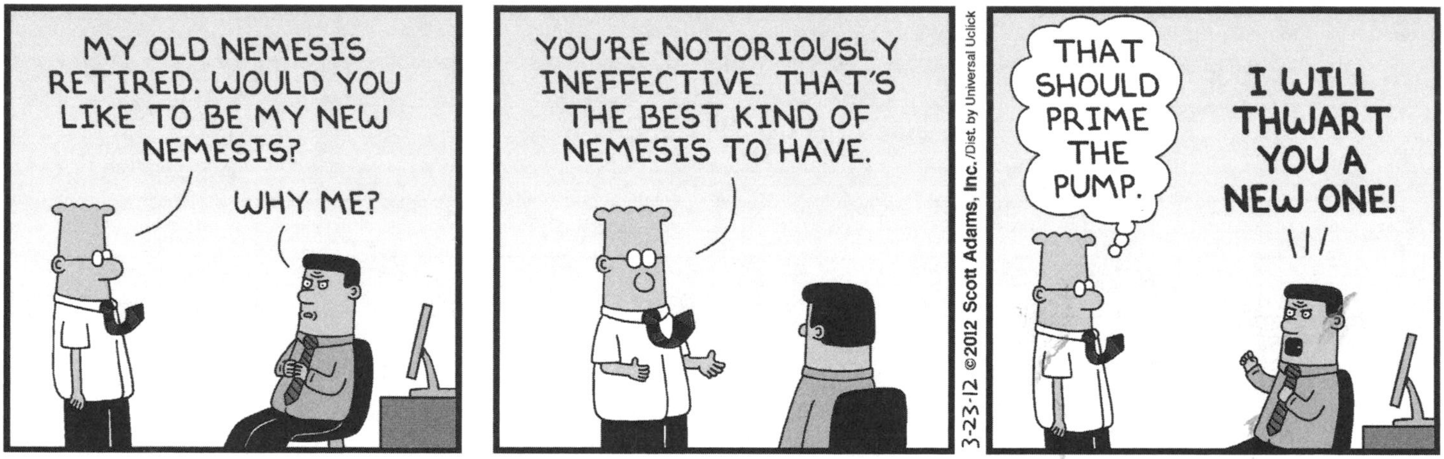
MY OLD NEMESIS RETIRED. WOULD YOU LIKE TO BE MY NEW NEMESIS?
WHY ME?
YOU'RE NOTORIOUSLY INEFFECTIVE. THAT'S THE BEST KIND OF NEMESIS TO HAVE.
3-23-12 ©2012 Scott Adams, Inc./Dist. by Universal Uclick
THAT SHOULD PRIME THE PUMP.
I WILL THWART YOU A NEW ONE!

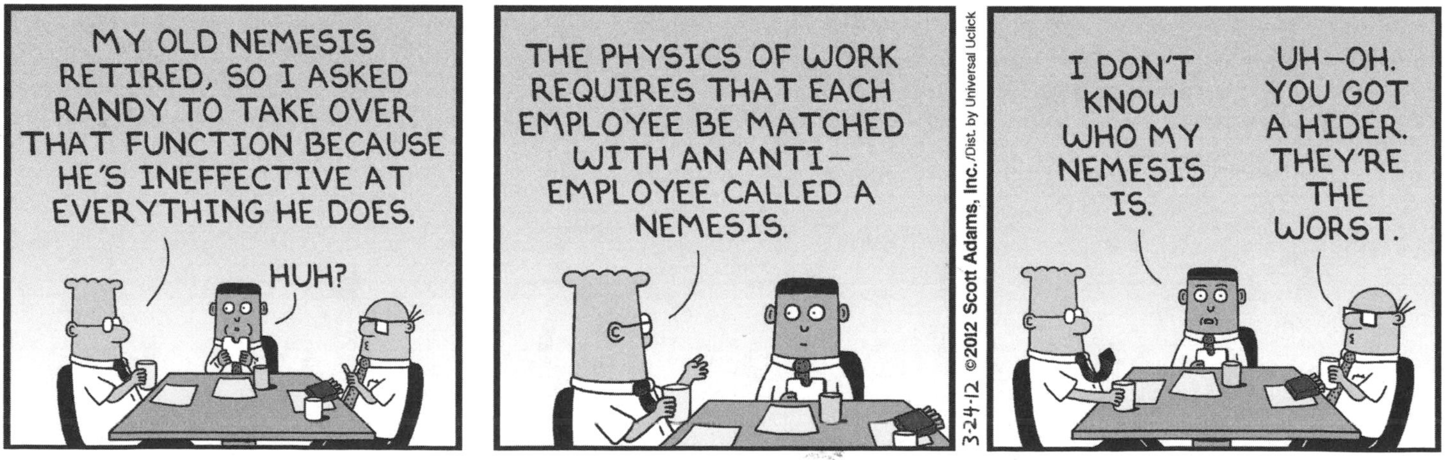
MY OLD NEMESIS RETIRED, SO I ASKED RANDY TO TAKE OVER THAT FUNCTION BECAUSE HE'S INEFFECTIVE AT EVERYTHING HE DOES.
HUH?
THE PHYSICS OF WORK REQUIRES THAT EACH EMPLOYEE BE MATCHED WITH AN ANTI-EMPLOYEE CALLED A NEMESIS.
3-24-12 ©2012 Scott Adams, Inc./Dist. by Universal Uclick
I DON'T KNOW WHO MY NEMESIS IS.
UH-OH. YOU GOT A HIDER. THEY'RE THE WORST.

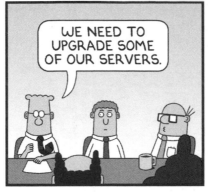

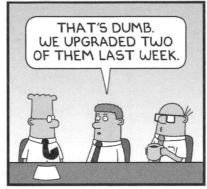

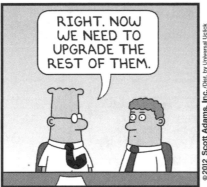

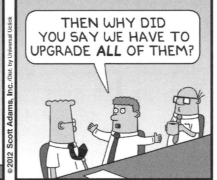

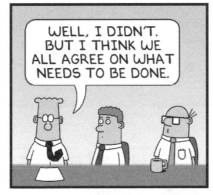

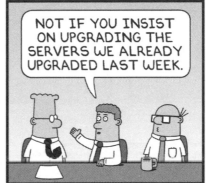

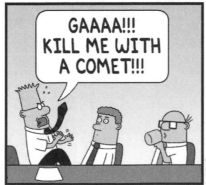

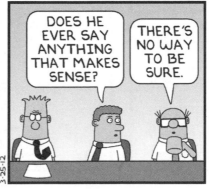

WE NEED TO UPGRADE SOME OF OUR SERVERS.
THAT'S DUMB. WE UPGRADED TWO OF THEM LAST WEEK.
RIGHT. NOW WE NEED TO UPGRADE THE REST OF THEM.
THEN WHY DID YOU SAY WE HAVE TO UPGRADE **ALL** OF THEM?
WELL, I DIDN'T. BUT I THINK WE ALL AGREE ON WHAT NEEDS TO BE DONE.
NOT IF YOU INSIST ON UPGRADING THE SERVERS WE ALREADY UPGRADED LAST WEEK.
GAAAA!!! KILL ME WITH A COMET!!!
DOES HE EVER SAY ANYTHING THAT MAKES SENSE?
THERE'S NO WAY TO BE SURE.
© 2012 Scott Adams, Inc./Dist. by Universal Uclick
3-25-12

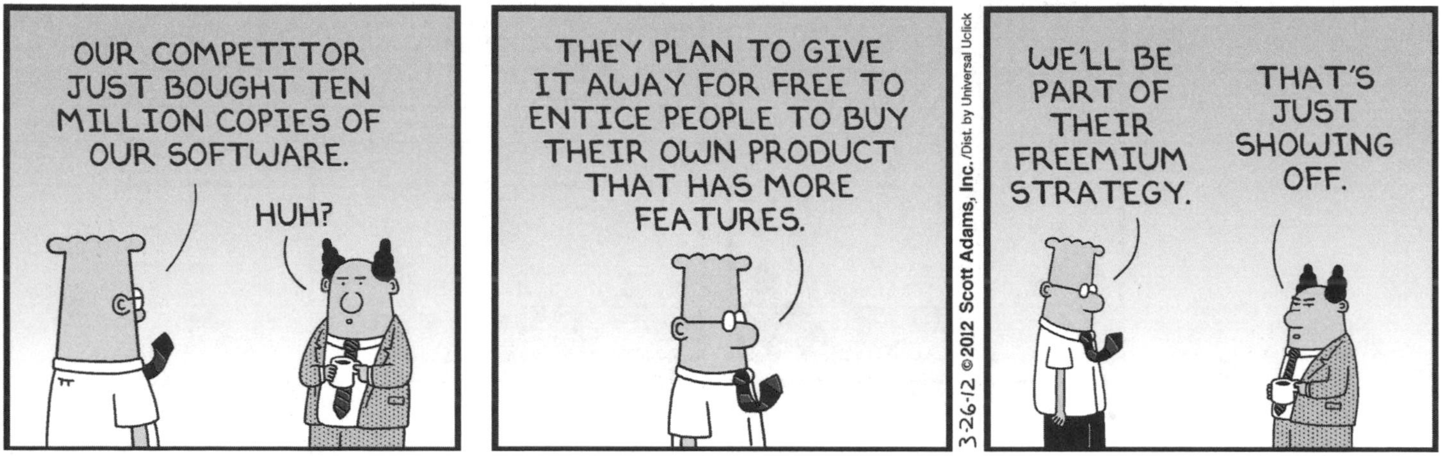
OUR COMPETITOR JUST BOUGHT TEN MILLION COPIES OF OUR SOFTWARE.
HUH?
THEY PLAN TO GIVE IT AWAY FOR FREE TO ENTICE PEOPLE TO BUY THEIR OWN PRODUCT THAT HAS MORE FEATURES.
3-26-12 ©2012 Scott Adams, Inc./Dist. by Universal Uclick
WE'LL BE PART OF THEIR FREEMIUM STRATEGY.
THAT'S JUST SHOWING OFF.

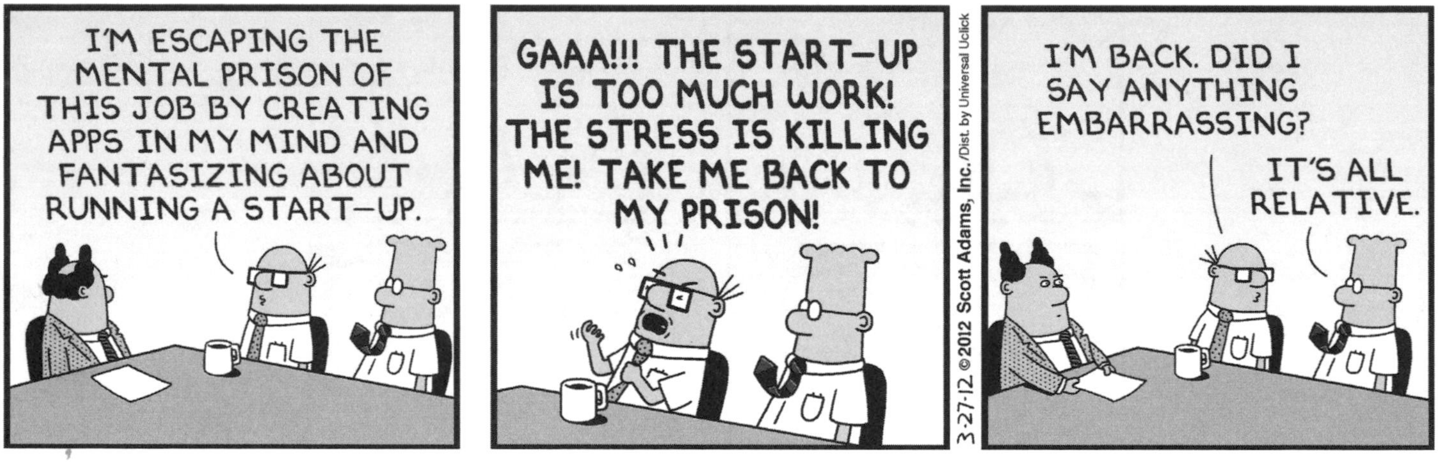
I'M ESCAPING THE MENTAL PRISON OF THIS JOB BY CREATING APPS IN MY MIND AND FANTASIZING ABOUT RUNNING A START-UP.
GAAA!!! THE START-UP IS TOO MUCH WORK! THE STRESS IS KILLING ME! TAKE ME BACK TO MY PRISON!
3-27-12 ©2012 Scott Adams, Inc./Dist. by Universal Uclick
I'M BACK. DID I SAY ANYTHING EMBARRASSING?
IT'S ALL RELATIVE.

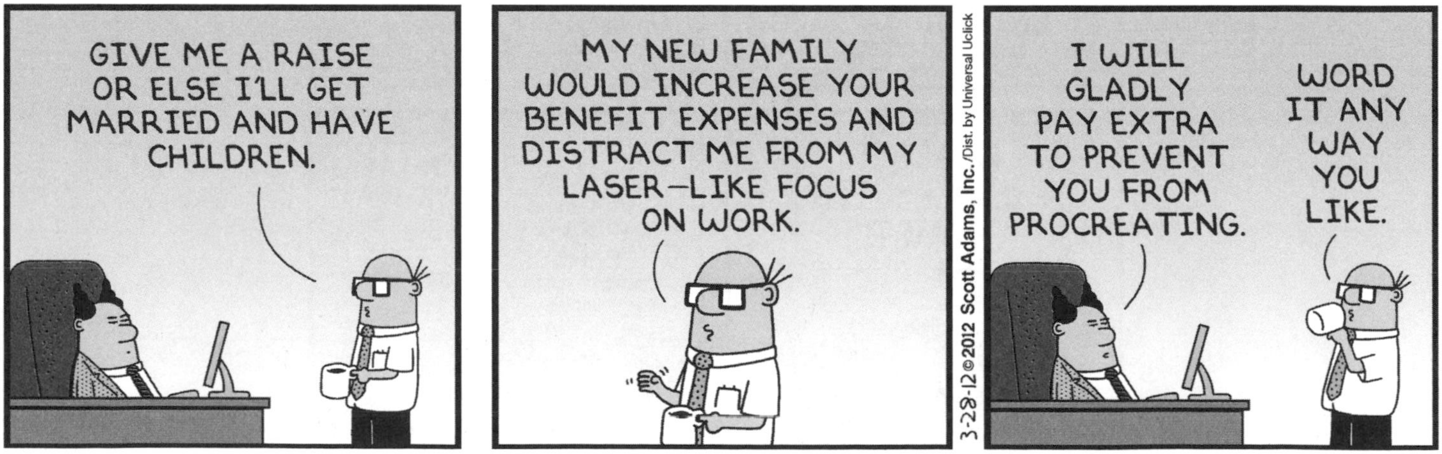
GIVE ME A RAISE OR ELSE I'LL GET MARRIED AND HAVE CHILDREN.
MY NEW FAMILY WOULD INCREASE YOUR BENEFIT EXPENSES AND DISTRACT ME FROM MY LASER-LIKE FOCUS ON WORK.
3-28-12 ©2012 Scott Adams, Inc./Dist. by Universal Uclick
I WILL GLADLY PAY EXTRA TO PREVENT YOU FROM PROCREATING.
WORD IT ANY WAY YOU LIKE.

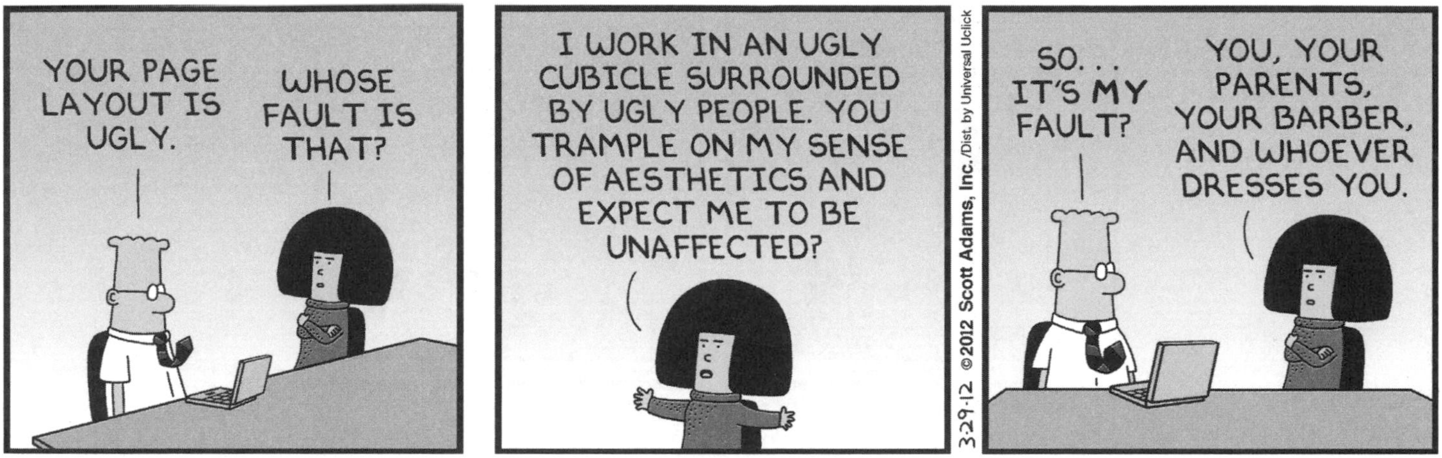
YOUR PAGE LAYOUT IS UGLY.
WHOSE FAULT IS THAT?
I WORK IN AN UGLY CUBICLE SURROUNDED BY UGLY PEOPLE. YOU TRAMPLE ON MY SENSE OF AESTHETICS AND EXPECT ME TO BE UNAFFECTED?
3·29·12 ©2012 Scott Adams, Inc./Dist. by Universal Uclick
SO... IT'S MY FAULT?
YOU, YOUR PARENTS, YOUR BARBER, AND WHOEVER DRESSES YOU.

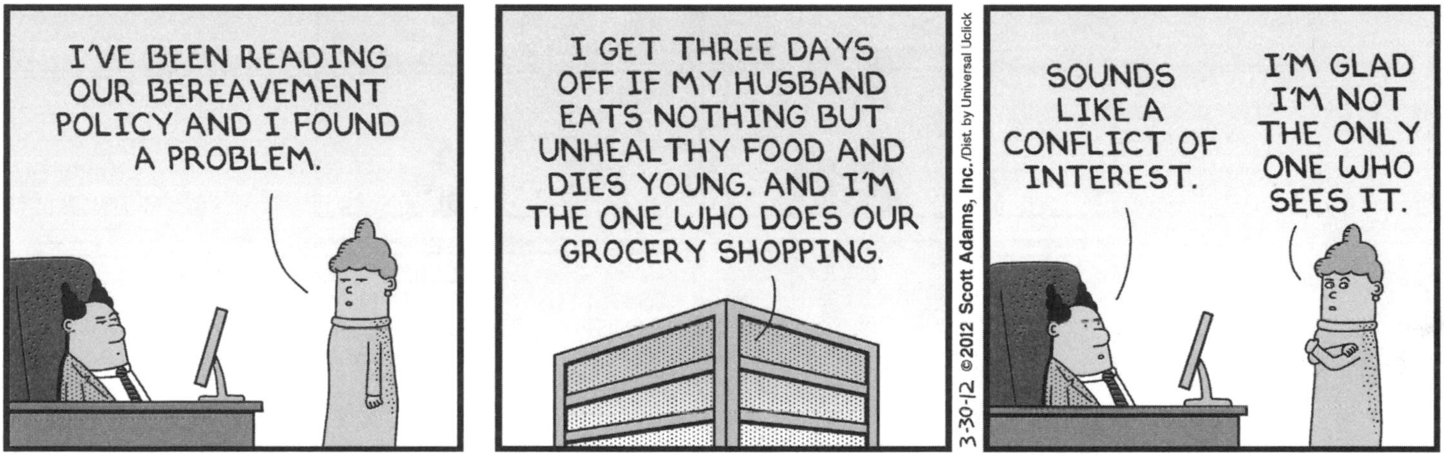
I'VE BEEN READING OUR BEREAVEMENT POLICY AND I FOUND A PROBLEM.
I GET THREE DAYS OFF IF MY HUSBAND EATS NOTHING BUT UNHEALTHY FOOD AND DIES YOUNG. AND I'M THE ONE WHO DOES OUR GROCERY SHOPPING.
3·30·12 ©2012 Scott Adams, Inc./Dist. by Universal Uclick
SOUNDS LIKE A CONFLICT OF INTEREST.
I'M GLAD I'M NOT THE ONLY ONE WHO SEES IT.

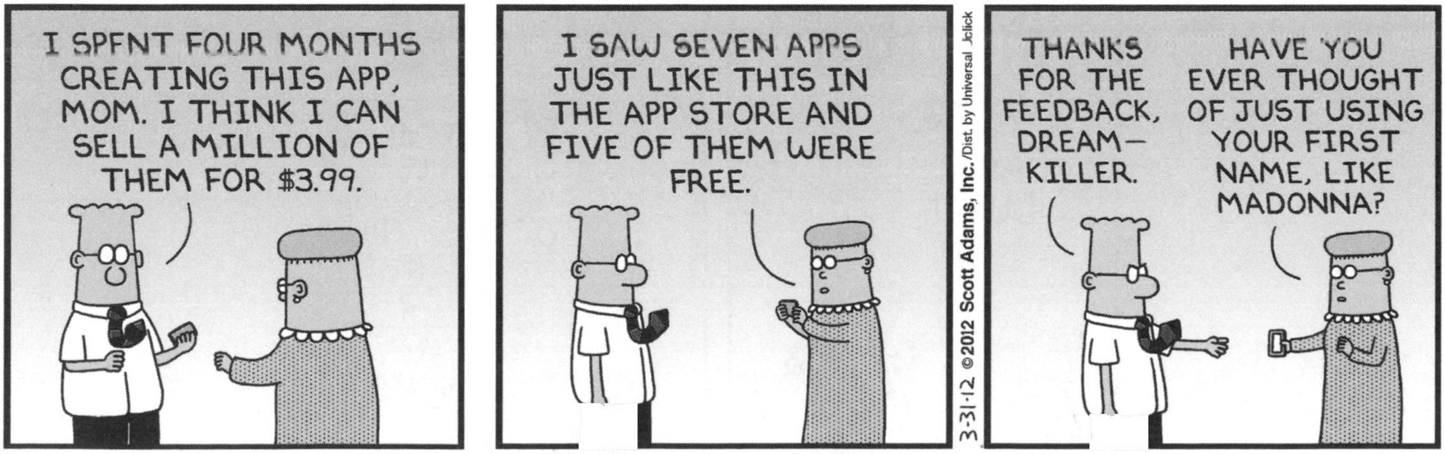
I SPENT FOUR MONTHS CREATING THIS APP, MOM. I THINK I CAN SELL A MILLION OF THEM FOR $3.99.
I SAW SEVEN APPS JUST LIKE THIS IN THE APP STORE AND FIVE OF THEM WERE FREE.
3·31·12 ©2012 Scott Adams, Inc./Dist. by Universal Uclick
THANKS FOR THE FEEDBACK, DREAM-KILLER.
HAVE YOU EVER THOUGHT OF JUST USING YOUR FIRST NAME, LIKE MADONNA?

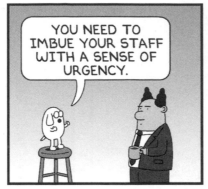

YOU NEED TO IMBUE YOUR STAFF WITH A SENSE OF URGENCY.
GAAA!!! OUR TECHNOLOGY PLATFORMS ARE OBSOLETE!
TRY IT AGAIN WITH LESS PANIC.
©2012 Scott Adams, Inc./Dist. by Universal Uclick
WE'RE DOOMED, AND YET, I AM NOT THE LEAST BIT WORRIED.
THAT ONE HAD A CREEPY VIBE.
A SENSE OF URGENCY IS HALFWAY BETWEEN BEING TOO FRIGHTENED TO ACT AND TOO DUMB TO KNOW WHAT TO DO.
GAAA!!! DUH!!!
4-1-12
YOU DIDN'T QUITE THREAD THE NEEDLE.
HERE COMES LEAD-ERSHIP!

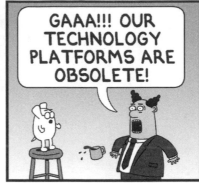

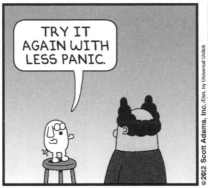

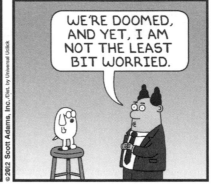

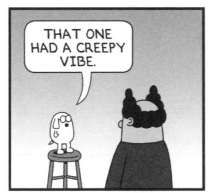

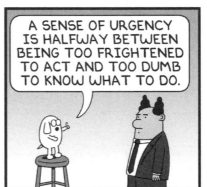

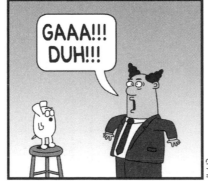

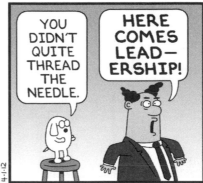

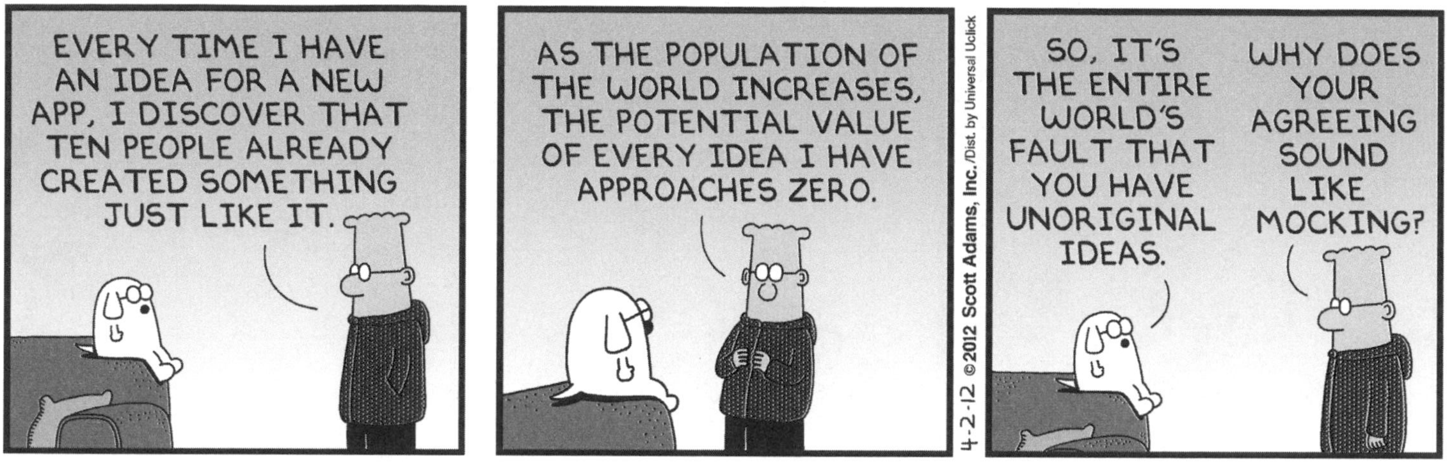
EVERY TIME I HAVE AN IDEA FOR A NEW APP, I DISCOVER THAT TEN PEOPLE ALREADY CREATED SOMETHING JUST LIKE IT.
AS THE POPULATION OF THE WORLD INCREASES, THE POTENTIAL VALUE OF EVERY IDEA I HAVE APPROACHES ZERO.
SO, IT'S THE ENTIRE WORLD'S FAULT THAT YOU HAVE UNORIGINAL IDEAS.
WHY DOES YOUR AGREEING SOUND LIKE MOCKING?
4-2-12

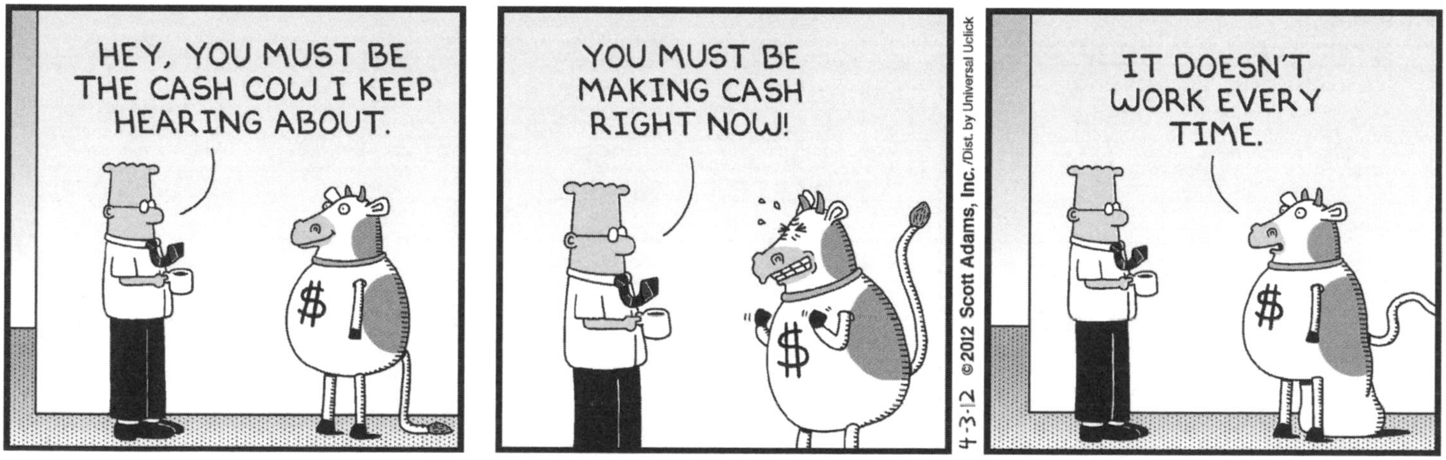
HEY, YOU MUST BE THE CASH COW I KEEP HEARING ABOUT.
$
YOU MUST BE MAKING CASH RIGHT NOW!
$
IT DOESN'T WORK EVERY TIME.
$
4-3-12

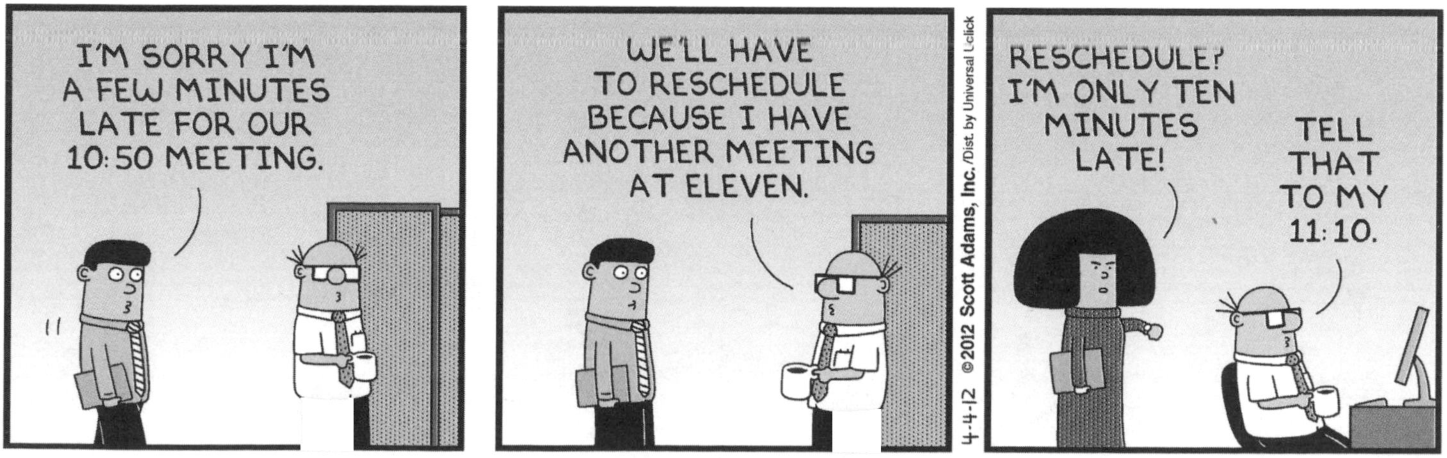
I'M SORRY I'M A FEW MINUTES LATE FOR OUR 10:50 MEETING.
WE'LL HAVE TO RESCHEDULE BECAUSE I HAVE ANOTHER MEETING AT ELEVEN.
RESCHEDULE? I'M ONLY TEN MINUTES LATE!
TELL THAT TO MY 11:10.
4-4-12

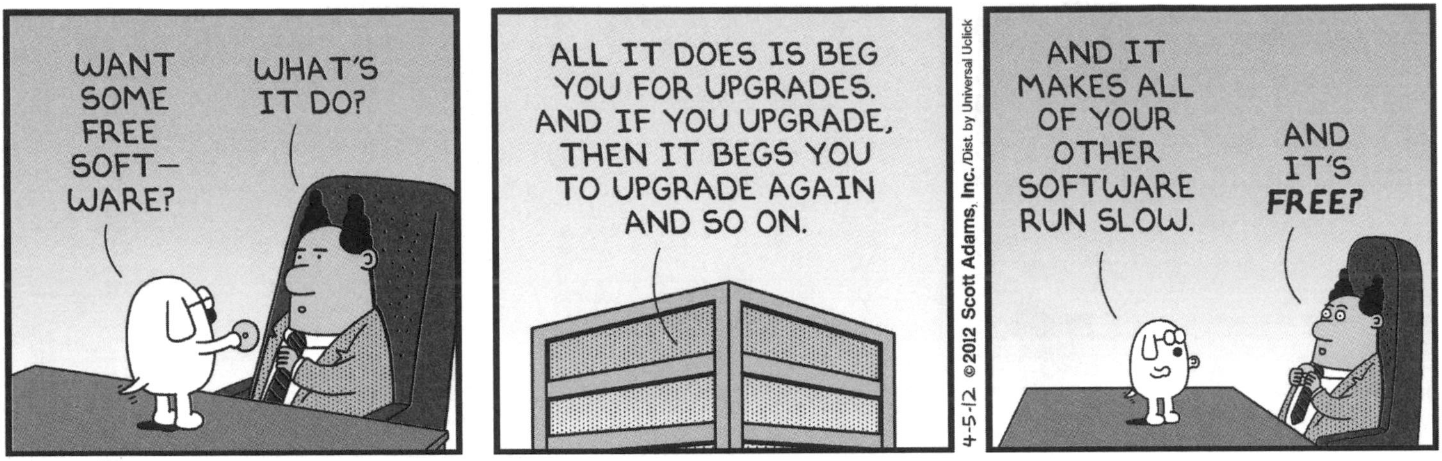
WANT SOME FREE SOFT-WARE?
WHAT'S IT DO?
ALL IT DOES IS BEG YOU FOR UPGRADES. AND IF YOU UPGRADE, THEN IT BEGS YOU TO UPGRADE AGAIN AND SO ON.
4-5-12 ©2012 Scott Adams, Inc./Dist. by Universal Uclick
AND IT MAKES ALL OF YOUR OTHER SOFTWARE RUN SLOW.
AND IT'S FREE?

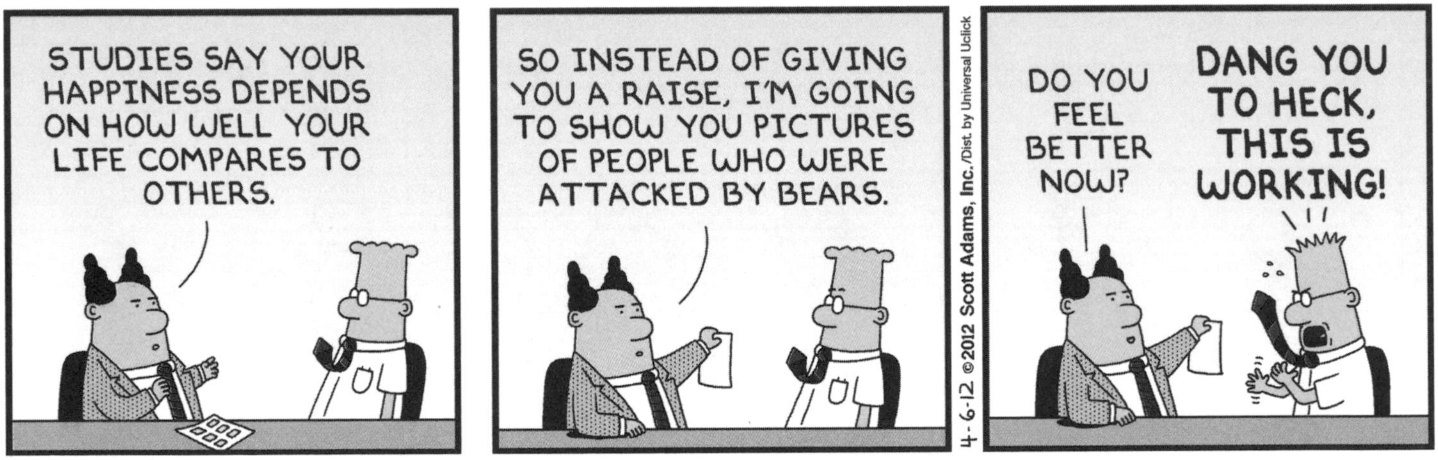
STUDIES SAY YOUR HAPPINESS DEPENDS ON HOW WELL YOUR LIFE COMPARES TO OTHERS.
SO INSTEAD OF GIVING YOU A RAISE, I'M GOING TO SHOW YOU PICTURES OF PEOPLE WHO WERE ATTACKED BY BEARS.
4-6-12 ©2012 Scott Adams, Inc./Dist. by Universal Uclick
DO YOU FEEL BETTER NOW?
DANG YOU TO HECK, THIS IS WORKING!

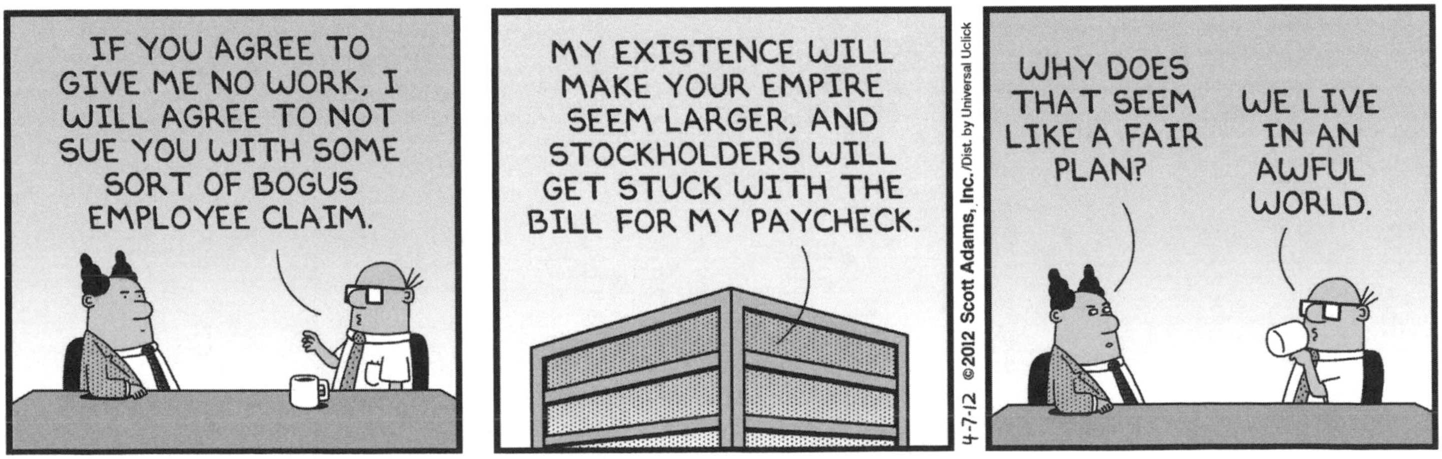
IF YOU AGREE TO GIVE ME NO WORK, I WILL AGREE TO NOT SUE YOU WITH SOME SORT OF BOGUS EMPLOYEE CLAIM.
MY EXISTENCE WILL MAKE YOUR EMPIRE SEEM LARGER, AND STOCKHOLDERS WILL GET STUCK WITH THE BILL FOR MY PAYCHECK.
4-7-12 ©2012 Scott Adams, Inc./Dist. by Universal Uclick
WHY DOES THAT SEEM LIKE A FAIR PLAN?
WE LIVE IN AN AWFUL WORLD.

WALLY, DO YOU WANT TO GO TO LUNCH?
NO, THANKS. I'M A DIGISEXUAL NOW.
WHAT?
I'M NO LONGER ATTRACTED TO PEOPLE.
I ONLY LIKE TECHNOLOGY.
PEOPLE CREEP ME OUT. YOU'RE BASICALLY A DELIVERY SYSTEM FOR VIRUSES, GERMS, AND UNREASONABLE FAVOR REQUESTS.
I'M WILLING TO TAKE A PICTURE OF YOU, BUT THAT'S AS FAR AS I'LL GO.
THIS IS THE MOST DISTURBING CONVERSATION I'VE EVER HAD.
CLICK
THANK GOODNESS FOR PHOTOSHOP.
©2012 Scott Adams, Inc./Dist. by Universal Uclick
4-8-12

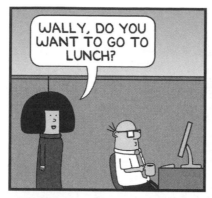

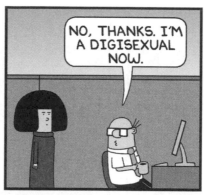

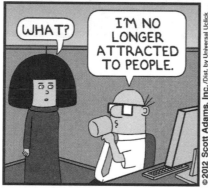

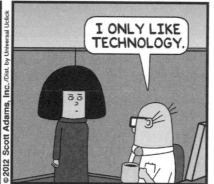

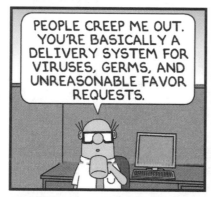

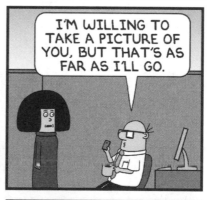

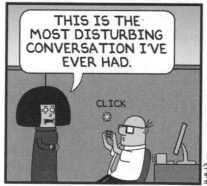

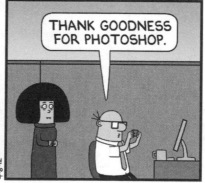

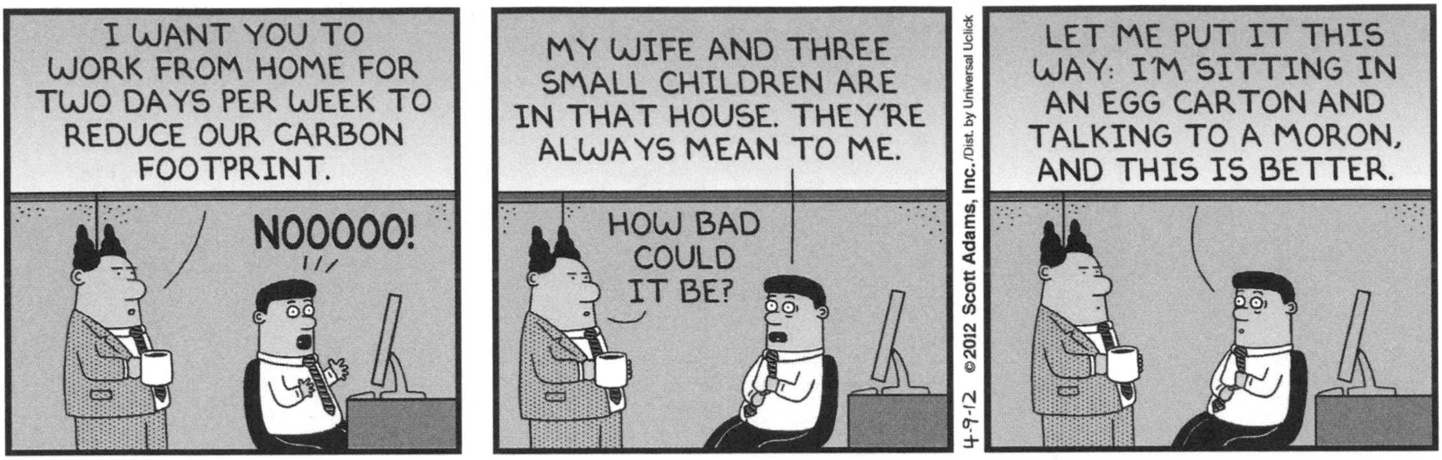
I WANT YOU TO WORK FROM HOME FOR TWO DAYS PER WEEK TO REDUCE OUR CARBON FOOTPRINT.
NOOOOO!
MY WIFE AND THREE SMALL CHILDREN ARE IN THAT HOUSE. THEY'RE ALWAYS MEAN TO ME.
HOW BAD COULD IT BE?
LET ME PUT IT THIS WAY: I'M SITTING IN AN EGG CARTON AND TALKING TO A MORON, AND THIS IS BETTER.
4-9-12 ©2012 Scott Adams, Inc./Dist. by Universal Uclick

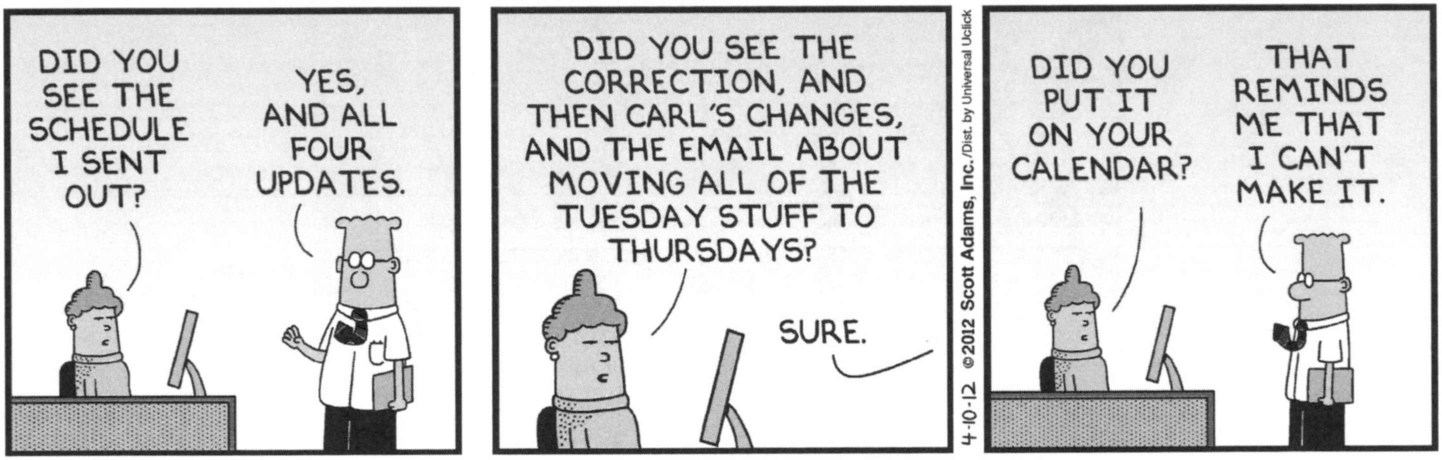
DID YOU SEE THE SCHEDULE I SENT OUT?
YES, AND ALL FOUR UPDATES.
DID YOU SEE THE CORRECTION, AND THEN CARL'S CHANGES, AND THE EMAIL ABOUT MOVING ALL OF THE TUESDAY STUFF TO THURSDAYS?
SURE.
DID YOU PUT IT ON YOUR CALENDAR?
THAT REMINDS ME THAT I CAN'T MAKE IT.
4-10-12 ©2012 Scott Adams, Inc./Dist. by Universal Uclick

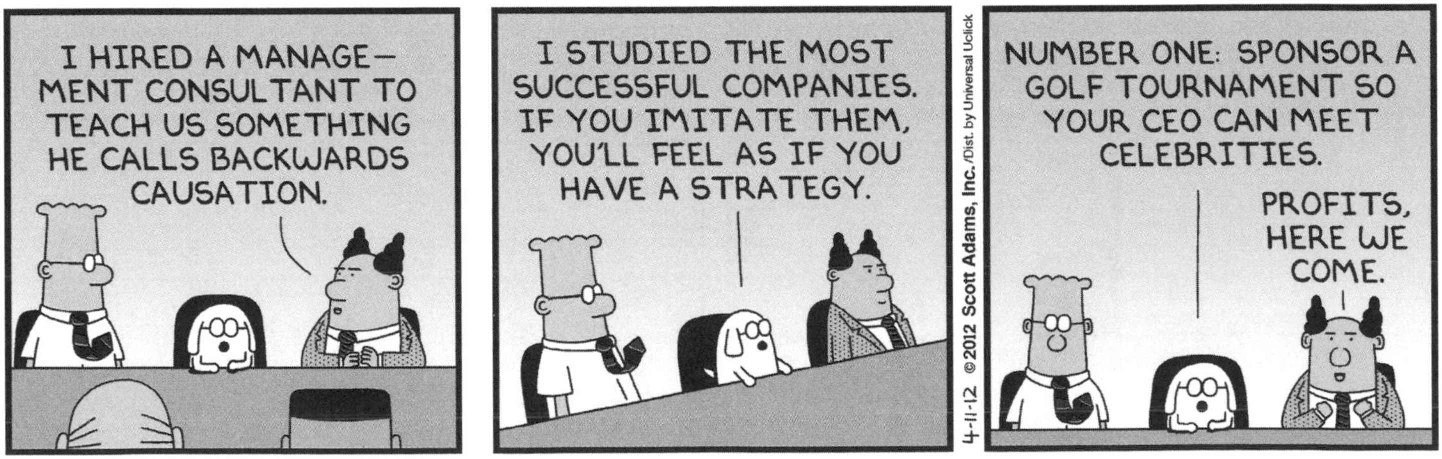
I HIRED A MANAGE-MENT CONSULTANT TO TEACH US SOMETHING HE CALLS BACKWARDS CAUSATION.
I STUDIED THE MOST SUCCESSFUL COMPANIES. IF YOU IMITATE THEM, YOU'LL FEEL AS IF YOU HAVE A STRATEGY.
NUMBER ONE: SPONSOR A GOLF TOURNAMENT SO YOUR CEO CAN MEET CELEBRITIES.
PROFITS, HERE WE COME.
4-11-12 ©2012 Scott Adams, Inc./Dist. by Universal Uclick

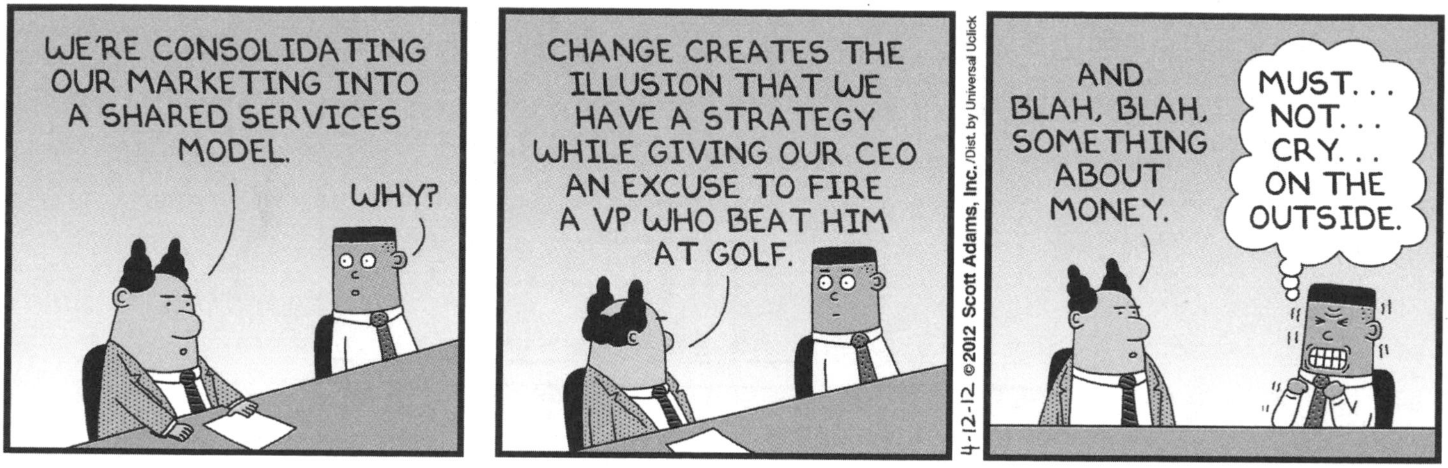
WE'RE CONSOLIDATING OUR MARKETING INTO A SHARED SERVICES MODEL.
WHY?
CHANGE CREATES THE ILLUSION THAT WE HAVE A STRATEGY WHILE GIVING OUR CEO AN EXCUSE TO FIRE A VP WHO BEAT HIM AT GOLF.
4-12-12 ©2012 Scott Adams, Inc./Dist. by Universal Uclick
AND BLAH, BLAH, SOMETHING ABOUT MONEY.
MUST... NOT... CRY... ON THE OUTSIDE.

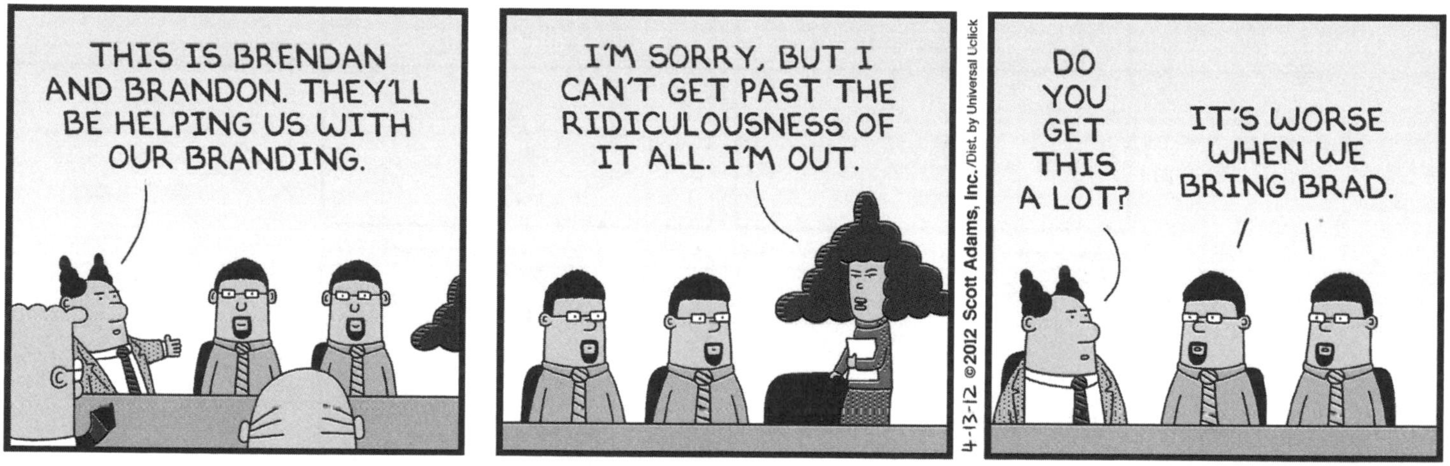
THIS IS BRENDAN AND BRANDON. THEY'LL BE HELPING US WITH OUR BRANDING.
I'M SORRY, BUT I CAN'T GET PAST THE RIDICULOUSNESS OF IT ALL. I'M OUT.
4-13-12 ©2012 Scott Adams, Inc./Dist. by Universal Uclick
DO YOU GET THIS A LOT?
IT'S WORSE WHEN WE BRING BRAD.

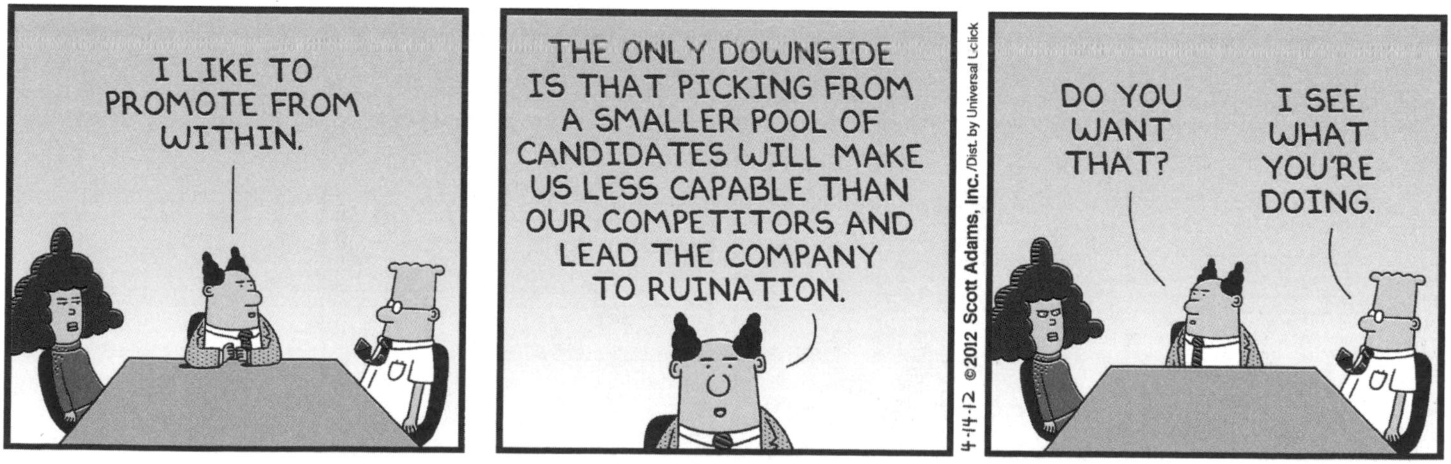
I LIKE TO PROMOTE FROM WITHIN.
THE ONLY DOWNSIDE IS THAT PICKING FROM A SMALLER POOL OF CANDIDATES WILL MAKE US LESS CAPABLE THAN OUR COMPETITORS AND LEAD THE COMPANY TO RUINATION.
4-14-12 ©2012 Scott Adams, Inc./Dist. by Universal Uclick
DO YOU WANT THAT?
I SEE WHAT YOU'RE DOING.

I DID A STUDY OF OUR PAST BUSINESS PLANS AND FOUND SOMETHING.
THERE'S NO CORRELATION BETWEEN OUR PREDICTED AND ACTUAL OUTCOMES.
THAT MIGHT BE A PROBLEM FOR YOU.
YOUR ENORMOUS CEO COMPENSATION IS BASED ON THE MYTH THAT YOU HAVE SOME CONTROL OVER OUR PROFITABILITY.
HA!
CLICK
HA!
IS IT JUST ME, OR IS THIS AWKWARD?
NO, I'M FEELING IT TOO.
©2012 Scott Adams, Inc./Dist. by Universal Uclick
4-15-12

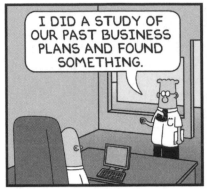

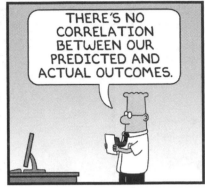

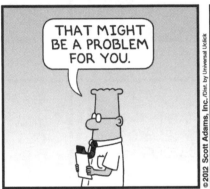

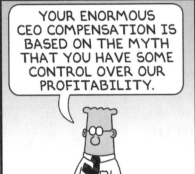

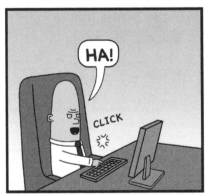

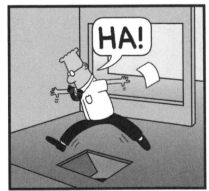

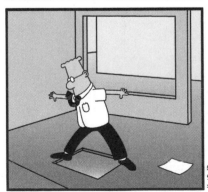

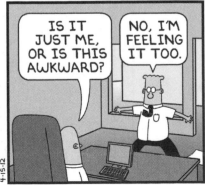

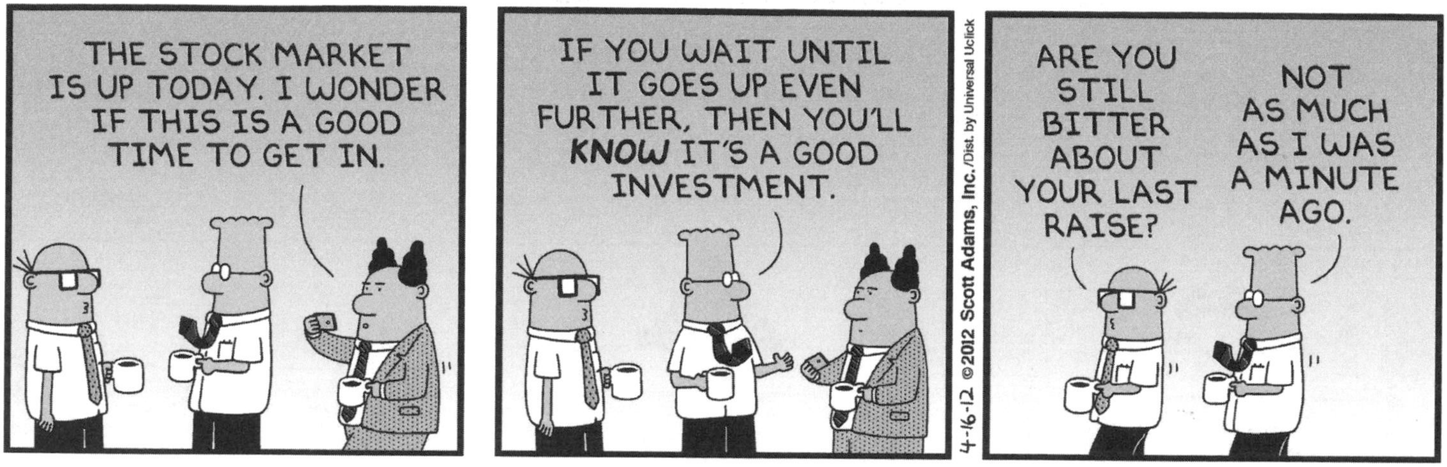
THE STOCK MARKET IS UP TODAY. I WONDER IF THIS IS A GOOD TIME TO GET IN.
IF YOU WAIT UNTIL IT GOES UP EVEN FURTHER, THEN YOU'LL *KNOW* IT'S A GOOD INVESTMENT.
4-16-12 ©2012 Scott Adams, Inc./Dist. by Universal Uclick
ARE YOU STILL BITTER ABOUT YOUR LAST RAISE?
NOT AS MUCH AS I WAS A MINUTE AGO.

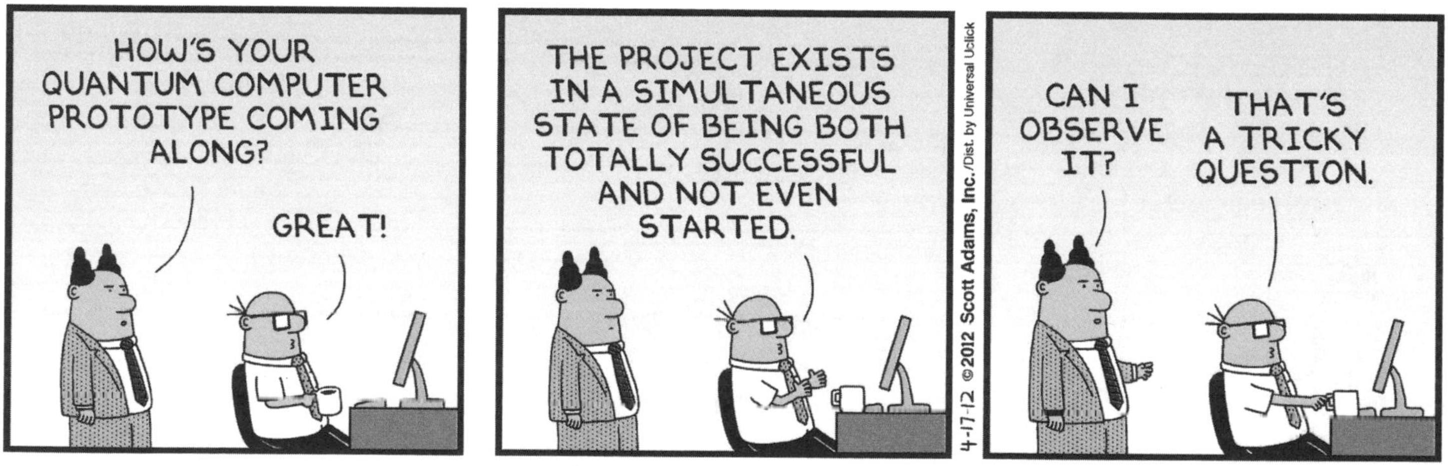
HOW'S YOUR QUANTUM COMPUTER PROTOTYPE COMING ALONG?
GREAT!
THE PROJECT EXISTS IN A SIMULTANEOUS STATE OF BEING BOTH TOTALLY SUCCESSFUL AND NOT EVEN STARTED.
4-17-12 ©2012 Scott Adams, Inc./Dist. by Universal Uclick
CAN I OBSERVE IT?
THAT'S A TRICKY QUESTION.

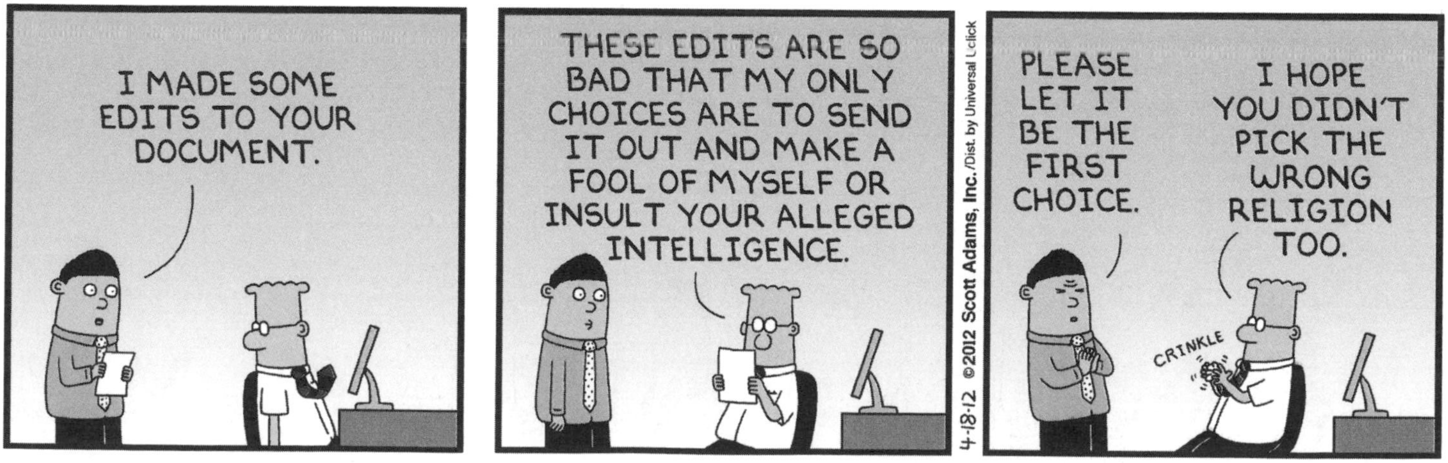
I MADE SOME EDITS TO YOUR DOCUMENT.
THESE EDITS ARE SO BAD THAT MY ONLY CHOICES ARE TO SEND IT OUT AND MAKE A FOOL OF MYSELF OR INSULT YOUR ALLEGED INTELLIGENCE.
4-18-12 ©2012 Scott Adams, Inc./Dist. by Universal Uclick
PLEASE LET IT BE THE FIRST CHOICE.
I HOPE YOU DIDN'T PICK THE WRONG RELIGION TOO.
CRINKLE

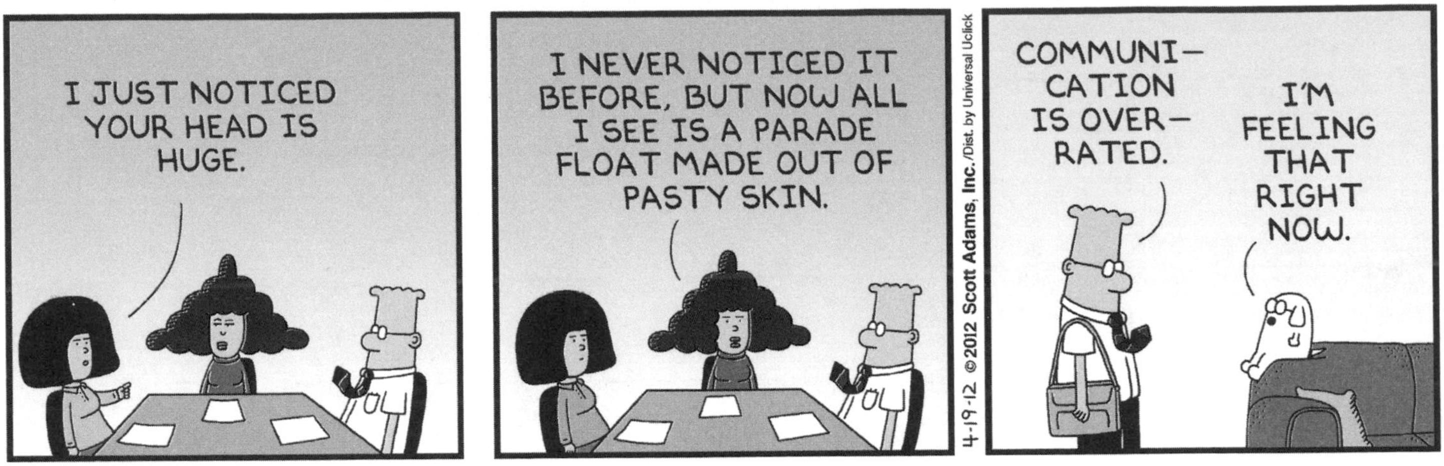
I JUST NOTICED YOUR HEAD IS HUGE.
I NEVER NOTICED IT BEFORE, BUT NOW ALL I SEE IS A PARADE FLOAT MADE OUT OF PASTY SKIN.
4-19-12 ©2012 Scott Adams, Inc./Dist. by Universal Uclick
COMMUNI-CATION IS OVER-RATED.
I'M FEELING THAT RIGHT NOW.

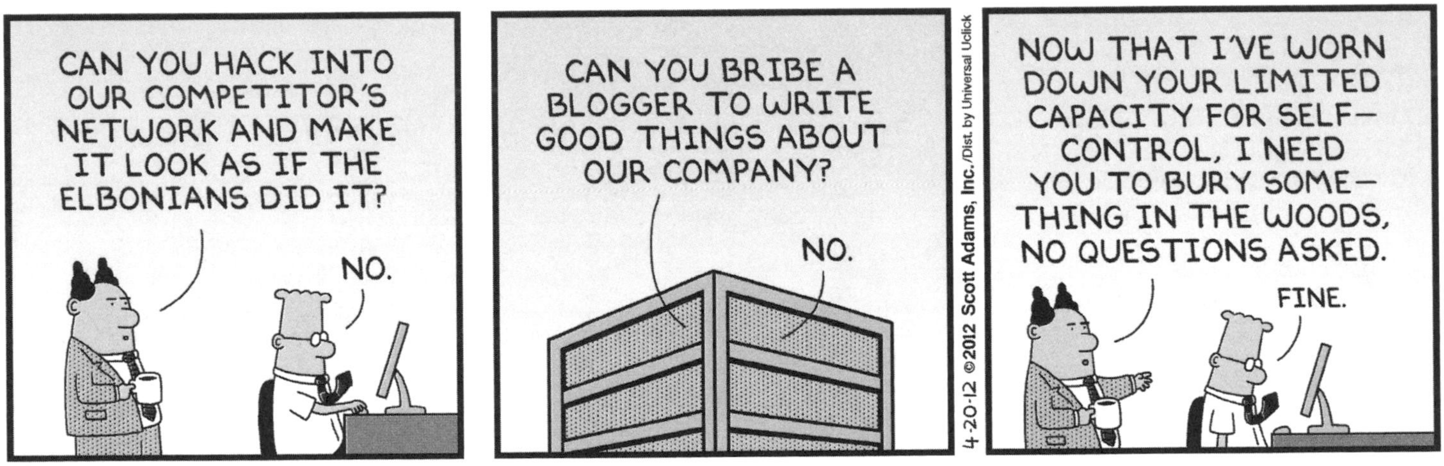
CAN YOU HACK INTO OUR COMPETITOR'S NETWORK AND MAKE IT LOOK AS IF THE ELBONIANS DID IT?
NO.
CAN YOU BRIBE A BLOGGER TO WRITE GOOD THINGS ABOUT OUR COMPANY?
NO.
4-20-12 ©2012 Scott Adams, Inc./Dist. by Universal Uclick
NOW THAT I'VE WORN DOWN YOUR LIMITED CAPACITY FOR SELF-CONTROL, I NEED YOU TO BURY SOME-THING IN THE WOODS, NO QUESTIONS ASKED.
FINE.

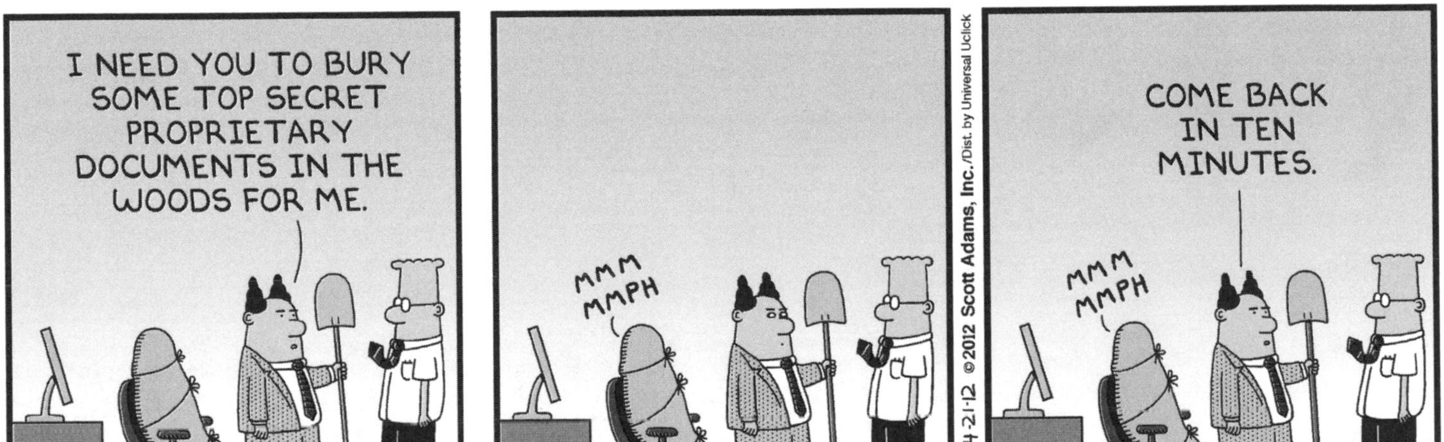
I NEED YOU TO BURY SOME TOP SECRET PROPRIETARY DOCUMENTS IN THE WOODS FOR ME.
MMM MMPH
4-21-12 ©2012 Scott Adams, Inc./Dist. by Universal Uclick
MMM MMPH
COME BACK IN TEN MINUTES.

ANY COMMENTS ON THE PROJECT PLAN?

WHEN YOU CONSIDER ALL OF THE TASKS TOGETHER, THEY FORM A RATIONAL PLAN.

BUT OUR INDIVIDUAL TASKS ARE SO FAR REMOVED FROM THE BIG PICTURE THAT THEY ARE STRIPPED OF MEANING.

YOU'VE MANAGED TO REMOVE ALL SENSE OF PURPOSE FROM MY LIFE.

ON AN INTELLECTUAL LEVEL, I UNDERSTAND THE BENEFITS OF BREAKING TASKS INTO SMALL CHUNKS.

BUT YOU'VE LEFT ME EMOTIONALLY GUTTED. AS I READ YOUR PLAN, I'M LOSING MY WILL TO LIVE.

CAN'T YOU FIND MEANING IN YOUR PERSONAL LIFE?

HE'S AN ENGINEER.

NOW YOU'RE JUST BEING A JERK.

© 2012 Scott Adams, Inc./Dist. by Universal Uclick

4-2-12

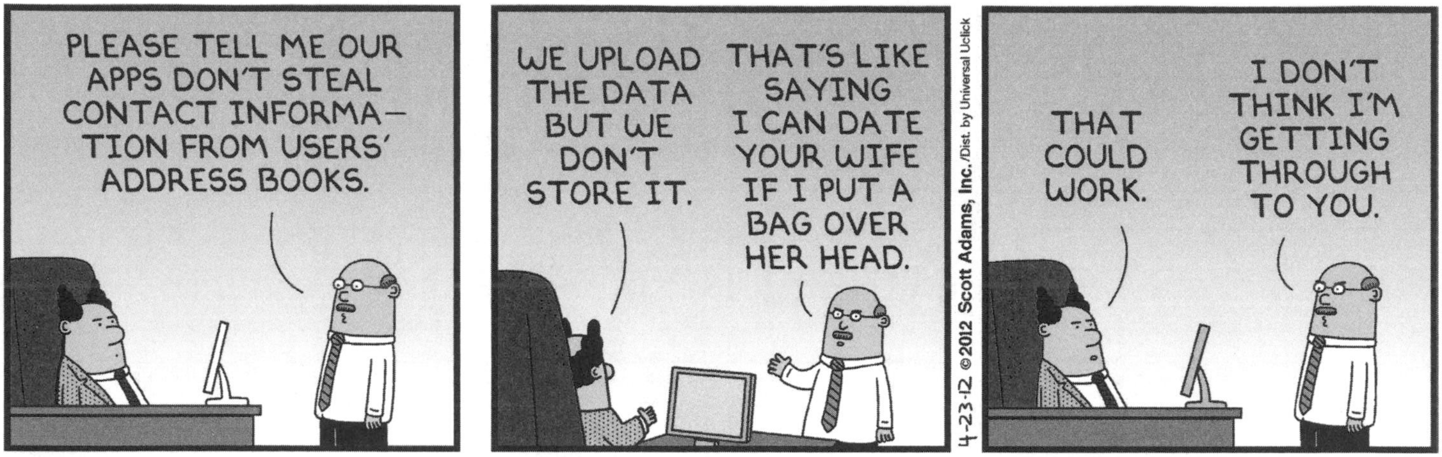
PLEASE TELL ME OUR APPS DON'T STEAL CONTACT INFORMATION FROM USERS' ADDRESS BOOKS.
WE UPLOAD THE DATA BUT WE DON'T STORE IT.
THAT'S LIKE SAYING I CAN DATE YOUR WIFE IF I PUT A BAG OVER HER HEAD.
4-23-12 ©2012 Scott Adams, Inc./Dist. by Universal Uclick
THAT COULD WORK.
I DON'T THINK I'M GETTING THROUGH TO YOU.

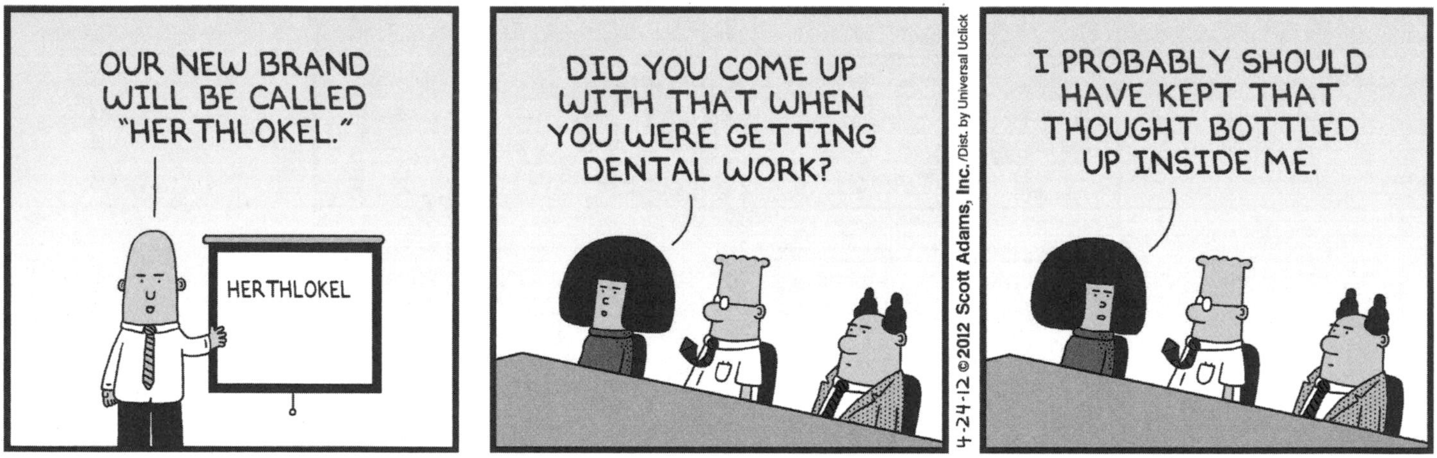
OUR NEW BRAND WILL BE CALLED "HERTHLOKEL."
HERTHLOKEL
DID YOU COME UP WITH THAT WHEN YOU WERE GETTING DENTAL WORK?
4-24-12 ©2012 Scott Adams, Inc./Dist. by Universal Uclick
I PROBABLY SHOULD HAVE KEPT THAT THOUGHT BOTTLED UP INSIDE ME.

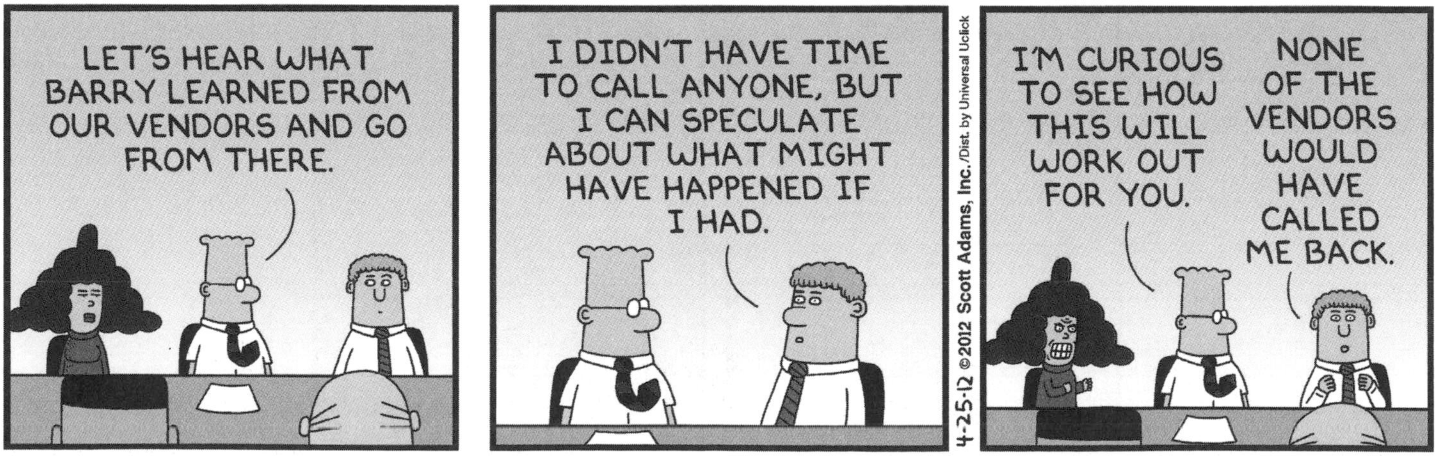
LET'S HEAR WHAT BARRY LEARNED FROM OUR VENDORS AND GO FROM THERE.
I DIDN'T HAVE TIME TO CALL ANYONE, BUT I CAN SPECULATE ABOUT WHAT MIGHT HAVE HAPPENED IF I HAD.
4-25-12 ©2012 Scott Adams, Inc./Dist. by Universal Uclick
I'M CURIOUS TO SEE HOW THIS WILL WORK OUT FOR YOU.
NONE OF THE VENDORS WOULD HAVE CALLED ME BACK.

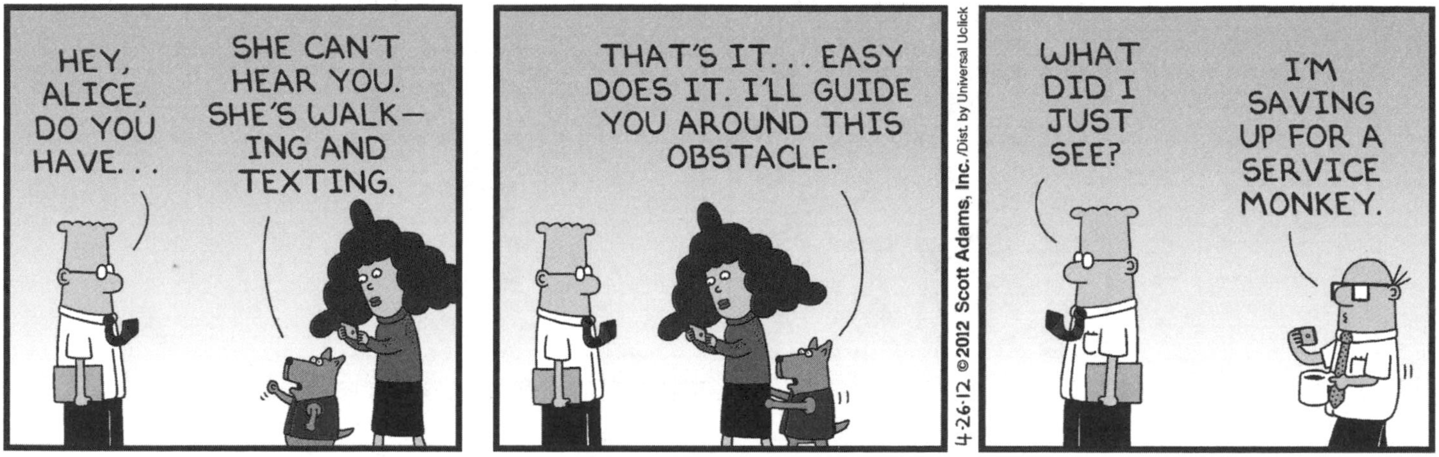
HEY, ALICE, DO YOU HAVE. . .
SHE CAN'T HEAR YOU. SHE'S WALK–ING AND TEXTING.
THAT'S IT. . . EASY DOES IT. I'LL GUIDE YOU AROUND THIS OBSTACLE.
4·26·12 ©2012 Scott Adams, Inc./Dist. by Universal Uclick
WHAT DID I JUST SEE?
I'M SAVING UP FOR A SERVICE MONKEY.

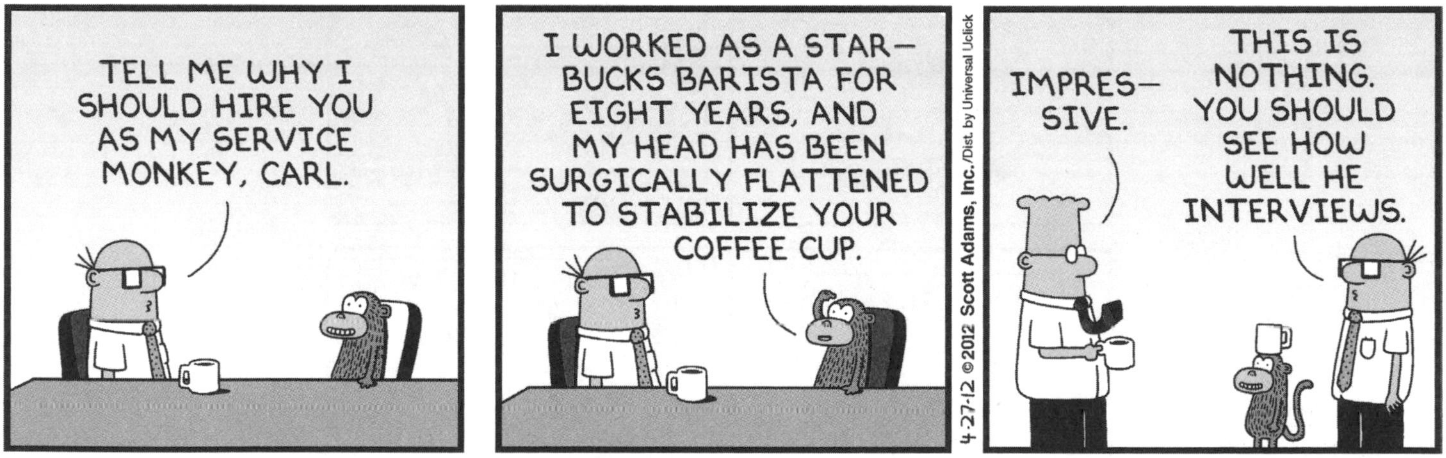
TELL ME WHY I SHOULD HIRE YOU AS MY SERVICE MONKEY, CARL.
I WORKED AS A STAR–BUCKS BARISTA FOR EIGHT YEARS, AND MY HEAD HAS BEEN SURGICALLY FLATTENED TO STABILIZE YOUR COFFEE CUP.
4·27·12 ©2012 Scott Adams, Inc./Dist. by Universal Uclick
IMPRES–SIVE.
THIS IS NOTHING. YOU SHOULD SEE HOW WELL HE INTERVIEWS.

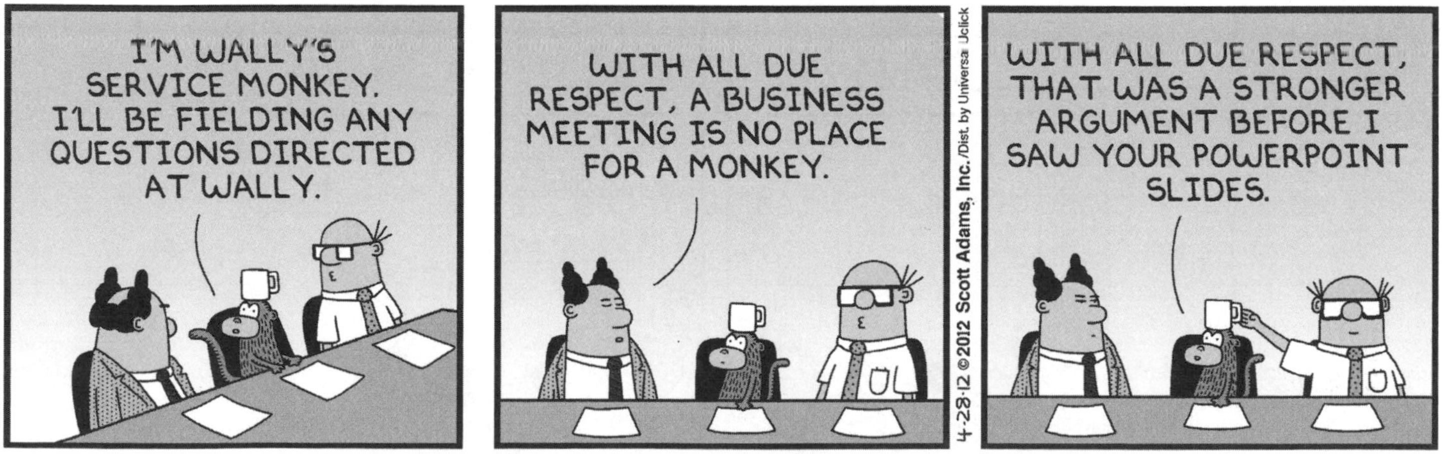
I'M WALLY'S SERVICE MONKEY. I'LL BE FIELDING ANY QUESTIONS DIRECTED AT WALLY.
WITH ALL DUE RESPECT, A BUSINESS MEETING IS NO PLACE FOR A MONKEY.
4·28·12 ©2012 Scott Adams, Inc./Dist. by Universal Uclick
WITH ALL DUE RESPECT, THAT WAS A STRONGER ARGUMENT BEFORE I SAW YOUR POWERPOINT SLIDES.

PEOPLE ALWAYS TRY TO TAKE ADVANTAGE OF ME.
I KNOW WHAT YOU MEAN.
I LOST FIVE POUNDS AND MY HUSBAND DIDN'T NOTICE!
I CAME HOME LAST NIGHT AND HE HADN'T EVEN CLEANED THE GARAGE LIKE HE PROMISED.
I HAD TO PARK ON THE STREET!
IS IT MY IMAGINA-TION, OR HAVE YOU FOUND A CLEVER WAY TO MAKE PEOPLE PAY TO LISTEN TO YOU COMPLAIN?
TELL ME MORE ABOUT HOW YOU THINK I'M CLEVER.
©2012 Scott Adams, Inc./Dist. by Universal Uclick
4-29-12

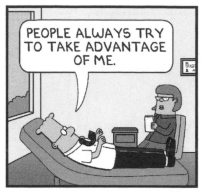

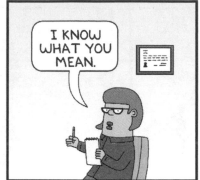

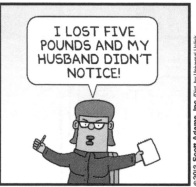

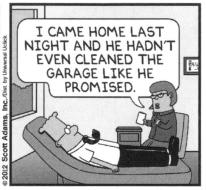

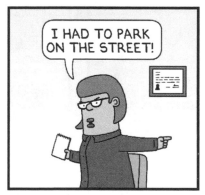

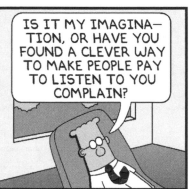

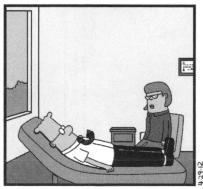

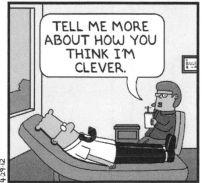

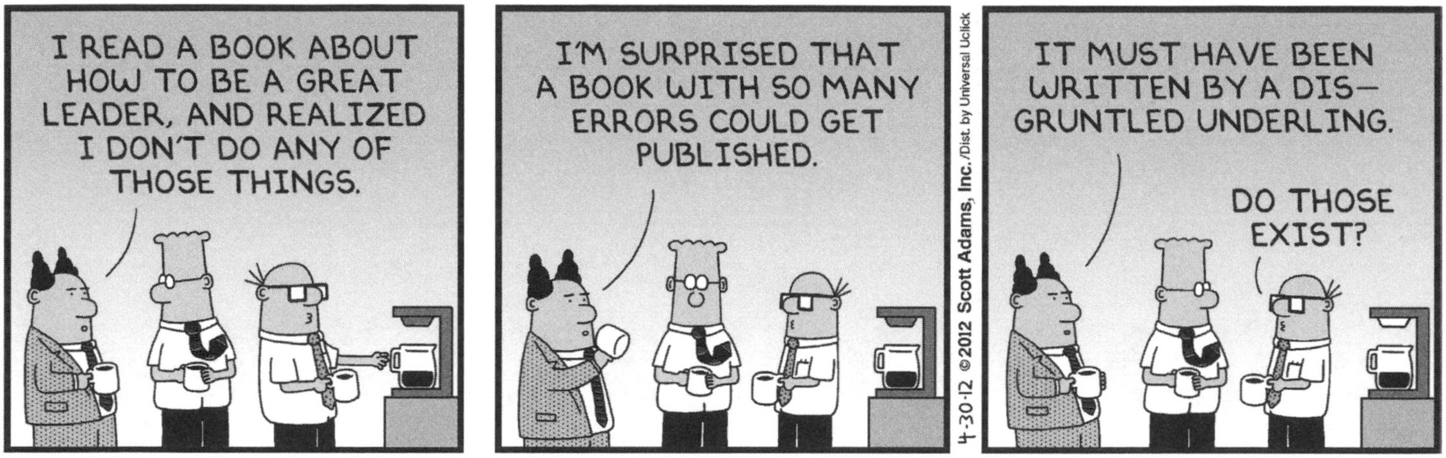
I READ A BOOK ABOUT HOW TO BE A GREAT LEADER, AND REALIZED I DON'T DO ANY OF THOSE THINGS.
I'M SURPRISED THAT A BOOK WITH SO MANY ERRORS COULD GET PUBLISHED.
4-30-12 ©2012 Scott Adams, Inc./Dist. by Universal Uclick
IT MUST HAVE BEEN WRITTEN BY A DIS-GRUNTLED UNDERLING.
DO THOSE EXIST?

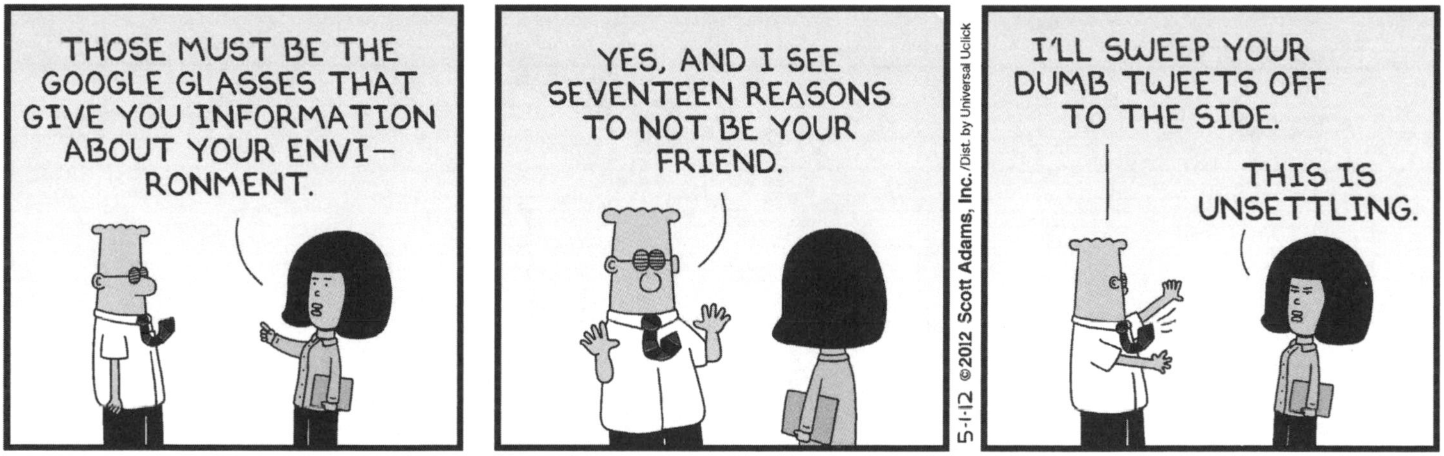
THOSE MUST BE THE GOOGLE GLASSES THAT GIVE YOU INFORMATION ABOUT YOUR ENVI-RONMENT.
YES, AND I SEE SEVENTEEN REASONS TO NOT BE YOUR FRIEND.
5-1-12 ©2012 Scott Adams, Inc./Dist. by Universal Uclick
I'LL SWEEP YOUR DUMB TWEETS OFF TO THE SIDE.
THIS IS UNSETTLING.

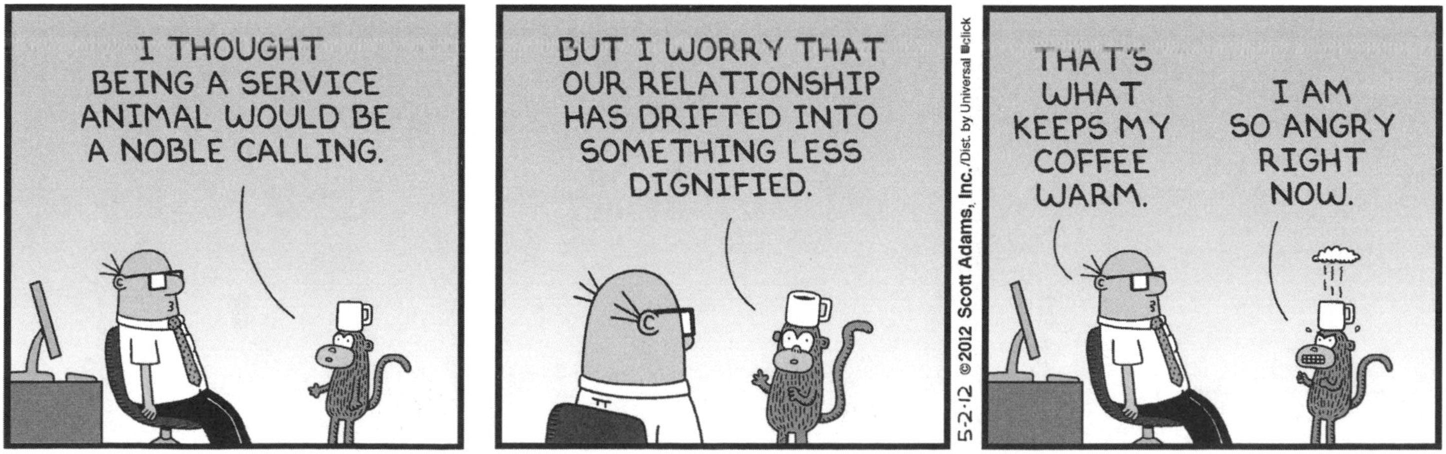
I THOUGHT BEING A SERVICE ANIMAL WOULD BE A NOBLE CALLING.
BUT I WORRY THAT OUR RELATIONSHIP HAS DRIFTED INTO SOMETHING LESS DIGNIFIED.
5-2-12 ©2012 Scott Adams, Inc./Dist. by Universal Uclick
THAT'S WHAT KEEPS MY COFFEE WARM.
I AM SO ANGRY RIGHT NOW.

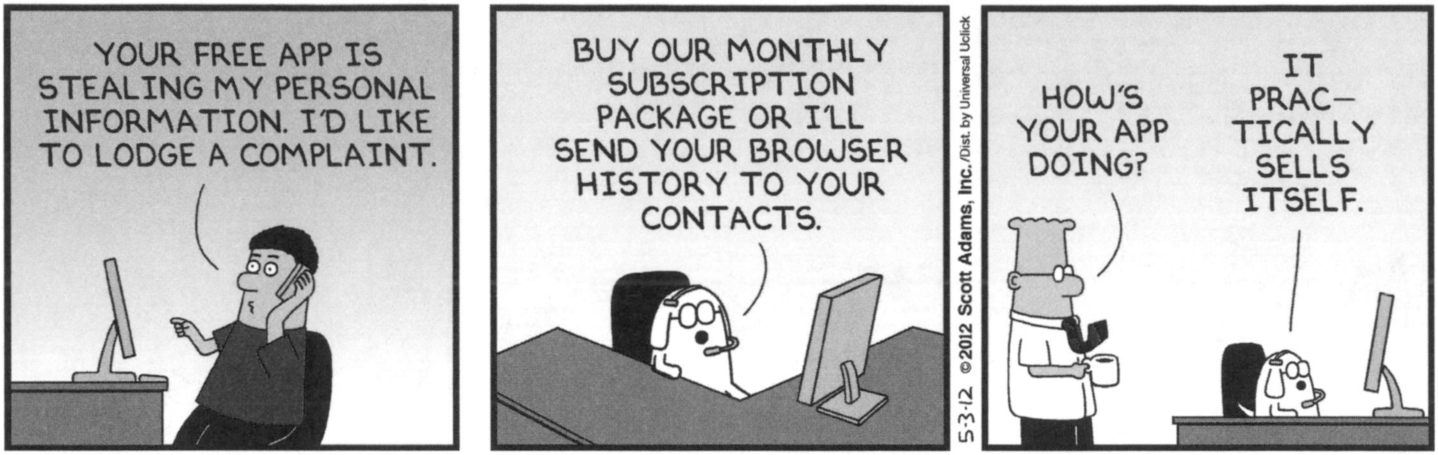
YOUR FREE APP IS STEALING MY PERSONAL INFORMATION. I'D LIKE TO LODGE A COMPLAINT.
BUY OUR MONTHLY SUBSCRIPTION PACKAGE OR I'LL SEND YOUR BROWSER HISTORY TO YOUR CONTACTS.
5-3-12 ©2012 Scott Adams, Inc./Dist. by Universal Uclick
HOW'S YOUR APP DOING?
IT PRAC–TICALLY SELLS ITSELF.

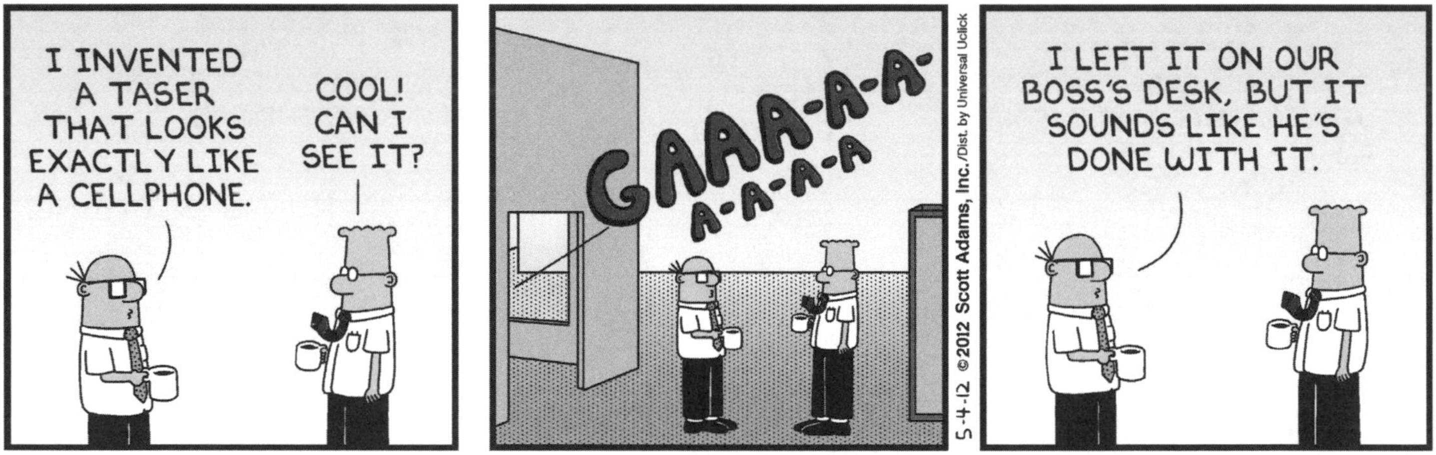
I INVENTED A TASER THAT LOOKS EXACTLY LIKE A CELLPHONE.
COOL! CAN I SEE IT?
GAAA-A-A-A-A-A-A
5-4-12 ©2012 Scott Adams, Inc./Dist. by Universal Uclick
I LEFT IT ON OUR BOSS'S DESK, BUT IT SOUNDS LIKE HE'S DONE WITH IT.

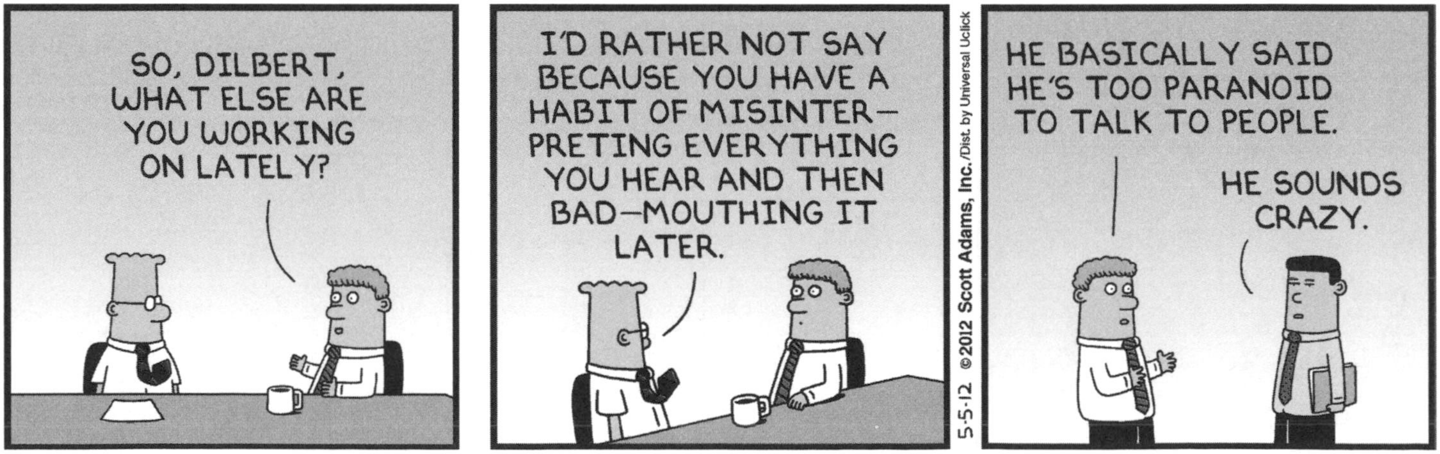
SO, DILBERT, WHAT ELSE ARE YOU WORKING ON LATELY?
I'D RATHER NOT SAY BECAUSE YOU HAVE A HABIT OF MISINTER–PRETING EVERYTHING YOU HEAR AND THEN BAD–MOUTHING IT LATER.
5-5-12 ©2012 Scott Adams, Inc./Dist. by Universal Uclick
HE BASICALLY SAID HE'S TOO PARANOID TO TALK TO PEOPLE.
HE SOUNDS CRAZY.

HOW DID WE DO AT THE TRADE SHOW?

WE HAD A HUGE CROWD AROUND OUR BOOTH THE ENTIRE TIME.

BUT IT WAS JUST THE SPILLOVER FROM THE POPULAR BOOTH NEXT TO US.

THE ONLY PERSON WHO ASKED FOR OUR BROCHURE USED IT TO KILL A SPIDER.

SOME GUY TRIED TO STEAL OUR EXTRA CHAIR AND THEN ALICE BEAT HIM SENSELESS WITH OUR LOGO SIGN.

A VIDEO OF THE INCIDENT IS ALREADY ON YOUTUBE.

IT COST US $200,000 TO BE AN EXHIBITOR AND WE GAINED ZERO NEW CUSTOMERS.

SO IT WAS JUST LIKE THE LAST ELEVEN YEARS.

I FEEL GOOD ABOUT NEXT YEAR!

©2012 Scott Adams, Inc./Dist. by Universal Uclick

5-6-12

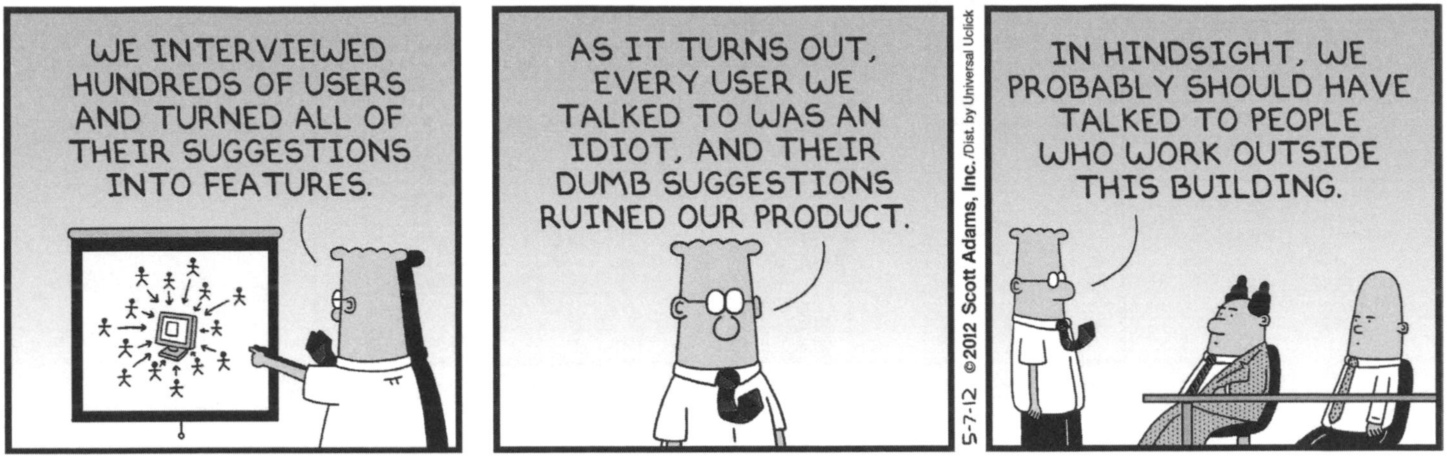
WE INTERVIEWED HUNDREDS OF USERS AND TURNED ALL OF THEIR SUGGESTIONS INTO FEATURES.
AS IT TURNS OUT, EVERY USER WE TALKED TO WAS AN IDIOT, AND THEIR DUMB SUGGESTIONS RUINED OUR PRODUCT.
5-7-12 ©2012 Scott Adams, Inc./Dist. by Universal Uclick
IN HINDSIGHT, WE PROBABLY SHOULD HAVE TALKED TO PEOPLE WHO WORK OUTSIDE THIS BUILDING.

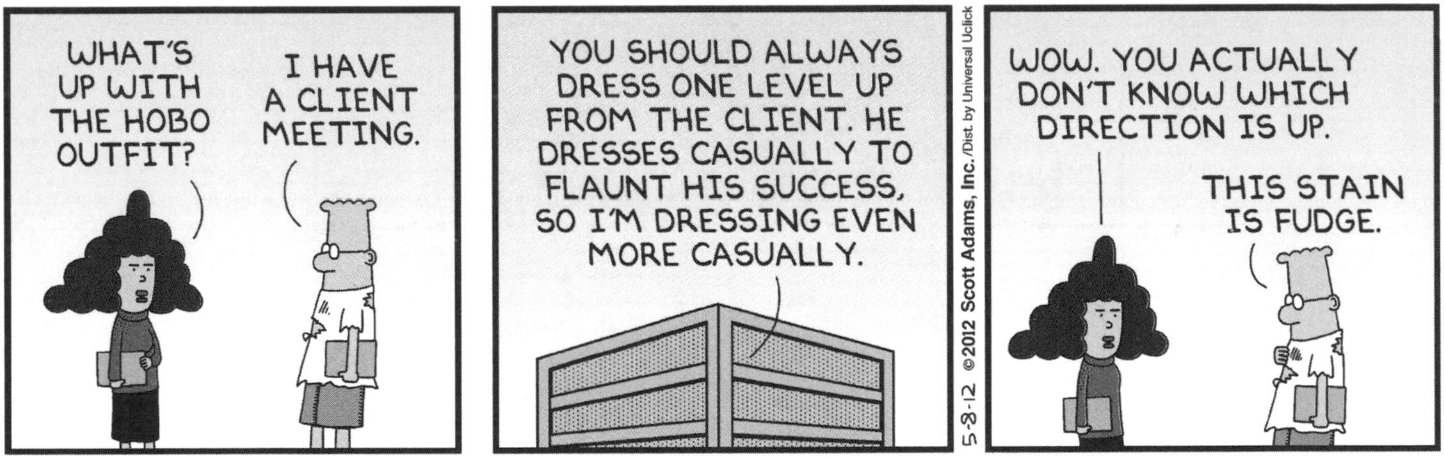
WHAT'S UP WITH THE HOBO OUTFIT?
I HAVE A CLIENT MEETING.
YOU SHOULD ALWAYS DRESS ONE LEVEL UP FROM THE CLIENT. HE DRESSES CASUALLY TO FLAUNT HIS SUCCESS, SO I'M DRESSING EVEN MORE CASUALLY.
5-8-12 ©2012 Scott Adams, Inc./Dist. by Universal Uclick
WOW. YOU ACTUALLY DON'T KNOW WHICH DIRECTION IS UP.
THIS STAIN IS FUDGE.

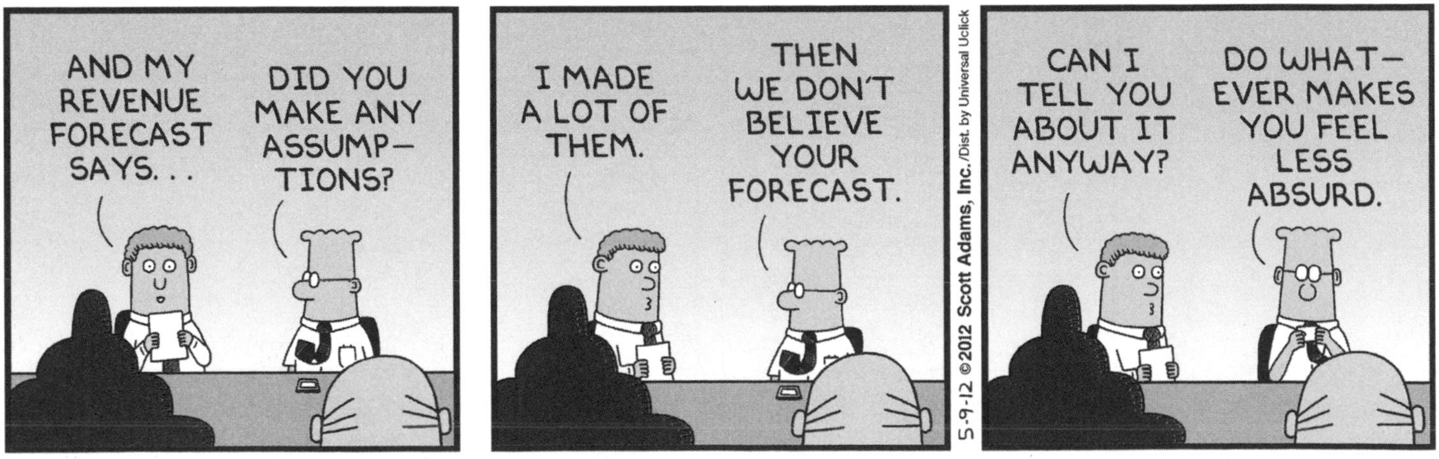
AND MY REVENUE FORECAST SAYS. . .
DID YOU MAKE ANY ASSUMP-TIONS?
I MADE A LOT OF THEM.
THEN WE DON'T BELIEVE YOUR FORECAST.
5-9-12 ©2012 Scott Adams, Inc./Dist. by Universal Uclick
CAN I TELL YOU ABOUT IT ANYWAY?
DO WHAT-EVER MAKES YOU FEEL LESS ABSURD.

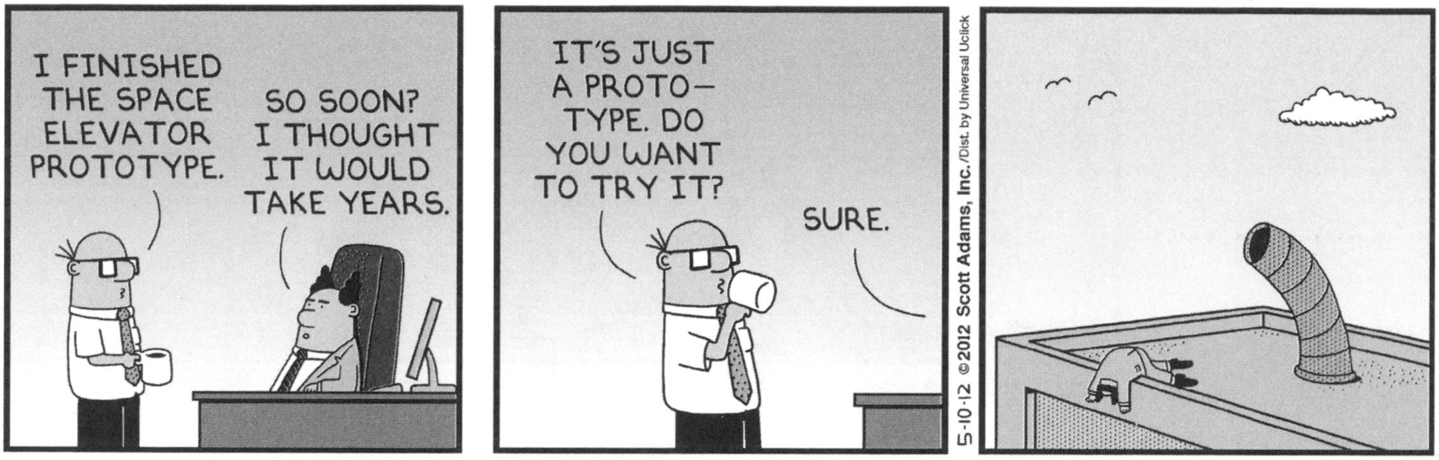
I FINISHED THE SPACE ELEVATOR PROTOTYPE.
SO SOON? I THOUGHT IT WOULD TAKE YEARS.
IT'S JUST A PROTO-TYPE. DO YOU WANT TO TRY IT?
SURE.
5-10-12 ©2012 Scott Adams, Inc./Dist. by Universal Uclick

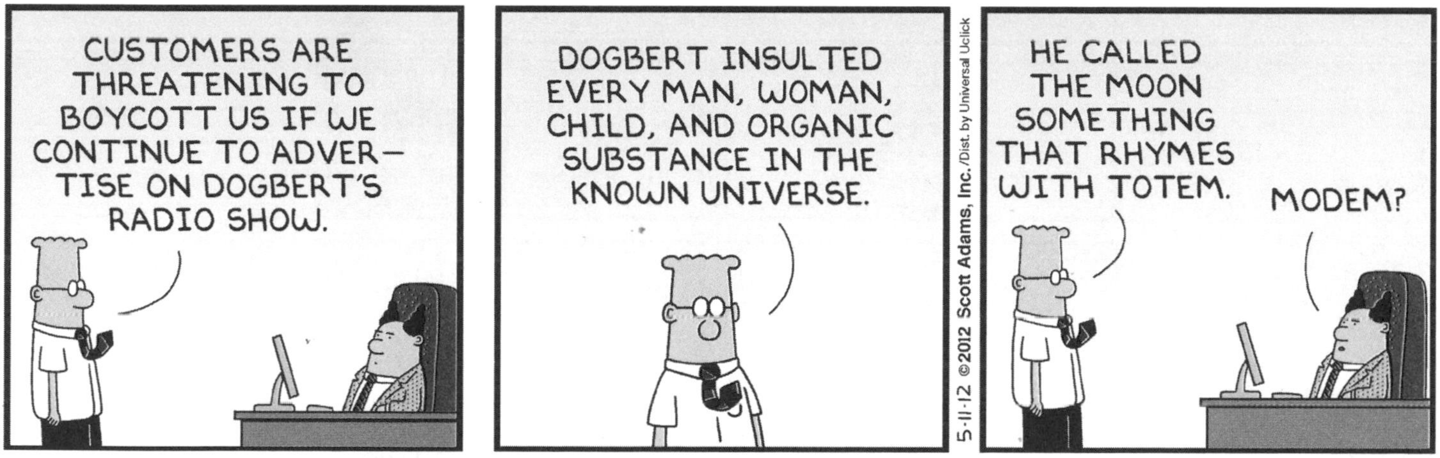
CUSTOMERS ARE THREATENING TO BOYCOTT US IF WE CONTINUE TO ADVER-TISE ON DOGBERT'S RADIO SHOW.
DOGBERT INSULTED EVERY MAN, WOMAN, CHILD, AND ORGANIC SUBSTANCE IN THE KNOWN UNIVERSE.
HE CALLED THE MOON SOMETHING THAT RHYMES WITH TOTEM.
MODEM?
5-11-12 ©2012 Scott Adams, Inc./Dist. by Universal Uclick

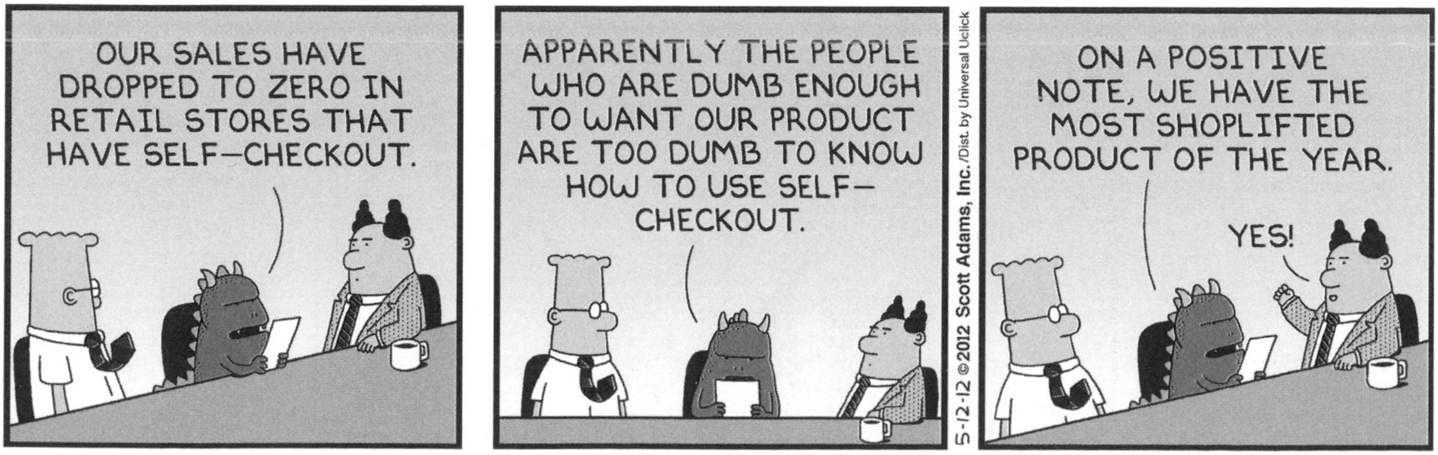
OUR SALES HAVE DROPPED TO ZERO IN RETAIL STORES THAT HAVE SELF-CHECKOUT.
APPARENTLY THE PEOPLE WHO ARE DUMB ENOUGH TO WANT OUR PRODUCT ARE TOO DUMB TO KNOW HOW TO USE SELF-CHECKOUT.
ON A POSITIVE NOTE, WE HAVE THE MOST SHOPLIFTED PRODUCT OF THE YEAR.
YES!
5-12-12 ©2012 Scott Adams, Inc./Dist. by Universal Uclick

. . . AND THAT'S MY SUGGESTION FOR OUR NEXT PRODUCT.
HOW DO WE KNOW THAT TEN OTHER COMPANIES AREN'T WORKING ON THE SAME IDEA?
WELL, THAT'S ALWAYS A POSSIBILITY.
THERE ARE SEVEN BILLION PEOPLE ON EARTH. I'LL BET A MILLION OF THEM HAD THIS IDEA.
IT'S IRRATIONAL TO THINK THAT ANY NEW PRODUCT IS LIKELY TO BE A HIT.
ON THE OTHER HAND, WE ONLY GET PAID IF WE PRETEND TO BE OPTIMISTIC ABOUT NEW PRODUCTS.
ALL IN FAVOR OF FAKING OUR OPTIMISM, RAISE YOUR HANDS.
ALL I COULD GET WAS FAKE BUY—IN.
THAT'S THE ONLY KIND THERE IS.
©2012 Scott Adams, Inc./Dist. by Universal Uclick
5-13-12

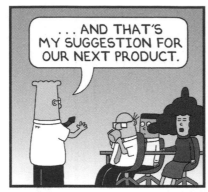

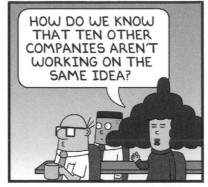

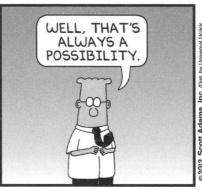

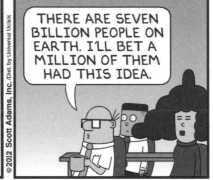

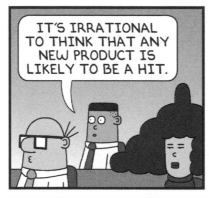

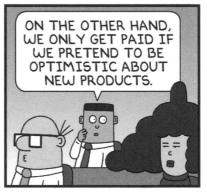

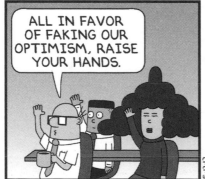

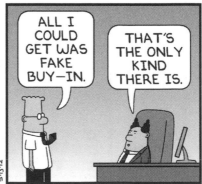

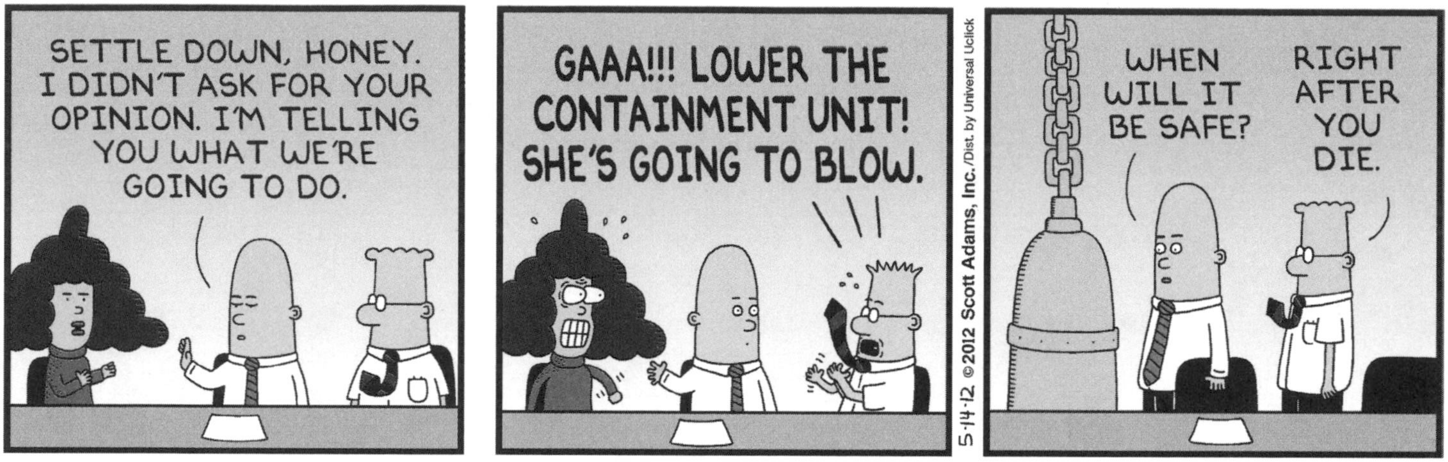
SETTLE DOWN, HONEY. I DIDN'T ASK FOR YOUR OPINION. I'M TELLING YOU WHAT WE'RE GOING TO DO.
GAAA!!! LOWER THE CONTAINMENT UNIT! SHE'S GOING TO BLOW.
5-14-12 ©2012 Scott Adams, Inc./Dist. by Universal Uclick
WHEN WILL IT BE SAFE?
RIGHT AFTER YOU DIE.

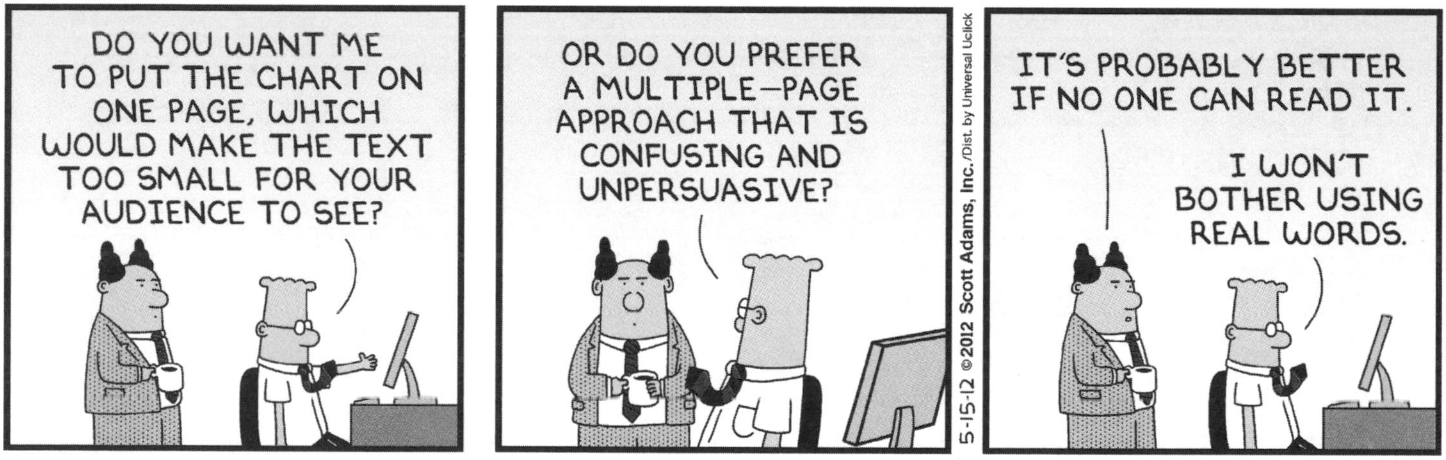
DO YOU WANT ME TO PUT THE CHART ON ONE PAGE, WHICH WOULD MAKE THE TEXT TOO SMALL FOR YOUR AUDIENCE TO SEE?
OR DO YOU PREFER A MULTIPLE—PAGE APPROACH THAT IS CONFUSING AND UNPERSUASIVE?
5-15-12 ©2012 Scott Adams, Inc./Dist. by Universal Uclick
IT'S PROBABLY BETTER IF NO ONE CAN READ IT.
I WON'T BOTHER USING REAL WORDS.

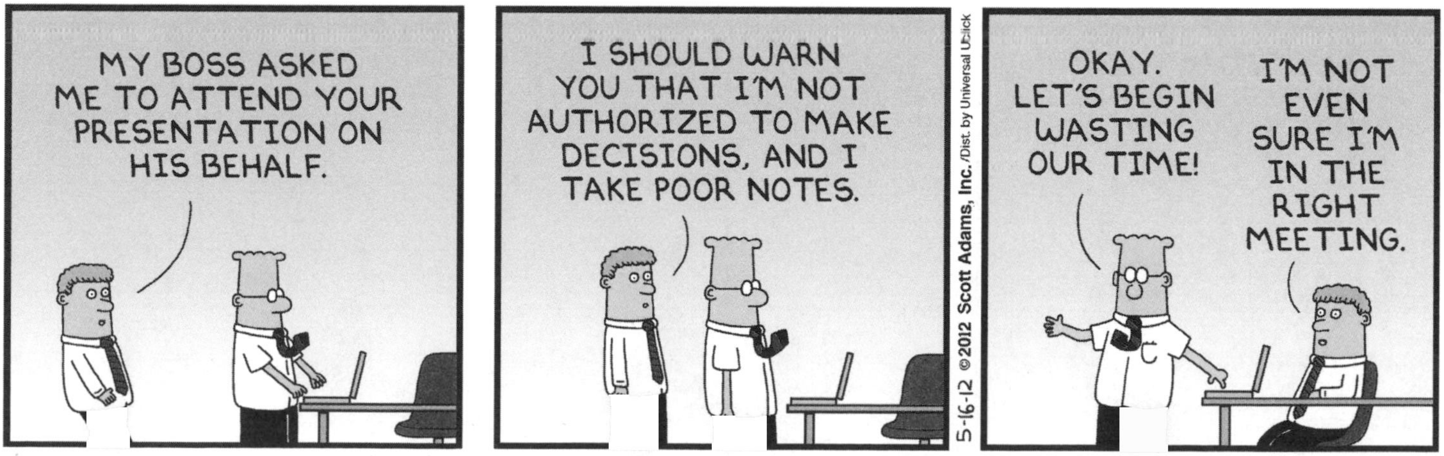
MY BOSS ASKED ME TO ATTEND YOUR PRESENTATION ON HIS BEHALF.
I SHOULD WARN YOU THAT I'M NOT AUTHORIZED TO MAKE DECISIONS, AND I TAKE POOR NOTES.
5-16-12 ©2012 Scott Adams, Inc./Dist. by Universal Uclick
OKAY. LET'S BEGIN WASTING OUR TIME!
I'M NOT EVEN SURE I'M IN THE RIGHT MEETING.

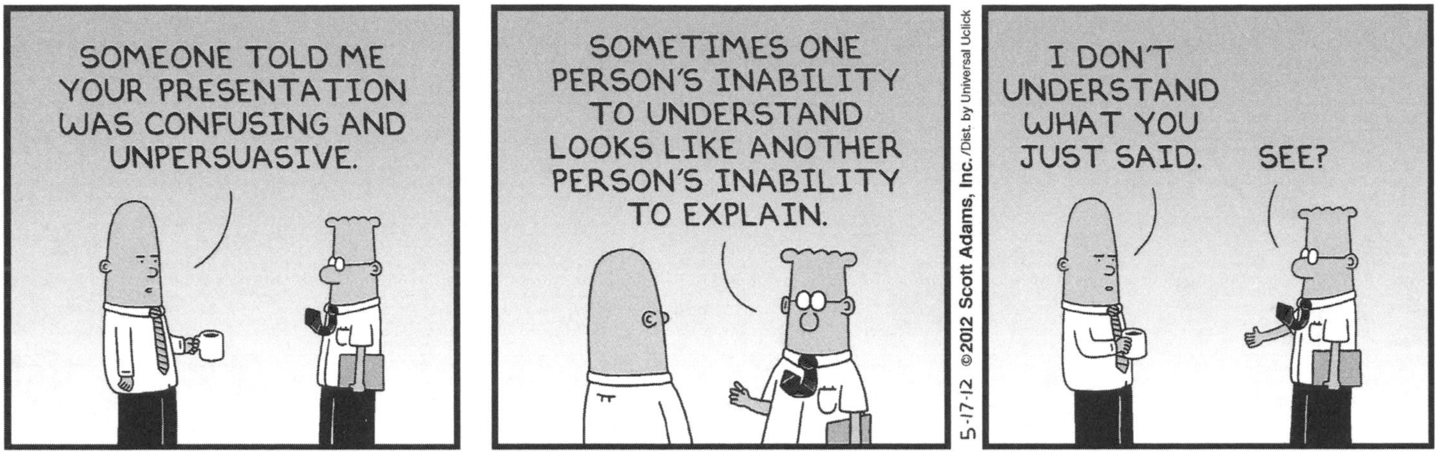
SOMEONE TOLD ME YOUR PRESENTATION WAS CONFUSING AND UNPERSUASIVE.
SOMETIMES ONE PERSON'S INABILITY TO UNDERSTAND LOOKS LIKE ANOTHER PERSON'S INABILITY TO EXPLAIN.
I DON'T UNDERSTAND WHAT YOU JUST SAID.
SEE?
5-17-12 ©2012 Scott Adams, Inc./Dist. by Universal Uclick

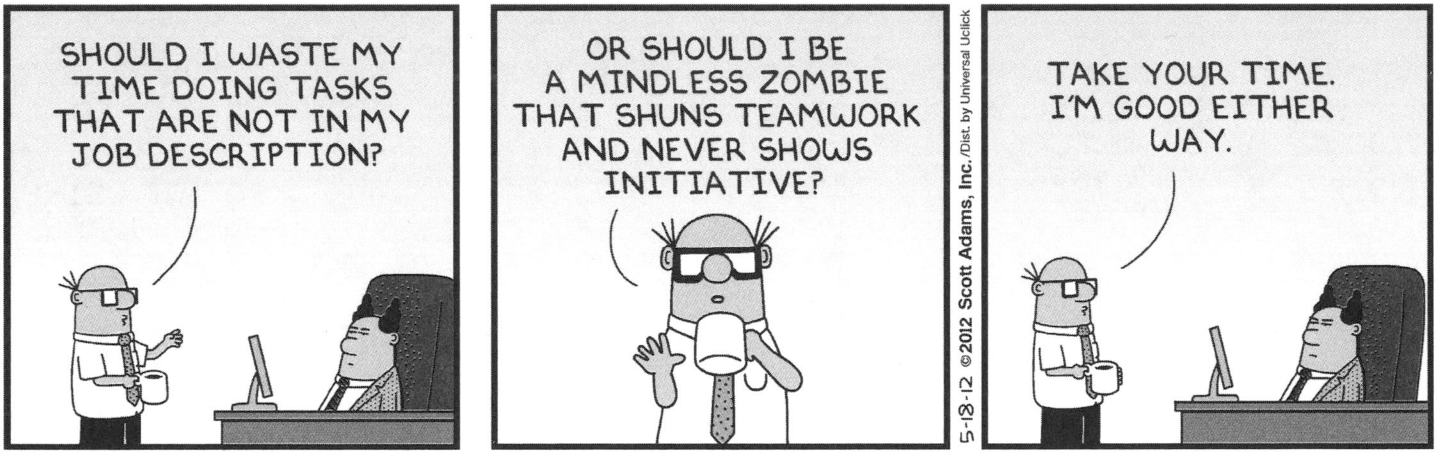
SHOULD I WASTE MY TIME DOING TASKS THAT ARE NOT IN MY JOB DESCRIPTION?
OR SHOULD I BE A MINDLESS ZOMBIE THAT SHUNS TEAMWORK AND NEVER SHOWS INITIATIVE?
TAKE YOUR TIME. I'M GOOD EITHER WAY.
5-18-12 ©2012 Scott Adams, Inc./Dist. by Universal Uclick

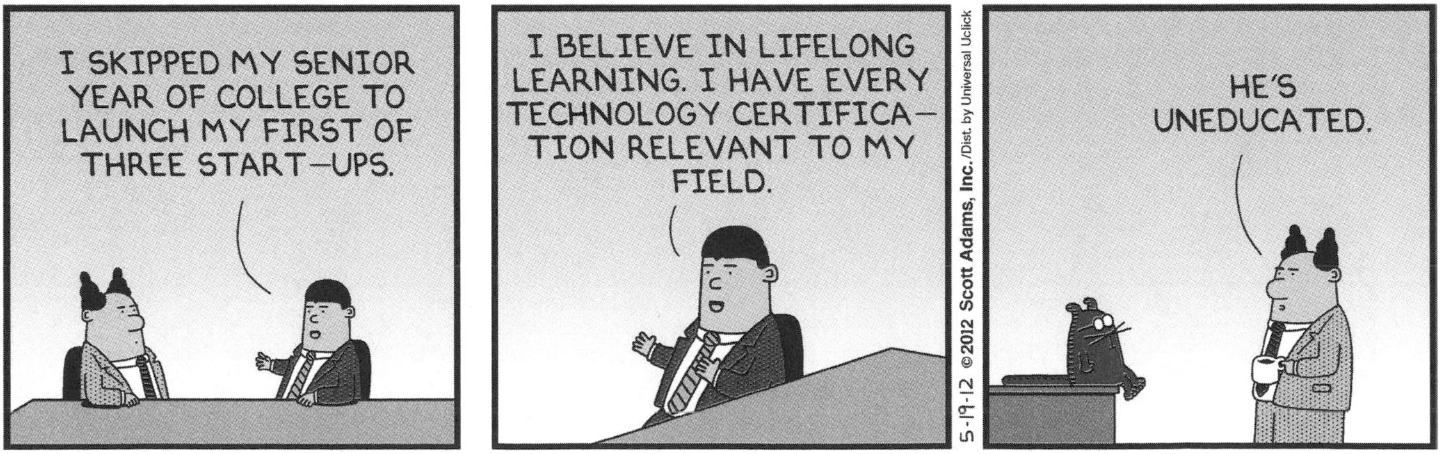
I SKIPPED MY SENIOR YEAR OF COLLEGE TO LAUNCH MY FIRST OF THREE START-UPS.
I BELIEVE IN LIFELONG LEARNING. I HAVE EVERY TECHNOLOGY CERTIFICATION RELEVANT TO MY FIELD.
HE'S UNEDUCATED.
5-19-12 ©2012 Scott Adams, Inc./Dist. by Universal Uclick

WAIT. HOLD THAT CRAZY THOUGHT.
I NEED TO GET A WITNESS IN THE ROOM.
ALICE, WOULD YOU MIND COMING TO THE CONFERENCE ROOM FOR A MINUTE?
WHAT FRESH HECK IS THIS?
LARRY IS A SADIST AND A SOCIOPATH, BUT HE HIDES IT WHEN THERE'S MORE THAN ONE WITNESS.
SO, LARRY, WHAT DO YOU THINK OF MY PROJECT?
IT LOOKS GREAT! I'LL BE HAPPY TO HELP YOU IN ANY WAY I CAN!
AM I DONE HERE?
DON'T TURN YOUR BACK!
5-20-12

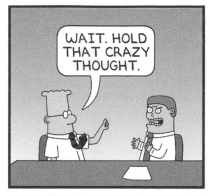

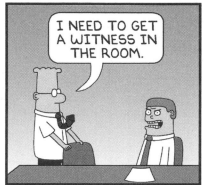

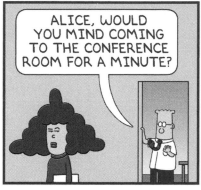

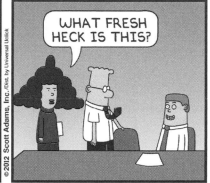

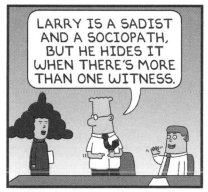

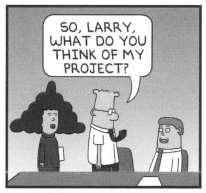

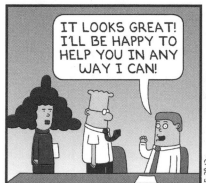

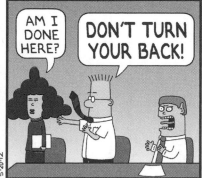

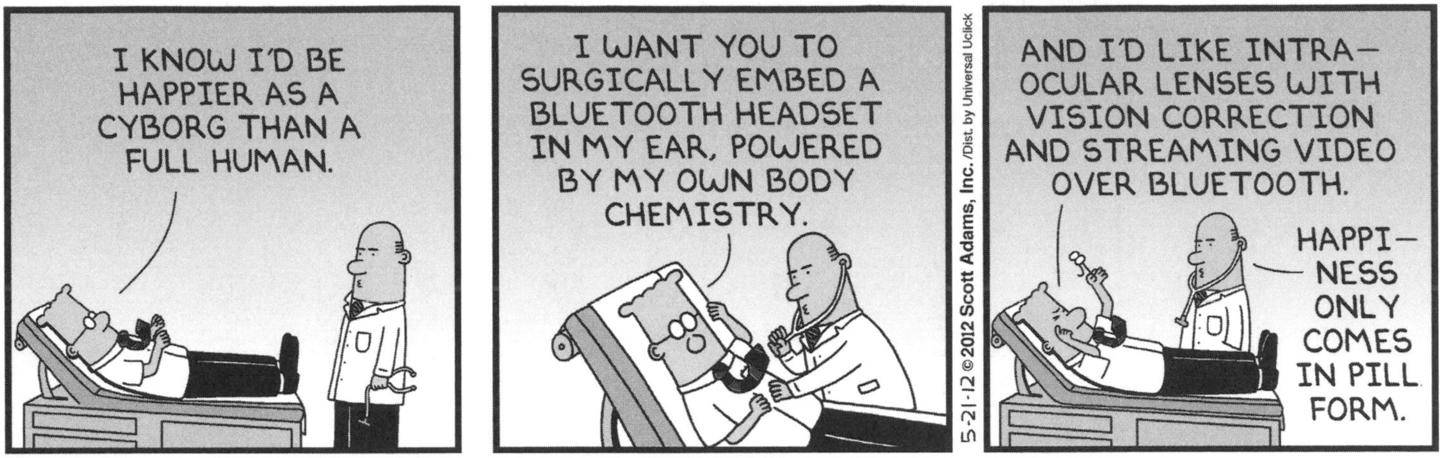
I KNOW I'D BE HAPPIER AS A CYBORG THAN A FULL HUMAN.
I WANT YOU TO SURGICALLY EMBED A BLUETOOTH HEADSET IN MY EAR, POWERED BY MY OWN BODY CHEMISTRY.
5-21-12 ©2012 Scott Adams, Inc. /Dist. by Universal Uclick
AND I'D LIKE INTRA-OCULAR LENSES WITH VISION CORRECTION AND STREAMING VIDEO OVER BLUETOOTH.
HAPPI-NESS ONLY COMES IN PILL FORM.

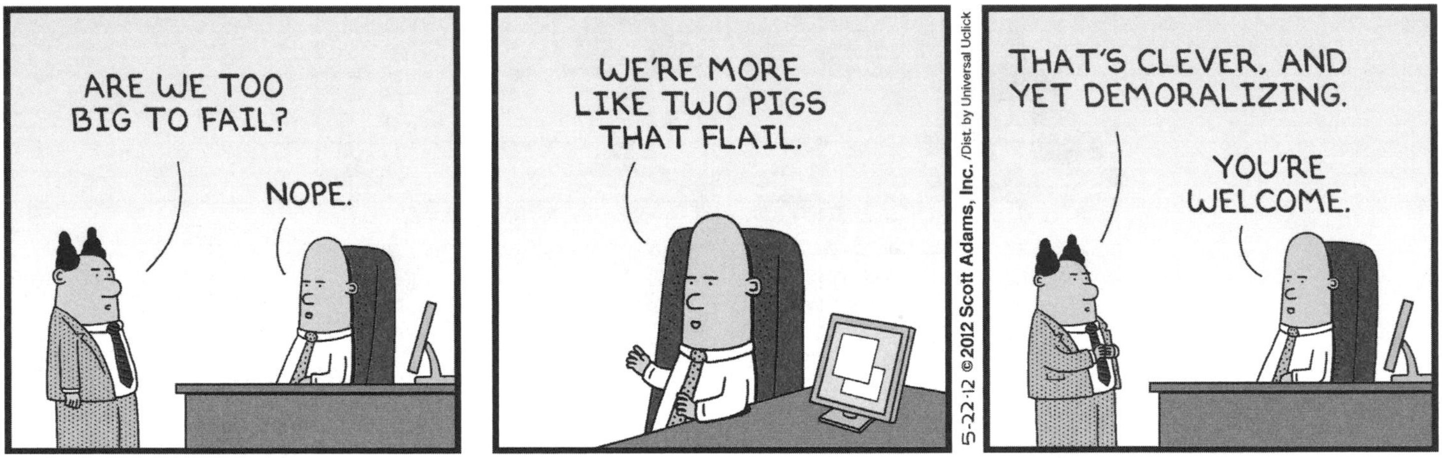
ARE WE TOO BIG TO FAIL?
NOPE.
WE'RE MORE LIKE TWO PIGS THAT FLAIL.
5-22-12 ©2012 Scott Adams, Inc. /Dist. by Universal Uclick
THAT'S CLEVER, AND YET DEMORALIZING.
YOU'RE WELCOME.

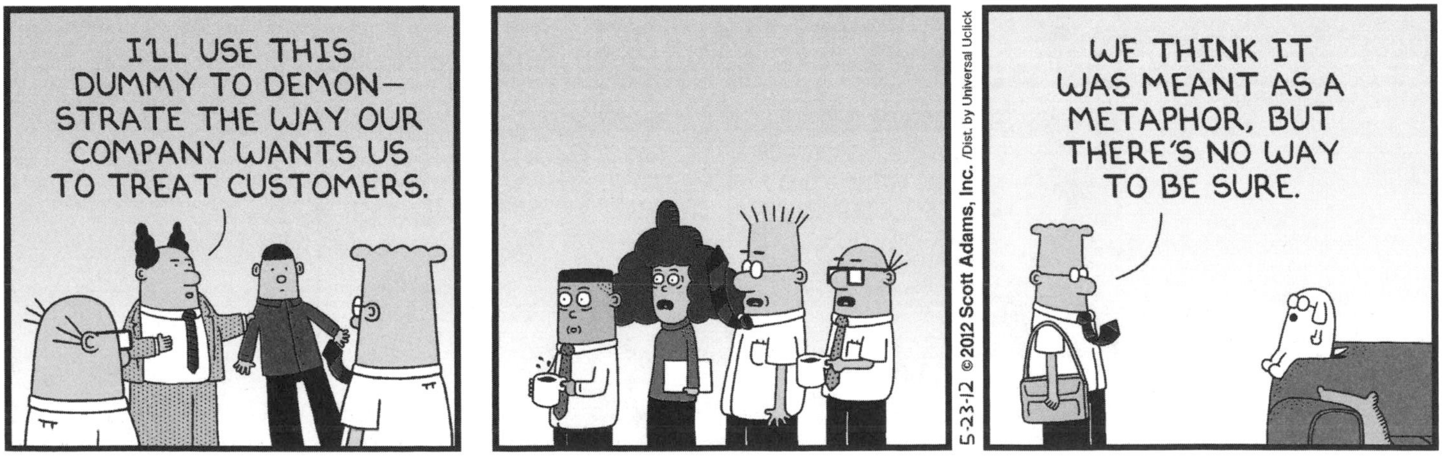
I'LL USE THIS DUMMY TO DEMON-STRATE THE WAY OUR COMPANY WANTS US TO TREAT CUSTOMERS.
5-23-12 ©2012 Scott Adams, Inc. /Dist. by Universal Uclick
WE THINK IT WAS MEANT AS A METAPHOR, BUT THERE'S NO WAY TO BE SURE.

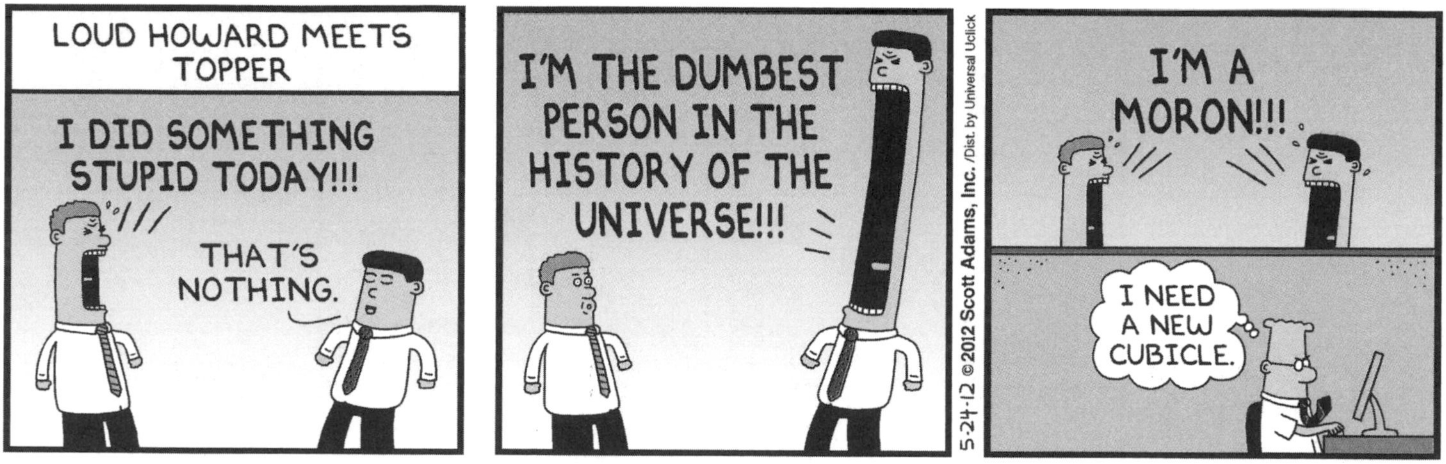
LOUD HOWARD MEETS TOPPER
I DID SOMETHING STUPID TODAY!!!
THAT'S NOTHING.
I'M THE DUMBEST PERSON IN THE HISTORY OF THE UNIVERSE!!!
5-24-12 ©2012 Scott Adams, Inc. /Dist. by Universal Uclick
I'M A MORON!!!
I NEED A NEW CUBICLE.

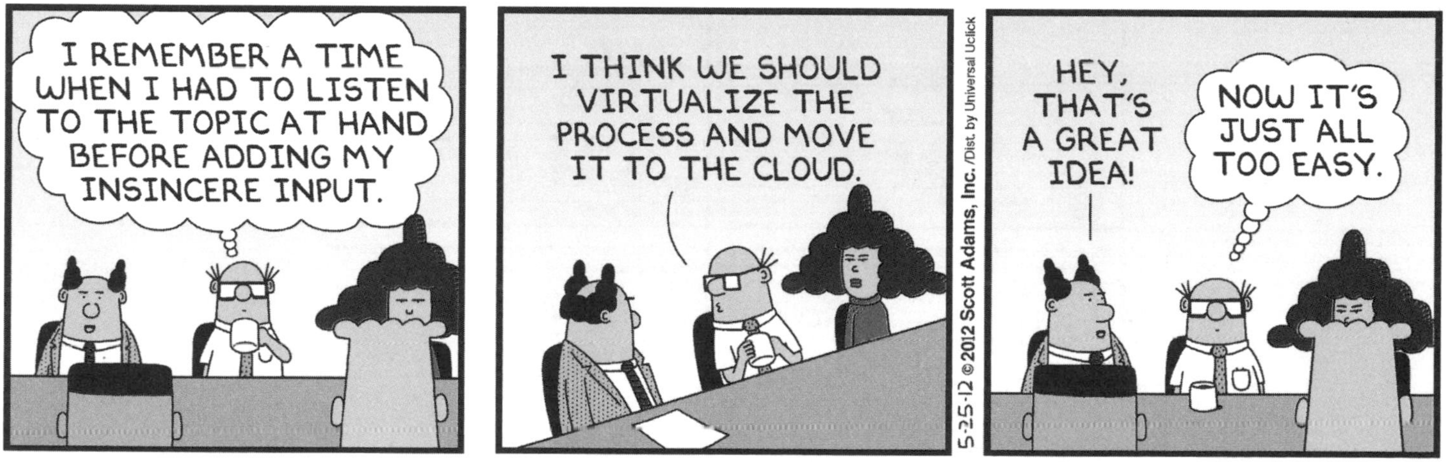
I REMEMBER A TIME WHEN I HAD TO LISTEN TO THE TOPIC AT HAND BEFORE ADDING MY INSINCERE INPUT.
I THINK WE SHOULD VIRTUALIZE THE PROCESS AND MOVE IT TO THE CLOUD.
5-25-12 ©2012 Scott Adams, Inc. /Dist. by Universal Uclick
HEY, THAT'S A GREAT IDEA!
NOW IT'S JUST ALL TOO EASY.

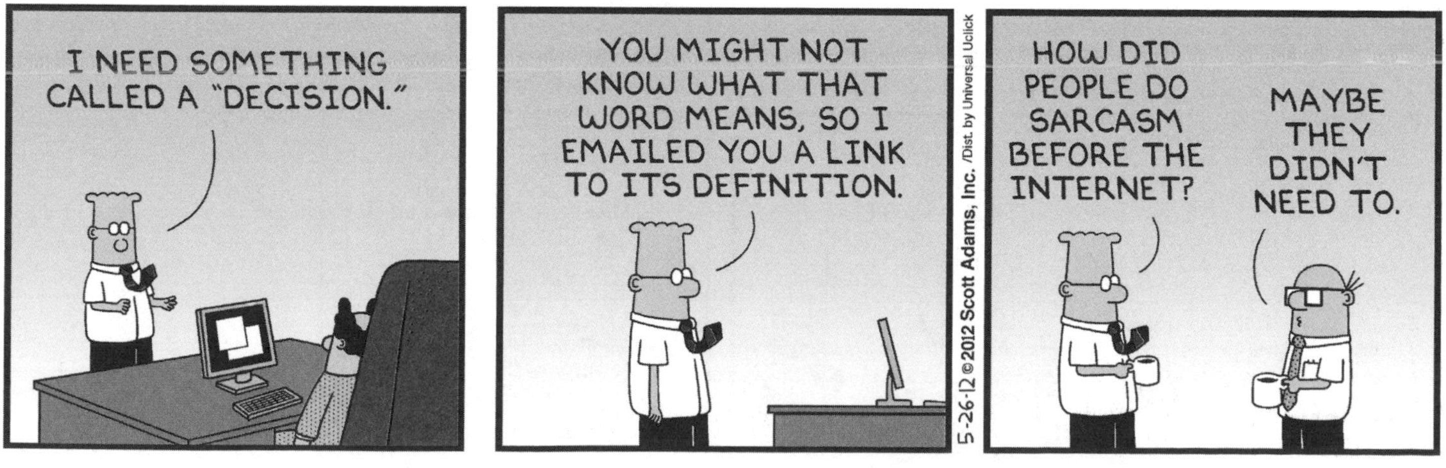
I NEED SOMETHING CALLED A "DECISION."
YOU MIGHT NOT KNOW WHAT THAT WORD MEANS, SO I EMAILED YOU A LINK TO ITS DEFINITION.
5-26-12 ©2012 Scott Adams, Inc. /Dist. by Universal Uclick
HOW DID PEOPLE DO SARCASM BEFORE THE INTERNET?
MAYBE THEY DIDN'T NEED TO.

WE'VE BEEN ASKED TO CUT OUR BUDGET BY 30%.
THAT DOESN'T MAKE SENSE. WE MET ALL OF OUR OBJECTIVES LAST YEAR.
A DIFFERENT PART OF OUR COMPANY HAD A HUGE LOSS.
SHOULDN'T YOU CUT THEIR BUDGET, NOT OURS?
THEIR BUDGET ISN'T BIG ENOUGH TO MAKE A DIFFERENCE TO THE BOTTOM LINE.
SO OUR STRATEGY IS TO PUNISH SUCCESS, AND REWARD FAILURE?
JUST DO YOUR JOB AND LEAVE THE STRATEGY TO MANAGEMENT.
HYPOTHETICALLY, IF I DO MY JOB POORLY, WOULD THAT BE GOOD OR BAD FOR ME?
©2012 Scott Adams, Inc./Dist. by Universal Uclick
5-27-12

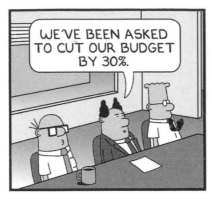

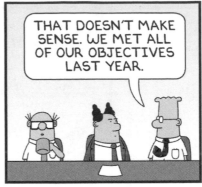

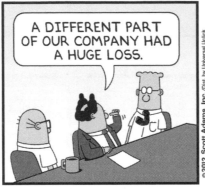

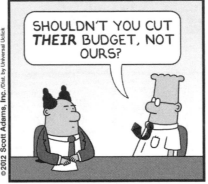

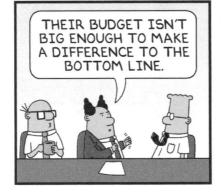

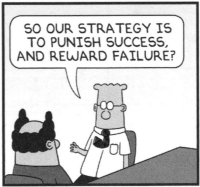

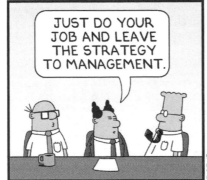

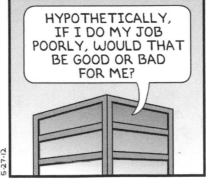

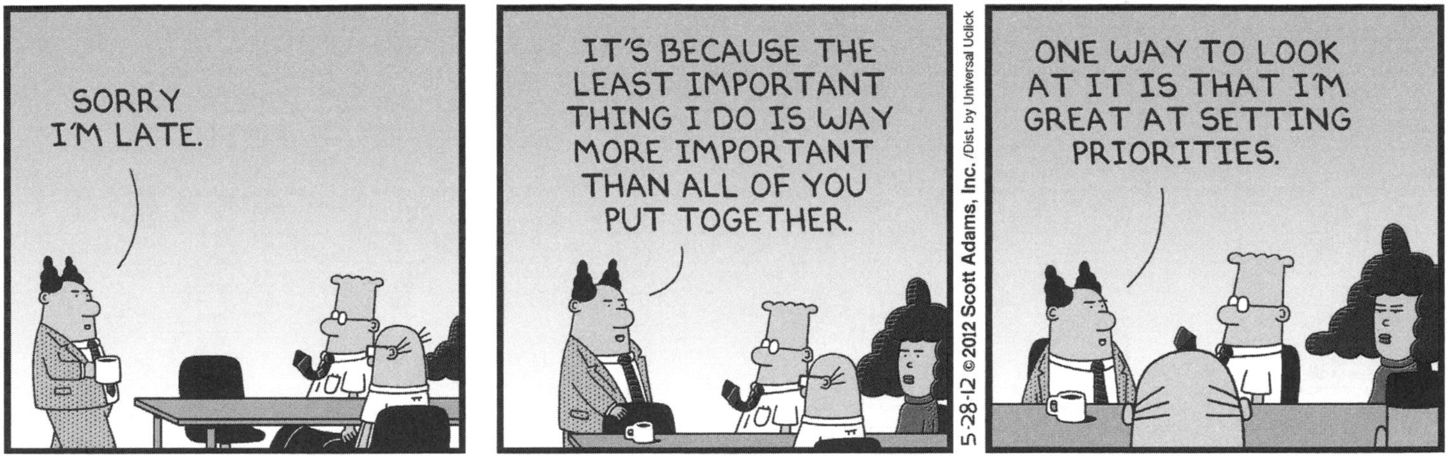
SORRY I'M LATE.
IT'S BECAUSE THE LEAST IMPORTANT THING I DO IS WAY MORE IMPORTANT THAN ALL OF YOU PUT TOGETHER.
5-28-12 ©2012 Scott Adams, Inc. /Dist. by Universal Uclick
ONE WAY TO LOOK AT IT IS THAT I'M GREAT AT SETTING PRIORITIES.

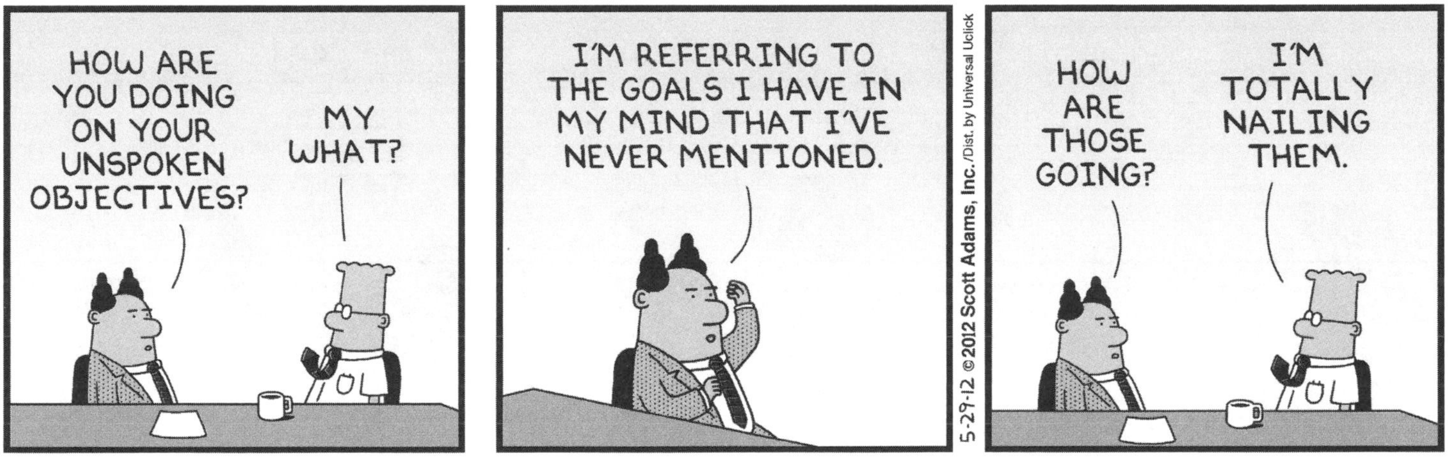
HOW ARE YOU DOING ON YOUR UNSPOKEN OBJECTIVES?
MY WHAT?
I'M REFERRING TO THE GOALS I HAVE IN MY MIND THAT I'VE NEVER MENTIONED.
5-29-12 ©2012 Scott Adams, Inc. /Dist. by Universal Uclick
HOW ARE THOSE GOING?
I'M TOTALLY NAILING THEM.

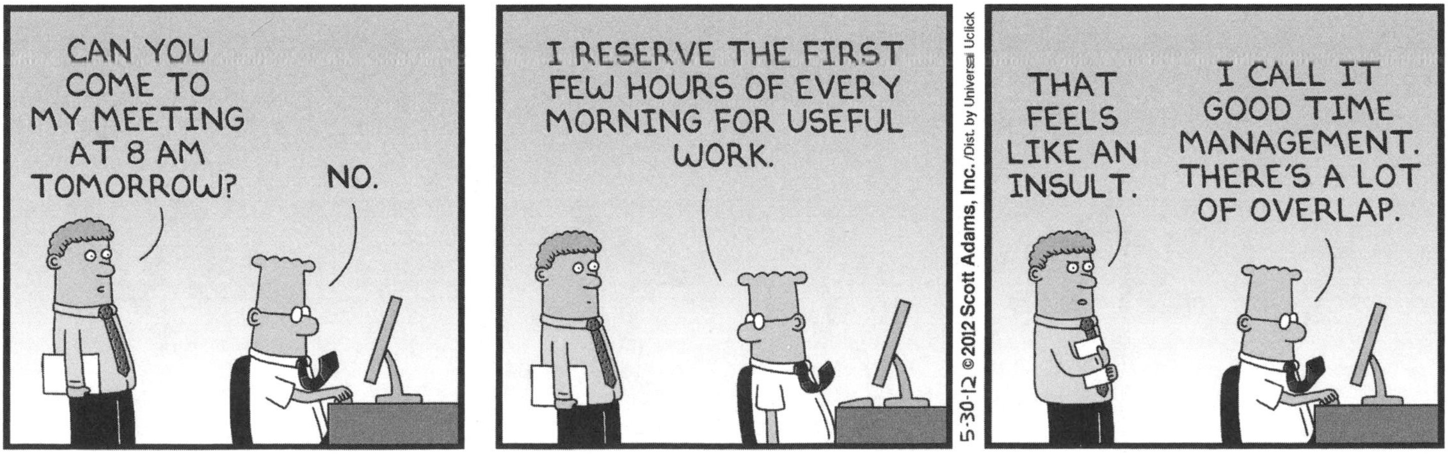
CAN YOU COME TO MY MEETING AT 8 AM TOMORROW?
NO.
I RESERVE THE FIRST FEW HOURS OF EVERY MORNING FOR USEFUL WORK.
5-30-12 ©2012 Scott Adams, Inc. /Dist. by Universal Uclick
THAT FEELS LIKE AN INSULT.
I CALL IT GOOD TIME MANAGEMENT. THERE'S A LOT OF OVERLAP.

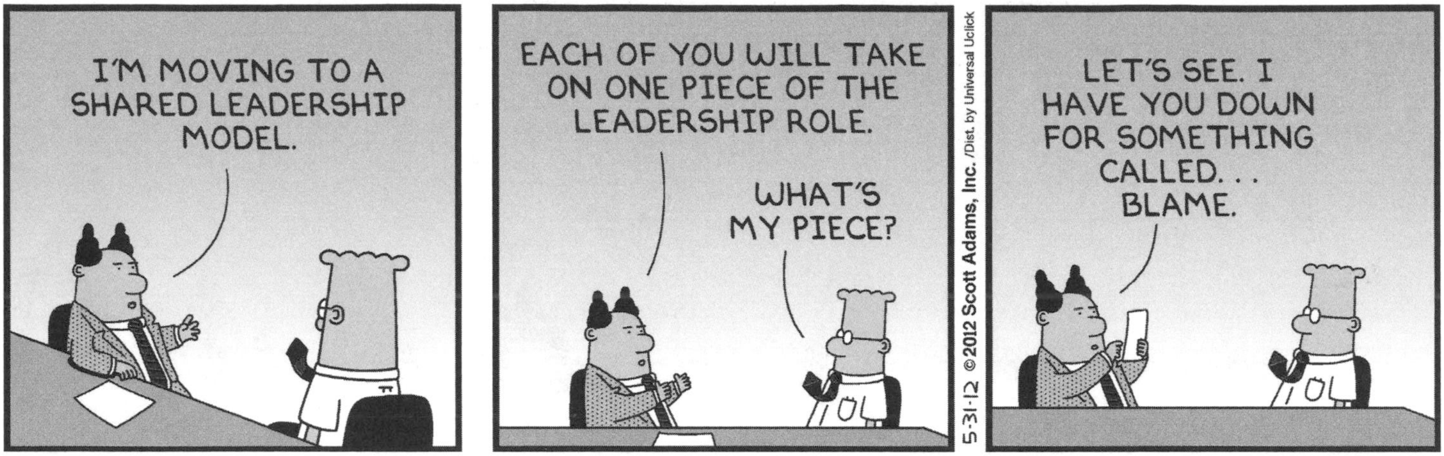
I'M MOVING TO A SHARED LEADERSHIP MODEL.
EACH OF YOU WILL TAKE ON ONE PIECE OF THE LEADERSHIP ROLE.
WHAT'S MY PIECE?
5-31-12 © 2012 Scott Adams, Inc. /Dist. by Universal Uclick
LET'S SEE. I HAVE YOU DOWN FOR SOMETHING CALLED. . . BLAME.

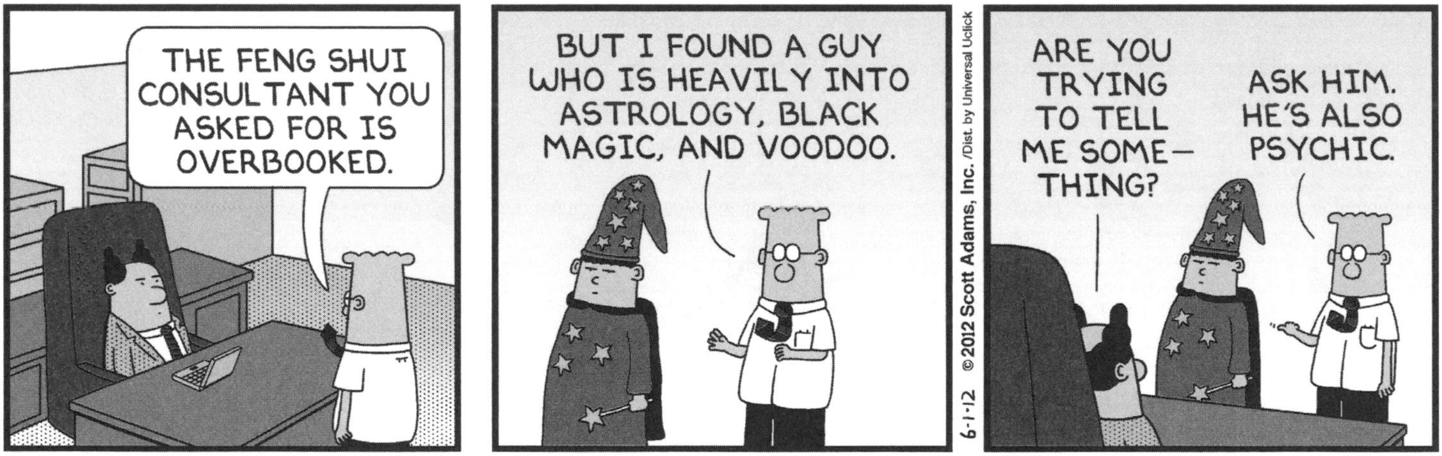
THE FENG SHUI CONSULTANT YOU ASKED FOR IS OVERBOOKED.
BUT I FOUND A GUY WHO IS HEAVILY INTO ASTROLOGY, BLACK MAGIC, AND VOODOO.
6-1-12 © 2012 Scott Adams, Inc. /Dist. by Universal Uclick
ARE YOU TRYING TO TELL ME SOME-THING?
ASK HIM. HE'S ALSO PSYCHIC.

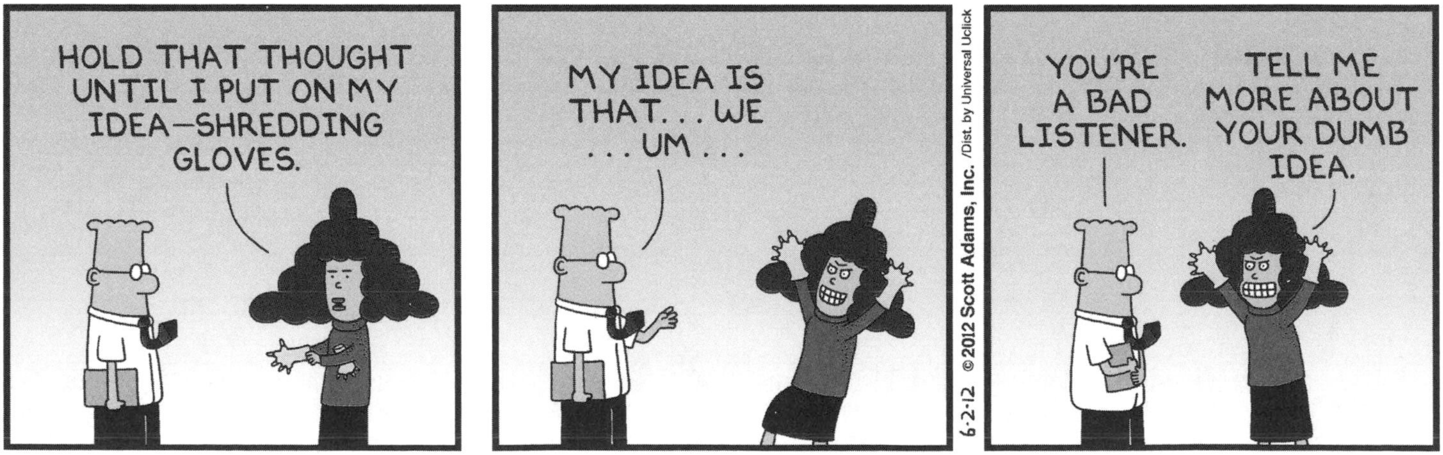
HOLD THAT THOUGHT UNTIL I PUT ON MY IDEA-SHREDDING GLOVES.
MY IDEA IS THAT. . . WE . . . UM . . .
6-2-12 © 2012 Scott Adams, Inc. /Dist. by Universal Uclick
YOU'RE A BAD LISTENER.
TELL ME MORE ABOUT YOUR DUMB IDEA.

WALLY, YOU CAN'T FLOAT THROUGH LIFE WITH NO GOALS AND NO AMBITION.

YOU MISJUDGE ME. I HAVE MY ENTIRE CAREER PLANNED OUT.

MY FIVE-YEAR PLAN IS TO AVOID ANY SORT OF WORK IN WHICH MY INDIVIDUAL ACCOMP-LISHMENTS CAN BE MEASURED.

I'LL HOARD KNOWLEDGE ABOUT ONE OF OUR LEGACY SYSTEMS SO I SEEM INDISPENSIBLE.

WHEN I GET TO WITHIN FOUR YEARS OF RETIREMENT, I'LL ONLY WORK ON PROJECTS THAT HAVE A FIVE-YEAR PAYBACK.

I'LL PROTECT MY CARDIOVASCULAR SYSTEM BY GETTING PLENTY OF NAPS AND NOT CARING ABOUT THE QUALITY OF MY WORK.

THEN I'LL STICK A STRAW IN OUR PENSION FUND AND SUCK ON IT FOR THE NEXT FORTY YEARS.

DID YOU GET HIM STRAIGHT-ENED OUT?

NO, BUT I GOT A NEW CAREER PLAN FOR MYSELF.

©2012 Scott Adams, Inc. /Dist. by Universal Uclick

6-3-12

91

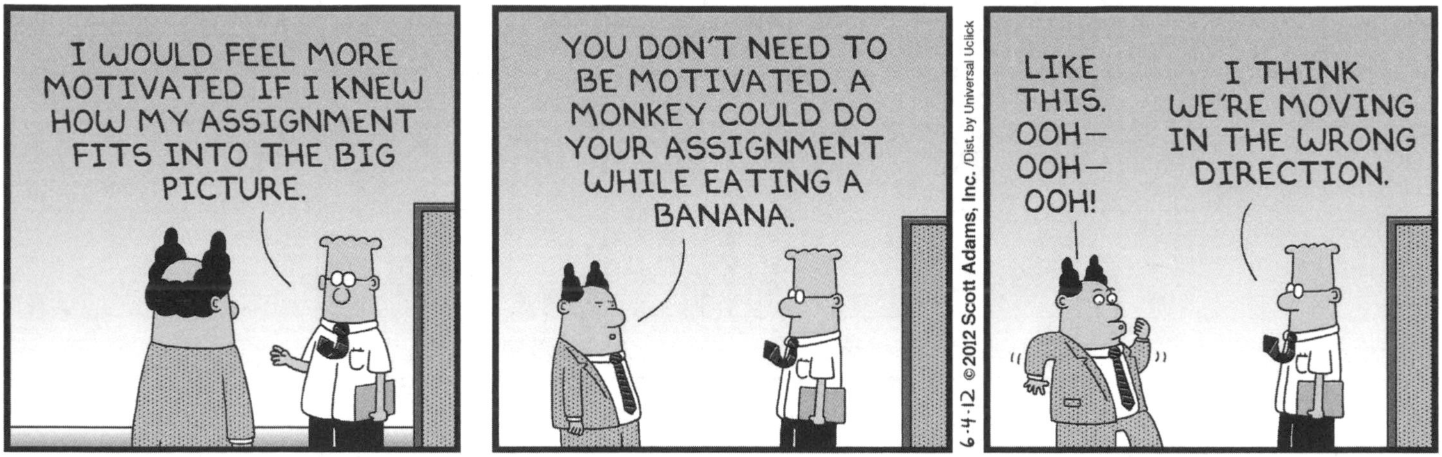
I WOULD FEEL MORE MOTIVATED IF I KNEW HOW MY ASSIGNMENT FITS INTO THE BIG PICTURE.
YOU DON'T NEED TO BE MOTIVATED. A MONKEY COULD DO YOUR ASSIGNMENT WHILE EATING A BANANA.
6·4·12 © 2012 Scott Adams, Inc. /Dist. by Universal Uclick
LIKE THIS. OOH— OOH— OOH!
I THINK WE'RE MOVING IN THE WRONG DIRECTION.

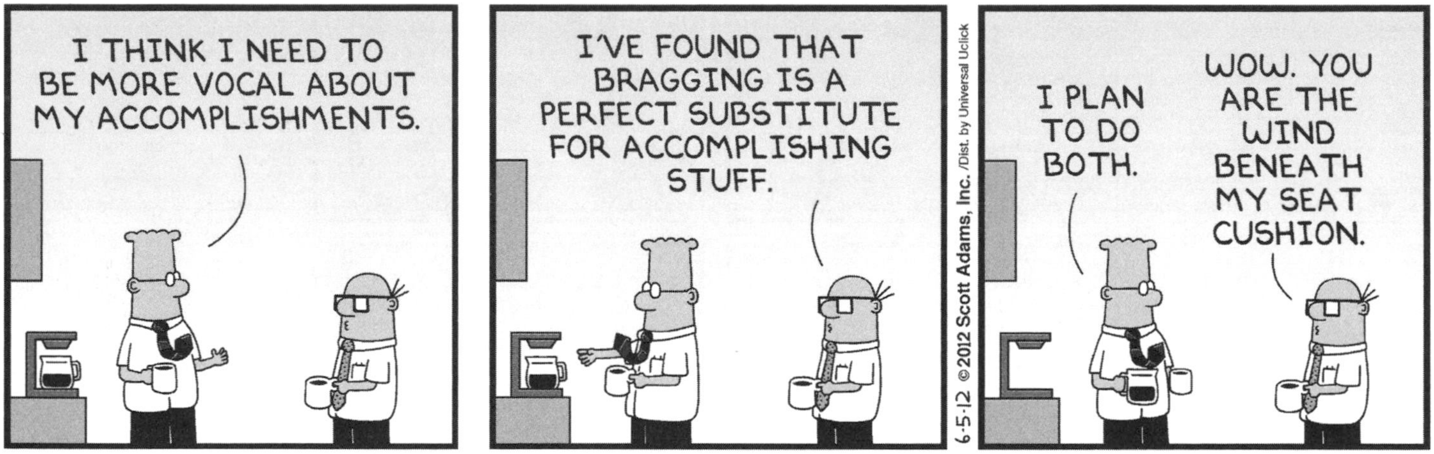
I THINK I NEED TO BE MORE VOCAL ABOUT MY ACCOMPLISHMENTS.
I'VE FOUND THAT BRAGGING IS A PERFECT SUBSTITUTE FOR ACCOMPLISHING STUFF.
6·5·12 © 2012 Scott Adams, Inc. /Dist. by Universal Uclick
I PLAN TO DO BOTH.
WOW. YOU ARE THE WIND BENEATH MY SEAT CUSHION.

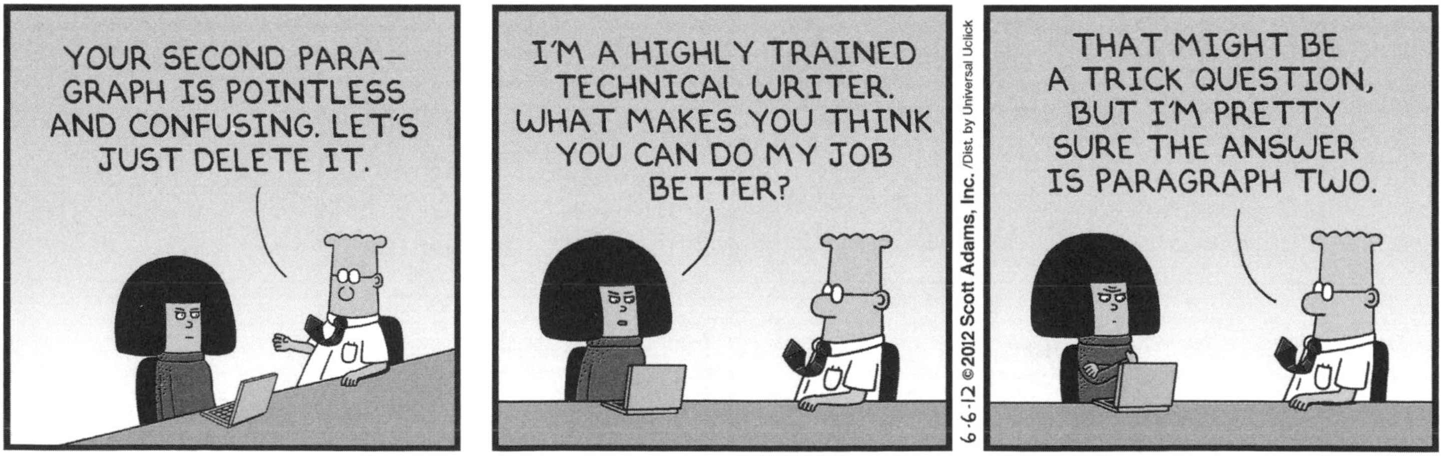
YOUR SECOND PARA-GRAPH IS POINTLESS AND CONFUSING. LET'S JUST DELETE IT.
I'M A HIGHLY TRAINED TECHNICAL WRITER. WHAT MAKES YOU THINK YOU CAN DO MY JOB BETTER?
6·6·12 © 2012 Scott Adams, Inc. /Dist. by Universal Uclick
THAT MIGHT BE A TRICK QUESTION, BUT I'M PRETTY SURE THE ANSWER IS PARAGRAPH TWO.

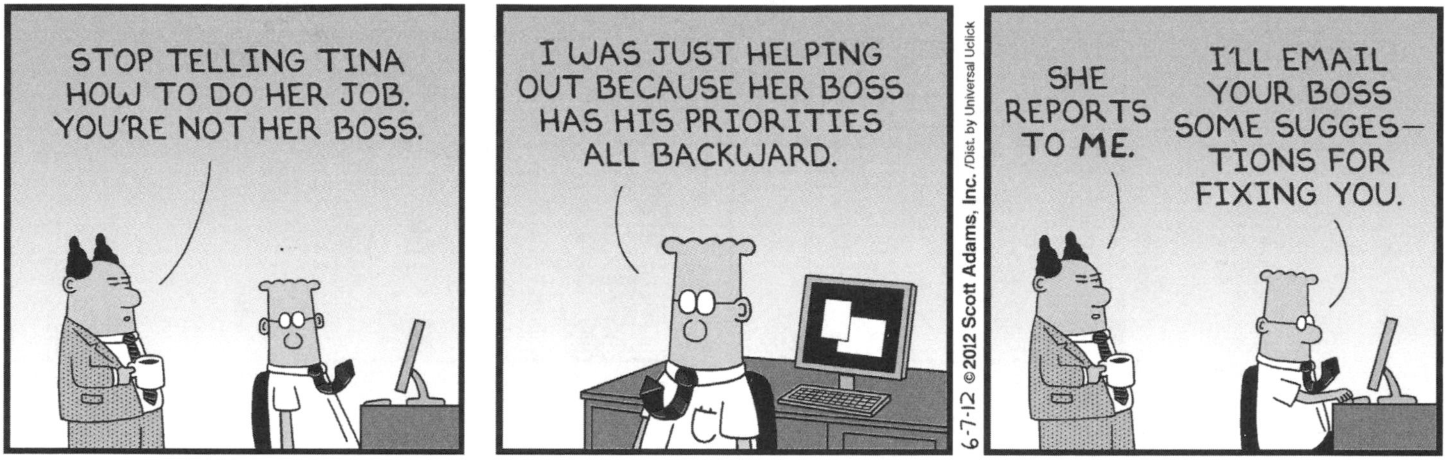
STOP TELLING TINA HOW TO DO HER JOB. YOU'RE NOT HER BOSS.
I WAS JUST HELPING OUT BECAUSE HER BOSS HAS HIS PRIORITIES ALL BACKWARD.
6-7-12 © 2012 Scott Adams, Inc. /Dist. by Universal Uclick
SHE REPORTS TO **ME.**
I'LL EMAIL YOUR BOSS SOME SUGGES- TIONS FOR FIXING YOU.

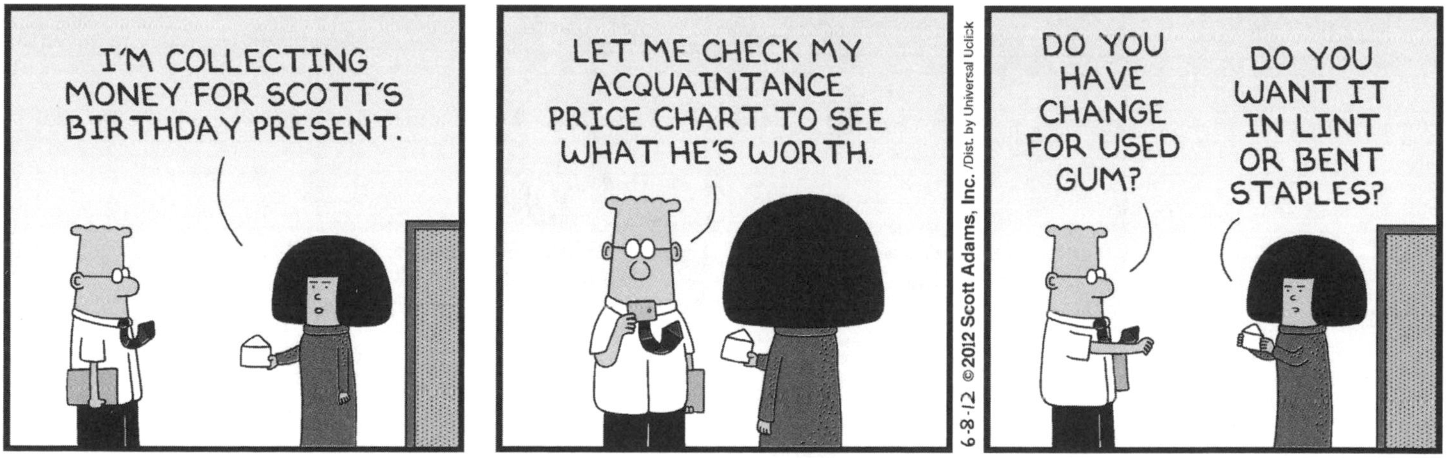
I'M COLLECTING MONEY FOR SCOTT'S BIRTHDAY PRESENT.
LET ME CHECK MY ACQUAINTANCE PRICE CHART TO SEE WHAT HE'S WORTH.
6-8-12 © 2012 Scott Adams, Inc. /Dist. by Universal Uclick
DO YOU HAVE CHANGE FOR USED GUM?
DO YOU WANT IT IN LINT OR BENT STAPLES?

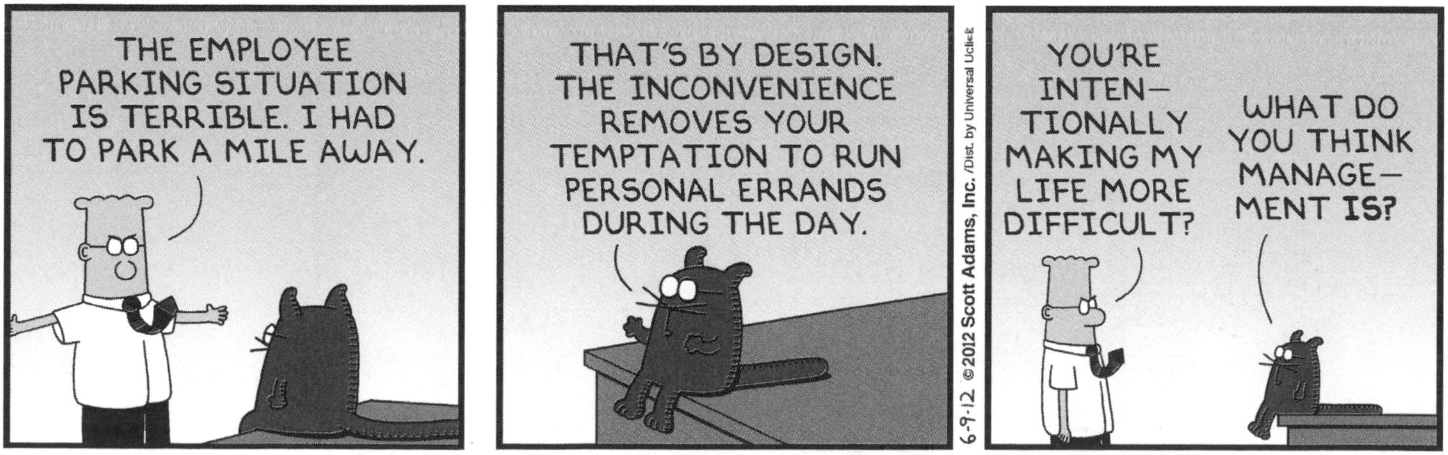
THE EMPLOYEE PARKING SITUATION IS TERRIBLE. I HAD TO PARK A MILE AWAY.
THAT'S BY DESIGN. THE INCONVENIENCE REMOVES YOUR TEMPTATION TO RUN PERSONAL ERRANDS DURING THE DAY.
6-9-12 © 2012 Scott Adams, Inc. /Dist. by Universal Uclick
YOU'RE INTEN- TIONALLY MAKING MY LIFE MORE DIFFICULT?
WHAT DO YOU THINK MANAGE- MENT **IS?**

I NEED TO GET THIS TECHNOLOGY CERTIFICATION.
WHOA! NO WAY.
IF I PAY FOR YOUR TRAINING, YOU'LL USE YOUR CERTIFICATION TO GET A BETTER JOB.
© 2012 Scott Adams, Inc./Dist. by Universal Uclick
AT THE MOMENT, YOU'RE IN WHAT WE MANAGERS CALL THE GOLDILOCKS ZONE.
YOU'RE NOT HOT ENOUGH TO GET A BETTER JOB, AND YOU'RE NOT YET INCOMPETENT AT THE ONE YOU HAVE.
WHEN YOUR SKILLS EXPIRE, IN THE NEXT YEAR OR TWO, I'LL REPLACE YOU WITH SOMEONE YOUNGER.
YOU'RE A MONSTER! I'LL PAY FOR MY OWN TRAINING AND LEAVE YOU TO MARINATE IN YOUR OWN STENCH!
6-10-12
HOW DID YOU KEEP YOUR TRAINING EXPENSES SO LOW?
I MARI-NATED IN MY OWN STENCH.

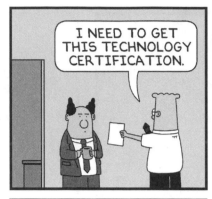

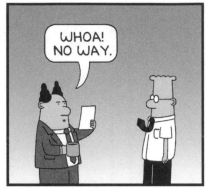

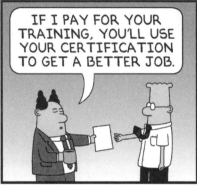

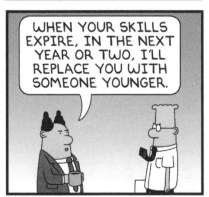

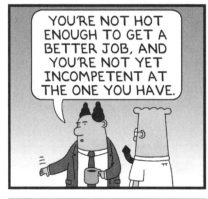

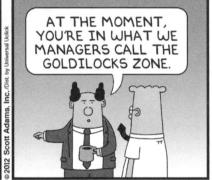

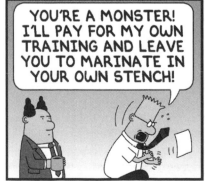

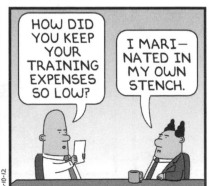

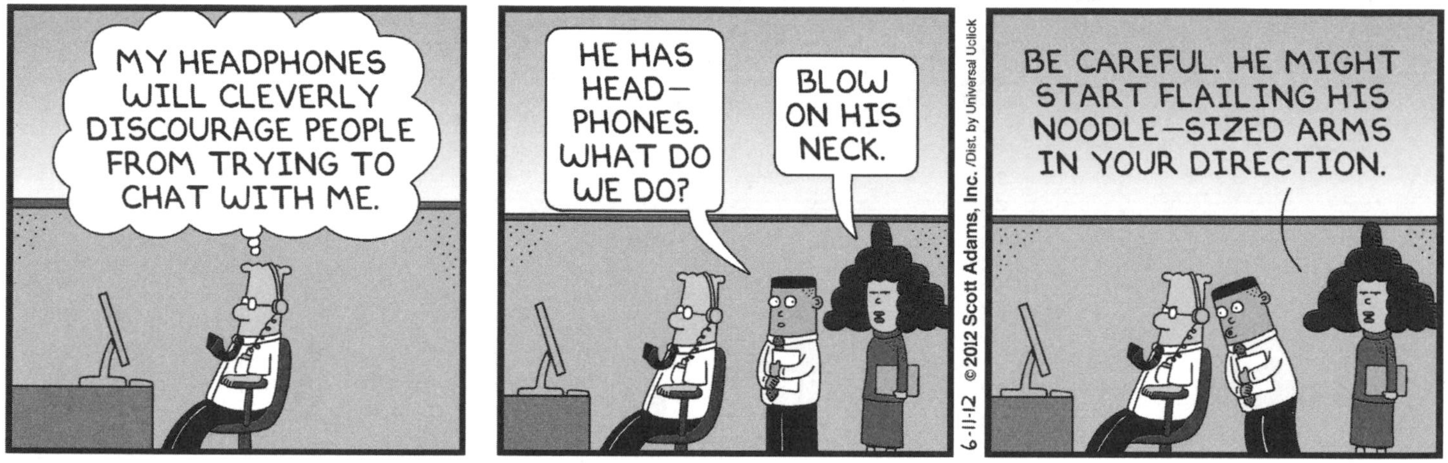
MY HEADPHONES WILL CLEVERLY DISCOURAGE PEOPLE FROM TRYING TO CHAT WITH ME.
HE HAS HEAD–PHONES. WHAT DO WE DO?
BLOW ON HIS NECK.
BE CAREFUL. HE MIGHT START FLAILING HIS NOODLE–SIZED ARMS IN YOUR DIRECTION.
6-11-12 © 2012 Scott Adams, Inc. /Dist. by Universal Uclick

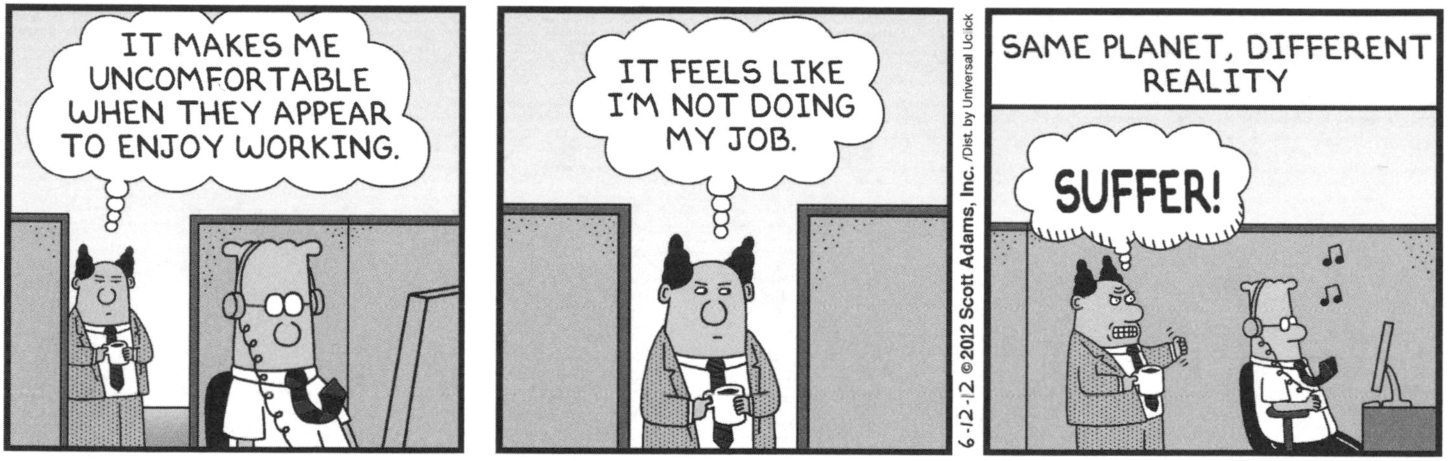
IT MAKES ME UNCOMFORTABLE WHEN THEY APPEAR TO ENJOY WORKING.
IT FEELS LIKE I'M NOT DOING MY JOB.
SAME PLANET, DIFFERENT REALITY
SUFFER!
6-12-12 © 2012 Scott Adams, Inc. /Dist. by Universal Uclick

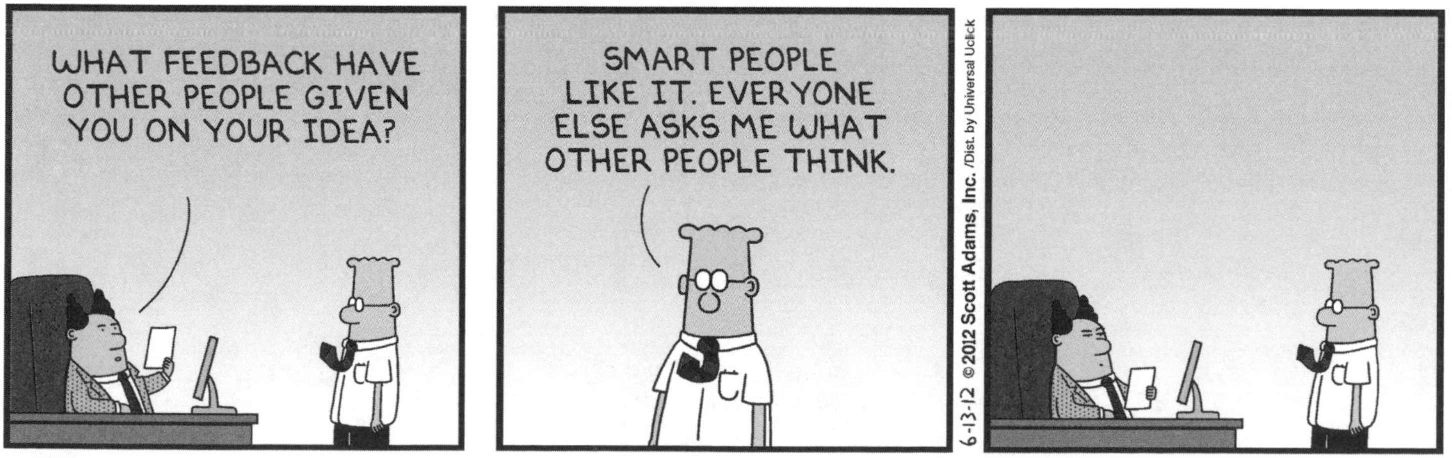
WHAT FEEDBACK HAVE OTHER PEOPLE GIVEN YOU ON YOUR IDEA?
SMART PEOPLE LIKE IT. EVERYONE ELSE ASKS ME WHAT OTHER PEOPLE THINK.
6-13-12 © 2012 Scott Adams, Inc. /Dist. by Universal Uclick

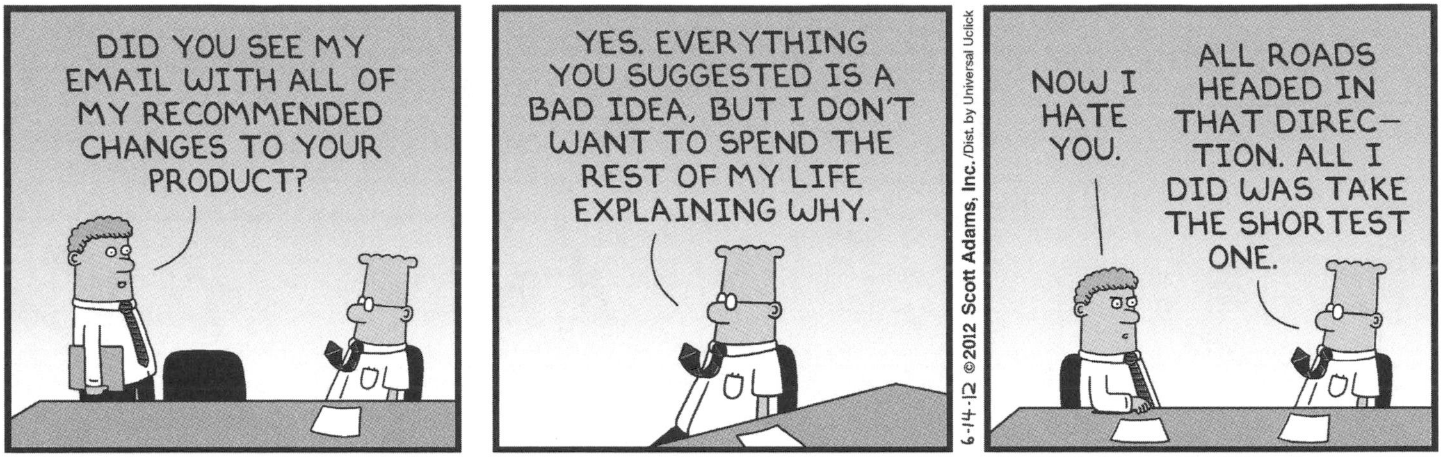
DID YOU SEE MY EMAIL WITH ALL OF MY RECOMMENDED CHANGES TO YOUR PRODUCT?
YES. EVERYTHING YOU SUGGESTED IS A BAD IDEA, BUT I DON'T WANT TO SPEND THE REST OF MY LIFE EXPLAINING WHY.
6-14-12 ©2012 Scott Adams, Inc./Dist. by Universal Uclick
NOW I HATE YOU.
ALL ROADS HEADED IN THAT DIREC- TION. ALL I DID WAS TAKE THE SHORTEST ONE.

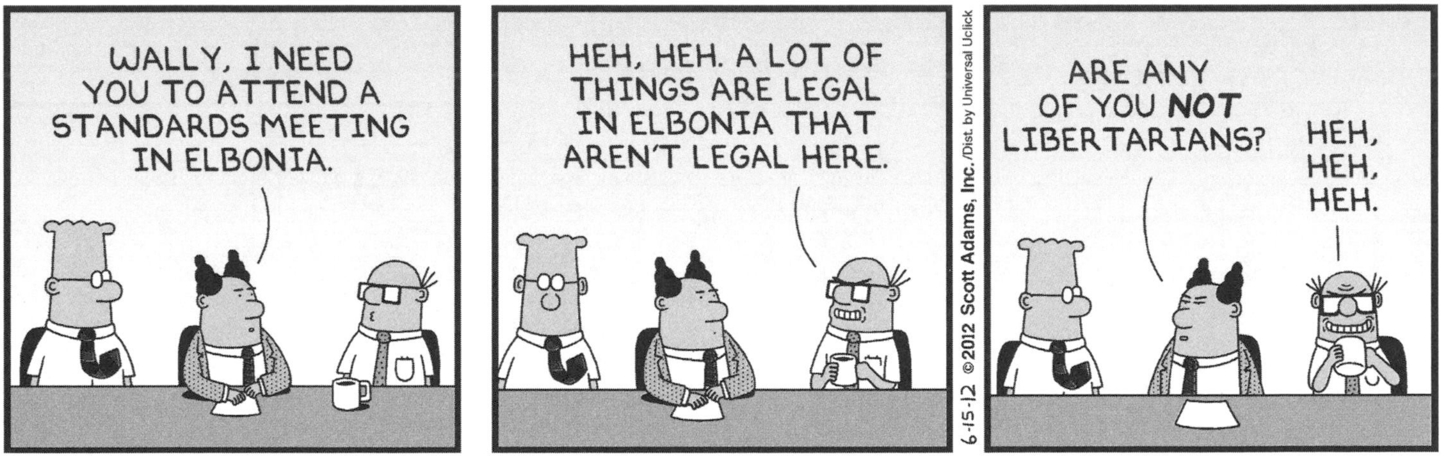
WALLY, I NEED YOU TO ATTEND A STANDARDS MEETING IN ELBONIA.
HEH, HEH. A LOT OF THINGS ARE LEGAL IN ELBONIA THAT AREN'T LEGAL HERE.
6-15-12 ©2012 Scott Adams, Inc./Dist. by Universal Uclick
ARE ANY OF YOU **NOT** LIBERTARIANS?
HEH, HEH, HEH.

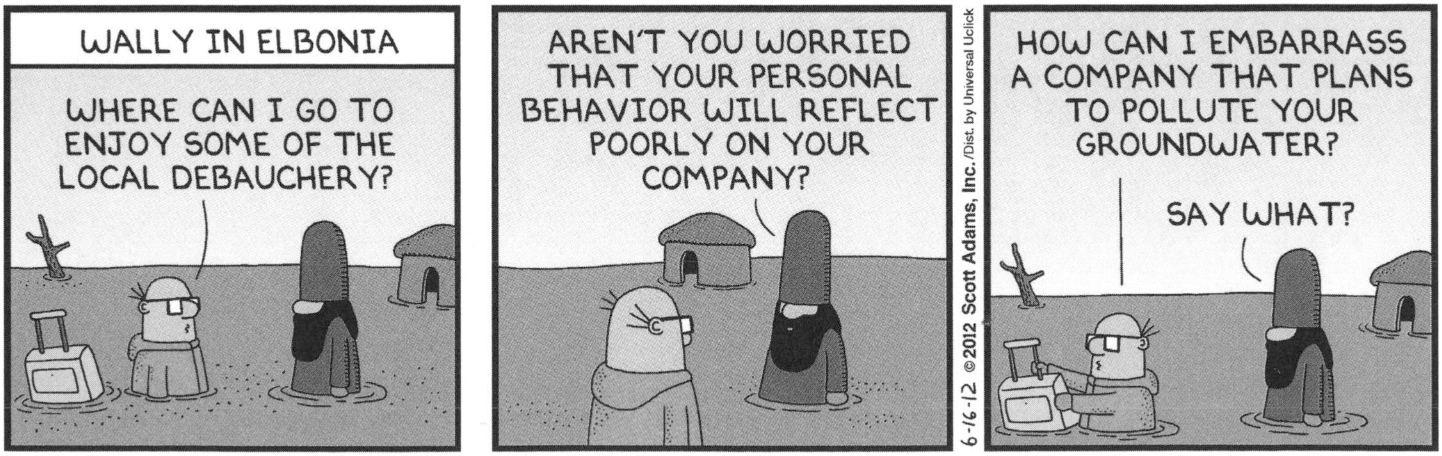
WALLY IN ELBONIA
WHERE CAN I GO TO ENJOY SOME OF THE LOCAL DEBAUCHERY?
AREN'T YOU WORRIED THAT YOUR PERSONAL BEHAVIOR WILL REFLECT POORLY ON YOUR COMPANY?
6-16-12 ©2012 Scott Adams, Inc./Dist. by Universal Uclick
HOW CAN I EMBARRASS A COMPANY THAT PLANS TO POLLUTE YOUR GROUNDWATER?
SAY WHAT?

I REPROGRAMMED OUR POINTY-HAIRED BOSS' SPEED DIAL ON HIS DESK PHONE.

NOW EVERY TIME HE TRIES TO USE SPEED DIAL, IT CALLS HIS OWN CELLPHONE.

IT'S LIKE AN INTELLIGENCE TEST. I WANT TO SEE HOW LONG IT TAKES HIM TO FIGURE IT OUT.

RING

I'D BETTER TAKE THIS.

RING

HELLO? HELLO?

HELLO? HELLO?

HOLD ON.

HOLD ON.

FOR THE HUNDREDTH TIME, DON'T TELL **ME** TO HOLD ON! I'M TELLING **YOU** TO HOLD ON!

TWENTY MINUTES SO FAR.

© 2012 Scott Adams, Inc. /Dist. by Universal Uclick

6-17-12

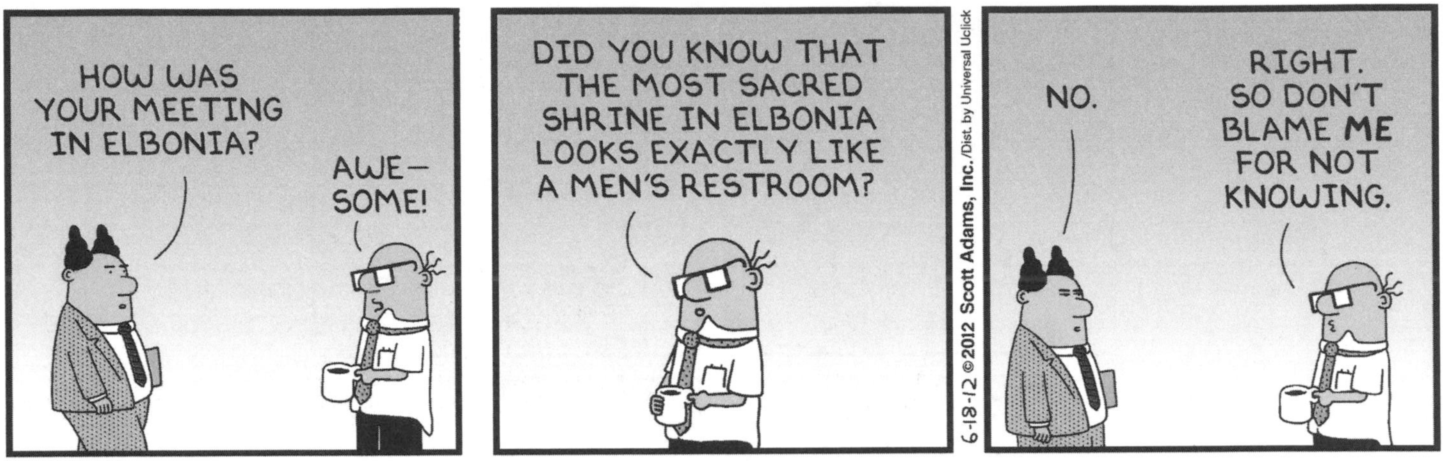
HOW WAS YOUR MEETING IN ELBONIA?
AWE-SOME!
DID YOU KNOW THAT THE MOST SACRED SHRINE IN ELBONIA LOOKS EXACTLY LIKE A MEN'S RESTROOM?
NO.
RIGHT. SO DON'T BLAME **ME** FOR NOT KNOWING.
6-18-12 ©2012 Scott Adams, Inc./Dist. by Universal Uclick

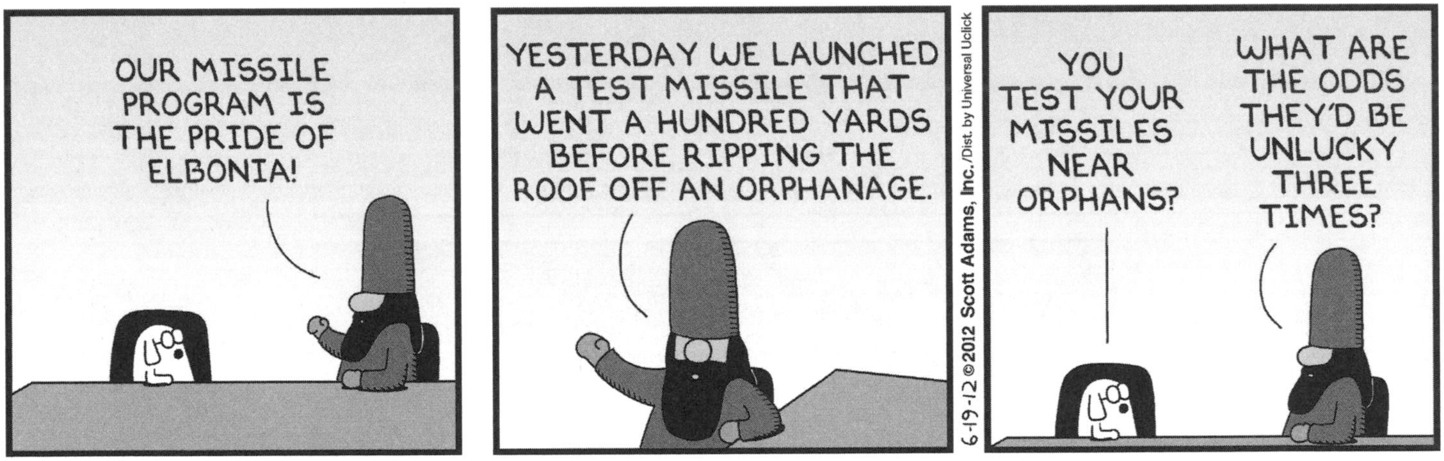
OUR MISSILE PROGRAM IS THE PRIDE OF ELBONIA!
YESTERDAY WE LAUNCHED A TEST MISSILE THAT WENT A HUNDRED YARDS BEFORE RIPPING THE ROOF OFF AN ORPHANAGE.
YOU TEST YOUR MISSILES NEAR ORPHANS?
WHAT ARE THE ODDS THEY'D BE UNLUCKY THREE TIMES?
6-19-12 ©2012 Scott Adams, Inc./Dist. by Universal Uclick

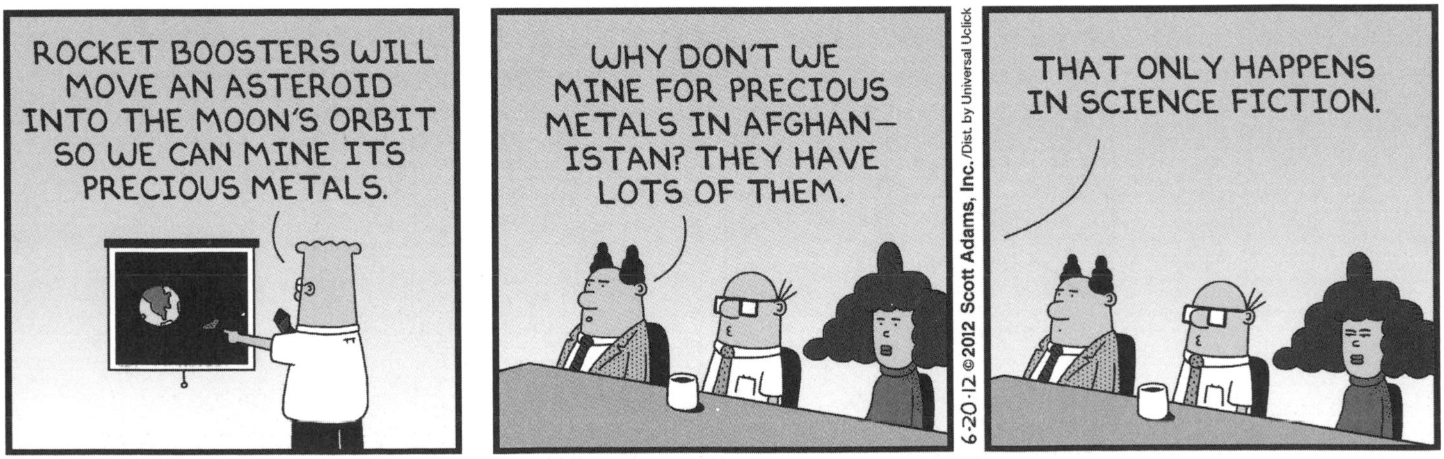
ROCKET BOOSTERS WILL MOVE AN ASTEROID INTO THE MOON'S ORBIT SO WE CAN MINE ITS PRECIOUS METALS.
WHY DON'T WE MINE FOR PRECIOUS METALS IN AFGHAN-ISTAN? THEY HAVE LOTS OF THEM.
THAT ONLY HAPPENS IN SCIENCE FICTION.
6-20-12 ©2012 Scott Adams, Inc./Dist. by Universal Uclick

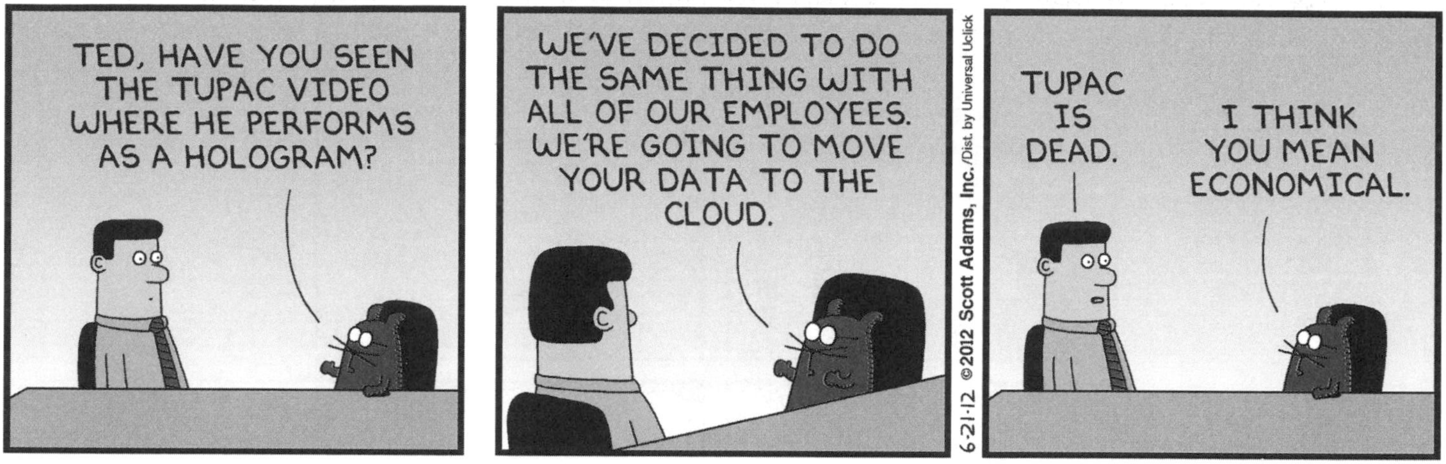
TED, HAVE YOU SEEN THE TUPAC VIDEO WHERE HE PERFORMS AS A HOLOGRAM?
WE'VE DECIDED TO DO THE SAME THING WITH ALL OF OUR EMPLOYEES. WE'RE GOING TO MOVE YOUR DATA TO THE CLOUD.
6-21-12 ©2012 Scott Adams, Inc./Dist. by Universal Uclick
TUPAC IS DEAD.
I THINK YOU MEAN ECONOMICAL.

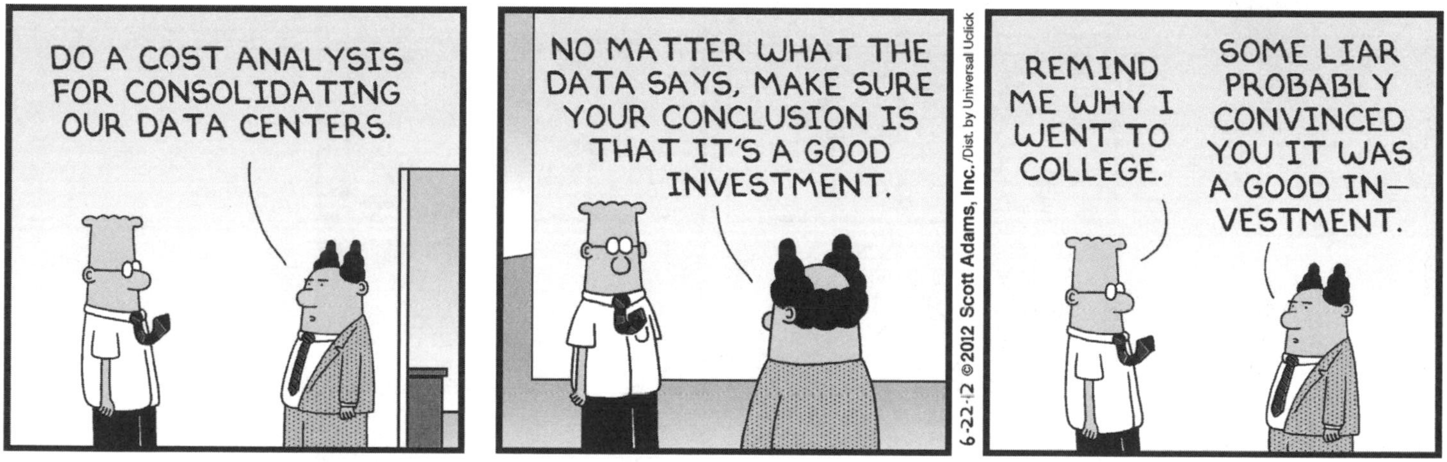
DO A COST ANALYSIS FOR CONSOLIDATING OUR DATA CENTERS.
NO MATTER WHAT THE DATA SAYS, MAKE SURE YOUR CONCLUSION IS THAT IT'S A GOOD INVESTMENT.
6-22-12 ©2012 Scott Adams, Inc./Dist. by Universal Uclick
REMIND ME WHY I WENT TO COLLEGE.
SOME LIAR PROBABLY CONVINCED YOU IT WAS A GOOD IN-VESTMENT.

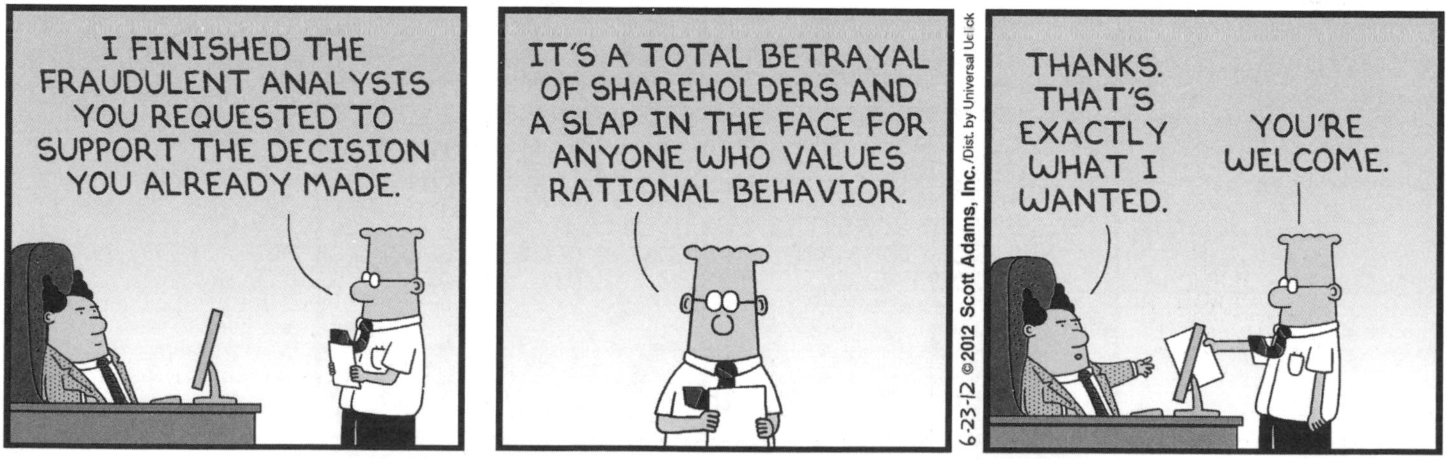
I FINISHED THE FRAUDULENT ANALYSIS YOU REQUESTED TO SUPPORT THE DECISION YOU ALREADY MADE.
IT'S A TOTAL BETRAYAL OF SHAREHOLDERS AND A SLAP IN THE FACE FOR ANYONE WHO VALUES RATIONAL BEHAVIOR.
6-23-12 ©2012 Scott Adams, Inc./Dist. by Universal Uclick
THANKS. THAT'S EXACTLY WHAT I WANTED.
YOU'RE WELCOME.

MY DAUGHTER IS TRAINING FOR THE OLYMPICS. MY SON IS GOING TO HARVARD.
I HAVE NO SPAWN OF MY OWN, SO I CLAIM THE RIGHT TO NAME A PROXY TO BRAG ON MY BEHALF.
TOPPER, I NEED YOU.
OF COURSE YOU DO.
©2012 Scott Adams, Inc./Dist. by Universal Uclick
MY DAUGHTER DISCOVERED THE HIGGS BOSON PARTICLE USING NOTHING BUT LICORICE AND A FLASHLIGHT.
MY SON INHALES CARBON DIOXIDE AND EXHALES ENDANGERED SPECIES WHILE PLAYING IN THE NATIONAL FOOTBALL LEAGUE.
THIS ISN'T FAIR! YOU CAN'T JUST MAKE UP STUFF!
ACCORDING TO THE PRESIDENT OF THE INTERNATIONAL SOCIETY OF BOASTERS, FABRICATIONS ARE ACCEPTABLE.
6-24-12
I'D LIKE TO TALK TO THAT GUY.
YOU'RE LOOKING AT HIM.
I WIN.

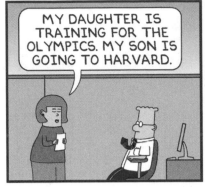

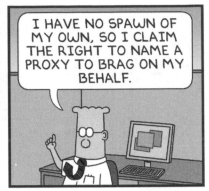

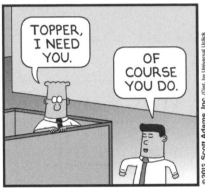

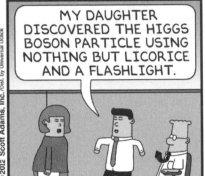

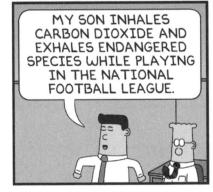

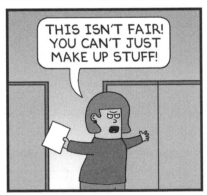

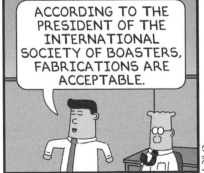

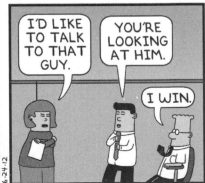

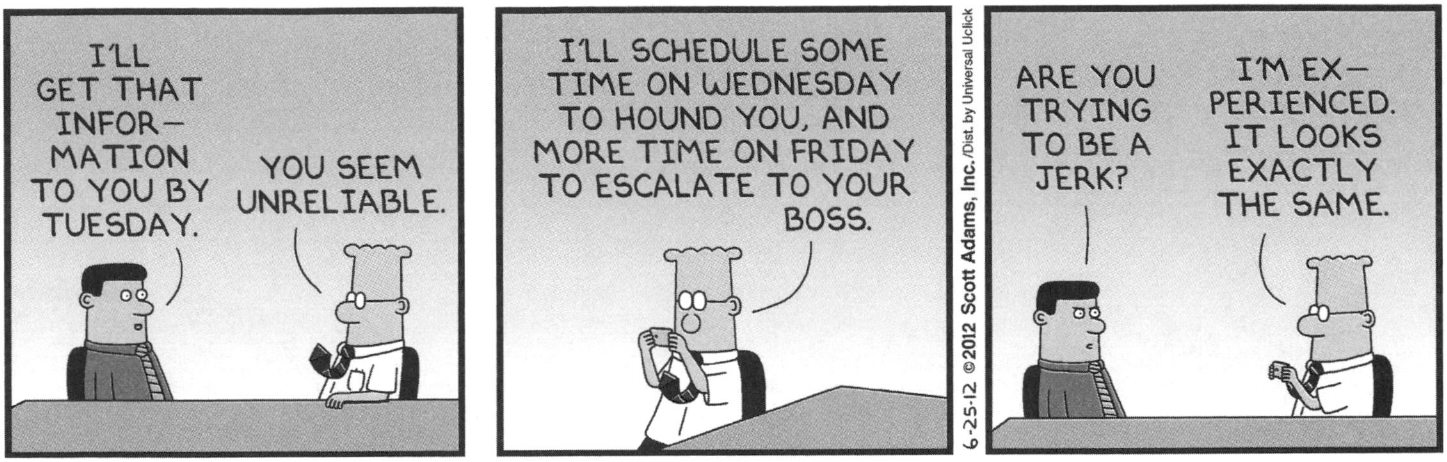
I'LL GET THAT INFORMATION TO YOU BY TUESDAY.
YOU SEEM UNRELIABLE.
I'LL SCHEDULE SOME TIME ON WEDNESDAY TO HOUND YOU, AND MORE TIME ON FRIDAY TO ESCALATE TO YOUR BOSS.
6-25-12 ©2012 Scott Adams, Inc./Dist. by Universal Uclick
ARE YOU TRYING TO BE A JERK?
I'M EXPERIENCED. IT LOOKS EXACTLY THE SAME.

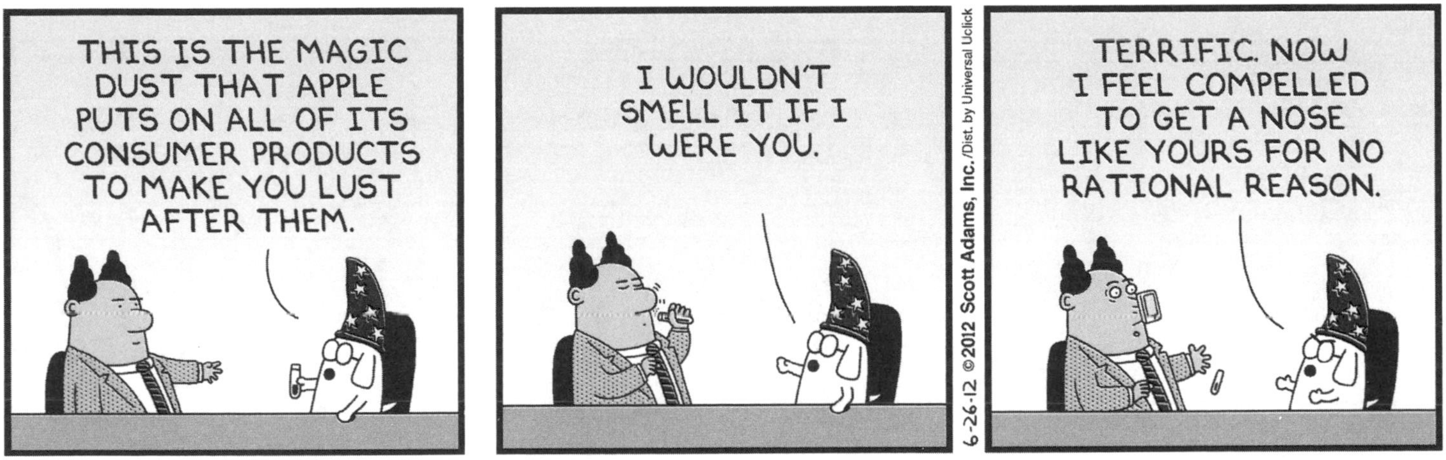
THIS IS THE MAGIC DUST THAT APPLE PUTS ON ALL OF ITS CONSUMER PRODUCTS TO MAKE YOU LUST AFTER THEM.
I WOULDN'T SMELL IT IF I WERE YOU.
6-26-12 ©2012 Scott Adams, Inc./Dist. by Universal Uclick
TERRIFIC. NOW I FEEL COMPELLED TO GET A NOSE LIKE YOURS FOR NO RATIONAL REASON.

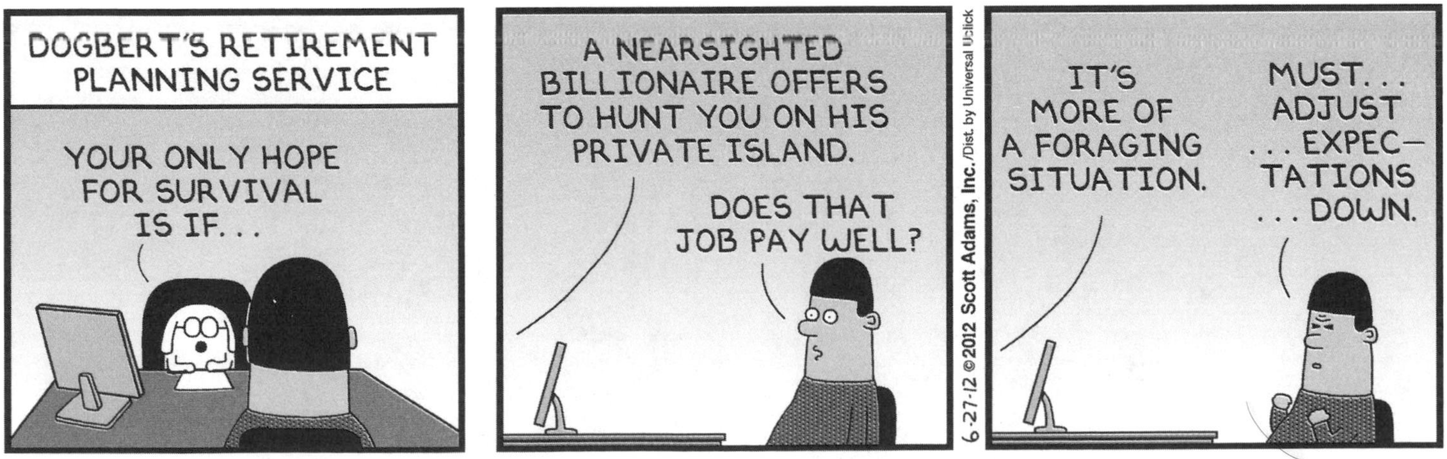
DOGBERT'S RETIREMENT PLANNING SERVICE
YOUR ONLY HOPE FOR SURVIVAL IS IF...
A NEARSIGHTED BILLIONAIRE OFFERS TO HUNT YOU ON HIS PRIVATE ISLAND.
DOES THAT JOB PAY WELL?
6-27-12 ©2012 Scott Adams, Inc./Dist. by Universal Uclick
IT'S MORE OF A FORAGING SITUATION.
MUST... ADJUST ... EXPECTATIONS ... DOWN.

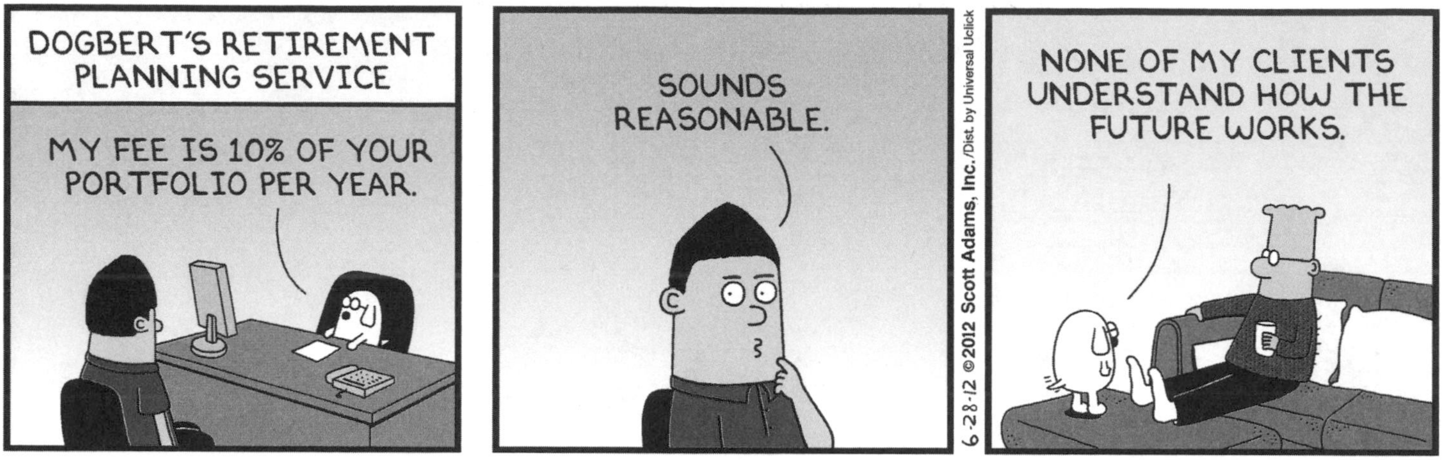
DOGBERT'S RETIREMENT PLANNING SERVICE
MY FEE IS 10% OF YOUR PORTFOLIO PER YEAR.
SOUNDS REASONABLE.
6-28-12 ©2012 Scott Adams, Inc./Dist. by Universal Uclick
NONE OF MY CLIENTS UNDERSTAND HOW THE FUTURE WORKS.

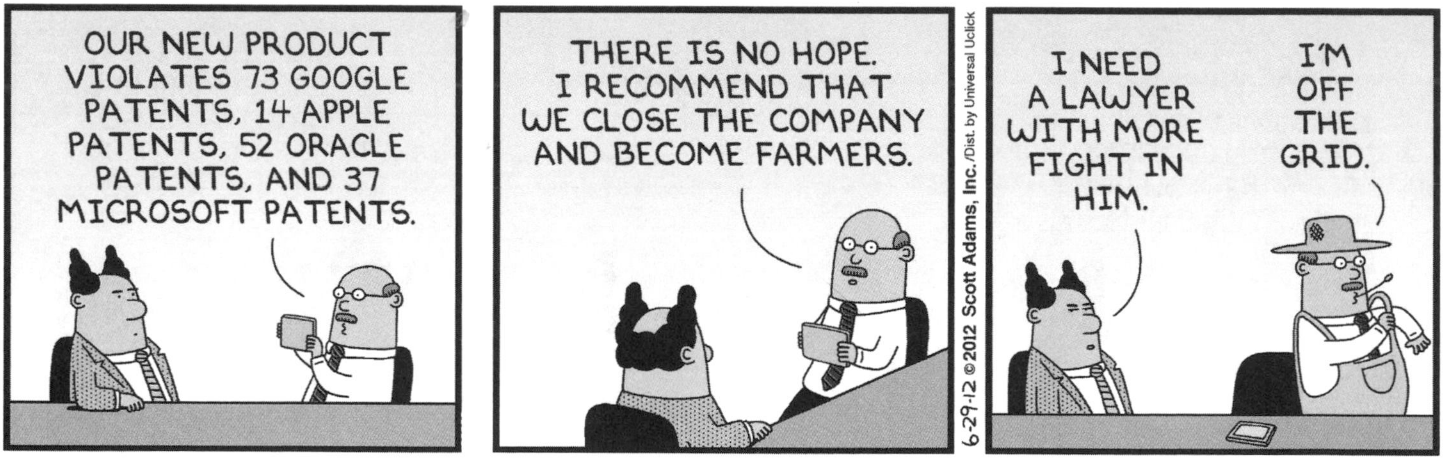
OUR NEW PRODUCT VIOLATES 73 GOOGLE PATENTS, 14 APPLE PATENTS, 52 ORACLE PATENTS, AND 37 MICROSOFT PATENTS.
THERE IS NO HOPE. I RECOMMEND THAT WE CLOSE THE COMPANY AND BECOME FARMERS.
6-29-12 ©2012 Scott Adams, Inc./Dist. by Universal Uclick
I NEED A LAWYER WITH MORE FIGHT IN HIM.
I'M OFF THE GRID.

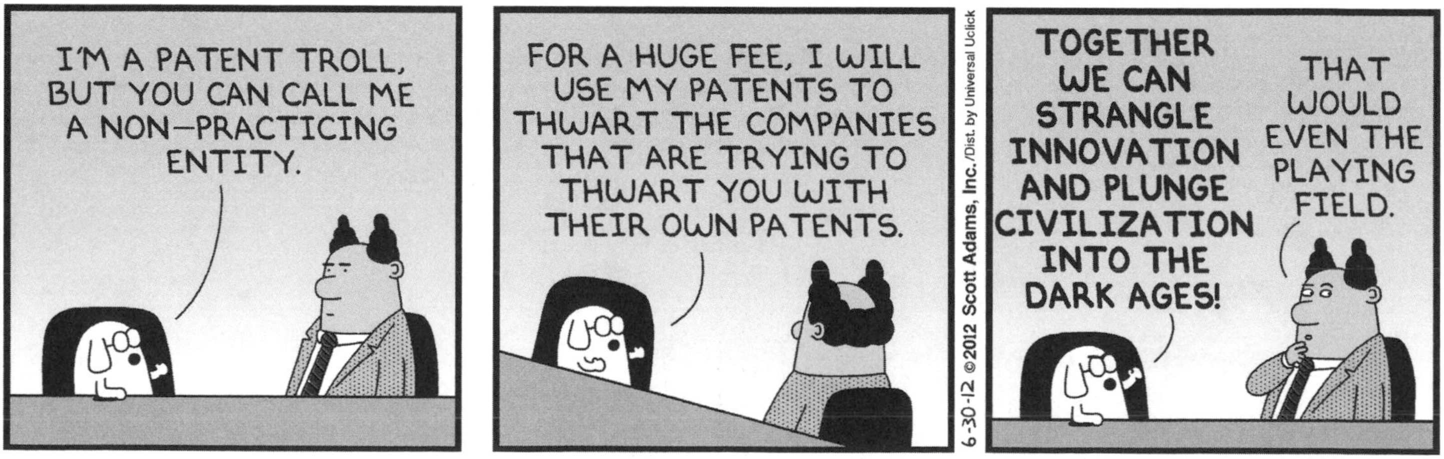
I'M A PATENT TROLL, BUT YOU CAN CALL ME A NON-PRACTICING ENTITY.
FOR A HUGE FEE, I WILL USE MY PATENTS TO THWART THE COMPANIES THAT ARE TRYING TO THWART YOU WITH THEIR OWN PATENTS.
6-30-12 ©2012 Scott Adams, Inc./Dist. by Universal Uclick
TOGETHER WE CAN STRANGLE INNOVATION AND PLUNGE CIVILIZATION INTO THE DARK AGES!
THAT WOULD EVEN THE PLAYING FIELD.

I AM MORDAC, THE PREVENTER OF INFORMATION SERVICES.
I KNOW. WE'VE WORKED TOGETHER FOR YEARS.
AND IT STILL SOUNDS AWESOME WHEN I SAY IT.
ANYWAY, I UP-GRADED OUR NETWORK SECURITY TO INCLUDE FACIAL RECOGNITION.
YOUR TEMPORARY PASSWORD IS THIS FACE.
YOU'LL NEED EXTENSIVE PLASTIC SURGERY TO LOG ON THE FIRST TIME.
YOU'VE GONE TOO FAR, MORDAC! I WILL ESCALATE THIS!
I WISH WE'D HAD THIS CONVERSATION A WEEK AGO.
©2012 Scott Adams, Inc./Dist. by Universal Uclick
7-1-12

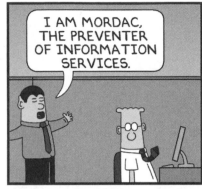

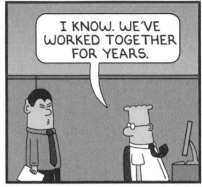

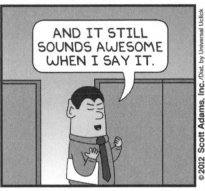

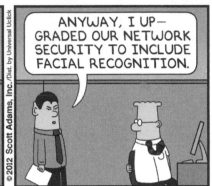

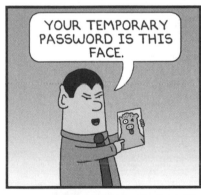

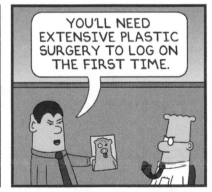

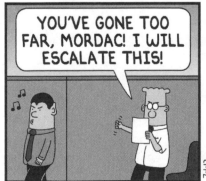

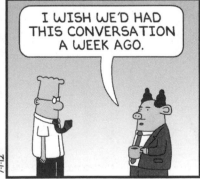

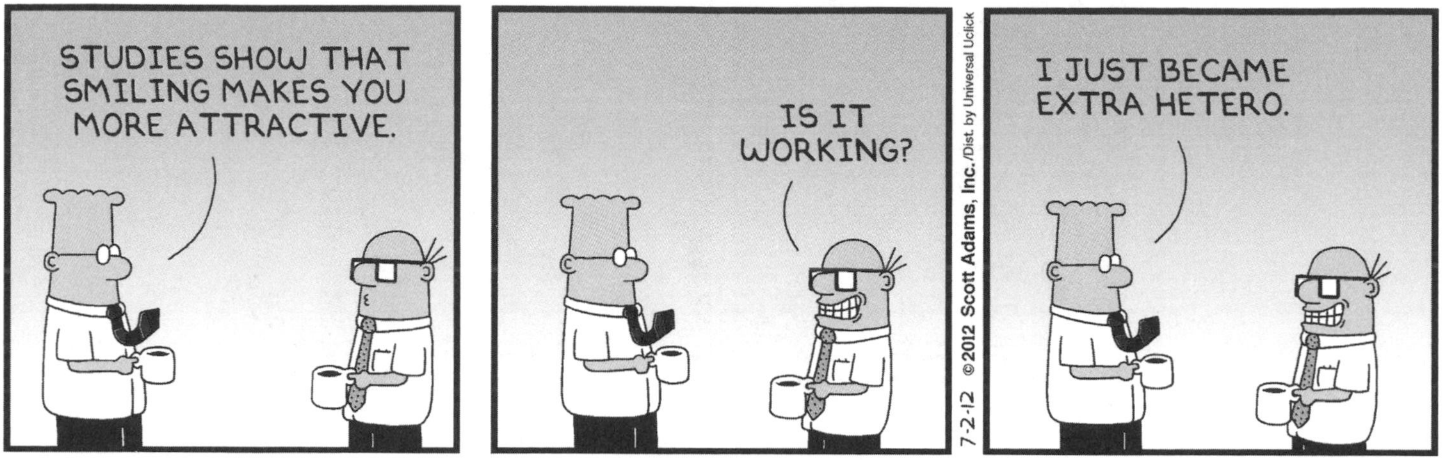
STUDIES SHOW THAT SMILING MAKES YOU MORE ATTRACTIVE.
IS IT WORKING?
7-2-12 ©2012 Scott Adams, Inc./Dist. by Universal Uclick
I JUST BECAME EXTRA HETERO.

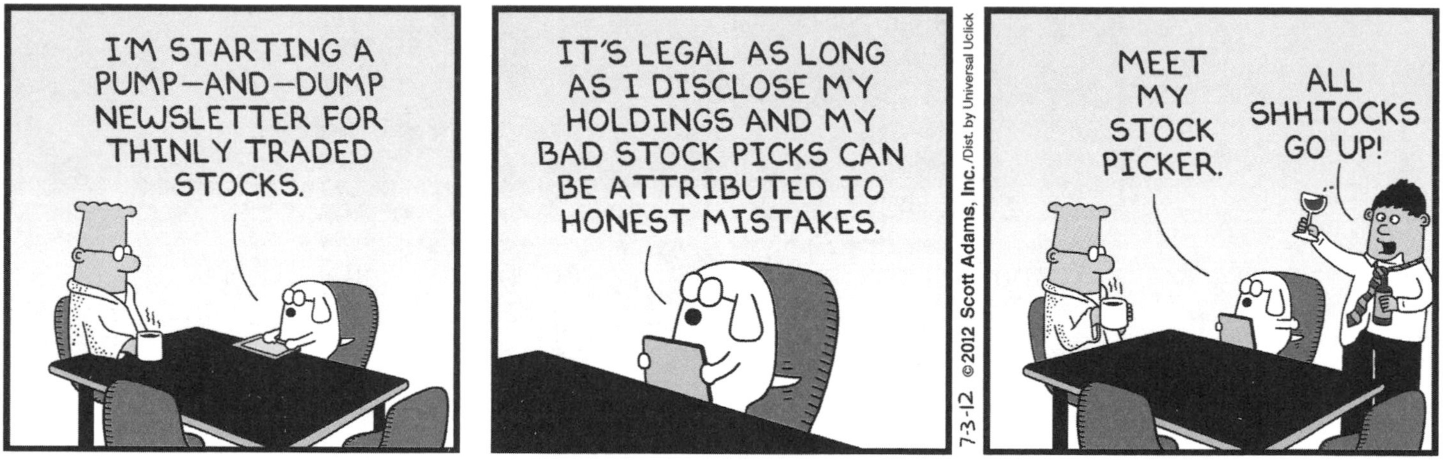
I'M STARTING A PUMP–AND–DUMP NEWSLETTER FOR THINLY TRADED STOCKS.
IT'S LEGAL AS LONG AS I DISCLOSE MY HOLDINGS AND MY BAD STOCK PICKS CAN BE ATTRIBUTED TO HONEST MISTAKES.
7-3-12 ©2012 Scott Adams, Inc./Dist. by Universal Uclick
MEET MY STOCK PICKER.
ALL SHHTOCKS GO UP!

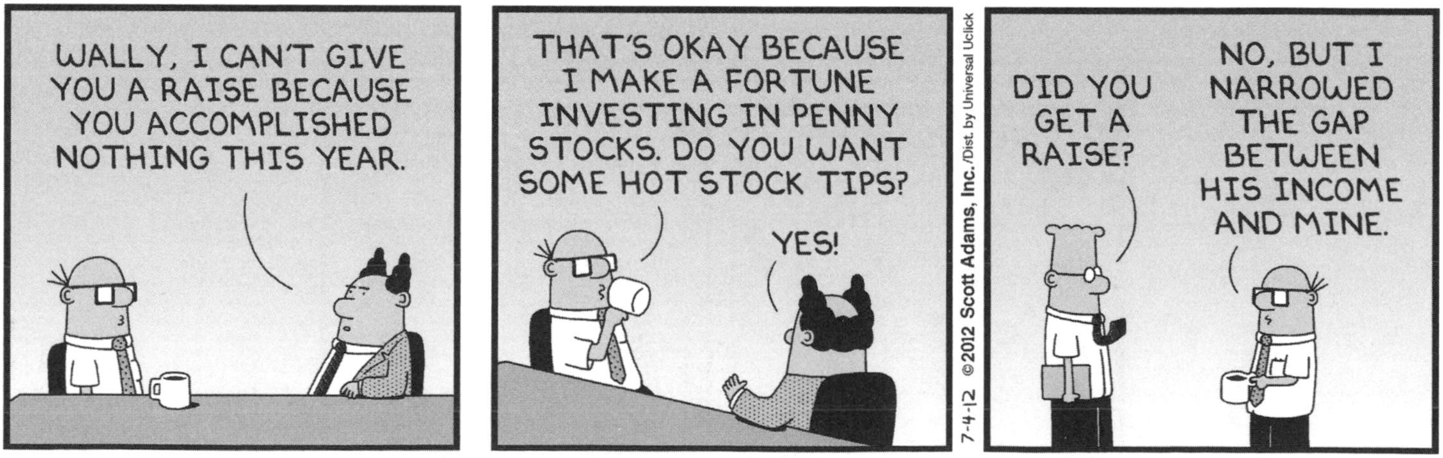
WALLY, I CAN'T GIVE YOU A RAISE BECAUSE YOU ACCOMPLISHED NOTHING THIS YEAR.
THAT'S OKAY BECAUSE I MAKE A FORTUNE INVESTING IN PENNY STOCKS. DO YOU WANT SOME HOT STOCK TIPS?
YES!
7-4-12 ©2012 Scott Adams, Inc./Dist. by Universal Uclick
DID YOU GET A RAISE?
NO, BUT I NARROWED THE GAP BETWEEN HIS INCOME AND MINE.

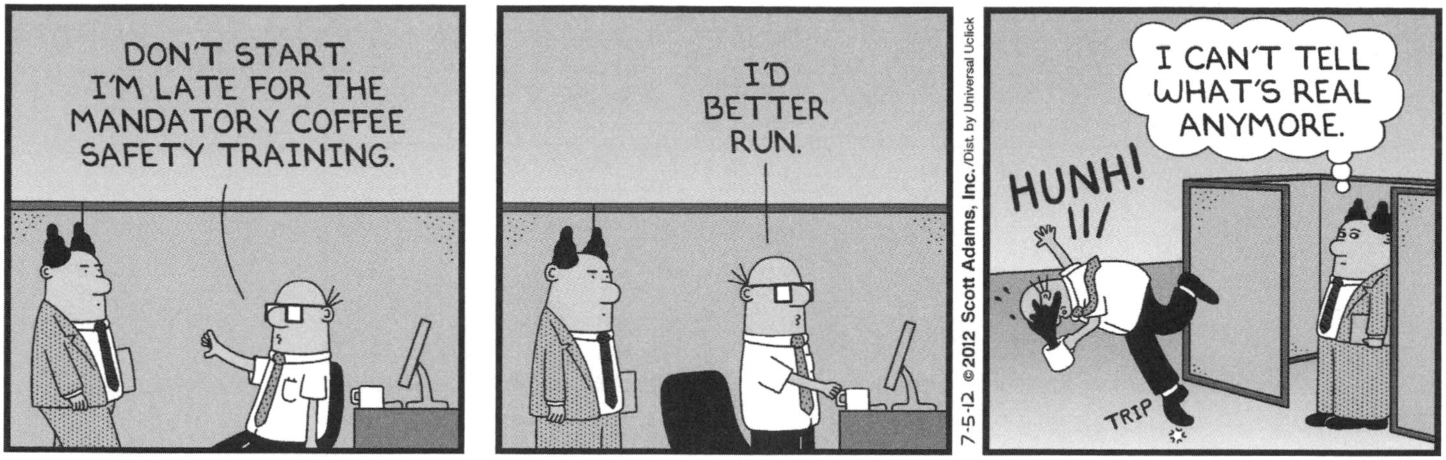
DON'T START. I'M LATE FOR THE MANDATORY COFFEE SAFETY TRAINING.
I'D BETTER RUN.
7-5-12 ©2012 Scott Adams, Inc./Dist. by Universal Uclick
HUNH!
TRIP
I CAN'T TELL WHAT'S REAL ANYMORE.

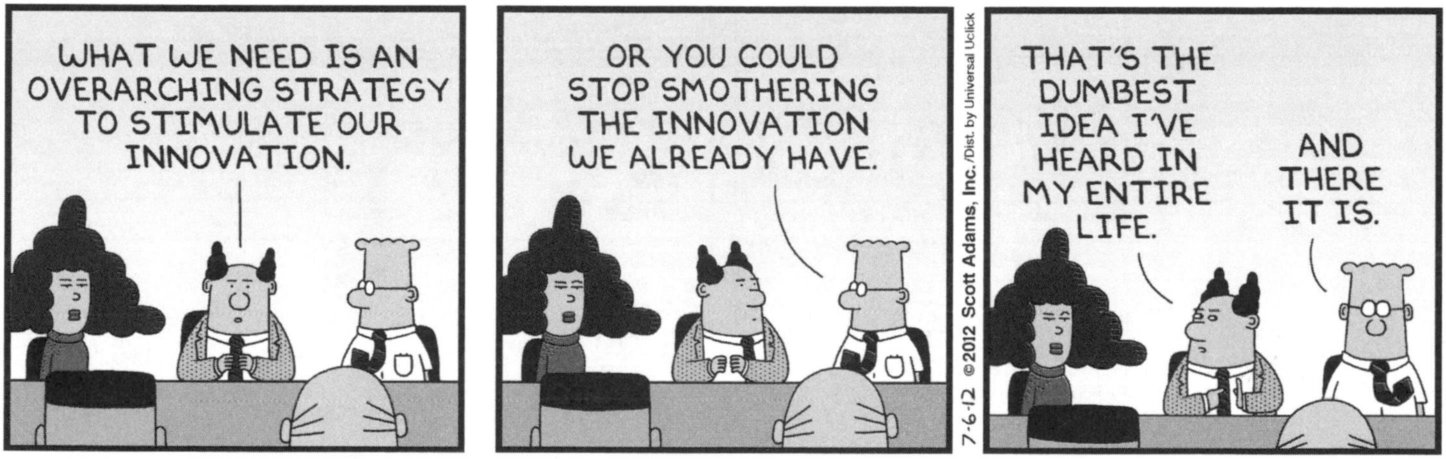
WHAT WE NEED IS AN OVERARCHING STRATEGY TO STIMULATE OUR INNOVATION.
OR YOU COULD STOP SMOTHERING THE INNOVATION WE ALREADY HAVE.
7-6-12 ©2012 Scott Adams, Inc./Dist. by Universal Uclick
THAT'S THE DUMBEST IDEA I'VE HEARD IN MY ENTIRE LIFE.
AND THERE IT IS.

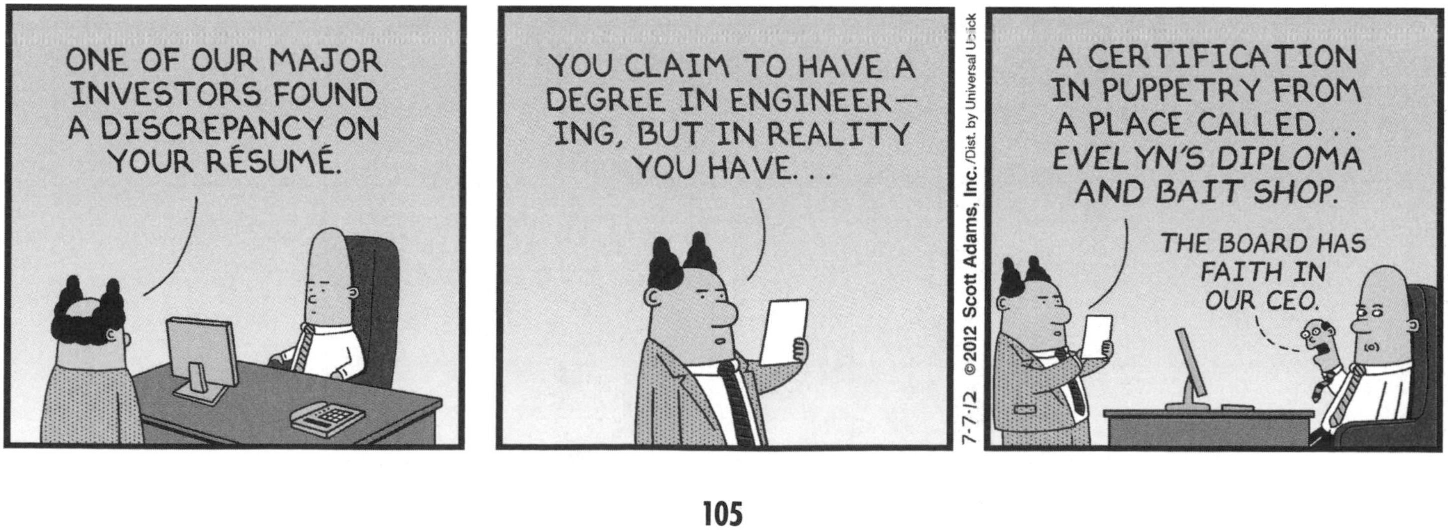
ONE OF OUR MAJOR INVESTORS FOUND A DISCREPANCY ON YOUR RÉSUMÉ.
YOU CLAIM TO HAVE A DEGREE IN ENGINEER-ING, BUT IN REALITY YOU HAVE...
7-7-12 ©2012 Scott Adams, Inc./Dist. by Universal Uclick
A CERTIFICATION IN PUPPETRY FROM A PLACE CALLED... EVELYN'S DIPLOMA AND BAIT SHOP.
THE BOARD HAS FAITH IN OUR CEO.

LET'S BRAINSTORM NEW PRODUCT IDEAS.
REMEMBER, THE MOST IMPORTANT RULE OF BRAINSTORMING IS *NO CRITICIZING.*
I'LL GO FIRST.
RESEARCH SHOWS THAT BRAINSTORMING IS LESS EFFECTIVE THAN PEOPLE WORKING BY THEMSELVES AND LATER COMPARING IDEAS.
MY IDEA IS TO USE STEM CELL TECHNOLOGY TO DESIGN BOSSES WHO AREN'T IGNORAMUSES.
REMEMBER, YOU'RE NOT SUPPOSED TO CRITICIZE IDEAS.
BUT IF YOU DECIDE TO DO IT ANYWAY, IT SORT OF PROVES MY POINT.
I UNDERSTAND WHY BRAINSTORMING HAS A BAD REPUTATION, BUT IT DOESN'T STOP ME FROM ENJOYING IT.
©2012 Scott Adams, Inc./Dist. by Universal Uclick
7-8-12

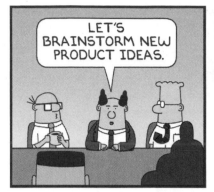

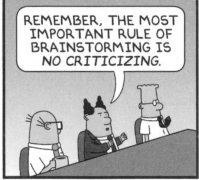

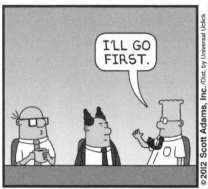

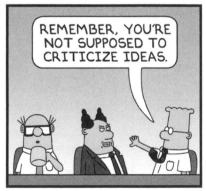

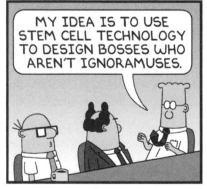

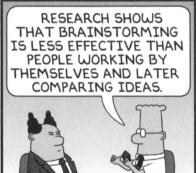

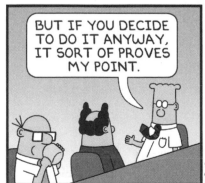

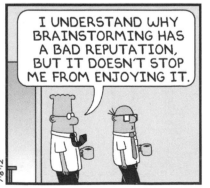

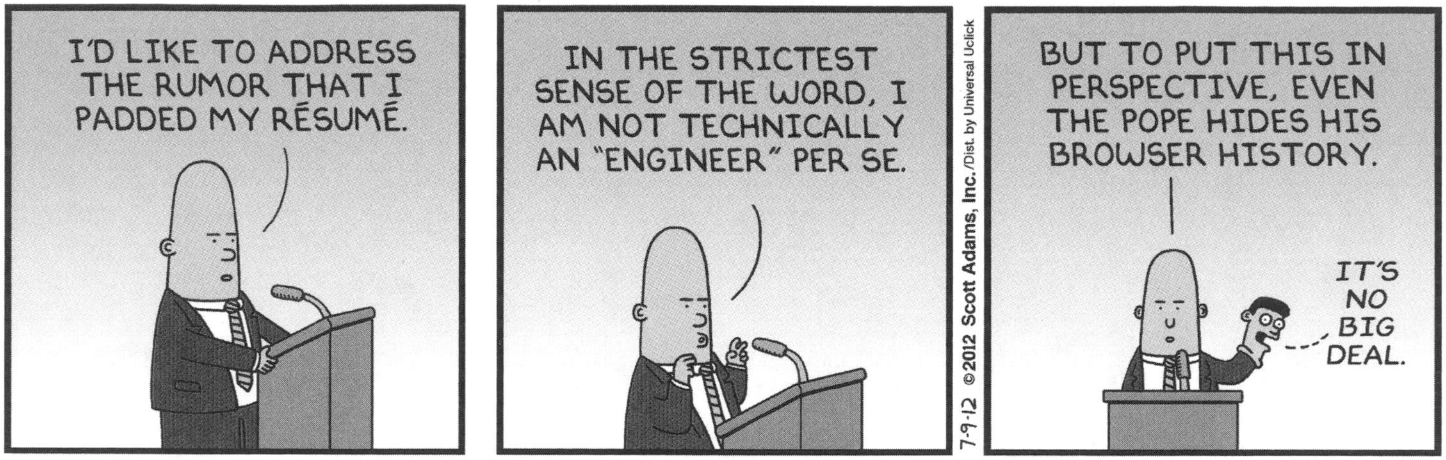
I'D LIKE TO ADDRESS THE RUMOR THAT I PADDED MY RÉSUMÉ.
IN THE STRICTEST SENSE OF THE WORD, I AM NOT TECHNICALLY AN "ENGINEER" PER SE.
7-9-12 ©2012 Scott Adams, Inc./Dist. by Universal Uclick
BUT TO PUT THIS IN PERSPECTIVE, EVEN THE POPE HIDES HIS BROWSER HISTORY.
IT'S NO BIG DEAL.

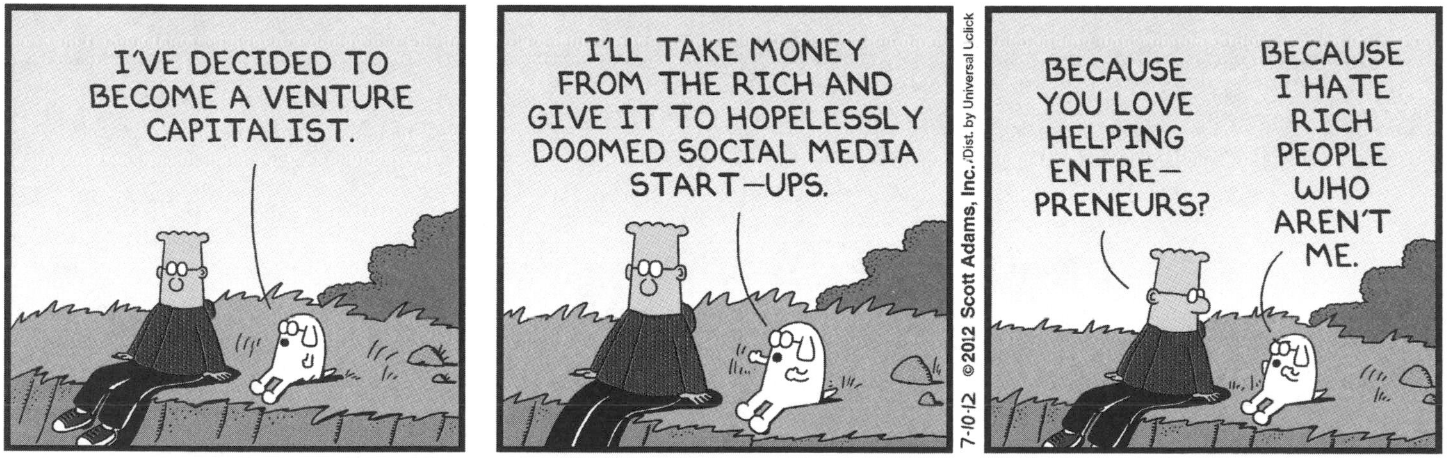
I'VE DECIDED TO BECOME A VENTURE CAPITALIST.
I'LL TAKE MONEY FROM THE RICH AND GIVE IT TO HOPELESSLY DOOMED SOCIAL MEDIA START-UPS.
7-10-12 ©2012 Scott Adams, Inc./Dist. by Universal Uclick
BECAUSE YOU LOVE HELPING ENTRE-PRENEURS?
BECAUSE I HATE RICH PEOPLE WHO AREN'T ME.

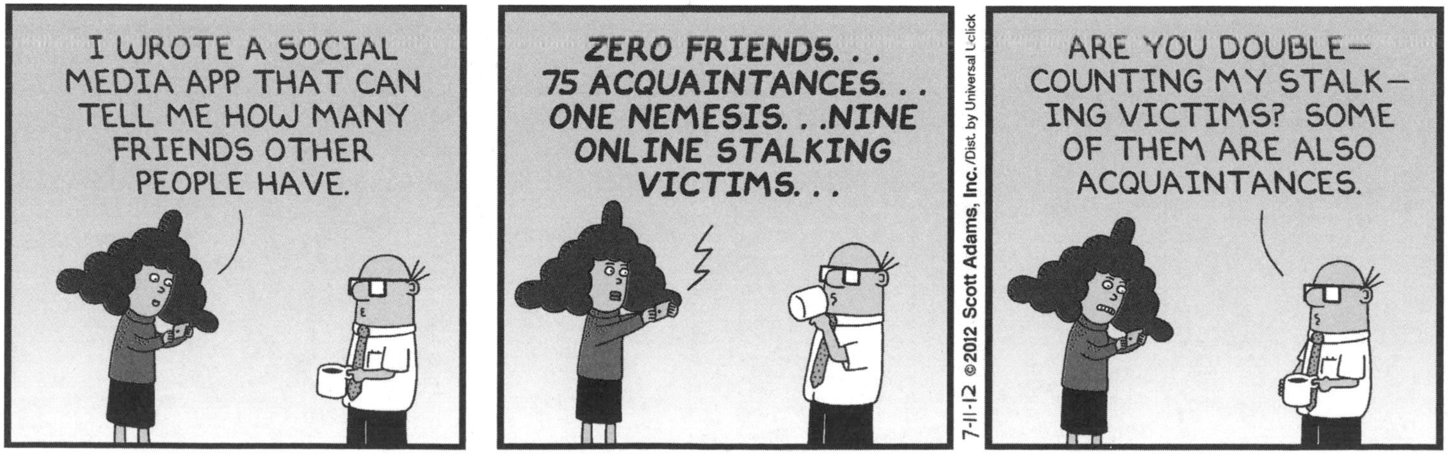
I WROTE A SOCIAL MEDIA APP THAT CAN TELL ME HOW MANY FRIENDS OTHER PEOPLE HAVE.
ZERO FRIENDS... 75 ACQUAINTANCES... ONE NEMESIS...NINE ONLINE STALKING VICTIMS...
7-11-12 ©2012 Scott Adams, Inc./Dist. by Universal Uclick
ARE YOU DOUBLE-COUNTING MY STALK-ING VICTIMS? SOME OF THEM ARE ALSO ACQUAINTANCES.

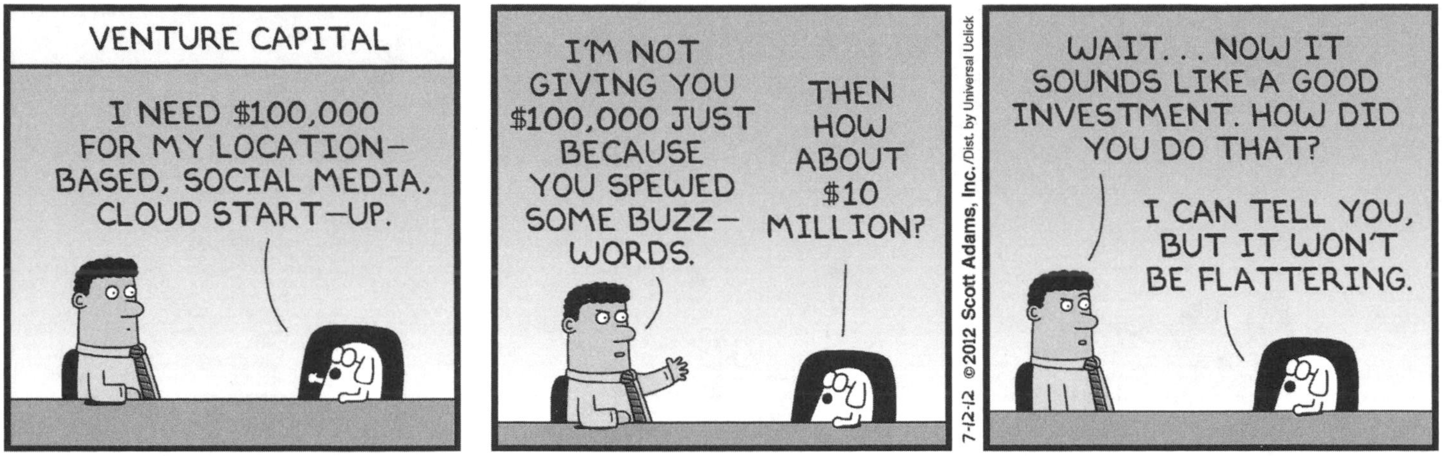
VENTURE CAPITAL
I NEED $100,000 FOR MY LOCATION-BASED, SOCIAL MEDIA, CLOUD START-UP.
I'M NOT GIVING YOU $100,000 JUST BECAUSE YOU SPEWED SOME BUZZWORDS.
THEN HOW ABOUT $10 MILLION?
7-12-12 © 2012 Scott Adams, Inc./Dist. by Universal Uclick
WAIT. . . NOW IT SOUNDS LIKE A GOOD INVESTMENT. HOW DID YOU DO THAT?
I CAN TELL YOU, BUT IT WON'T BE FLATTERING.

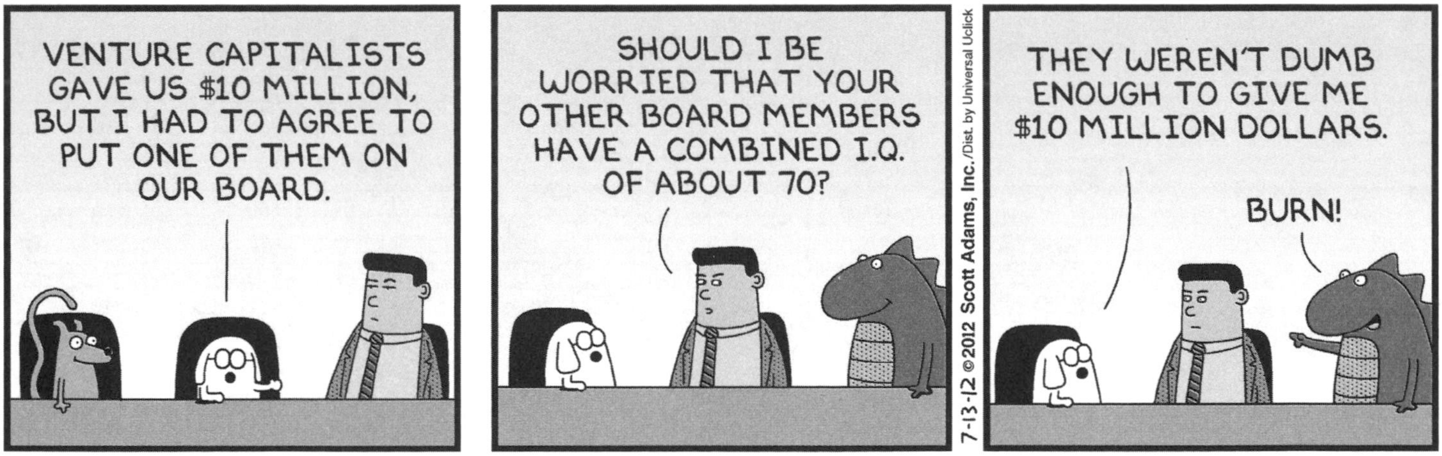
VENTURE CAPITALISTS GAVE US $10 MILLION, BUT I HAD TO AGREE TO PUT ONE OF THEM ON OUR BOARD.
SHOULD I BE WORRIED THAT YOUR OTHER BOARD MEMBERS HAVE A COMBINED I.Q. OF ABOUT 70?
7-13-12 © 2012 Scott Adams, Inc./Dist. by Universal Uclick
THEY WEREN'T DUMB ENOUGH TO GIVE ME $10 MILLION DOLLARS.
BURN!

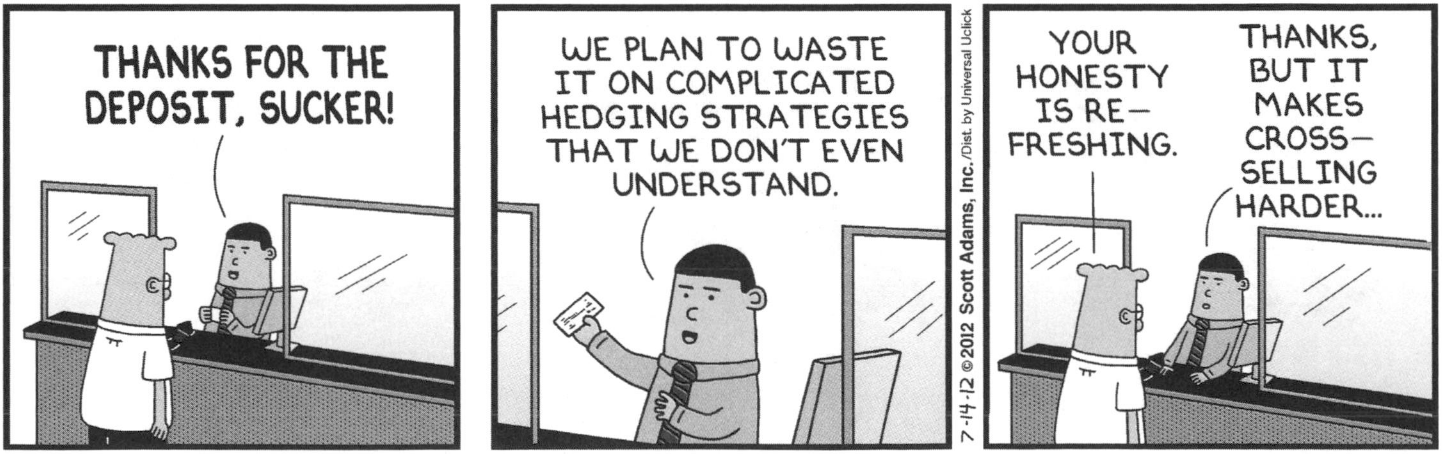
THANKS FOR THE DEPOSIT, SUCKER!
WE PLAN TO WASTE IT ON COMPLICATED HEDGING STRATEGIES THAT WE DON'T EVEN UNDERSTAND.
7-14-12 © 2012 Scott Adams, Inc./Dist. by Universal Uclick
YOUR HONESTY IS RE-FRESHING.
THANKS, BUT IT MAKES CROSS-SELLING HARDER...

STOP WHATEVER YOU'RE DOING AND GO RESEARCH THE ANSWER TO THIS QUESTION.
I DON'T HAVE TIME TO WORK ON LOW-PRIORITY TASKS.
GIVE ME TEN MINUTES TO TRANSFORM IT INTO AN EMERGENCY.
BRAD IS BEING UNHELPFUL. I NEED YOU TO TALK TO HIS BOSS.
SURE.
BRAD REFUSES TO HELP ALICE.
HELP HER DO WHAT?
I DON'T KNOW, BUT OBVIOUSLY IT'S VERY IMPORTANT BECAUSE IT GOT ESCALATED.
IT MUST BE AN EMERGENCY BECAUSE EVERYONE IS ALL WORKED UP ABOUT IT.
NOW HUM A HAPPY TUNE OR I'LL COMPLAIN ABOUT YOUR ATTITUDE.
©2012 Scott Adams, Inc./Dist. by Universal Uclick
7-15-12

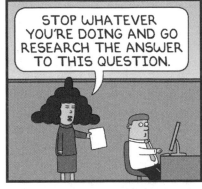

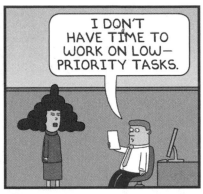

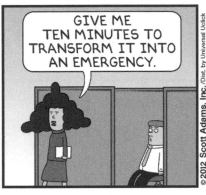

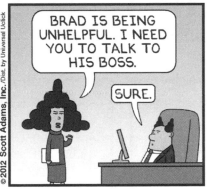

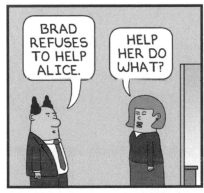

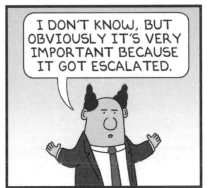

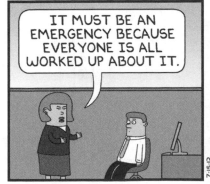

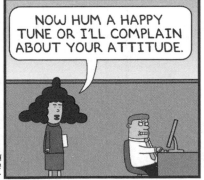

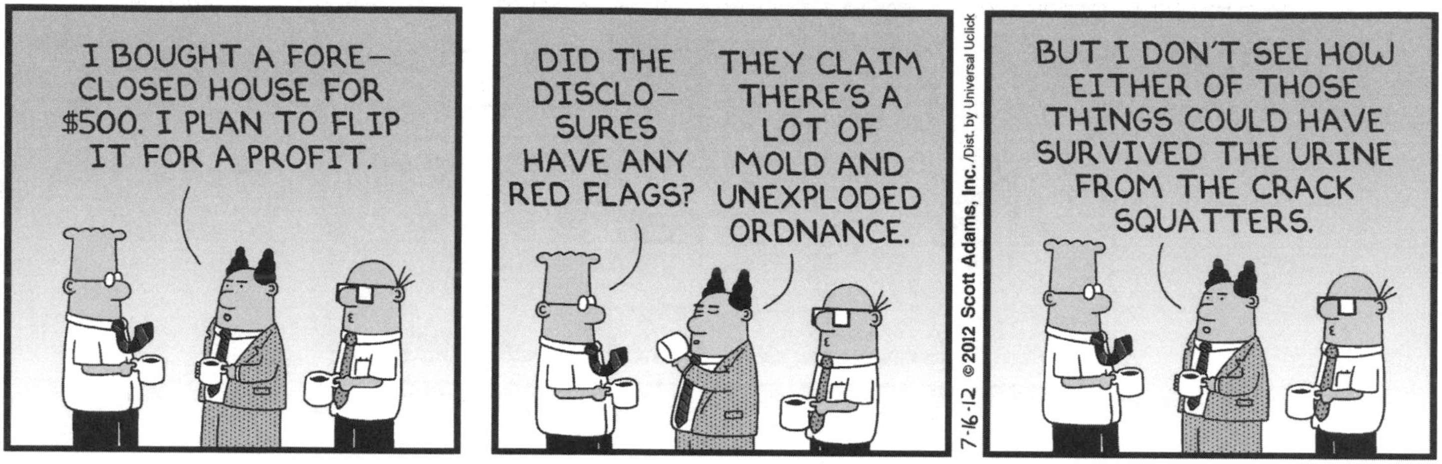
I BOUGHT A FORE-CLOSED HOUSE FOR $500. I PLAN TO FLIP IT FOR A PROFIT.
DID THE DISCLO-SURES HAVE ANY RED FLAGS?
THEY CLAIM THERE'S A LOT OF MOLD AND UNEXPLODED ORDNANCE.
7-16-12 ©2012 Scott Adams, Inc./Dist. by Universal Uclick
BUT I DON'T SEE HOW EITHER OF THOSE THINGS COULD HAVE SURVIVED THE URINE FROM THE CRACK SQUATTERS.

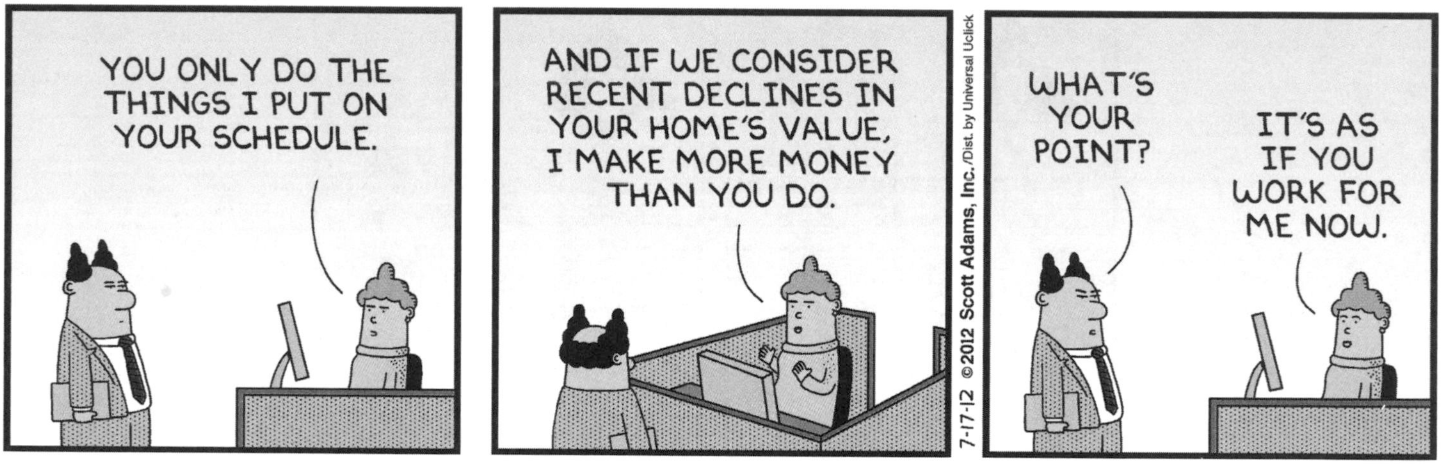
YOU ONLY DO THE THINGS I PUT ON YOUR SCHEDULE.
AND IF WE CONSIDER RECENT DECLINES IN YOUR HOME'S VALUE, I MAKE MORE MONEY THAN YOU DO.
7-17-12 ©2012 Scott Adams, Inc./Dist. by Universal Uclick
WHAT'S YOUR POINT?
IT'S AS IF YOU WORK FOR ME NOW.

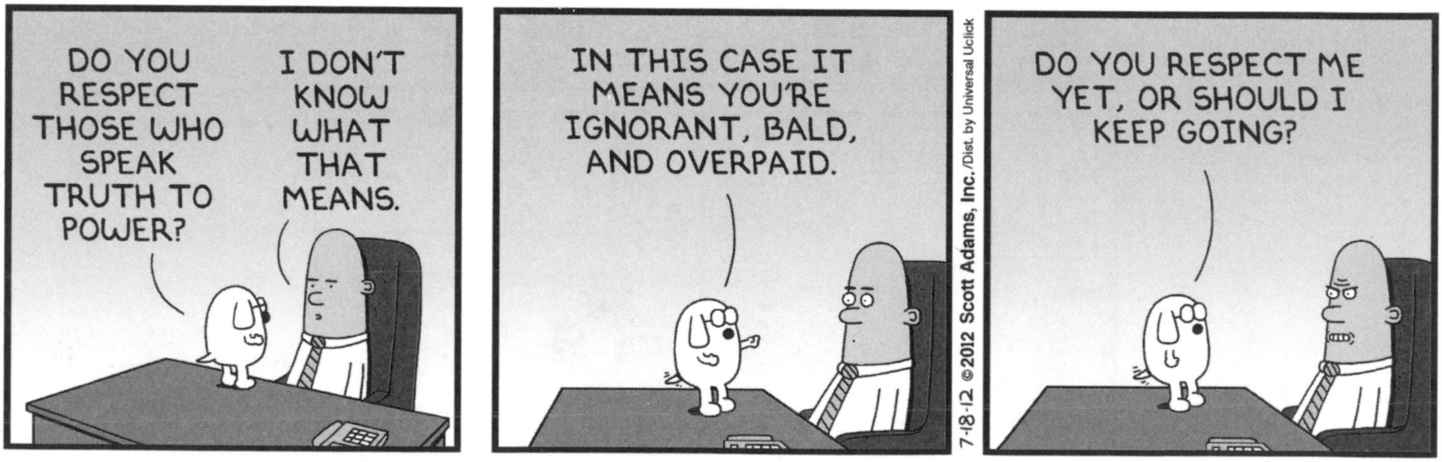
DO YOU RESPECT THOSE WHO SPEAK TRUTH TO POWER?
I DON'T KNOW WHAT THAT MEANS.
IN THIS CASE IT MEANS YOU'RE IGNORANT, BALD, AND OVERPAID.
7-18-12 ©2012 Scott Adams, Inc./Dist. by Universal Uclick
DO YOU RESPECT ME YET, OR SHOULD I KEEP GOING?

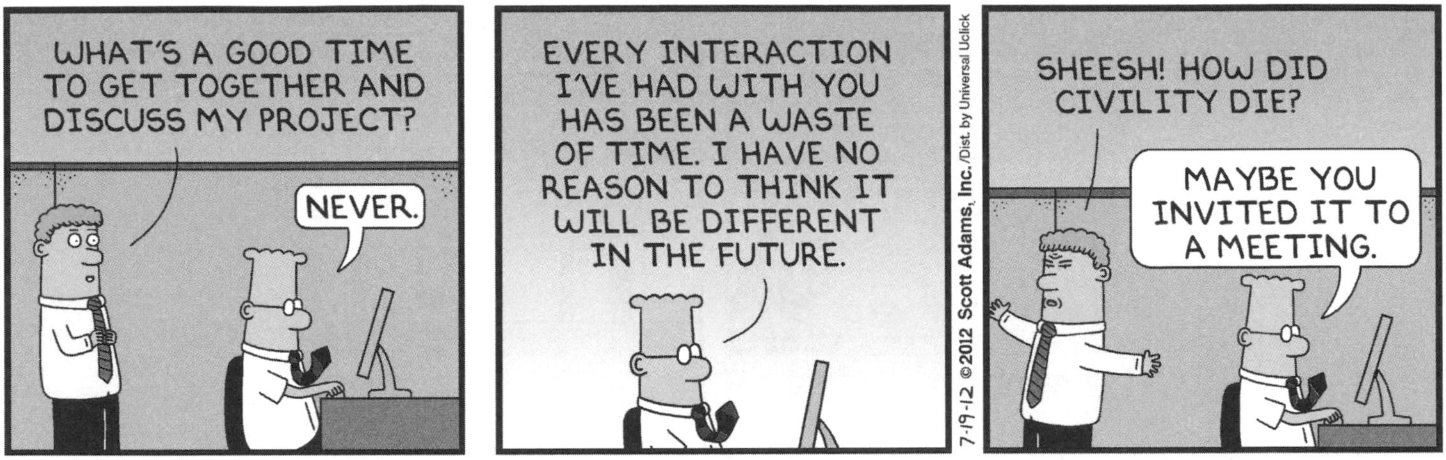
WHAT'S A GOOD TIME TO GET TOGETHER AND DISCUSS MY PROJECT?
NEVER.
EVERY INTERACTION I'VE HAD WITH YOU HAS BEEN A WASTE OF TIME. I HAVE NO REASON TO THINK IT WILL BE DIFFERENT IN THE FUTURE.
SHEESH! HOW DID CIVILITY DIE?
MAYBE YOU INVITED IT TO A MEETING.
7-19-12 ©2012 Scott Adams, Inc./Dist. by Universal Uclick

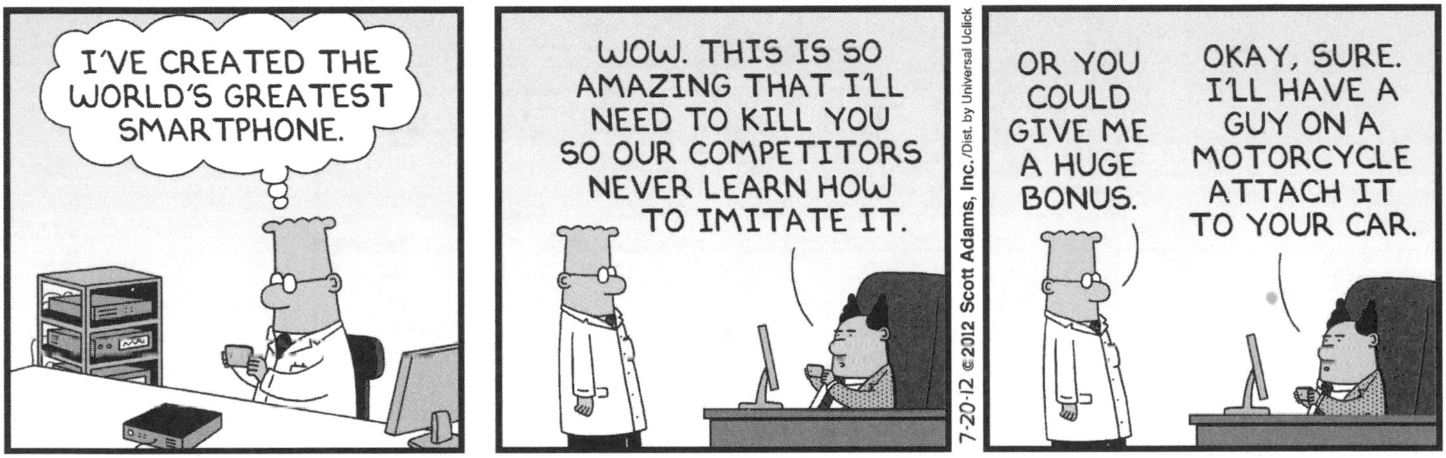
I'VE CREATED THE WORLD'S GREATEST SMARTPHONE.
WOW. THIS IS SO AMAZING THAT I'LL NEED TO KILL YOU SO OUR COMPETITORS NEVER LEARN HOW TO IMITATE IT.
OR YOU COULD GIVE ME A HUGE BONUS.
OKAY, SURE. I'LL HAVE A GUY ON A MOTORCYCLE ATTACH IT TO YOUR CAR.
7-20-12 ©2012 Scott Adams, Inc./Dist. by Universal Uclick

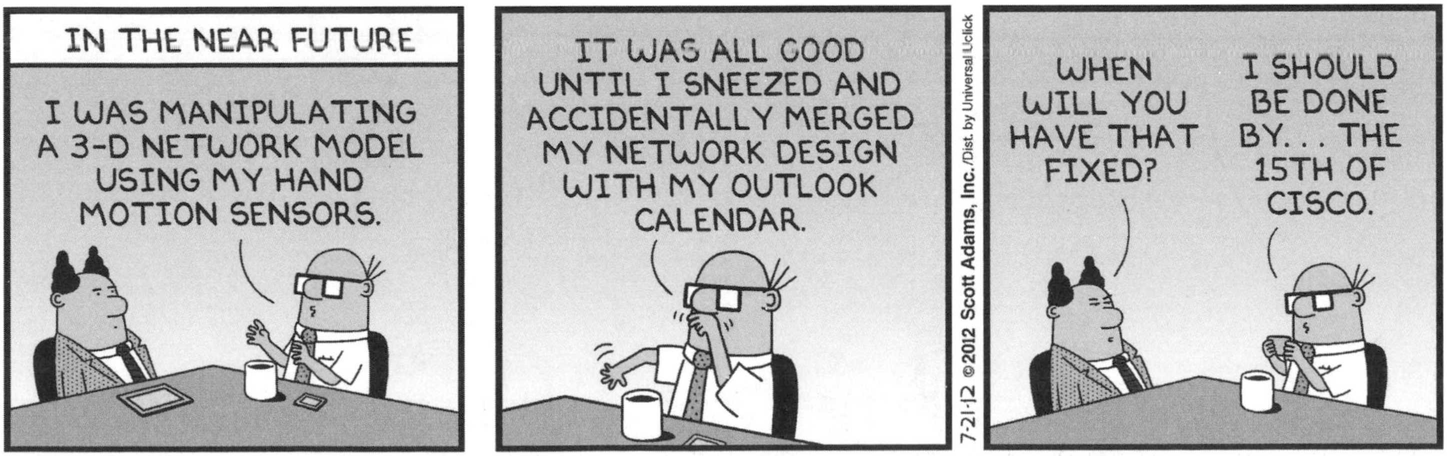
IN THE NEAR FUTURE
I WAS MANIPULATING A 3-D NETWORK MODEL USING MY HAND MOTION SENSORS.
IT WAS ALL GOOD UNTIL I SNEEZED AND ACCIDENTALLY MERGED MY NETWORK DESIGN WITH MY OUTLOOK CALENDAR.
WHEN WILL YOU HAVE THAT FIXED?
I SHOULD BE DONE BY. . . THE 15TH OF CISCO.
7-21-12 ©2012 Scott Adams, Inc./Dist. by Universal Uclick

BASED ON A TRUE STORY
I COMPLETED THE WIREFRAME AND PASSED IT OFF TO OUR CODERS.
THAT'S GREAT. DID YOU INCORPORATE ALL OF MY SPECS?
I DIDN'T SEE ANY SPECS FROM YOU. MAYBE MY SPAM FILTER ATE YOUR EMAIL.
NO PROBLEM. I'LL RESEND THEM AND YOU CAN START FROM SCRATCH.
©2012 Scott Adams, Inc./Dist. by Universal Uclick
YES, I CERTAINLY COULD DO THAT.
OR I COULD IGNORE YOUR INPUT, ENJOY MY DEEP FEELING OF ACCOMPLISHMENT, AND HOPE FOR THE BEST.
THAT SOUNDS EASIER.
I ACCEPT YOUR WISE COUNSEL, WALLY.
7-22-12
I GUESS YOUR SEARCH FOR RELEVANCE MARCHES ON.

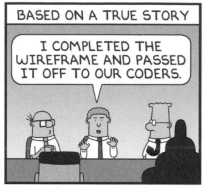

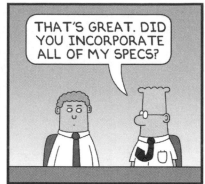

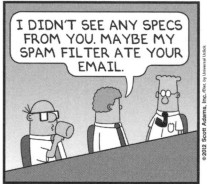

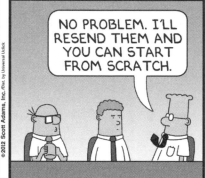

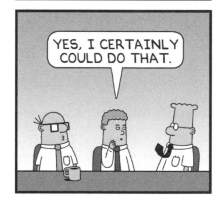

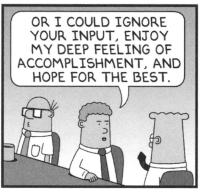

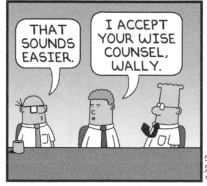

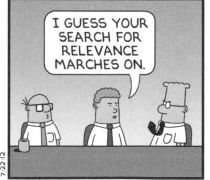

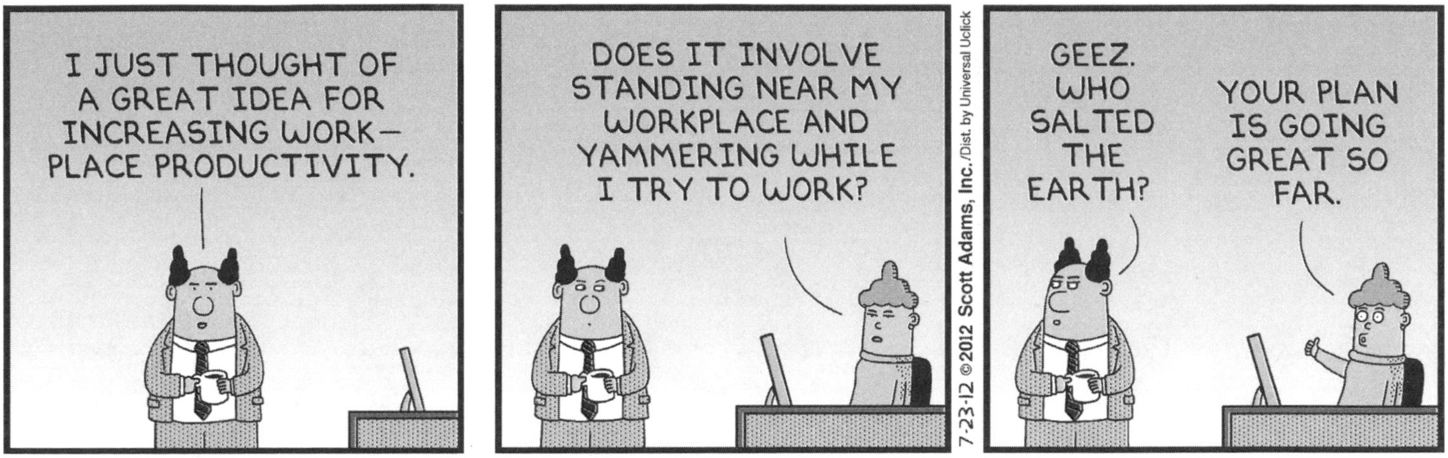
I JUST THOUGHT OF A GREAT IDEA FOR INCREASING WORK-PLACE PRODUCTIVITY.
DOES IT INVOLVE STANDING NEAR MY WORKPLACE AND YAMMERING WHILE I TRY TO WORK?
GEEZ. WHO SALTED THE EARTH?
YOUR PLAN IS GOING GREAT SO FAR.
7-23-12 © 2012 Scott Adams, Inc./Dist. by Universal Uclick

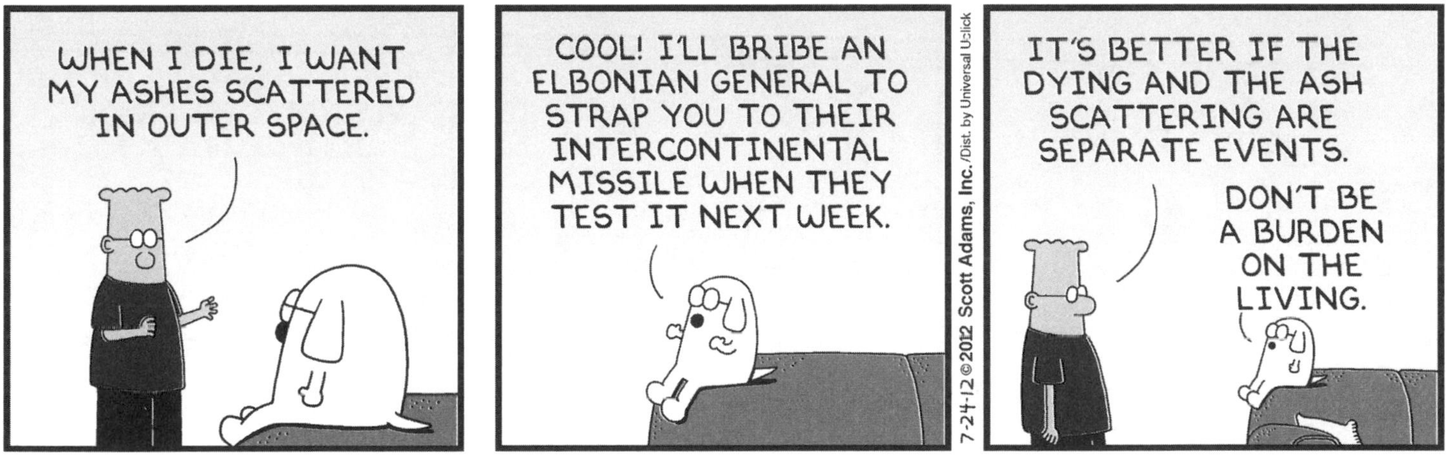
WHEN I DIE, I WANT MY ASHES SCATTERED IN OUTER SPACE.
COOL! I'LL BRIBE AN ELBONIAN GENERAL TO STRAP YOU TO THEIR INTERCONTINENTAL MISSILE WHEN THEY TEST IT NEXT WEEK.
IT'S BETTER IF THE DYING AND THE ASH SCATTERING ARE SEPARATE EVENTS.
DON'T BE A BURDEN ON THE LIVING.
7-24-12 © 2012 Scott Adams, Inc./Dist. by Universal Uclick

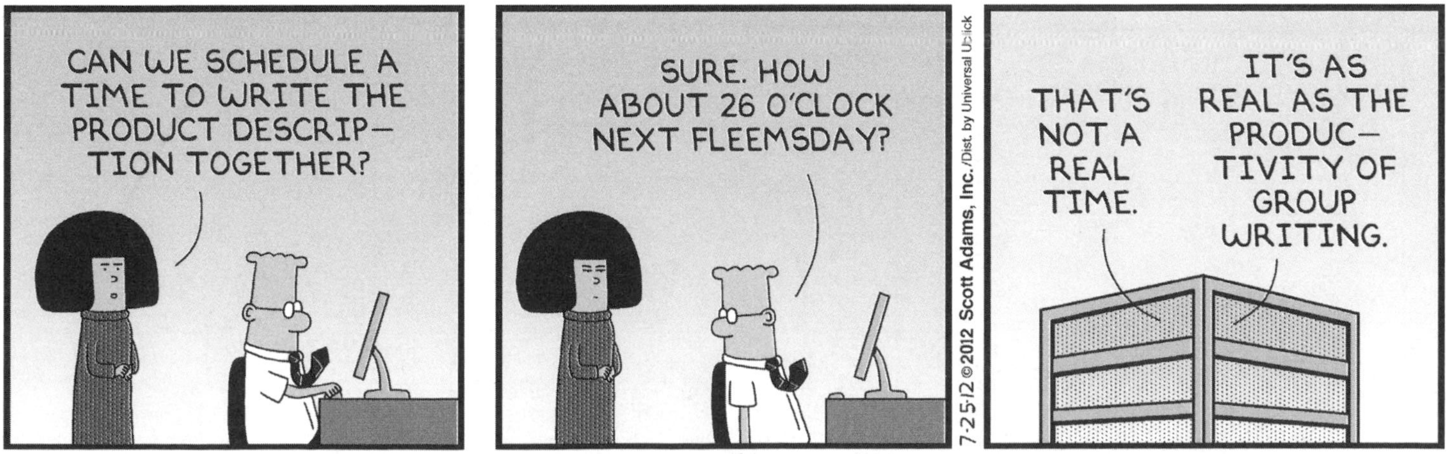
CAN WE SCHEDULE A TIME TO WRITE THE PRODUCT DESCRIP-TION TOGETHER?
SURE. HOW ABOUT 26 O'CLOCK NEXT FLEEMSDAY?
THAT'S NOT A REAL TIME.
IT'S AS REAL AS THE PRODUC-TIVITY OF GROUP WRITING.
7-25-12 © 2012 Scott Adams, Inc./Dist. by Universal Uclick

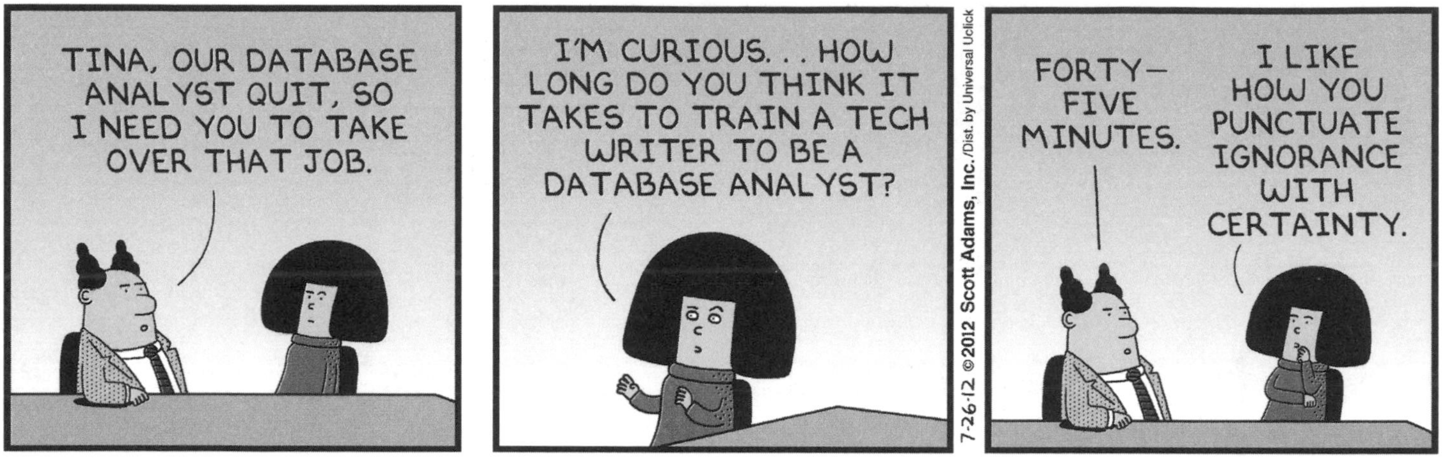
TINA, OUR DATABASE ANALYST QUIT, SO I NEED YOU TO TAKE OVER THAT JOB.
I'M CURIOUS. . . HOW LONG DO YOU THINK IT TAKES TO TRAIN A TECH WRITER TO BE A DATABASE ANALYST?
7-26-12 ©2012 Scott Adams, Inc./Dist. by Universal Uclick
FORTY-FIVE MINUTES.
I LIKE HOW YOU PUNCTUATE IGNORANCE WITH CERTAINTY.

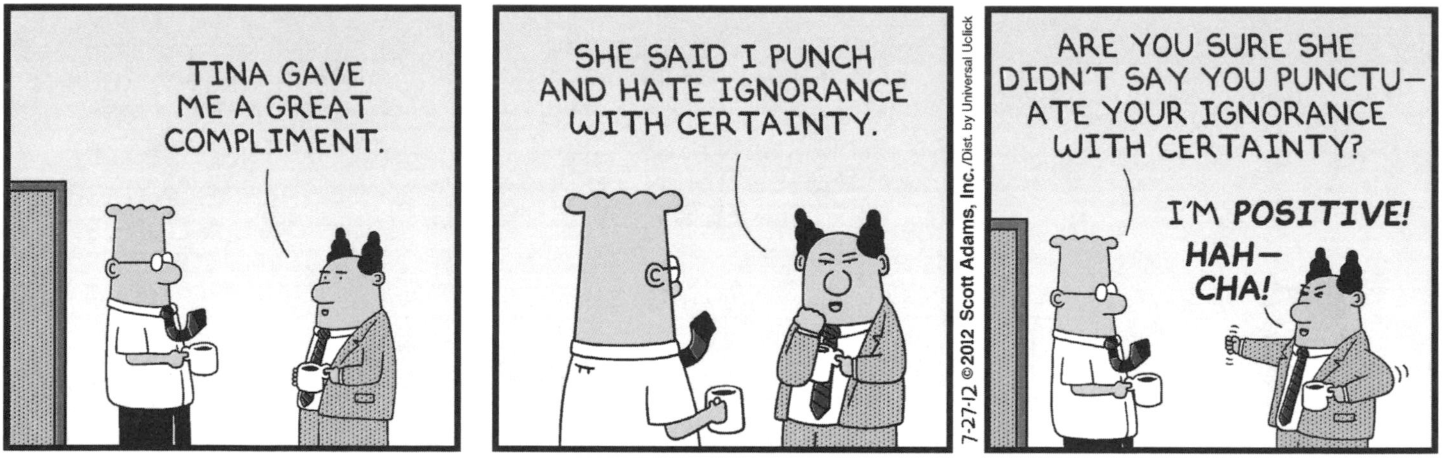
TINA GAVE ME A GREAT COMPLIMENT.
SHE SAID I PUNCH AND HATE IGNORANCE WITH CERTAINTY.
7-27-12 ©2012 Scott Adams, Inc./Dist. by Universal Uclick
ARE YOU SURE SHE DIDN'T SAY YOU PUNCTU-ATE YOUR IGNORANCE WITH CERTAINTY?
I'M POSITIVE!
HAH-CHA!

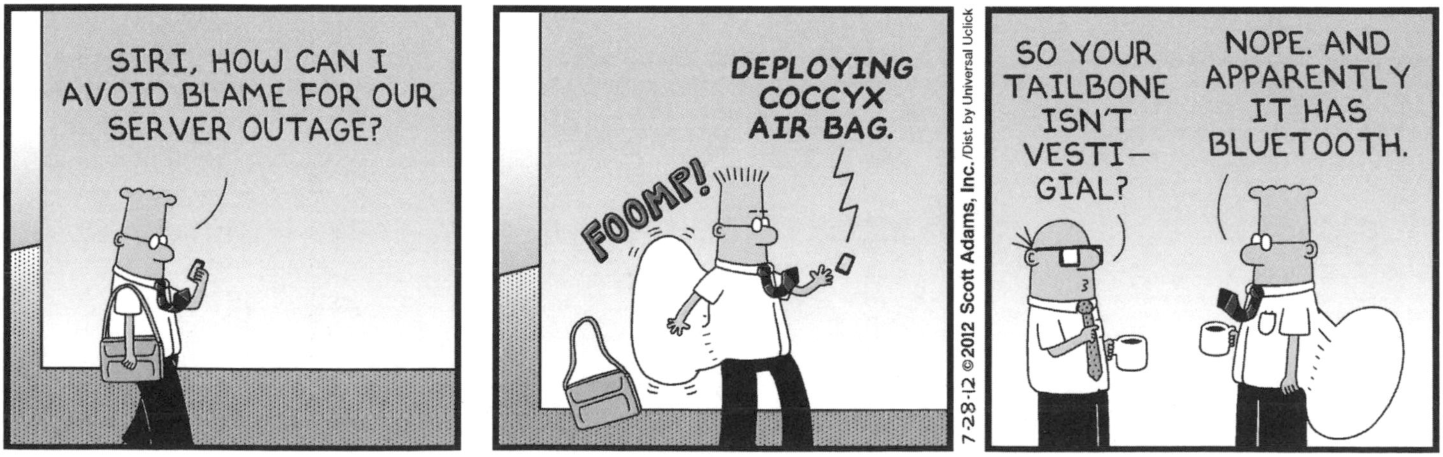
SIRI, HOW CAN I AVOID BLAME FOR OUR SERVER OUTAGE?
DEPLOYING COCCYX AIR BAG.
FOOMP!
7-28-12 ©2012 Scott Adams, Inc./Dist. by Universal Uclick
SO YOUR TAILBONE ISN'T VESTI-GIAL?
NOPE. AND APPARENTLY IT HAS BLUETOOTH.

CONSULTANTS SAY THREE QUINTILLION BYTES OF DATA ARE CREATED EVERY DAY.
IT COMES FROM EVERYWHERE. IT KNOWS ALL.
ACCORDING TO THE BOOK OF WIKIPEDIA, ITS NAME IS "BIG DATA."
BIG DATA
BIG DATA LIVES IN THE CLOUD. IT KNOWS WHAT WE DO.
IN THE PAST, OUR COMPANY DID MANY EVIL THINGS.
BUT IF WE ACCEPT BIG DATA IN OUR SERVERS, WE WILL BE SAVED FROM BANKRUPTCY.
LET US PAY.
$
IS IT TOO LATE TO SIDE WITH EVIL?
SHHHH! IT HEARS YOU.
©2012 Scott Adams, Inc./Dist. by Universal Uclick
7-29-12

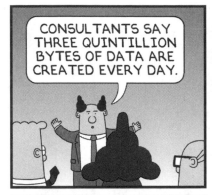

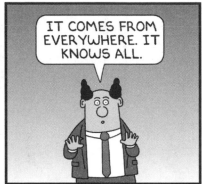

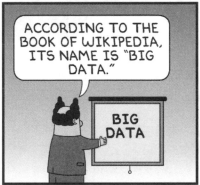

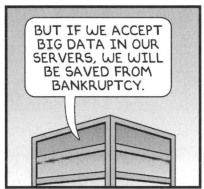

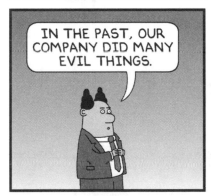

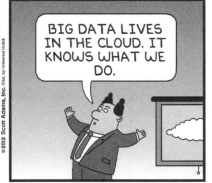

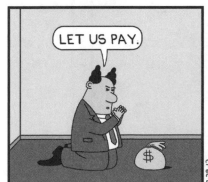

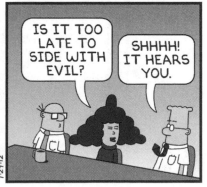

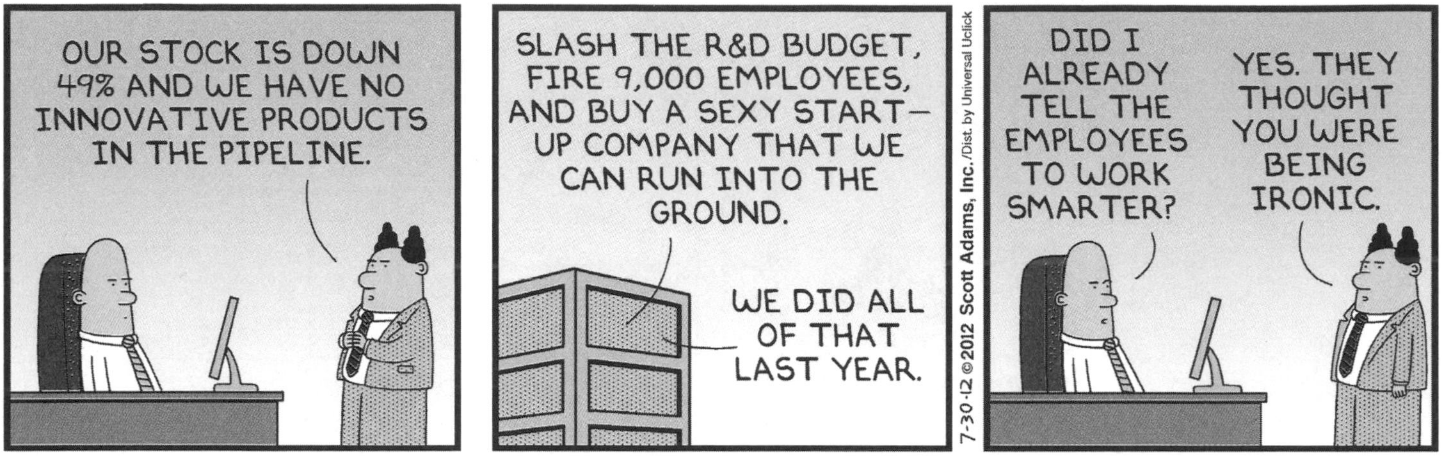
OUR STOCK IS DOWN 49% AND WE HAVE NO INNOVATIVE PRODUCTS IN THE PIPELINE.
SLASH THE R&D BUDGET, FIRE 9,000 EMPLOYEES, AND BUY A SEXY START-UP COMPANY THAT WE CAN RUN INTO THE GROUND.
WE DID ALL OF THAT LAST YEAR.
7-30-12 ©2012 Scott Adams, Inc./Dist. by Universal Uclick
DID I ALREADY TELL THE EMPLOYEES TO WORK SMARTER?
YES. THEY THOUGHT YOU WERE BEING IRONIC.

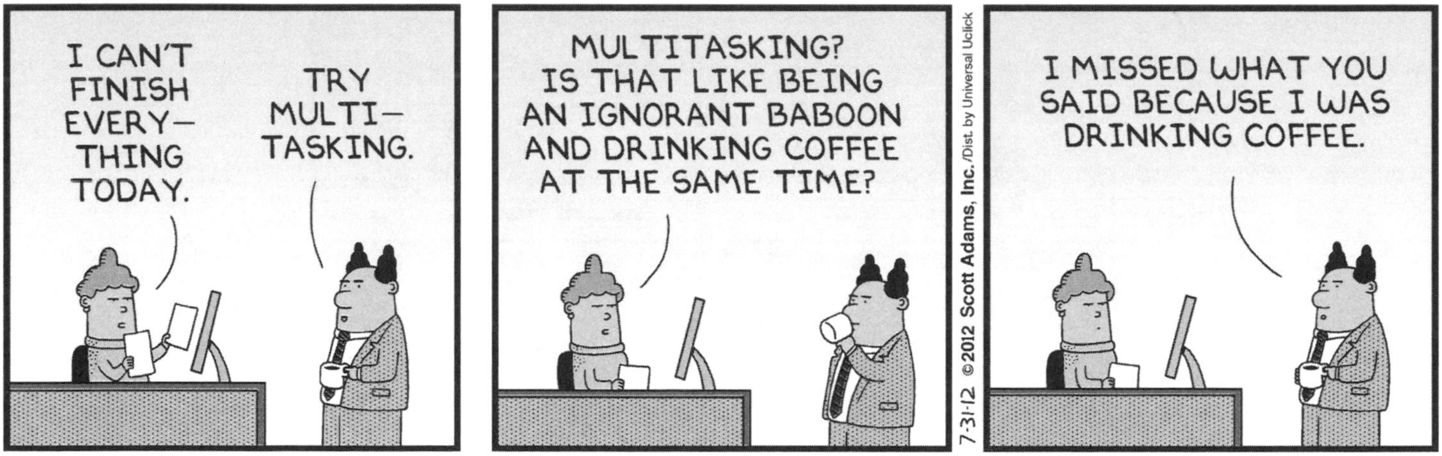
I CAN'T FINISH EVERY-THING TODAY.
TRY MULTI-TASKING.
MULTITASKING? IS THAT LIKE BEING AN IGNORANT BABOON AND DRINKING COFFEE AT THE SAME TIME?
7-31-12 ©2012 Scott Adams, Inc./Dist. by Universal Uclick
I MISSED WHAT YOU SAID BECAUSE I WAS DRINKING COFFEE.

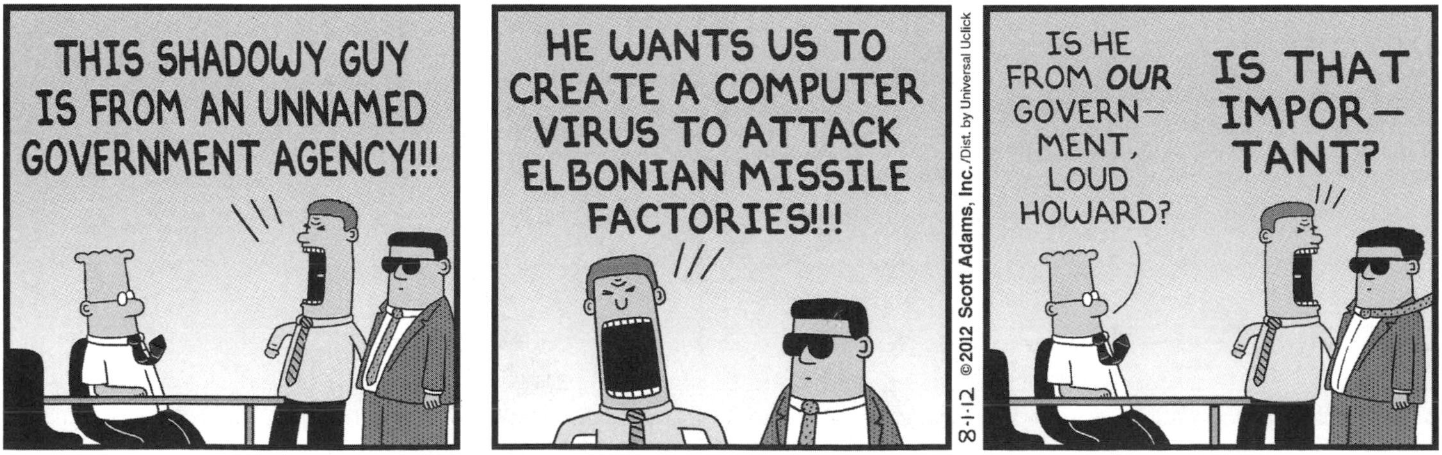
THIS SHADOWY GUY IS FROM AN UNNAMED GOVERNMENT AGENCY!!!
HE WANTS US TO CREATE A COMPUTER VIRUS TO ATTACK ELBONIAN MISSILE FACTORIES!!!
8-1-12 ©2012 Scott Adams, Inc./Dist. by Universal Uclick
IS HE FROM *OUR* GOVERN-MENT, LOUD HOWARD?
IS THAT IMPOR-TANT?

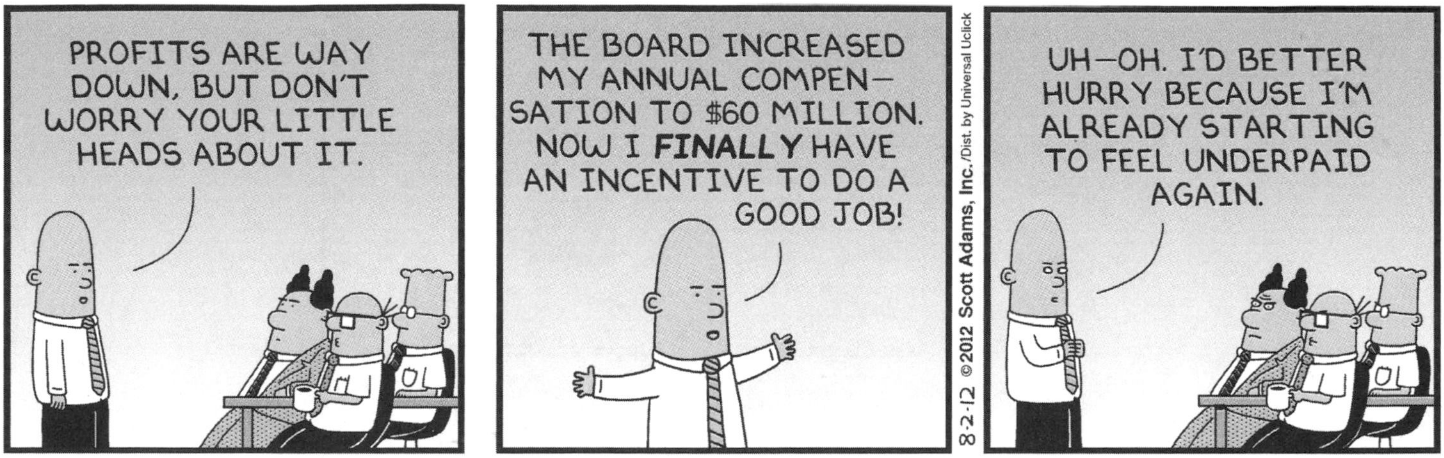
PROFITS ARE WAY DOWN, BUT DON'T WORRY YOUR LITTLE HEADS ABOUT IT.
THE BOARD INCREASED MY ANNUAL COMPEN-SATION TO $60 MILLION. NOW I **FINALLY** HAVE AN INCENTIVE TO DO A GOOD JOB!
8-2-12 ©2012 Scott Adams, Inc./Dist. by Universal Uclick
UH-OH. I'D BETTER HURRY BECAUSE I'M ALREADY STARTING TO FEEL UNDERPAID AGAIN.

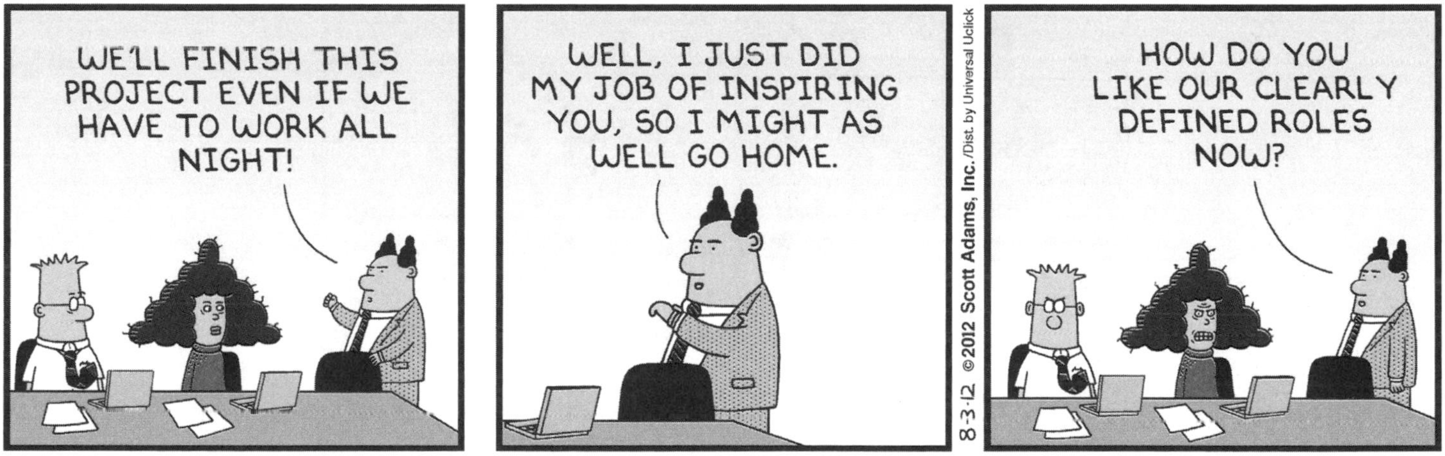
WE'LL FINISH THIS PROJECT EVEN IF WE HAVE TO WORK ALL NIGHT!
WELL, I JUST DID MY JOB OF INSPIRING YOU, SO I MIGHT AS WELL GO HOME.
8-3-12 ©2012 Scott Adams, Inc./Dist. by Universal Uclick
HOW DO YOU LIKE OUR CLEARLY DEFINED ROLES NOW?

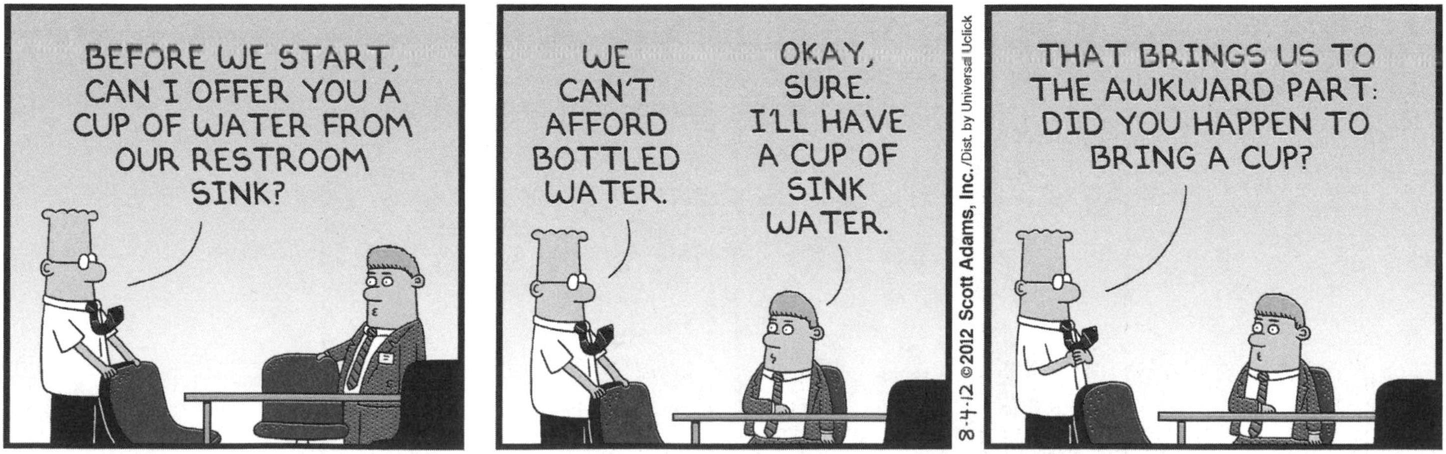
BEFORE WE START, CAN I OFFER YOU A CUP OF WATER FROM OUR RESTROOM SINK?
WE CAN'T AFFORD BOTTLED WATER.
OKAY, SURE. I'LL HAVE A CUP OF SINK WATER.
8-4-12 ©2012 Scott Adams, Inc./Dist. by Universal Uclick
THAT BRINGS US TO THE AWKWARD PART: DID YOU HAPPEN TO BRING A CUP?

WALLY, I'M SENDING YOU TO A CONFERENCE FOR THE WORLD'S TOP ENGINEERS.
WITH ANY LUCK, ONE OF OUR COMPETITORS WILL TRY TO POACH YOU.
THAT WILL SAVE ME THE TROUBLE OF FIRING YOU.
YOU'LL BE GOING WITH FIVE OTHER PEOPLE I WANT TO GET RID OF.
©2012 Scott Adams, Inc./Dist. by Universal Uclick
I TOOK THE LIBERTY OF UPDATING YOUR RÉSUMÉ.
IF THIS GOES AS PLANNED, YOU'LL DESTROY ONE OF OUR COMPETITORS FROM WITHIN, LIKE A HIDEOUS DISEASE.
MAKE ME PROUD!
8-5-12
IT WAS THE FIRST TIME I EVER FELT USEFUL.
I DIDN'T LIKE IT.

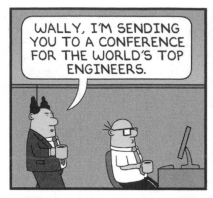

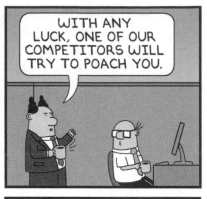

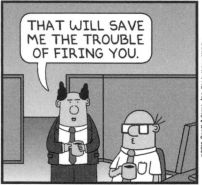

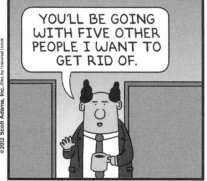

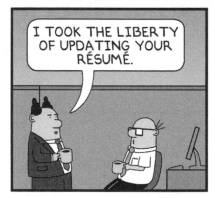

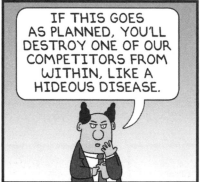

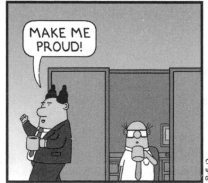

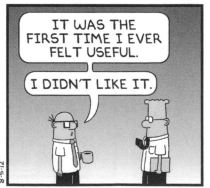

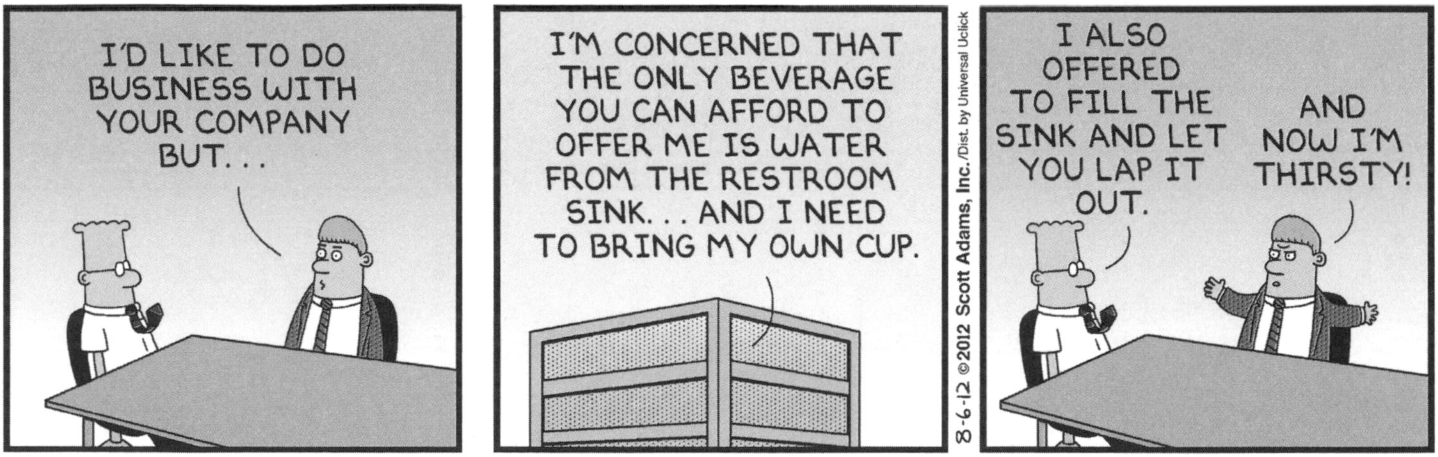
I'D LIKE TO DO BUSINESS WITH YOUR COMPANY BUT. . .
I'M CONCERNED THAT THE ONLY BEVERAGE YOU CAN AFFORD TO OFFER ME IS WATER FROM THE RESTROOM SINK. . . AND I NEED TO BRING MY OWN CUP.
8-6-12 ©2012 Scott Adams, Inc./Dist. by Universal Uclick
I ALSO OFFERED TO FILL THE SINK AND LET YOU LAP IT OUT.
AND NOW I'M THIRSTY!

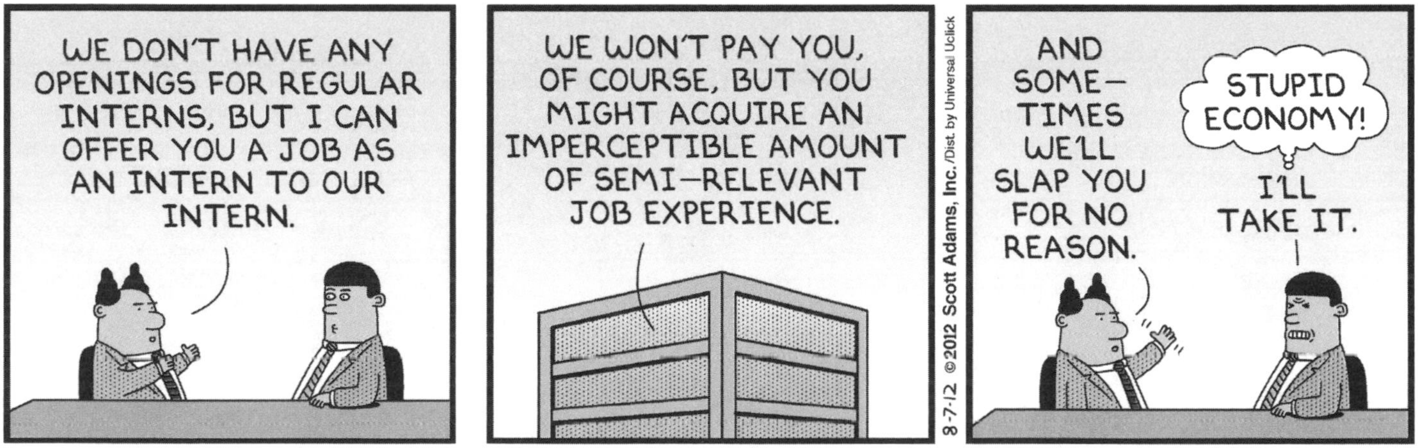
WE DON'T HAVE ANY OPENINGS FOR REGULAR INTERNS, BUT I CAN OFFER YOU A JOB AS AN INTERN TO OUR INTERN.
WE WON'T PAY YOU, OF COURSE, BUT YOU MIGHT ACQUIRE AN IMPERCEPTIBLE AMOUNT OF SEMI-RELEVANT JOB EXPERIENCE.
8-7-12 ©2012 Scott Adams, Inc./Dist. by Universal Uclick
AND SOME-TIMES WE'LL SLAP YOU FOR NO REASON.
STUPID ECONOMY!
I'LL TAKE IT.

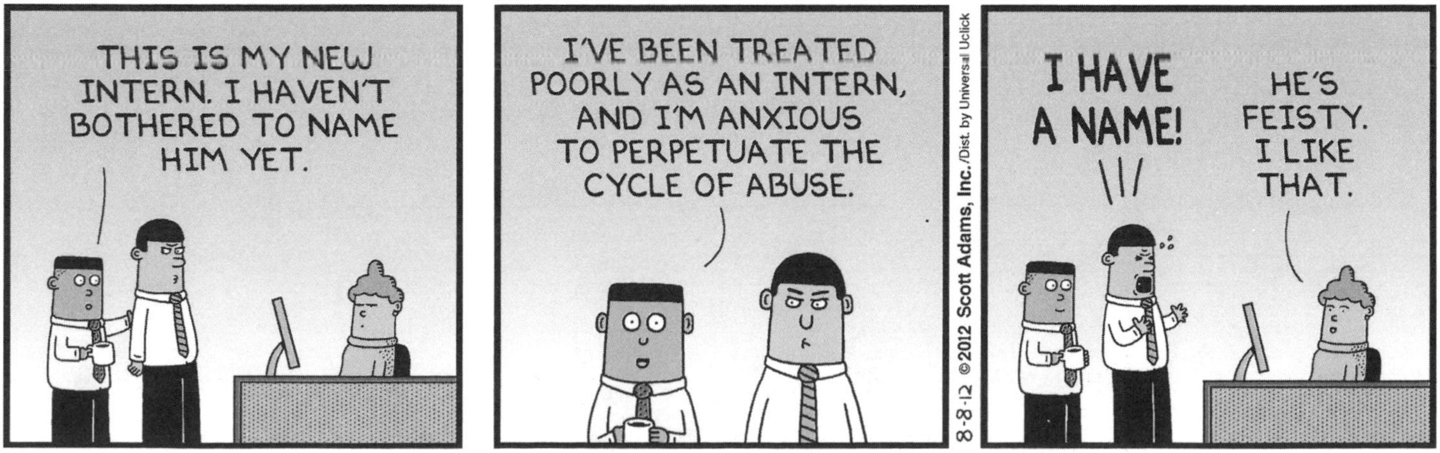
THIS IS MY NEW INTERN. I HAVEN'T BOTHERED TO NAME HIM YET.
I'VE BEEN TREATED POORLY AS AN INTERN, AND I'M ANXIOUS TO PERPETUATE THE CYCLE OF ABUSE.
8-8-12 ©2012 Scott Adams, Inc./Dist. by Universal Uclick
I HAVE A NAME!
HE'S FEISTY. I LIKE THAT.

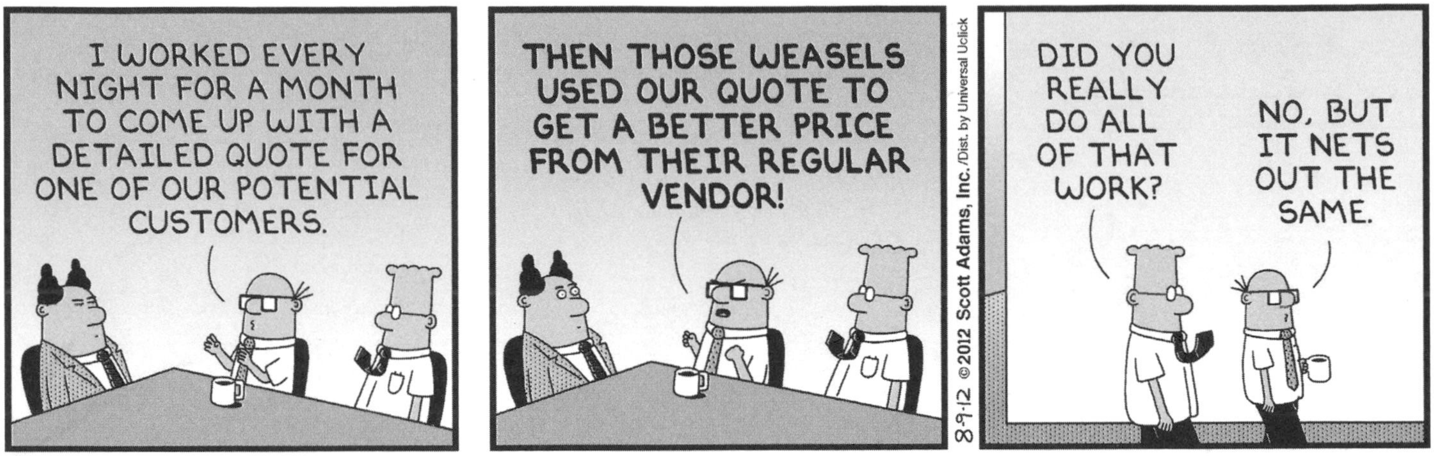
I WORKED EVERY NIGHT FOR A MONTH TO COME UP WITH A DETAILED QUOTE FOR ONE OF OUR POTENTIAL CUSTOMERS.
THEN THOSE WEASELS USED OUR QUOTE TO GET A BETTER PRICE FROM THEIR REGULAR VENDOR!
8-9-12 ©2012 Scott Adams, Inc./Dist. by Universal Uclick
DID YOU REALLY DO ALL OF THAT WORK?
NO, BUT IT NETS OUT THE SAME.

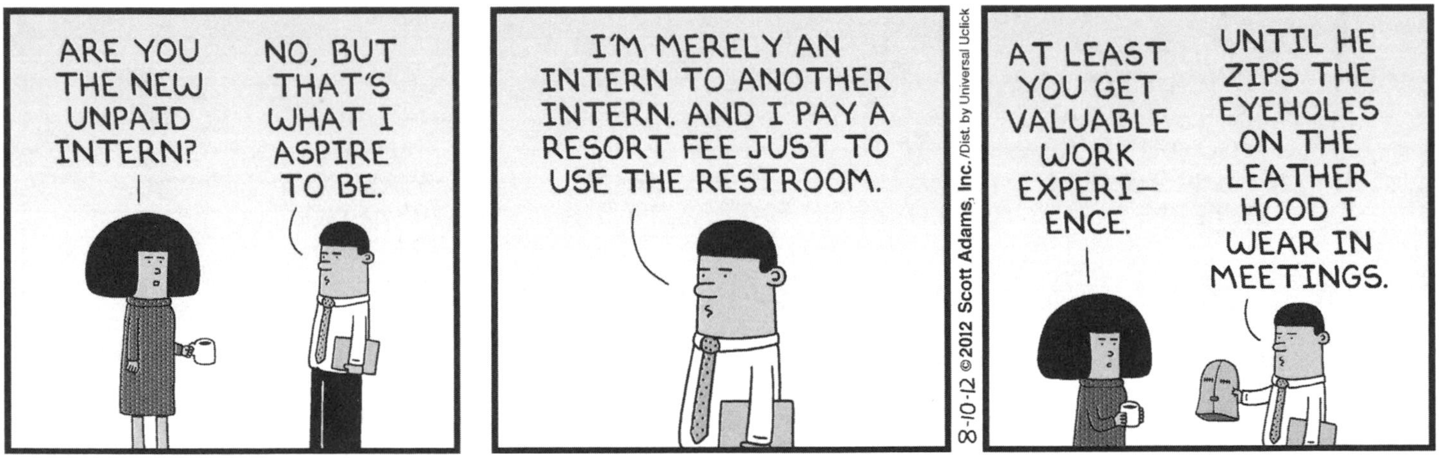
ARE YOU THE NEW UNPAID INTERN?
NO, BUT THAT'S WHAT I ASPIRE TO BE.
I'M MERELY AN INTERN TO ANOTHER INTERN. AND I PAY A RESORT FEE JUST TO USE THE RESTROOM.
8-10-12 ©2012 Scott Adams, Inc./Dist. by Universal Uclick
AT LEAST YOU GET VALUABLE WORK EXPERI-ENCE.
UNTIL HE ZIPS THE EYEHOLES ON THE LEATHER HOOD I WEAR IN MEETINGS.

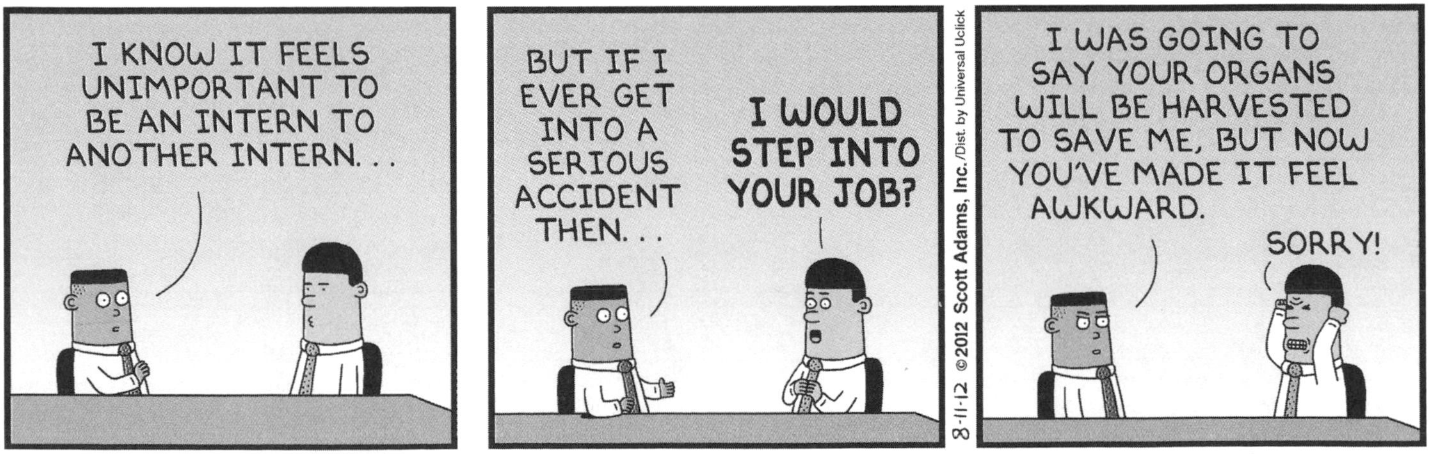
I KNOW IT FEELS UNIMPORTANT TO BE AN INTERN TO ANOTHER INTERN. . .
BUT IF I EVER GET INTO A SERIOUS ACCIDENT THEN. . .
I WOULD STEP INTO YOUR JOB?
8-11-12 ©2012 Scott Adams, Inc./Dist. by Universal Uclick
I WAS GOING TO SAY YOUR ORGANS WILL BE HARVESTED TO SAVE ME, BUT NOW YOU'VE MADE IT FEEL AWKWARD.
SORRY!

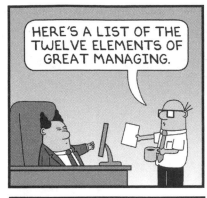

HERE'S A LIST OF THE TWELVE ELEMENTS OF GREAT MANAGING.
IF YOU DO EVERY-THING ON THAT LIST, IT WILL MAKE ME FEEL WHAT EXPERTS CALL "ENGAGED."
IF YOU FAIL TO DO YOUR JOB PROPERLY, I WILL FEEL ALL DISENGAGED AND DO POOR WORK.
THIS WOULD BE A CONVENIENT TIME TO GIVE ME SOME PRAISE AND RECOGNITION.
YOU MIGHT ALSO WANT TO ENCOURAGE MY DEVELOPMENT AND TELL ME MY JOB IS IMPORTANT.
REMEMBER TO CARE ABOUT ME AS A PERSON AND TELL ME MY OPINIONS COUNT.
IF YOU DO ALL OF THAT, PLUS SEVEN MORE THINGS ON THE LIST, YOU MIGHT GET SOME PRODUC-TIVITY OUT OF ME.
LEAVE MY OFFICE AND DROP DEAD.
WILL THAT HELP ME LEARN AND GROW?
©2012 Scott Adams, Inc./Dist. by Universal Uclick
8-12-12

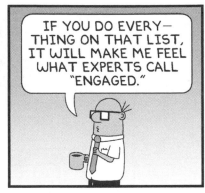

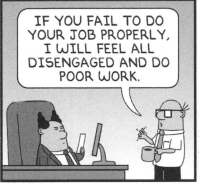

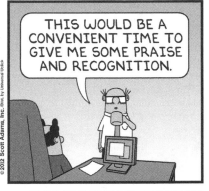

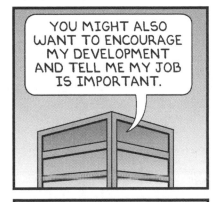

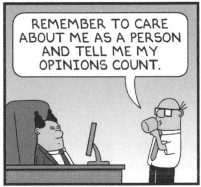

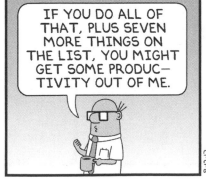

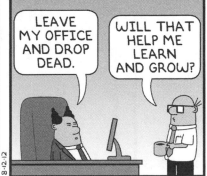

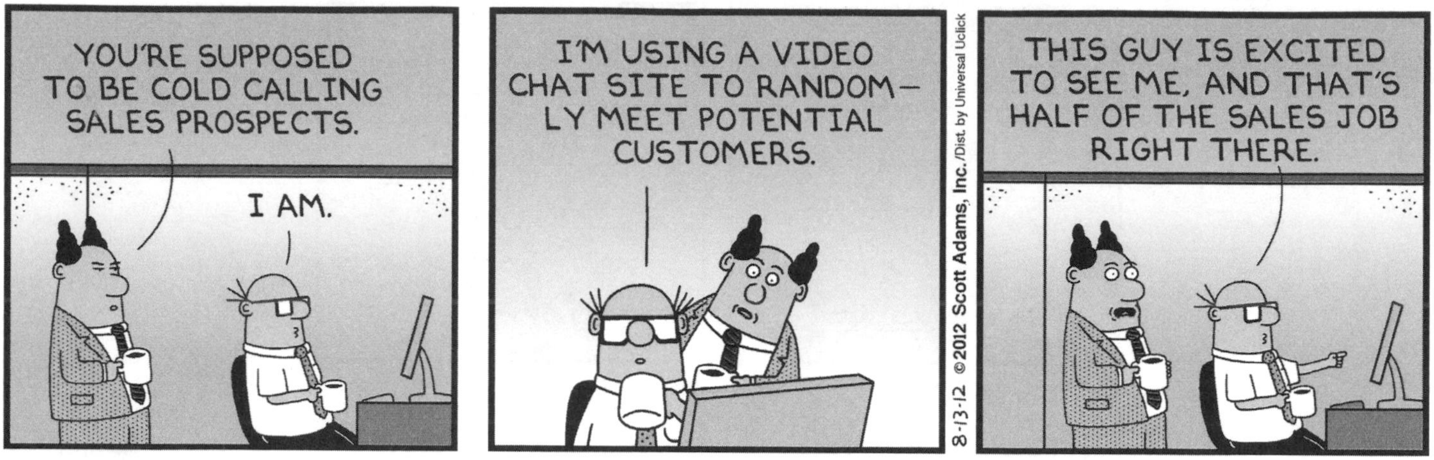
YOU'RE SUPPOSED TO BE COLD CALLING SALES PROSPECTS.
I AM.
I'M USING A VIDEO CHAT SITE TO RANDOM-LY MEET POTENTIAL CUSTOMERS.
8-13-12 ©2012 Scott Adams, Inc./Dist. by Universal Uclick
THIS GUY IS EXCITED TO SEE ME, AND THAT'S HALF OF THE SALES JOB RIGHT THERE.

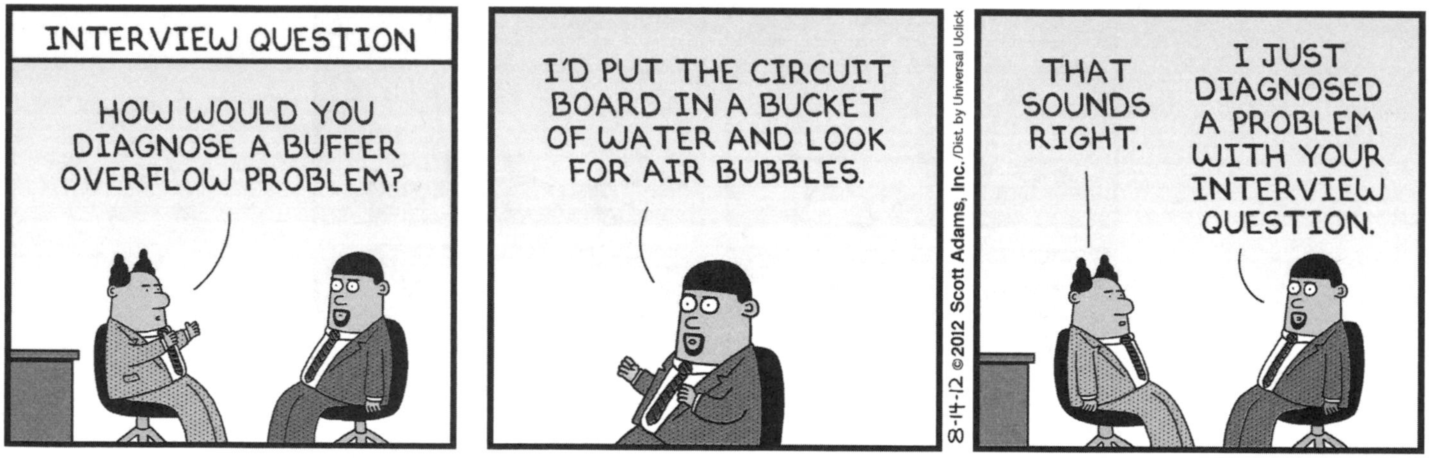
INTERVIEW QUESTION
HOW WOULD YOU DIAGNOSE A BUFFER OVERFLOW PROBLEM?
I'D PUT THE CIRCUIT BOARD IN A BUCKET OF WATER AND LOOK FOR AIR BUBBLES.
8-14-12 ©2012 Scott Adams, Inc./Dist. by Universal Uclick
THAT SOUNDS RIGHT.
I JUST DIAGNOSED A PROBLEM WITH YOUR INTERVIEW QUESTION.

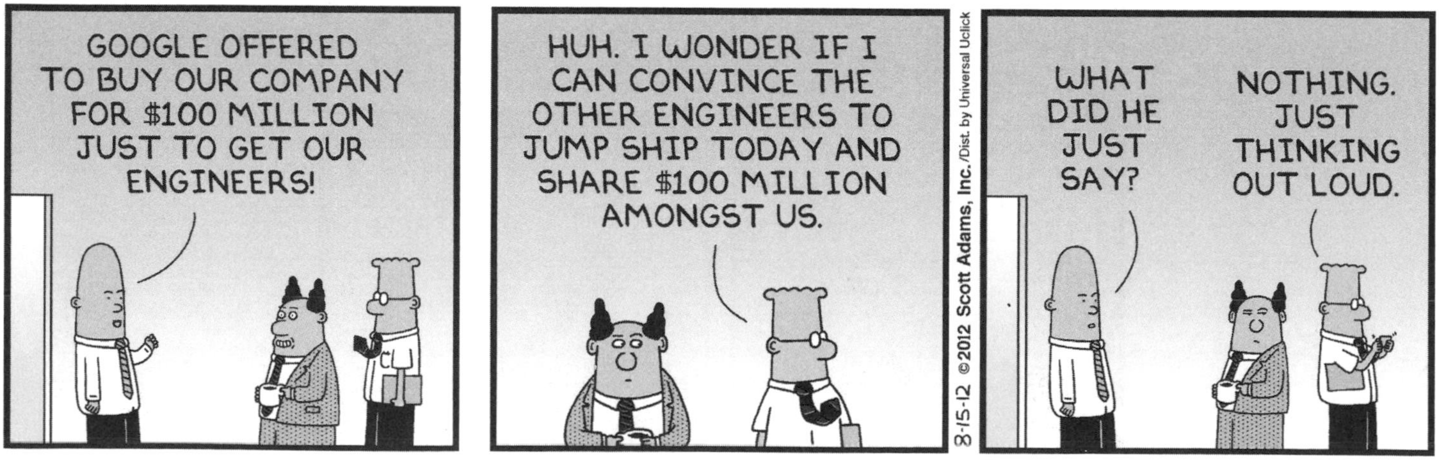
GOOGLE OFFERED TO BUY OUR COMPANY FOR $100 MILLION JUST TO GET OUR ENGINEERS!
HUH. I WONDER IF I CAN CONVINCE THE OTHER ENGINEERS TO JUMP SHIP TODAY AND SHARE $100 MILLION AMONGST US.
8-15-12 ©2012 Scott Adams, Inc./Dist. by Universal Uclick
WHAT DID HE JUST SAY?
NOTHING. JUST THINKING OUT LOUD.

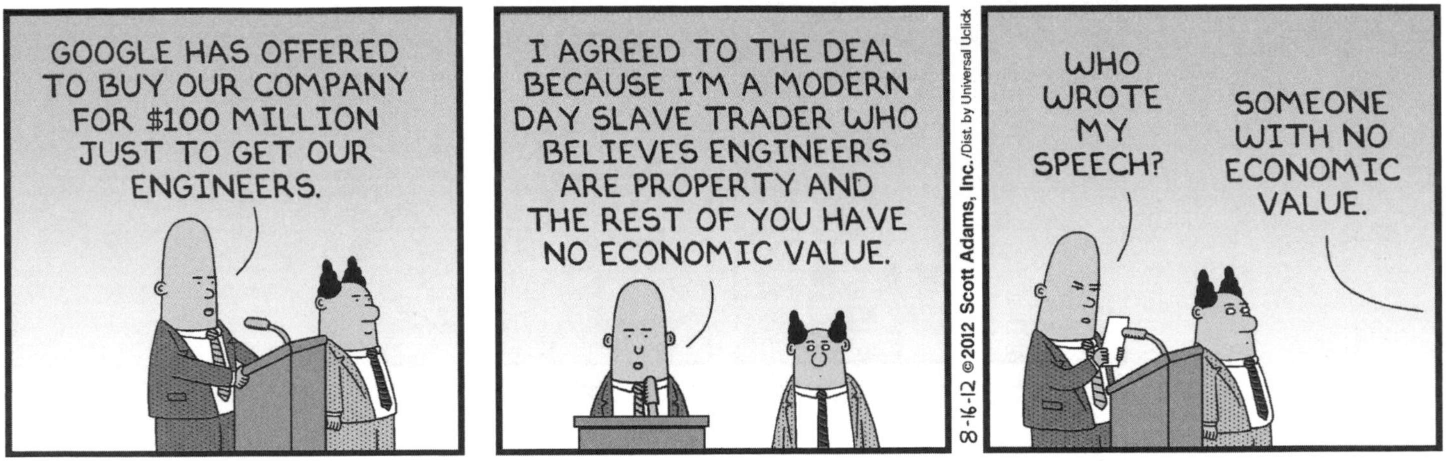
GOOGLE HAS OFFERED TO BUY OUR COMPANY FOR $100 MILLION JUST TO GET OUR ENGINEERS.
I AGREED TO THE DEAL BECAUSE I'M A MODERN DAY SLAVE TRADER WHO BELIEVES ENGINEERS ARE PROPERTY AND THE REST OF YOU HAVE NO ECONOMIC VALUE.
8-16-12 ©2012 Scott Adams, Inc./Dist. by Universal Uclick
WHO WROTE MY SPEECH?
SOMEONE WITH NO ECONOMIC VALUE.

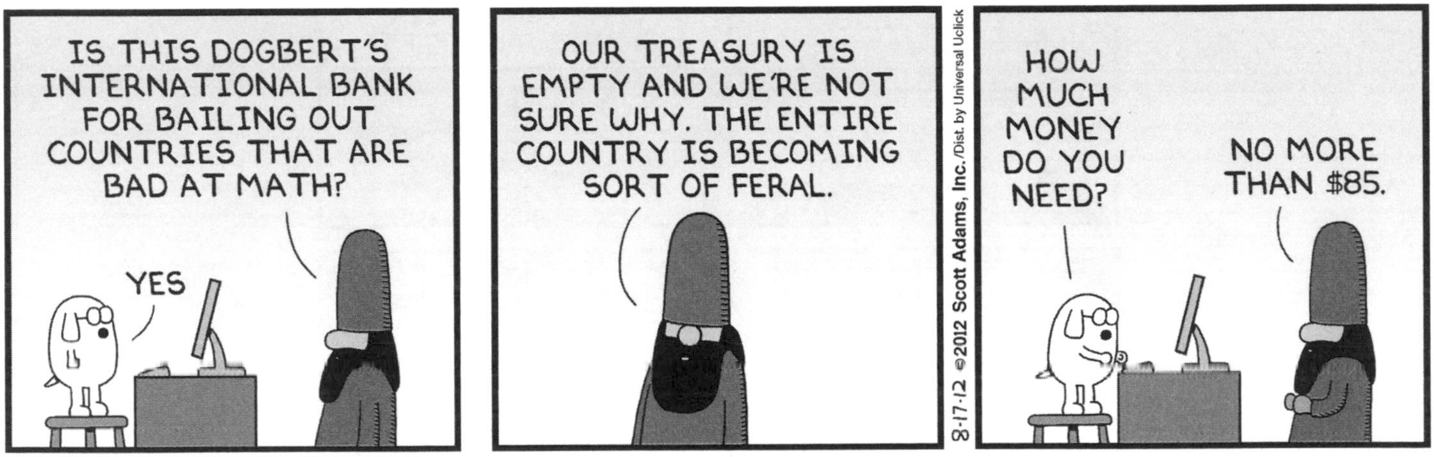
IS THIS DOGBERT'S INTERNATIONAL BANK FOR BAILING OUT COUNTRIES THAT ARE BAD AT MATH?
YES
OUR TREASURY IS EMPTY AND WE'RE NOT SURE WHY. THE ENTIRE COUNTRY IS BECOMING SORT OF FERAL.
8-17-12 ©2012 Scott Adams, Inc./Dist. by Universal Uclick
HOW MUCH MONEY DO YOU NEED?
NO MORE THAN $85.

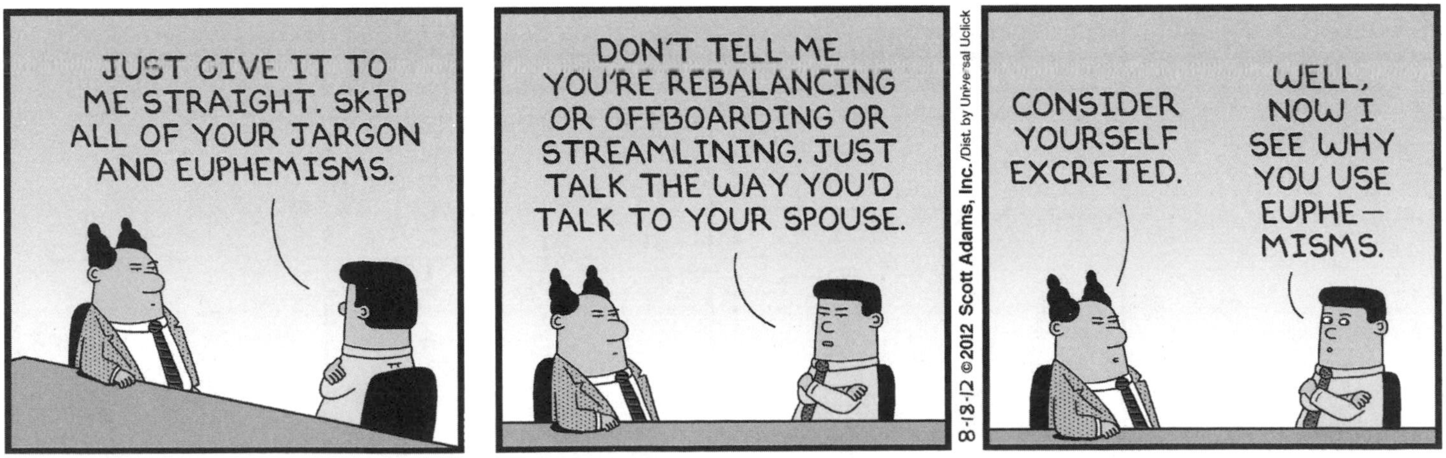
JUST GIVE IT TO ME STRAIGHT. SKIP ALL OF YOUR JARGON AND EUPHEMISMS.
DON'T TELL ME YOU'RE REBALANCING OR OFFBOARDING OR STREAMLINING. JUST TALK THE WAY YOU'D TALK TO YOUR SPOUSE.
8-18-12 ©2012 Scott Adams, Inc./Dist. by Universal Uclick
CONSIDER YOURSELF EXCRETED.
WELL, NOW I SEE WHY YOU USE EUPHE-MISMS.

YOU NEED TO ACT MORE LIKE AN ENTREPRENEUR.
ENTREPRENEURS MAKE DECISIONS THAT WILL END IN FAILURE 90% OF THE TIME.
THEY MOTIVATE PEOPLE THROUGH BULLYING, LYING, MANIPULATION, AND VERBAL ABUSE.
ENTREPRENEURS MAKE THEIR EMPLOYEES WORK SO MANY HOURS THAT THEIR PERSONAL LIVES AND THEIR BODIES FALL APART.
I'VE BEEN DOING ALL OF THAT STUFF FOR YEARS.
HAS IT WORKED?
NO.
WELL, IN THAT CASE, YOU'RE NOT AN ENTREPRENEUR.
YOU'RE JUST A HUGE JERK.
IS THAT WHY NO ONE IS WRITING MY BIOG-RAPHY?
©2012 Scott Adams, Inc./Dist. by Universal Uclick
8-19-12

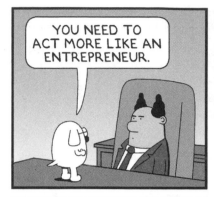

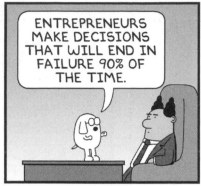

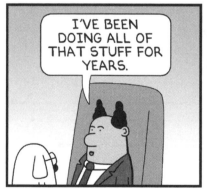

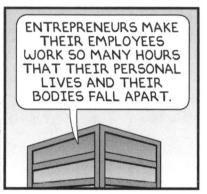

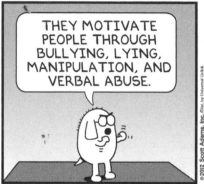

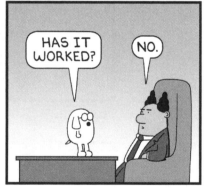

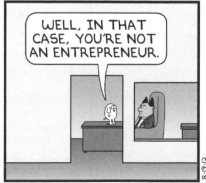

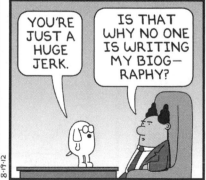

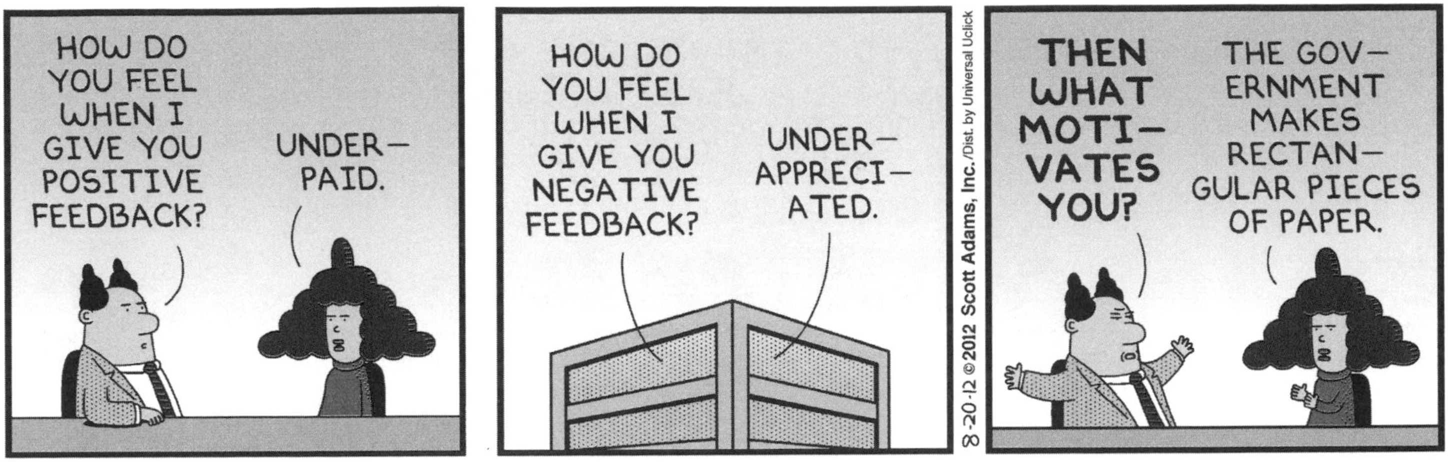
HOW DO YOU FEEL WHEN I GIVE YOU POSITIVE FEEDBACK?
UNDER-PAID.
HOW DO YOU FEEL WHEN I GIVE YOU NEGATIVE FEEDBACK?
UNDER-APPRECI-ATED.
8-20-12 ©2012 Scott Adams, Inc./Dist. by Universal Uclick
THEN WHAT MOTI-VATES YOU?
THE GOV-ERNMENT MAKES RECTAN-GULAR PIECES OF PAPER.

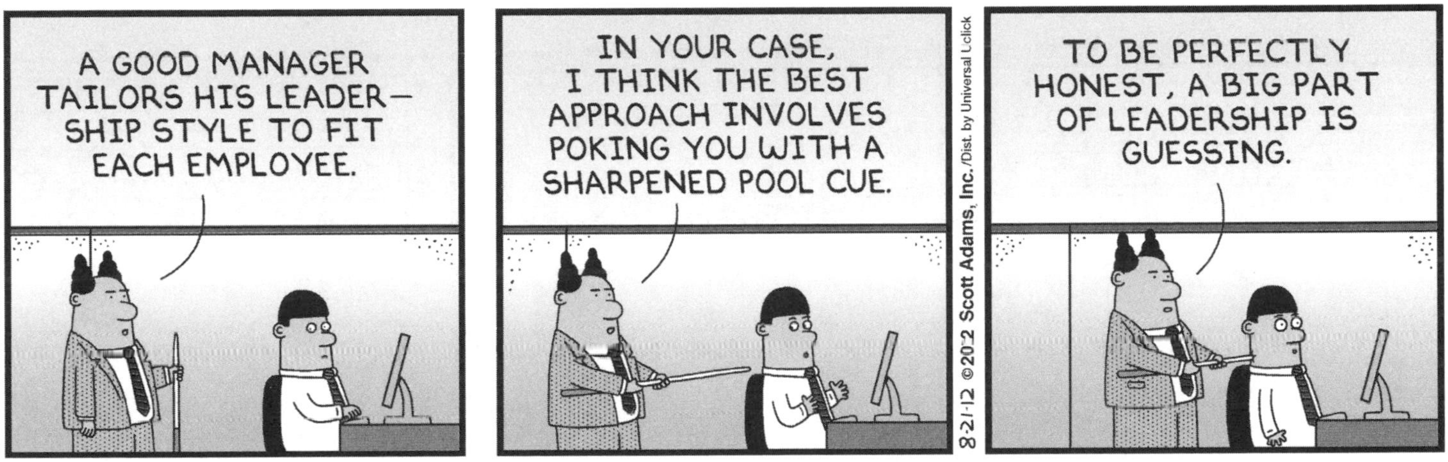
A GOOD MANAGER TAILORS HIS LEADER-SHIP STYLE TO FIT EACH EMPLOYEE.
IN YOUR CASE, I THINK THE BEST APPROACH INVOLVES POKING YOU WITH A SHARPENED POOL CUE.
8-21-12 ©2012 Scott Adams, Inc./Dist. by Universal Uclick
TO BE PERFECTLY HONEST, A BIG PART OF LEADERSHIP IS GUESSING.

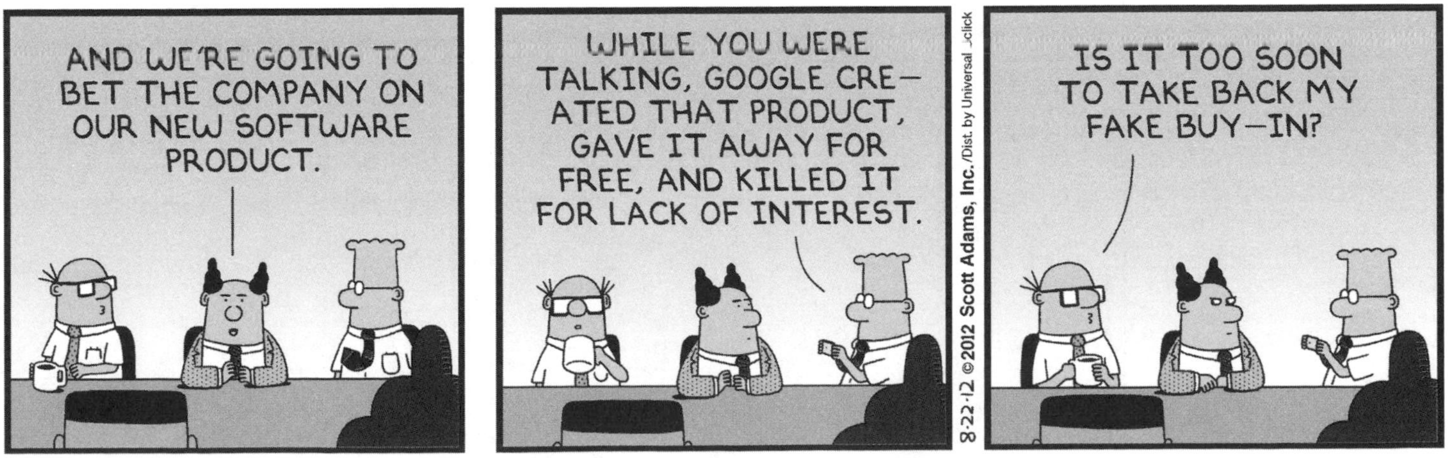
AND WE'RE GOING TO BET THE COMPANY ON OUR NEW SOFTWARE PRODUCT.
WHILE YOU WERE TALKING, GOOGLE CRE-ATED THAT PRODUCT, GAVE IT AWAY FOR FREE, AND KILLED IT FOR LACK OF INTEREST.
8-22-12 ©2012 Scott Adams, Inc./Dist. by Universal
IS IT TOO SOON TO TAKE BACK MY FAKE BUY-IN?

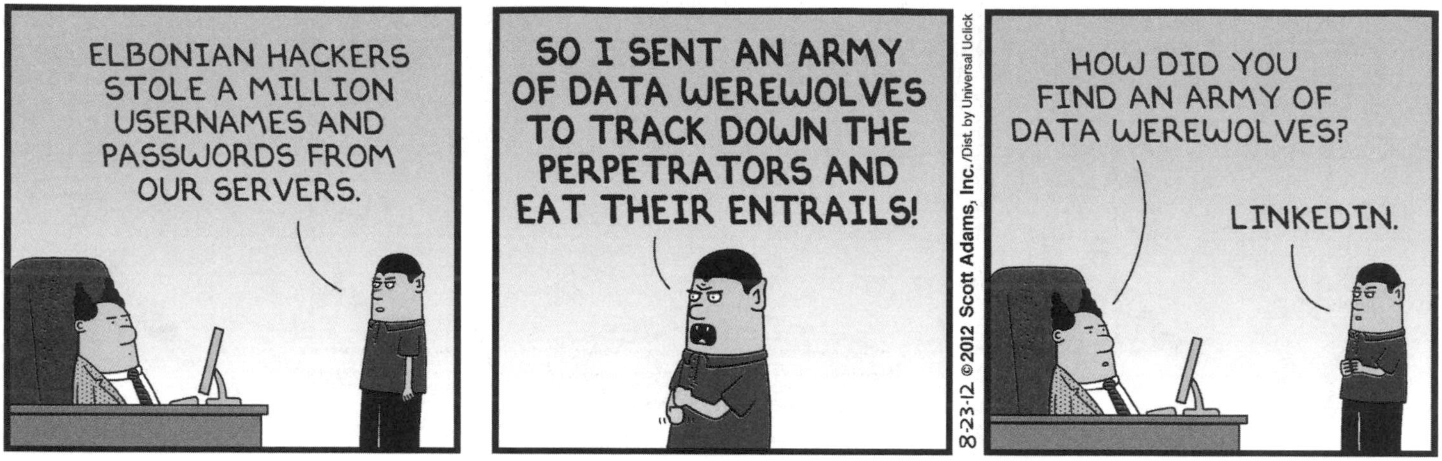
ELBONIAN HACKERS STOLE A MILLION USERNAMES AND PASSWORDS FROM OUR SERVERS.
SO I SENT AN ARMY OF DATA WEREWOLVES TO TRACK DOWN THE PERPETRATORS AND EAT THEIR ENTRAILS!
8-23-12 ©2012 Scott Adams, Inc./Dist. by Universal Uclick
HOW DID YOU FIND AN ARMY OF DATA WEREWOLVES?
LINKEDIN.

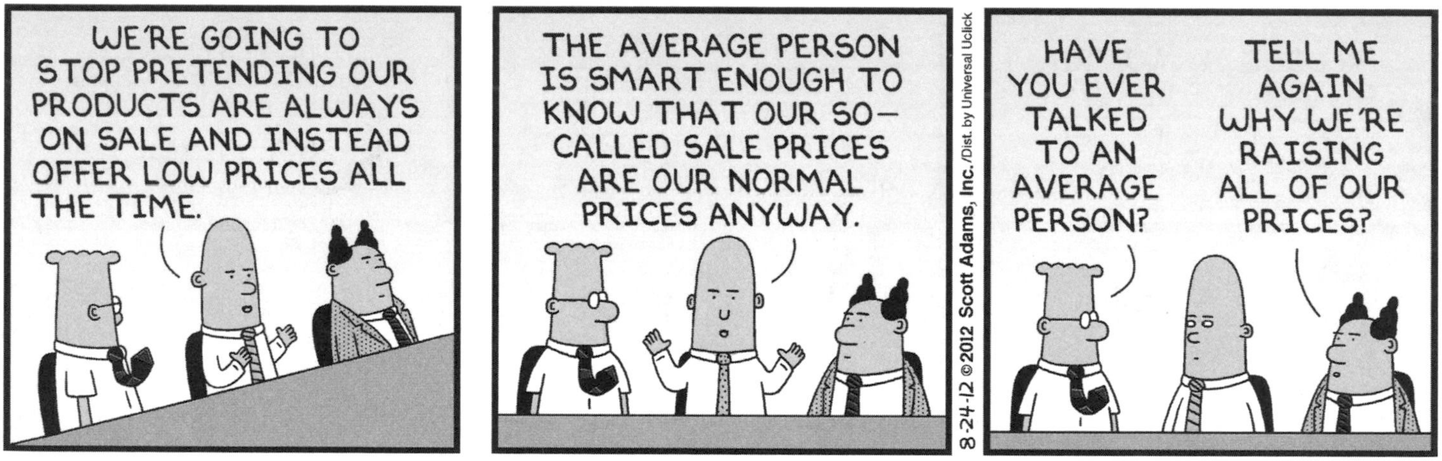
WE'RE GOING TO STOP PRETENDING OUR PRODUCTS ARE ALWAYS ON SALE AND INSTEAD OFFER LOW PRICES ALL THE TIME.
THE AVERAGE PERSON IS SMART ENOUGH TO KNOW THAT OUR SO-CALLED SALE PRICES ARE OUR NORMAL PRICES ANYWAY.
8-24-12 ©2012 Scott Adams, Inc./Dist. by Universal Uclick
HAVE YOU EVER TALKED TO AN AVERAGE PERSON?
TELL ME AGAIN WHY WE'RE RAISING ALL OF OUR PRICES?

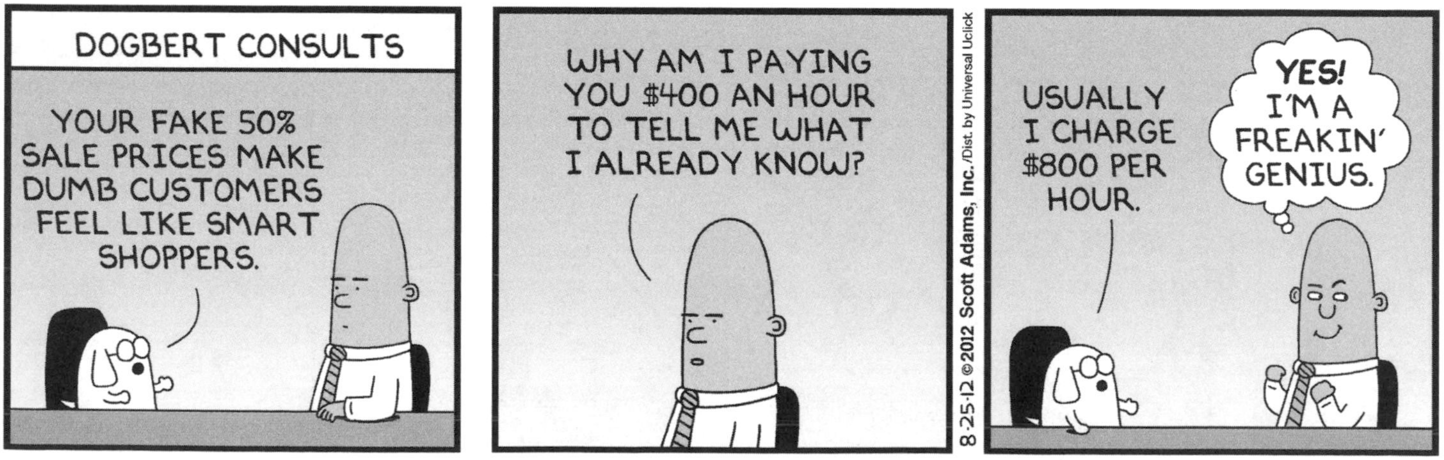
DOGBERT CONSULTS
YOUR FAKE 50% SALE PRICES MAKE DUMB CUSTOMERS FEEL LIKE SMART SHOPPERS.
WHY AM I PAYING YOU $400 AN HOUR TO TELL ME WHAT I ALREADY KNOW?
8-25-12 ©2012 Scott Adams, Inc./Dist. by Universal Uclick
USUALLY I CHARGE $800 PER HOUR.
YES! I'M A FREAKIN' GENIUS.

I CAN'T GIVE YOU THE RAISE YOU DESERVE BECAUSE IT WOULD MAKE YOUR PAY HIGHER THAN MINE.
I DON'T SEE HOW THAT'S A PROBLEM.
LET ME EXPLAIN IT TO YOU THIS WAY, ALICE.
IF YOU MAKE MORE MONEY THAN I DO. . .
YOUR COMPENSATION WOULD BE GREATER THAN MINE.
THAT'S NOT A REASON, YOU IGNORANT BABOON!
OKAY, HOW ABOUT . . . I MUST BE SMARTER THAN YOU BECAUSE MY INCOME IS HIGHER?
GAAA!!!
WHEN I DON'T HAVE REASONS FOR THINGS, IS THAT CALLED INTUITION OR JUST COMMON SENSE?
©2012 Scott Adams, Inc./Dist. by Universal Uclick
8-26-12

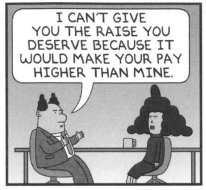

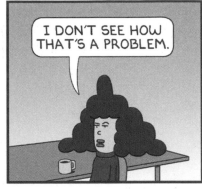

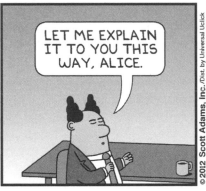

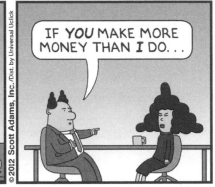

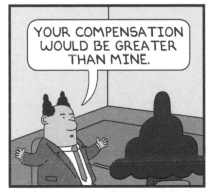

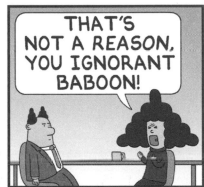

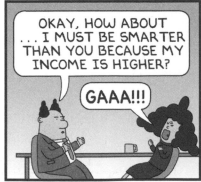

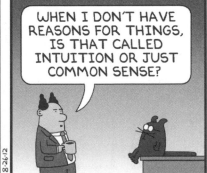